Made to Be Seen

Made to Be Seen

*Perspectives on the History
of Visual Anthropology*

EDITED BY MARCUS BANKS
AND JAY RUBY

The University of Chicago Press   Chicago and London

MARCUS BANKS is professor of visual anthropology at the University of Oxford and the author, most recently, of *Using Visual Data in Qualitative Research*. **JAY RUBY** is professor emeritus of anthropology at Temple University and the author or editor of numerous books, including *Picturing Culture: Essays on Film and Anthropology*, also published by the University of Chicago Press.

The University of Chicago Press, Chicago 60637
The University of Chicago Press, Ltd., London
© 2011 by The University of Chicago
All rights reserved. Published 2011
Printed in the United States of America
20 19 18 17 16 15 14 13 12   2 3 4 5

ISBN-13: 978-0-226-03661-8 (cloth)
ISBN-13: 978-0-226-03662-5 (paper)
ISBN-10: 0-226-03661-8 (cloth)
ISBN-10: 0-226-03662-6 (paper)

Library of Congress Cataloging-in-Publication Data

    Made to be seen : perspectives on the history of visual
anthropology / edited by Marcus Banks and Jay Ruby.
      p. cm.
    Includes bibliographical references and index.
    ISBN-13: 978-0-226-03661-8 (alk. paper)
    ISBN-10: 0-226-03661-8 (alk. paper)
    ISBN-13: 978-0-226-03662-5 (pbk. : alk. paper)
    ISBN-10: 0-226-03662-6 (pbk. : alk. paper)
    1. Visual anthropology.   I. Banks, Marcus. II. Ruby, Jay.
GN347.M33 2011
301—dc22   2010048748

Contents

Additional illustrations are posted at
http://www.press.uchicago.edu/books/banks.

Made to Be Seen: Historical Perspectives on Visual Anthropology

MARCUS BANKS AND JAY RUBY

History, Anthropology, and the History of Visual Anthropology

In Britain, the United States, and elsewhere in the Euro-American world the discipline of anthropology—in its broadest sense—is at least a century and half old. How much more or less is a matter of debate that need not concern us here, though we draw the line at claiming that Herodotus was an anthropologist or that Edward Curtis or the Lumière brothers were anthropological image creators. For the purposes of this volume we limit ourselves to the anthropological endeavors of those who recognized the contemporary anthropological project and the image-making activities of those who understood that project or were in other ways engaged with it. Even with this limitation (indeed, because of it), there remains the question of whether there is in fact a distinct history of visual anthropology that can be untwined from the history of the discipline as a whole. Below we demonstrate that such a history is not only possible but a worthwhile venture, but at the same time we acknowledge that those traces that historians of the subdiscipline have previously seized upon—the Balinese films and photographs of Mead and Bateson, the West African films of

1

Jean Rouch—exist only because those individuals were already conduct-ing field research relevant to the production of the images or were en-gaged in anthropological analyses for which image analysis was a part, but only a part.[1] While there is, in that sense, a visual strand, or strands, to be teased out, we and our contributors never lose sight of the fact that all anthropologists work on a variety of fronts and that anthropology is distinctive as a discipline precisely because of its ambition to produce holistic accounts, albeit with primary and secondary foci. A linguistic anthropologist, a political anthropologist, an anthropologist of global-ization can—and do—incorporate visual data and visual methods into their studies while contributing to their respective subfields. Authors in this volume note, for example, that the production and consumption of images plays only a part in the history of anthropological approaches to dress and textiles (Dudley) and to the built environment (Waterson). Even with regard to the anthropological uses of photography, Edwards notes that "in many ways work on photography is becoming more dif-fuse and dispersed across the anthropological field, no longer confined within visual anthropology." Our joint aim in this volume is therefore to give an account of the visual as it passes in and out of the discipline of anthropology.

As editors, we encouraged our contributors to reflect on the role of the visual within distinct fields of anthropological inquiry. Some of these fields are constitutive of what is generally thought to be the particular subject matter of visual anthropology (film, photography), while oth-ers (materiality, embodiment, the use of technology) make such use of the visual, or share common methodologies and approaches to such an extent, that they are often considered within the same ambit or that it would be intellectually hobbling to exclude them. This history is not a narrative of great men and their movies or photographs.[2] It is rather a his-tory of ideas and interests within the discipline that at some times have cried out for visual exploration (whether that call was heeded or not) and at others have apparently spurned the visual in favor of the written word as a mode of representation and language as an access route to the mind.

Perhaps the most closely examined period in this volume is those few decades before long-term field research became common, a time when the study of art and material culture was thought to yield evidence of cultural evolution (e.g., Haddon 1895). At this time, roughly between the 1880s and the 1920s, photography was vital as a form of evidence that could be circulated among ethnologists anxious to receive as much in-formation about as many "primitive" groups as possible—far more than they could ever hope to gather firsthand (Edwards 2001, chap. 2). The development of long-term fieldwork, with its Malinowskian emphasis on "the imponderabilia of everyday life," and the subsequent rise of interest in the comparative study of abstract institutions such as "kinship," "the economy," and so forth led to a setting aside of material culture studies for many decades. This, together with the costs and difficulties of publishing photographs in books and journals, contributed to a decline in the perceived value of the photomechanical image.

There have been several previous attempts to write a history of visual anthropology, some condensed (e.g., Banks and Morphy 1997, 4–13), others more elaborate (e.g., de France 1975; Pink 2006, 5–15). Many have focused largely or exclusively on the history of ethnographic film (several are discussed here by Durington and Ruby) or on a particular period, particularly the foundational period (Edwards 2001; Griffiths 2002). If we follow Ruby's strict definition of ethnographic film (2000, 239), as that produced by anthropologists for anthropological purposes, then the history of ethnographic film essentially begins after World War II, as there are very few such films from before that conflict and little in the way of institutional support. While the same is not true for still photography, which was put to explicitly anthropological uses starting in the late nineteenth century,[3] some contributors to this volume share this view of visual anthropology as an essentially postwar development when it comes to invoking the visual (through production or analysis) in other fields. While an interest in clothing and the built environment formed part of the Victorian and Edwardian anthropological project, the interest was largely technological, concerned with the relation between practical knowledge or skill and the "level" of a culture. As Dudley points out there was also an interest in dress as a marker of ethnicity, and photography was used to document this. While this could be taken as evidence of an early interest in the capacity of clothing to communicate visually, there is little to suggest that pre–World War II anthropologists were more than superficially interested in such visual communication between peoples, as opposed to their own scientific task of reading meaning from the surface of the photograph. Indeed, it was not until the 1970s that an anthropological model of visual communication was explicitly formulated (Worth 1981). Waterson finds even less historical evidence of attention to visual aspects of the built environment, situating the anthropological study of vernacular architecture firmly in the postwar period. When it comes to anthropological studies of the body and embodiment, Farnell states in her chapter that "visual representations of the body can be said to have permeated anthropology since its inception" (for example, in drawings and photographs of tattoos; see Gell 1993), yet the body was not problematized as such; nor, we might add, were its representations. So while anthropological interest in the body, its movement, its clothing, and its built environment would all seem fruitful ground for visual exploration and visual analysis, it seems this was not conducted in any systematic way until recently.

The study of art is perhaps the other field, alongside still photography, in which a prewar visual anthropology might be identified. The field is too rich and prolific for us to adequately cover here, beginning as it does with Haddon's now largely forgotten *Evolution in Art* (1895) and Boas's rather more influential *Primitive Art* (1927). Yet Haddon was little interested in the broader social context of the art discussed, and while Boas rejected Haddon's social evolutionary framework his approach is still almost entirely formalist and says little about either the artists or their social context. What both established, however, was a long-lasting distinction between "primitive art" and simply "art" (variously defined but including the Euro-American idea of "fine art"), with the former considered more as artifact than art, especially in societies that appeared to have no category or even term for art (Maquet's "art by metamorphosis"—objects created with non-art intentionality that become art through incorporation into the Euro-American art world; Maquet 1986, cited in Morphy (2009, 13). Though now collapsing, this divide continued through much of the twentieth century, and while art objects could occasionally move from the primitive art realm to the fine art realm, according to Morphy it wasn't really until relatively recently that the former category was challenged and deconstructed (Morphy 2009, 176). More importantly, however, the agendas of the anthropology of art were not specifically attuned to the very visuality of art, however paradoxical that may seem.[4] After Malinowski's functionalist "revolution" there was an increasing concern with what primitive art "does," and later, with the rise of structuralist and semiotic approaches in anthropology, with what primitive art "means" or says (e.g., Lévi-Strauss 1963). What was sometimes lacking was a consideration of how art "looks," with how it is seen (though see Morphy 1994 on "how" art means).

In the present volume, Schneider sets himself the task of mining the history of the anthropology of art for "veins of quartz," moments in the matrix of the past when a visual sensibility transcended narrow concerns of functionality or meaning. In this, his project resembles that of Grimshaw a decade earlier to uncover a counterhistory of the visual in anthropology (Grimshaw 1997, see also Grimshaw 2001). But where Grimshaw seeks to make connections between moments within anthropological history, Schneider also looks for connections across the boundary, particularly between anthropology and art history, but also between them and art practice. We return to such border crossings below.

For other contributors, those not dealing with substantive objects such as film, textiles, or bodies, the pursuit of a history of the visual in anthropology is more elusive. Pink, for example, considers a set of anthropological practices that, by definition, are no more than a decade or so old, although the desire that has led her and others to employ digital media is one with a deeper history, a search for representational forms that transcend the printed word. Pink's emphasis on collaboration and activism, activities facilitated by the use of digital media, is also a route to a further historical thread, that of engaged anthropology. While this alone does not have a deep history it provides another vein that can be productively mined.[5] Grasseni similarly deals with a formally short history, that of studies of "skilled vision," but it is one that crosses productively into other areas. More particularly, she notes that the technologies of vision, film in particular, are materializations of ideas that have greater historical depth. While the enskillment of vision obviously long predates these technologies (Baxandall's "period eye" for example [1988] can presumably be found in any period), the arrival of photomechanical recording devices enables a new and extremely powerful form of skilled envisioning, one that appears to deny its origins and promote pure naturalism.

In tracing outward to find historical roots, Pink and Grasseni are—like many of the other contributors to this volume—pointing toward a nexus of social relations that constitute visual anthropology. Hughes and Ramey make this particularly clear. For Ramey "experimental films" are artifacts embedded in a mesh of social relations that are actualized in activities such as screenings, distribution mechanisms, and review writing. Their history—and that of ethnographic film—is a history of the social relations involved in a field of cultural production (see also Durington and Ruby on the institutional structures that have facilitated ethnographic film production). Similarly, Ginsburg claims that feature films made by indigenous peoples ("First features") cannot be understood through textual readings alone, but only in the context of the "cultural and political labor of indigenous activists" engaged in complex relationships with the state structures in which they are embedded, relationships that have a deep history.

Hughes takes up this theme by highlighting yet another set of relationships. By privileging production over consumption in writing about ethnographic film, visual anthropologists were missing a vital part of the nexus. The task here then is to reinscribe the audience into the history of ethnographic film. Drawing on Griffiths's work (2002) on the early history of anthropology and visual culture, Hughes also sees the need to investigate the full social—and visual—context in which ethnographic film emerged (in this case, the visual culture of the late nineteenth century) and suggests that scholars should be examining the multiple "modes of address" inherent in the ethnographic films of each generation. While Hughes, following others such as MacDougall (e.g., 1978), is right to point to the dialogic nature of the relation between film production and film reception, the problem remains that it is not always clear who the audience actually was (as opposed to the "inscribed" audience presumed by the film). Durington and Ruby point out that, in the first half of the twentieth century at least, while the purpose of what then passed for ethnographic film was educational "there is no evidence that they were ever used in teaching," and while "teaching" is of course a narrower category than "education" it is still the case that the actual audiences of the time are largely unknown.

What is clear is that in the postwar period ethnographic film production and consumption was supported by an increasing number of institutional structures, in a way that was simply not the case for anthropological photography (the major exception being the use made of photography in ethnographic museums for exhibition display and documentation purposes). Although ethnographic museums provided the backing for some early ethnographic film work (e.g., the Field Museum in Chicago sponsored an anthropological film expedition to India as early as 1916),[6] institutionalization did not really get under way until the 1950s, with the establishment of the Comité du Film Ethnographique at the Musée de l'Homme in 1953 and the founding of the Film Study Center at Harvard's Peabody Museum of Archaeology and Ethnography in 1958. From the 1970s onward Film Australia and the Institute of Aboriginal and Torres Strait Islander Studies supported film production in Australia and the Pacific. Later, training programs were established in or with the collaboration of university anthropology departments, initially in the United States and then in Europe, that gave anthropologists the tools to create their own films, and for half a century there has been a steady growth in the number of ethnographic film festivals. Public and commercial television stations, such as Granada Television in the UK, have at various times sponsored ethnographic film production, though the so-called golden age of television production appears over, at least for the present.

Finally, for a complete history of visual anthropology to be understood there must be an understanding of paths not taken, of inconclusive experiments, of unfulfilled promises. As already noted, several contributors point to a lack of sustained anthropological interest until recently in areas such as vernacular architecture, clothing and textiles, and dance and movement. Such inherently visual forms demand attention and, as Waterson and particularly Dudley point out in this volume, they received it through early ethnographic photography and later film. But by and large such documentary processes mistook the means for the ends and were self-limiting, paths that became culs-de-sac; rather than use the camera to explore the visual systems and cultural forms to which it gave access, the shutters clicked and then moved on.

Schneider here provides instances of "practical experiments" as a form of anthropological exploration of visual systems that has not been fully realized. Through participation, anthropologists of course frequently practice actions and tasks performed by their research subjects: they learn to crew on fishing boats, they sit in meditation, they tipsily join in late-night song and dance sessions. Schneider has in mind, however, a specifically visual form of practiced mimesis, one in which the past can be embodied in the present, and in which the anthropologist exerts creative agency. Through engaging with visual practice, and specifically art practice, the anthropologist does not merely represent but contributes to emergent visual forms. This is consistent with Farnell's rejection of studies of the body as a site of representation in favor of the study of embodied, acting persons. Through this, as she notes, invisible cultural knowledge becomes meaningfully visible. The combination of practical action and visuality may not always be successful—Schneider quotes Russell, who claims that the filmmaker and dancer Maya Deren found her film work on Haitian Voudon ritual to be "inadequate" (Russell 1999). Instead, as Ramey says in this volume, Deren ceased to use the camera "as a capturing device" and joined the dance; however, as he goes on to point out, Deren died before editing the footage, and so in some sense the unrealized nature of the experiment may be due as much to personal as to methodological difficulties.

Like Schneider, Ramey points to a number of unexplored pathways, occasions when ethnographic filmmakers were offered alternative representational modes by experimental filmmakers that were—at least in the opinion of the experimental artists—rejected. Ramey and Schneider both point to the fact that visual artists and experimental filmmakers saw—and continue to see—anthropology as a "science," a discipline that does not fully appreciate other ways of seeing and is too strongly wedded to documentary realism as a representational mode. Historically of course this is largely true, as Edwards has shown in numerous publications and in this volume enlarges with her discussion of "pose." Dudley, Farnell, and other contributors also point to the scientistic aspirations of Victorian anthropology. Grasseni, however, goes on to highlight how very unstable the tools of scientific analysis, such as Munsell color coding charts, have proved to be in application. Scientism therefore becomes one more pathway, long abandoned, that may be fruitfully revisited once the socially contextualized nature of scientific practice is recognized and understood.

Ethnographic Film or Visual Anthropology?

The history of visual anthropology has been dominated by the production and use of ethnographic film. Indeed, despite its title, Hocking's pioneering edited collection, *Principles of Visual Anthropology* (1975), contained just six papers (of thirty-two) that dealt with anything other than film (including video and broadcast film). When the volume was reissued in a revised form in 1995, that number had actually shrunk, to five.[7] This conflation of visual anthropology with ethnographic film continues (e.g., El Guindi 2004), and it is worth considering the reasons. In a strongly worded defense of film, Taylor argues that the distinctiveness of a visual anthropological approach lies solely, but powerfully, in the medium: "It is not clear that anthropological interest in visual culture demands or would even benefit from the institutionalization of a discrete subdiscipline [i.e., visual anthropology]. On the other hand, an anthropology that is constitutively visual, that is conducted through principally visual rather than purely verbal media, is so radically different in kind . . . that it has a good claim to separate consideration" (Taylor 1998, 534–35). Similar sentiments are expressed by others such as Grimshaw (2002). We would not wish to argue against the distinctiveness and indeed power of film as a medium of anthropological communication; we have both been involved in film projects, have both written extensively on ethnographic film, and both continue to champion the medium, albeit in rather different ways.[8] Yet we would still argue that the medium should not be mistaken for the message. The issue is essentially one of context, by which we mean multiple things.

First, many films labeled "ethnographic" are nothing of the sort, except in a very loose sense of somehow being concerned with the human condition or indeed "any sort of image-making that can be seen to be *about* culture," as Ramey puts it. There are plenty of good, professionally made films from which anthropologists can learn a good deal (and

use in their teaching), but those that actually communicate anthropological concepts are far fewer and, by definition, can only be made with
sustained anthropological input. The context here then is the deep ethnographic insight and broad anthropological understanding from which
the film grows.

Following on from this, as we argue above and our contributors demonstrate in what follows, there is the intertextual dialogue between the
filming process, other investigations into visual forms, and the more conventional forms of ethnographic investigation, resulting in written as well
as visual outputs. While it is customary to draw a distinction between the
filmic representation and the pro-filmic event, within an anthropological context there are many more cross-cutting relationships beyond this
simple duality. Barbash and Taylor's film *In and Out of Africa* (1993) is a
good case in point. This is not simply the film of a book (Steiner's *African
Art in Transit* [1994]), and indeed the book does not "need" the film.
Rather, Steiner's investigations into the global market in African art and
Barbash and Taylor's film are complete but complementary exercises in
the analysis of a visual system (which includes not merely the semiotic aspect but also the materiality of forms, the processes of consumption and
exchange, and much more beside—in short, the whole art world; Becker
1982)—and each provides takeoff points for further investigation, which
could be conducted filmically or through written text as appropriate. The
contributions in this volume range from the highly visually abstract—
Grasseni on the sociology of skilled vision, for example—to the highly
concrete—Waterson on the built environment. In their chapters both
Grasseni and Waterson derive insight from moving images made by social scientists to craft their arguments,[9] but neither can complete their
arguments with that material alone. On the other hand, Hughes is not
(in his chapter in this volume, at least) interested in any particular ethnographic film or corpus of such films, but his argument concerning audiences and the media is constructed partly from the practitioner insights
of David MacDougall and partly from the purely "academic" insights of
visual anthropologists such as Sol Worth.

Finally, there is the context of reception. As Hughes says of ethnographic film "the perspectives of production have been privileged over
those of reception." One possible reason for this is that the audiences of
ethnographic film are—or are presumed to be—largely students, research
on whom is left to educational studies specialists (although we are not
aware of any such studies, at least on the use of ethnographic film). With
the exception of Wilton Martinez's much-cited unfinished study (e.g.,
1990, 1992, 1996), few anthropologists seem to have done any formal

research on this student audience, possibly because the educators in the classroom are very rarely the producers of the films they screen (by and large they will know little or nothing, for example, about the context of production). As far as we know, there has also been no formal research conducted on the domestic audiences for televised ethnographic film.[10] Equally, apart from reviews in journals such as *American Anthropologist*, *Visual Anthropology*, *Visual Anthropology Review*, *Anthropology Today*, and so on, there is very little known about what professional anthropologists think about ethnographic film—and these reviews are of course, like book reviews, the opinions of single individuals (albeit professionally informed). Taken together these factors mean that the claims made for the value of ethnographic film in the broader anthropological project are just that—claims. It is significant that, apart from writing concerned directly with ethnographic film(s), films are *very* rarely cited as data sources in written ethnography. This final example is thus about a context for which much is claimed yet remarkably little is known. Even when anthropologists such as Clifford, Fischer, Marcus, and others involved in the "writing culture"/"crisis of representation" critiques of the mid-1980s dealt with issues such as reflexivity, they failed to acknowledge that ethnographic filmmakers such as Rouch had been exploring such issues in their films since the 1960s (e.g., Rouch's *La pyramide humaine* [1961]).[11]

Art or Science?

While written scholarship in anthropology has never had to stand up to serious comparison with great works of literature,[12] visual anthropologists who produce their own images frequently face the question: But is it (also) art? As we use them here the terms "art" and "science" are, of course, shorthand. Film and photography, as representational media, invoke in the Euro-American viewer notions of deliberate aesthetic intention, or at the very least an authorial presence that is alert to the ways in which the form can represent: even the humblest amateur photographer has a vocabulary with which to speak of "good" and "bad" photographs. By contrast, "science" is the realm of the disinterested professional academic, who produces texts to communicate pure meaning that transcends whatever medium is used to convey it. The representations associated with art are fluid, the facts conveyed by science are rock stable. Of course, these positions are caricatures, but given the heat of the debate surrounding, say, the films of Robert Gardner (see, e.g., Loizos 1993; Ruby 1989), it is worth overstressing the point for heuristic purposes.

In earlier periods, the stylistic conventions of the day provided an almost certainly unconscious aesthetic model for visual anthropological image production: the posed compositions of Victorian anthropologists such as E. H. Man or J. W. Lindt read much like other photographs of the period,[13] and even when there is innovation, or little precedent to guide, there is an unself-conscious artlessness (the "no-style style," as Edwards terms it). The formal similarities between the image of Haddon and his team, and the image of the Torres Strait Islanders that Edwards reproduces in this volume testify to this. Yet as the discipline matured, and as the aesthetic imperative began to be felt first in photography and then in film, so the anthropological producers of photographs and films found their images to be in circulation in a much expanded visual universe, one in which images of the distant, the exotic, and the other were in competition with their own.

Durington and Ruby, in their chapter, comment that Flaherty's *Nanook of the North* (1922) is arguably neither documentary nor ethnography, yet for decades the film has been assigned to the "ethnographic" category by anthropologists and non-anthropologists alike, as well as praised for its stark beauty. Many more people know the Nuba people of Sudan through Leni Riefenstahl's photographic work (e.g., 1974) than through Faris's *Nuba Personal Art* (1972). More recently, films in the British television series *Tribe* have been assumed by critics and viewers to be in some way anthropological (Caplan 2005; Hughes-Freeland 2006).[14] Flaherty's film and Riefenstahl's photographs have certainly been admired for their aesthetic qualities, and while there is nothing particularly innovative visually about the *Tribe* films, they undoubtedly provided a gripping televisual experience for British viewers, despite being largely disowned by the anthropological community for, for want of a better term, their lack of "science"—that is, an absence of rigorous ethnographic investigation. Thus, despite their best intentions, visual anthropologists produce images that circulate in a world already full of similar product, a world that brings external aesthetic judgment to bear.

Equally, those anthropologists who study rather than create visual forms must at some level deal with the question "But is it art?" This is most sharply apparent in writing about "art," whether designated as such by the producers or not. The problem here is what should one do about the artness of the art object in communicating knowledge of it to the reader or viewer. The obvious answer is to discuss what it means to those who produce and consume it, just as one would discuss their religious beliefs and practices, or their understanding of personhood. Following on from that, the anthropologist would consider how appropriately English

MARCUS BANKS AND JAY RUBY

vernacular terms such as "art," "religion," and so forth can function as metalinguistic concepts (see Morphy 2007). Incorporating certain objects of material culture within the Euro-American category of fine art can and has been debated by anthropologists (see Morphy 2007, chap. 1) and still remains contentious. Such objects range from Duchamp's urinal to an Azande fishing net, the most obvious example being the discovery of "primitive art" and the celebration of, for example, African carving by Picasso and other artists.

Anthropology has always concerned itself with subject matters that other academic disciplines consider to be theirs—economics, politics, and so forth—and has had to stake out and defend its territory.[15] For most of the discipline's history this was done by concentrating study on the non-Western world. When it comes to the production and study of images and visual representation, a great number of people, academics, professionals, and others, take an interest, add their opinion, and shape the discursive space that anthropologists enter. Most contributors to this volume propose that instead of defending the academic boundary, maintaining the "science," as it were, visual anthropologists can (or should) collaborate with other professionals and indeed with the persons or objects of study. Hughes points to the insights into audience that have come from media studies, while Waterson advocates more direct collaboration with architects. Activism and active engagement emerges as a theme in the contributions of Pink, Ginsburg, and Dudley, while Grasseni draws upon ecological psychology, science and technology studies, and ethnomethodology to develop her approach to an anthropology of vision.

In an influential article Edwards has argued that "anthropologists should be aware of other ways of articulating their tradional territory . . . they should be responsive to resonances of representations of their own making beyond The Boundary" (1997, 75). In her chapter here, she considers further boundary crossings, such as that between anthroplogy and documentary photographic practice, while also drawing attention to photographic repatriation as a site where active collaboration between anthropologists and research subjects is facilitated. The idea of border crossing is not new, of course, nor is anthropological activism or intellectual engagement with the subjects of research—treating them as agents in the cocreation of knowledge—but visual anthropology is arguably the area of the discipline most prone to cross-border fertilization and the most invigorated by it. Schneider notes that recent writing on art and anthropology has come to view art "as a participating subject, not a passive object" and claims that through productive collaboration between art practice, art history and anthropology new directions will emerge. Farnell too, characterizes the "second somatic revolution" (in anthropological work on the body) as treating the body not as an object of study but as an agentive "biocultural resource." Ginsburg is well known for pointing to the "parallax effect," the result of a dialogue between ethnographic filmmakers and indigenous image-makers that ultimately offers "a fuller comprehension of the complexity . . . of the social phenomenon we call culture and those media representations that self-consciously engage with it." Similarly, while ethnographic filmmakers and visual anthropologists have generally had little to do with the world of experimental film, Ramey points to past border crossings, such as the work of Maya Deren and Chick Strand, as indicative not only of the productivity that might be found, but of the permeability of what she calls "communities of practice."

Seen from this perspective the apparent disjunction between art and science effectively dissolves. A focus on practices, both anthropological and of the research subjects, rather than representations inevitably entails boundary crossing and engagement, whether for political ends—as in the activism of indigenous filmmakers (Ginsburg)—or for intellectual ends—as in the developing model of visual enskillment (Grasseni). Representations, whether anthropological photographs or indigenous art, are static, and their aesthetics, veracity, and evidentiality can be debated within an objectivist paradigm. While ultimately visual anthropologists must resort to representations in their written work, the contributors to this volume point toward, in the language of Farnell, an agentic and dynamic approach to practice.

Beyond Visual Anthropology?

In her contribution to this volume Farnell charts three phases of anthropological interest in the body, the second two of which—dating from the 1980s to the 1990s and from the late 1990s to the present—she refers to as (somatic) "revolutions," compete overturnings of the ways in which the body had been conceptualized. While the periodicity is not the same, a similar schema could be used to conceptualize the history of visual anthropology.[16] The first phase is the same as that which Farnell identifies—a period of a century or so, from the mid-nineteenth to the mid-twentieth century, during which anthropologists shot film and took photographs (of bodies, weapons, house-building, and so forth) but in a largely unsystematized way, in connection with short-lived theoretical agendas (biometric validation of cultural variation, the culture and personality "school," etc.), or simply as self-evident documentation and (as Edwards puts it, in this volume) "scene-setting." With the exception of primitive art, little attention was paid in this period to the visual properties of buildings, textiles, or indeed to vision itself.

The second phase, which begins in the 1960s but comes to prominence in the 1970s and 1980s, is dominated by ethnographic film production and subsequent writing about ethnographic film. The first signs of a dissatisfaction with established paradigms of ethnographic representation began to appear in anthropology (e.g., Asad 1973), and while there is no obvious causal link, ethnographic film could then be looked on in a new light. No longer thought to be merely a form of transparent documentation, the strong narrative drive associated with the films of the MacDougalls and others provided new ways of considering socially embedded human experience. The earlier notion, toward which Mead and Bateson perhaps tended in their photographic and filmic work in Bali, is certainly evident in Mead's introduction to the first edition of Hockings's *Principles of Visual Anthropology* (1975/2003), which contains an uneasy mixture of articles, some of which point to new understandings of the power of film (e.g., those by Rouch and MacDougall) and some of which seek to revive the certainties of the Victorian scientific anthropology (e.g., those by Lomax and Scherer). At the same time, work had begun on reassessing the photographic archive (e.g., Edwards 1992),[17] and the journal *Studies in the Anthropology of Visual Communication*, with a much broader remit than ethnographic film and photography, began publication in 1974.

The third phase runs from the 1990s to the present, and consequently there must be a caveat concerning the short perspective we can adopt in assessing it. It is underpinned by the "pictorial turn" in anthropology generally (Hughes, in this volume, citing MacDougall, citing Mitchell), a shift away from language-based models of analysis, and a questioning of representational practices (Edwards). This ongoing phase is characterized by three main concerns: boundary crossing and collaboration; the use of new (digital) media; and a recognition of the full sensorium. Boundary crossing has been discussed above, and is in part facilitated by the use of new media. For example, in this volume Ramey points out that access to experimental film, of the kind that could or should be of interest to visual anthropologists, is easier to obtain than ever before thanks to the Internet, and Ginsburg is "cautiously" optimistic about the possibilities of the Internet for indigenous peoples, although she also highlights problems, such as the representation of Uluru (Ayers Rock) in Second Life. Pink also points to difficulties, ethical and representational, that can arise with visual anthropological use of the Internet, the principle one being loss of control over sensitive material. One solution advocated by Pink is some form of "hard copy" publishing, on CD-ROM or DVD, a strategy also suggested by Durington and Ruby. The debate surrounding the utility of digital media for visual anthropology goes further than matters of control and ethics, however. Durington and Ruby refer to the suggestion that (ethnographic) film is an "incomplete utterance," incapable of conveying anthropological concepts completely (see Asch 1972; Heider 1976/2006). Authored multimedia, with a mixture of text, sound, and still and moving images, allows the representational and communicative properties of each medium to achieve their potential, to the point where Durington and Ruby speculate that ethnographic film—as we currently know it—may be rendered obsolete. Pink does not predict such an outcome, although she notes that multimedia productions can enhance some of the capabilities that film has presented in the past, notably empathetic understanding, by providing greater context and more overt theoretical consideration (a point that might cause one to reassess Taylor's 1998 defense of film as a medium, mentioned above).

Another lauded property of film is that of communicating, or empathetically inducing, corporeality. This, a concept proposed in this context by David MacDougall (e.g., 2006; cf. Pinney's concept of "corpothetics," 2001), points to the embodied identification spectators are said to form with images and especially with the persons represented in film and photographs. While ostensibly mono-track (image-only photography) or twin-track (image-and-sound film) sensory channels are engaged, MacDougall, following Merleau-Ponty, argues that film viewing is a synesthetic experience, by means of which the full sensorium is evoked. Following the "pictorial turn," anthropology in its poststructuralist phase has (re)discovered the senses (e.g., Classen 1993; Stoller 1989; Edwards, Gosden, and Phillips 2006). This has led some to question whether there is, or can be, a distinctive visual anthropology. On the one hand, to segregate the visual from the other senses (synesthesia notwithstanding) is to slice off a portion of the full, embodied experience of those we study; on the other, it reifies the occularcentrism of which anthropology has been accused in all of its representational practices (e.g., Fabian 1983). The answer is yes, and no. No, for the reasons given above, but yes because nominally, visual anthropology exists and has been a productive force within the discipline. Our contributors point to the fact that the visual typically mediates (Dudley), providing access to otherwise invisible knowledges (Farnell) or in itself being the focus of cultural attention (Grasseni). It is at once solipsistic and public in a way that the other senses are not; indeed, Dudley points to the fact that while a primary sensory experience of textiles is their feel, this is sensible only for the wearer and perhaps her or his most intimate companions: it is the materials' look (and to a lesser extent their sound) that has public salience. Finally, the visual has the capacity of instantaneity, Cartier-Bresson's punctum held endlessly before us, the living snapshot as it were.

The essays in this volume all point to the inescapable entanglement of the visual in all areas of life, from the spontaneous act of seeing to the deeply considered artifice of film and art. While the book was originally conceived as an exploration of the history of the visual in a variety of anthropological fields, our contributors have gone far beyond this brief, not only highlighting past instances but also laying the groundwork for new engagements and new possibilities. At the start of this introduction we noted that there have been other histories of visual anthropology (though many are in fact histories of ethnographic film). On the whole, though, such accounts have been self-contained and self-defined, inasmuch as their authors are already self-identified as visual anthropologists and tend to rehearse a narrative that leads to their subjective position. Our aim in this volume is much more ambitious: we and our contributors—not all of whom would identify as visual anthropologists—aim to weave a narrative from many different strands within and without the anthropological project. One result is to demonstrate that the visual is inextricably threaded through most if not all areas of anthropological activity. There are areas where it is foregrounded—the study of indigenous media for example—and others where a subtle teasing apart of the fabric of the inquiry is required to see it.[18] We do not wish to end on a triumphalist note, but we do wish to stress that the visual has been and will continue to be a vital part of the anthropological endeavor. We hope this volume will provide a reflective and critical basis for considering future engagements.

Notes

Our first thanks must go to our contributors for their thoughtful, clear, and intelligent articles. Some of them we must thank for their patience too, as they waited while we commissioned the final chapters. David Brent, at the University of Chicago Press, again demonstrated his ability to be a patient and very supportive editor. Joshua Hatton worked long and hard to locate the many illustrations for this book and to secure permission to reproduce them. Janis Ruby greatly assisted in formatting and proofreading.

1.   Rouch is perhaps an anomaly here. Although trained as an anthropologist and working within a strongly anthropological context, he wrote compara-

tively little (the means by which most anthropologists communicate to their peers), and so the anthropological impetus behind his films is not always clear. He has, however, been firmly embraced by other anthropologists as having made significant contributions not simply to ethnographic film but to the anthropological project more generally (e.g., Stoller 1992b; Brink 2007).

2. While the pioneers of visual anthropology are almost exclusively men, reflecting the gender balance in the discipline until recently, contemporary visual anthropology draws heavily upon concerns introduced by way of feminism, such as reflexivity and subjectivity (Caplan 1988; but see also Ruby 1980a for discussion of a broader range of influences).

3. As Edwards (1992, 2001) and others have shown, Victorian and Edwardian anthropologists made much use of still photography, yet they did so largely using photographic prints alone; halftone reproduction in books and journals was uncommon before the twentieth century, and even after it was introduced the cost severely limited the number of images a publisher would permit.

4. We are well aware that not all art, however defined, is visual art. However, for the purposes of this discussion we are concerned with the visual dimension of those art objects that project it or that are sensible to visual perception. We are not, however, concerned with the debates over aesthetics and whether there can be a cross-cultural category of aesthetics (for which see Ingold 1993).

5. Bastide (1973) offers probably the first formal assessment of "applied" anthropology, though of course anthropologists had been applying—or helping others to apply—the results of their research for decades before this (see, e.g., Malinowski 1929).

6. We are conscious that we have not included a chapter on museums—ethnographic or otherwise—in this volume, and not given a great deal of attention to them as sites of visual production and consumption in this introduction. In part this is because many excellent studies have recently appeared (e.g., Bouquet 2001) and in part because we and our authors have preferred to emphasize individuals and practices rather than institutions.

7. To be fair, the total number of papers in the 1995 edition was also reduced, to twenty-seven.

8. As an example of our differences, compare Ruby 1989b with Banks 2008.

9. Somewhat paradoxically, it would seem, our argument here rests upon the use of moving image material that is not, by the claim of the earlier paragraph, ethnographic at all. Grasseni draws upon Charles Goodwin's video footage of fiber dyeing, which has more ethnomethodological significance than anthropological, for example, while Waterson chooses a very unambiguously ethnographic film (Engelbrecht's 1999 *Building Season in Tiébélé*). Meanwhile, Dudley draws upon a variety of films, such as Bole-Becker and Becker's *Unraveling the Stories* (1997) and Howes and Hardy's *Kafi's Story* (1989/2001), that were made with broad public audiences

(not just anthropologists) in mind, to make similar points to Waterson's concerning tactility, memory, and skill. But this is precisely our point: ethnographic films exist as a distinctive subset of nonfiction films, not as the exclusive focal point for visual anthropological analysis. Dudley, for example, uses the visual material contained in films about quilting to derive (in part) her anthropological analysis of textiles; Waterson by contrast recognizes the analysis concerning the female symbolism of the Kasena house already contained within Engelbrecht's film.

10. The British cultural studies "school" did conduct empirical research on domestic television audiences but concentrated largely on drama and news (e.g., Morley 1980; Gillespie 1995). Silverstone briefly discusses reception in his study of the making of a television science documentary, but his audience was a set of specially convened focus groups (1985).

11. There is no reference to (ethnographic) film in the articles collected together as *Writing Culture* (Clifford and Marcus 1986). "Ethnographic film" merits a single paragraph of discussion in Marcus and Fischer's *Anthropology as Cultural Critique* (1986), although its analytical power is (wrongly) attributed to outside influences.

12. Of course, individual authors are sometimes praised—or criticized—for the quality of their writing, and some have written about anthropological literary style in some detail (e.g., Rosaldo 1986), but this is not the same as making a direct comparison with works of literature per se.

13. We are talking here only of images produced by professional anthropologists with anthropological intent; clearly the photographs of non-anthropologists, such as Curtis, show a profoundly self-conscious aesthetic intent.

14. The series featured Bruce Parry, a former marine and "explorer," spending relatively short periods of time with "tribal" groups such as the Kombi people of Irian Jaya and the Babongo people of Gabon, and participating in what for him—and indeed for most Euro-American viewers—were relatively extreme experiences, such as penis inversion or the taking of hallucinogenic drugs.

15. The one possible exception to this is the study of kinship, which perhaps also accounts for why kinship was so central to the discipline in the UK and the US for so many decades.

16. Note, however, that Edwards cautions against too processual a reading of the history of photography and anthropology's engagement; the same caution would apply to visual anthropology more generally. We prefer the term "phase" to "revolution" (however apt the latter may be in the case of studies of the body) to simply indicate a dominant trend or trends.

17. Although Edwards's book was published in 1992, planning for the project had begun much earlier, in 1984.

18. There is much more work to be done on anthropologists' use of diagrams and other nontext modes of presenting material and analysis (see Banks 2001, 23–33) for an example, while recent studies of visualization in, for example, business studies suggest new methodological directions.

ONE

Skilled Visions: Toward an Ecology of Visual Inscriptions

CRISTINA GRASSENI

A large part of ethnographic research, of theoretical reflections, and of commonsense assumptions about vision presumes that those who see are individual spectators and/or social actors, who impose certain social representations on experience. The "skilled visions" approach considers vision as a social activity, a proactive engagement with the world, a realm of expertise that depends heavily on trained perception and on a structured environment. This concept of, and approach to, vision allows us to recontextualize the critique of visualism in the wider contemporary debate on the anthropology of practice and the construction of knowledge.

Introduction

This chapter proposes a survey of some of the approaches to visuality that proliferate at the margins and across the disciplinary boundaries of visual anthropology. It seeks to explain how they contribute methodological tools and insightful case studies that help in charting influences and intellectual hybridizations on and around the history of visual anthropology. In particular, I shall refer to the "skilled visions" approach in the anthropology of vision (Grasseni 2007b), to ethnomethodological studies of visualization in scientific practice (Lynch 1985, 1990, 2001; Lynch and Woolgar 1990), and to Latour's actor-network theory (1991)—in particular, his approach to visualization and cognition (1986). I shall also draw on cultural psychology and the study of the role of artifacts in communication and cognition (e.g., Hutchins 1986, 1993, 1995; Hutchins and Klausen 1998; Suchman 1987, 1998; Suchman and Trigg 1993). I shall highlight the convergence of visual analysis and discourse analysis, especially in the work of Charles Goodwin (1994, 1996, 1997, 2000; Goodwin and Goodwin 1998; Goodwin and Ueno 2000). I shall argue that these trends are interesting to visual anthropologists as they converge toward a notion of vision that investigates it as the action of a body in an environment, considering it as a form of practical, emotional, and sensual knowledge and privileging case studies that deal with apprenticeship, training, and routines of action.

The aim of this chapter is thus to propose a theoretical approach to the field of "visual anthropology," which not only interprets it as the study of visual and pictorial culture but poses the question of an "anthropology of vision" as a field of inquiry worth investigating through ethnographic means and methods. In order to roughly define these "strategies of the eye" (Faeta 2003), I propose the following preliminary considerations, which I will elaborate in the following section: First, looking is a technique of the body (Mauss 1935/1979); as such it is culturally inculcated and socially performed as *habitus* (Bourdieu 1972).[1] Second, learning how to look at the world, or how to visualize particular objects or phenomena, is a form of social apprenticeship. Learning a skilled way of looking, therefore, involves senses and emotions as the apprentice becomes proficient in carrying out a form of expertise. Third, the concepts of apprenticeship and of culturally competent ways of seeing lead the ethnographer to keep an analytical focus on different types of "schooling of the eye," or schools of seeing—for lack of a better word to translate *scuole dello sguardo*, literally "schools of gaze."

In alluding to the "gaze," I by no means mean to invoke a disembodied or abstracted way of looking; I am instead seeking to define an intent and skillful capacity for looking, which I have named elsewhere "skilled vision" (Grasseni 2004a). Schooling of the gaze, in this sense, permeates every aspect of our daily, professional, artistic, and emotional lives. As a result, an anthropology of the visual is not exhausted solely by the production, utilization and cultural analysis of audiovisual, digital, or multimedia texts but includes, too, a close ethnographic analysis of the contexts and protagonists of the schooling of the eye.

As a way of anticipating what is meant here by an "ecology of visual inscriptions," I refer mainly to the recent trend in ecological anthropology (Ingold 2000), which owes much to some key notions of ecological psychology, such as that of *affordance* (Gibson 1979), and to the study of perception and cognition as *participatory* and *embedded*. By that I mean a situated action performed in a guiding, structured environment (Rogoff 2003; Suchman 1987). If vision is to be explored as a situated practice, it will be of paramount importance to single out the constraints and possibilities offered by the material and social environment that structures visual practice (Ceruti 1986), in terms both of the artifacts employed to guide and channel it, and of the cognitive interactions and communications that help one to attune one's perceptions and actions to those of others in the same environment.

Exploring Vision as a Situated Practice

The misconception that visual anthropology is exclusively concerned with producing or analyzing images (whether filmic, photographic, or of other kinds) has led to the rather banal and objectionable distinction between a discipline of words and a discipline of images. On the one hand, texts would be both capable of and passively open to transparent analysis, objective critique, and exhaustive description, while images would be opaque, affording too many opportunities and possibilities of interpretation. Hence visual texts would be subjective and incomplete.

Without wishing to enter the vexed question of realism versus relativism (Hollis and Lukes 1982; Hacking 1983; Nichols 1991; Winston 1995), let us remember as a commonly held premise that vision is not an automatic, mimetic capacity for crafting "copies" of things, processes, and images—which must have important implications for the ways we practice visual anthropology, and anthropology *tout court*. Visual knowledge should not be interpreted as a "realist" *adequatio intellectus ad rem* but rather as a form of cultural construction of the world around us. This is just one possible way of posing "the epistemological question" in visual anthropology: How do we consider our representations of the world as valid?

I agree with Tim Ingold (1993c, 2000), that we should not think of looking as just a capacity for image-reading or for discerning a predetermined design already present in nature (2001). I would like to discuss here the possibility of carrying out an ethnographic analysis of ways of seeing which, in my interpretation at least, cannot be disjointed from specific ways of looking. This will lead me, in the following section, to consider some responses to the "epistemological question" within neighboring disciplines, such as the anthropology of science, that can be particularly relevant to an anthropology of vision, albeit not devoid of problematic aspects.

In a project that I have carried out in the last few years I have asked fellow anthropologists and professionals from other disciplines to contribute case studies of the ways in which people actually use their eyes.[2] I shall quote some of these examples in order to highlight what I mean by "skilled vision" and to explain how this notion may contribute a relativist, constructivist, and ecological solution to the epistemological question in visual anthropology.

The idea was to situate vision in a scenario of everyday skilled activities and to underline both the social and the material dimensions of visual training. Gathering different "ethnographies of sight" led to the conclusion that there is no "vision" as such; instead there are professional, aesthetic, ecstatic, sensual, and erotic exercises of vision, each a skilled and social activity in itself. Consequently, I have proposed the notion of "skilled visions," in the plural, to acknowledge a plurality of visual practices that employ different kinds of gestural competence, develop within different kinds of apprenticeship, and are differently embodied (Grasseni 2007c). Examples of visual training in high- and low-tech practices (from architecture to urban planning, from scientific laboratories to medical training, from botanical to artistic apprenticeship) stress the importance of local rules and highlight the processes by which consensus on notions of beauty, propriety, and exactness is achieved socially.

This opens up an important aside, which I shall not follow up here but which is worth considering as part of the issues framing the epistemological question, that is, the relation between power and knowledge. A critical focus on imaging technologies—meant as mediators of meaning, power, and knowledge—frequently leads to an often implicit equation between vision and the disembodied, abstracted and rationalizing ways of seeing. From the point of view of the rediscovery of the senses, of the body, and of the local dimensions of knowledge, "visualism" stands for the technification of seeing, for the global inculturation of shallow media images and for the loss of the capacity to "look for oneself."[3] To this, we can oppose two orders of considerations.

First, we are by now used to critiquing Cartesian, formalized, and disembodied forms of visualization as carrying the power of Western rationality or exercising forms of surveillance. But we should remember that the opposite does not necessarily hold: embodied vision is not powerless. On the contrary, the social exercise of sight can be "an activity through which certain social actors find the materials for the maintenance of power" (Herzfeld 2007, 207; see also Herzfeld 2004). For instance, artifacts such as icons, models, and imaging technologies have great importance in inculcating a sense of aesthetic propriety that is seized through the eyes but belongs, in fact, to the visceral, to the core itself of identity—professional and beyond.[4] So if vision is cultural, this does not only mean that different cultures hold radically different metaphors for, and hierarchies of, the senses (as the works of Constance Classen and David Howes convincingly demonstrate). It also means that the conditions for the construction of meaningful visual knowledge are local, situated, and contextual—even in the highly technified, standardized, and functional Western world. Some examples from the ethnography of science, in the next section, will substantiate this.

Second, we should consider that visual skill is often invisible! It is a capacity for *attention* before it can become productive of any kind of visual *representation*, and, as Brenda Farnell puts it in this volume, "analysis and interpretations must be grounded in the multiple and complex *invisible* forms of cultural knowledge that make that which is visible and meaningful to its practitioners." Therefore, we should find appropriate ways of investigating such tacit knowledge in its making, for instance, by studying the material and relational structure of its contexts of production. In the examples that follow, for instance, participant observation, analytic camerawork, and art-historical investigation have been used.

One "learns to see" in cultural ways. Visual training happens within forms of social (and sometimes, but not always, professional) apprenticeship. Francesco Ronzon (2007) elaborates ironically on visual skill from the margins of acceptable theatrical performance, following a group of drag queens acting on stage in the gay clubs of Verona, Italy. He *"follows the followers"* of Madame Sisi, a well-established drag performer posing particular attention to the artifacts and conversations exchanged by Madame Sisi's fans. Artifacts such as posters or photographs of gay "icons" support and acknowledge collective notions of "propriety" and "beauty." Appreciative and critical remarks about each other's looks further negotiate and contextualize such notions. Here, "skilled vision" is the result of verbal, social, and aesthetic training carried out as resistance in the face of discrimination and marginalization. The ethnographer, newly exposed to this form of life, has to "pick up" the relevant cues in an environment where commonsensical definitions of beauty and grace break down.

A second example uses the technique of the analytic revisitation of filmed images, in time-lapse and slow motion, to highlight cultural patterns of movement. Riccardo Putti (2005, 2008) refers to "cultural kinesics" (Carpitella 1981a, 1981b) to distill the patterned behavior of visitors at an exhibition in Siena dedicated to fourteenth-century Gothic art. In particular, he highlights the widespread use of indexicals and acts of pointing to direct the visitors' attention, notices that acts of orientation and self-disposition in the space are a fundamental factor in the overall aesthetic experience of the visitor, and underlines a commonality of experience created by the space and rhythm of movement of other people's bodies in space. He concludes that vision is not exclusively visual but a resonant, kinetic, synthetic mode of perception.

A historical analysis of botanical illustrations in eighteenth-century colonial science confirms this. Daniela Bleichmar has studied how naturalists were trained at length before going to the field, reading authoritative texts, memorizing and redrawing their illustrations. "Seeing was neither simple nor immediate, but a sophisticated technique that identified practitioners as belonging or not to a community of observers" (Bleichmar 2007, 175).[5] Bleichmar discusses how "the notion of sight went beyond the physiological act of seeing to involve rather *insight*—an accretion that the paradox of the *blind naturalist* brings to the fore. The acumen of observation became so characteristic of the very *persona* of the naturalist that one could even do without the eyes" (168). To substantiate this claim, she quotes the case of Georgius Everhardus Rumphius (1627–1702), a German botanist and collector employed by the Dutch East India Company, who lost his eyesight.

Despite this considerable challenge, over the second half of the seventeenth century Rumphius amassed an incomparable collection of natural objects, many of which he sold to the Grand Duke of Tuscany as the basis of an impressive natural history cabinet. Rumphius also had many items drawn, and wrote or dictated their scientific descriptions in preparation for publication. These images and texts furnished the material for two titles appearing posthumously over the first half of the eighteenth century, *The Ambonese Curiosity Cabinet* (1705) and *The Ambonese Herbarium* (1741–55). (167)

Bleichmar argues that it was the authority of this kind of skilled vision that was implicitly drawn upon, when organizing and producing completely different kinds of representation of local knowledge, namely taxonomies of race ordered by degrees of miscegenation. *Casta* paintings of the late eighteenth century typically compiled model images of individuals or couples of different ethnicities, according to a white-to-black gradation correlated to occupation, social standing, and disposition. The ideological nature of this kind of taxonomic enterprise stands out glaringly now. What I wish to stress here is that it was a form of figurative display of a shared and implicit visual knowledge about "race." The taxonomic classification and the diagrammatic disposition in space added to the analytical nature of such display (figure 1.1).

1.1   Vicente Albán, *Cuadros de mestizaje*, six pieces (Quito, 1783). Courtesy of the Museo de
América, Madrid.

1.1   (*continued*)

The final example highlights the enduring guiding influence of structured environments and cultural artifacts for the social inculcation of skilled visual tasks. I refer to my own study of breeding "aesthetics"—the educated capacity of perceiving the animal body in terms of functional beauty—among dairy breeders in particular (see Grasseni 2005a, 2005b). The ethnography was conducted among breeders of the Italian Brown, a milking cow "progeny" breed developed through artificial insemination and intensive inbreeding from the original Swiss Brown breed. Professional breeders learn to look at cows and appreciate their "beauty" in highly functional terms. They assess, by looking, which desirable "milking" traits have been developed, and to what degree, in any single cow. In order to understand how this sensibility is developed, we need to look at what Bruno Latour (1986) would call "the socio-technical system" of animal husbandry: that is, at the interactions between breeders, cows, and the artifacts that mediate their mutual perception. Among the children of breeders, for instance, toys play a *transparent* role in the social mimicry of adult expertise. Plastic toys mimic the ideal of good form that is found in champion specimens (Grasseni 2007c, 47–66), recalling in detail the "morpho-functional" traits that are evaluated favorably in both cattle fairs and inbreeding practices (see figure 1.2). By observing daily such icons of animal "perfection," the breeders' children incorporate them into their everyday ecology of attention.

The use of such toys parallels the cognitive and social role played by scale models of "ideal cows" in the settings of their parents' professional life. Scale models of prize cows serve, in fact, as trophies at cattle fairs. They are exhibited both in domestic and in professional contexts, thus serving both an educational purpose and one of social acknowledgment. Toys and trophies recapitulate both the historical development and the social inculcation of a professional aesthetics (Grasseni 2004a). This case study shows that what are or are not deemed to be "good looking" animals is often a question of how you learn to look at them. *Which kind* of visual training one is exposed to is often a case of professional history and of social hegemony. In this case the model Brown cow, mimicked by the plastic toy and the cattle fair trophy, is associated with a recent history of intensive dairy farming and with the ideological promotion of pure breeds with specialized functions.

The point of this ethnography was to stress the convergence of intellectual interest in cognitive artifacts—such as models and diagrams—with the practical concerns of technologies of power and simplification. This could not be clearer than in the works of Reviel Netz, author of *Barbed Wire: An Ecology of Modernity* (2004). Having shown in an earlier work

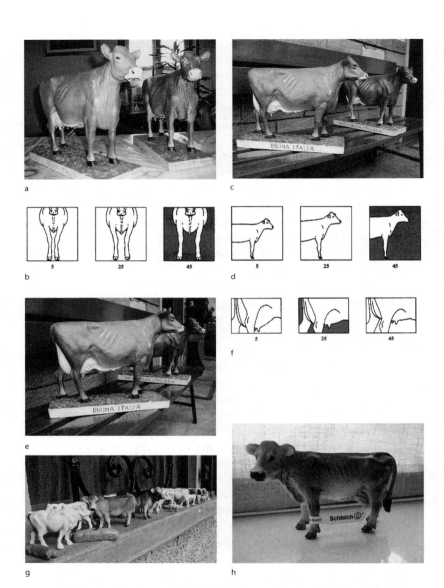

1.2   Artist's drawings based on technical specifications regarding the ideal body shape of the
       Italian Brown cow (2b, 2d, 2f), compared with relevant "traits" in the plastic body of a
       cattle fair trophy (2a, 2c, 2e) and with plastic toys of several breeds (2g, 2h). Drawings
       courtesy of A.N.A.R.B. Photos: Cristina Grasseni.

(1999) how the conservation of necessity in logical, mathematical, and geometrical deduction is a local invention that was amplified and disseminated through visual artifacts (the diagram), Netz devotes his study to the development of a more sinister controlling device: barbed wire, from a technology to control cattle during the colonization of the American West, to an architecture of containment in Nazi concentration camps and Soviet gulags. His ecology of modernity, drawing together the history of humans and animals, shows the interconnectedness of technology as a network, of the environment as a structured space, and of inscription as the powerful act of drawing a line (Ingold 2007).

To conclude this first section, I would propose that vision pervades our cultural forms of life in skilled ways that depend both on the way sight is physically trained and on social positioning. Skilled vision is certainly "sensuous knowledge" (Stoller 1997, 1989), or "corporeal" (Mac Dougall 2006), but it is also positional, political, and relational in important ways. Because skilled visions combine aspects of embodiment (as an educated capacity for selective perception) and of apprenticeship, they are both ecological and ideological, in the sense that they inform worldviews and practice (Grasseni 2007b).

Anthropologists are interested in how private views and expertise become representable and communicable in some way. What inside observers consider crucial to see, in order to participate competently in a standard practice, must be conveyed in a way that makes it visible as well to an outsider. This may include mutual understandings about what must be overlooked, or unremarked, by the expert onlooker.

This means facing the issue of the privacy of perception, or of the incommensurability of different worldviews. An operative perspective on the sharability of experience (including visual experience) can be found in the work of Harold Conklin, an ethnoscientist who worked for years among the Ifugao of the island of Luzon in the Philippines. For him, gaining a perspective of "intimacy" into the working knowledge of his informants could not in any way be the result of finding an "objective" stance. Veridicity was not a matter of how "naturally" things evolved under the eye of the (visual) anthropologist. If he wished to "represent" correctly the ecological knowledge that Ifugao agriculturalists had of their mountainous landscapes, he had to resort to "mediating devices" such as maps and elaborate diagrams of their seasonal activities. Here, I am concerned with how Conklin poses and solves the epistemological problem of representing Ifugao vision *for himself and for his readers*, rather than with Ifugao vision per se. Indeed, as Allison Jablonko puts it, Conklin, with his *Atlas* (1980), had transformed the complex environmental knowledge and practices of the various Ifugao communities into a form of printed communication that could communicate crucial information about phenomena that were otherwise largely invisible to out-siders. The Atlas which resulted from this multidisciplinary effort was used to "educate the gaze" of Philippine politicians." . . . With the Atlas in hand, local Ifugao leaders could go before the national government and win a fight against the construction of dams which would have destroyed a good part of their territory. (Jablonko 2008)

We shall return in the next section to this search for *oversight* as one way to solve the epistemological problem in visual anthropology. For the moment, I simply wish to enroll the workings of "icons" and "in-dexes" (Herzfeld 2007)—from cartography and diagrams to classificatory paintings and artifacts to cultural kinesics—as methods through which local constellations of knowledge (performative, bodily, corporeal, even visceral) are translated into formats that guarantee their sharability.

Ethnographers of science, and other authors from relevant disciplines, have toiled to develop a vocabulary that is apt to convey and analyze the stages of such transformation, from the intimacy of apprenticeship to the circulation of standard representations. In particular, seminal laboratory studies (Latour and Woolgar 1979; Lynch 1985) have focused on the me-diation of teamwork through technology. Ethnomethodological studies of science were among the first to focus on detailed analyses of the vari-ous technologies of vision and inscription that are effectively employed in situated practices, on their socialization through apprenticeship and on their hegemonic potential (see, e.g., Lynch and Woolgar 1990; Good-win and Ueno 2000). Garfinkel, Lynch, and Livingston's (1981) seminal study on the optical discovery of the pulsar shows how the act of *seeing* an entity whose existence had long been posited, but that had never been observed, depends on a complex interaction of communication with other humans and with visualizing machinery, an epistemological act they equate with the Gestalt experience of making out an animal amid thick foliage. In this case, it was a question of giving the *meaning* of seeing something out there (a pulsar) to a series of complex recording on a computer screen, a video display and a printout of mathematical data.

For Lynch and Woolgar (1990), scientific representations are veritable acts of *inscription*, which pass through the stages of selection (according to standards), modeling (highlighting), and mathematization (defini-tion) in order to "reveal" an object. Far from being an act of copying, this complex process amounts to an act of shaping or construction. The images thus produced in scientific practice are textual hybrids that serve the purpose of sharing representations in order to manage operational notions.

Following this line, some ethnographies of scientific, professional, and organizational contexts have argued forcefully that human activity is mediated by artifacts (Chaiklin and Lave 1993; Norman 1988, 1993; Cole 1997; Suchman 1998; Suchman and Trigg 1993) which often have a standardizing function that allows different "espistemic cultures" to co-exist and cooperate toward a functional end. Susan Leigh Star, who trained at the pragmatist school of social interactionism, has pinned down the apt notion of *boundary objects* as those artifacts that are capable of con-necting practices and routines characterized by disparate methods, problems, and theoretical premises. Being characterized by modularity, abstraction, standardization, and mobility across different contexts (Leigh Star and Griesemer 1989), boundary objects can be as functional as insur-ance claim forms, which single out the information necessary for a clerk to figure out whether a claim can be accepted (see Wenger 1998, 106–9). Leigh Star and Griesemer in fact refer to a much more complex historical case study: the foundation of the Zoology Museum at Berkeley, where director Joseph Grinnell succeeded in channeling the material interests and intellectual resources of such disparate partners as amateur collec-tors, taxidermists, hunters, professional biologists, university adminis-trators, researchers, and philanthropists. His uniform protocol for data gathering greatly contributed to establishing the notion of "ecological niche," systematizing the museum displays and archive as an immense database that in turn contributed to the founding of ecology as a distinc-tive subdiscipline. He made use of evolutionary, biogeographical, and physiological concepts (selection, distribution, interaction) that were paramount in defining the interplay of ecological and geographical fac-tors in the process of speciation.

The conviction that artifacts are powerful mediators and generators of sense is also widespread in some quarters of cultural psychology and cognitive research. A vast literature has specialized in ethnographic-style research on how the social and the material environment play a funda-mental role in the ways in which we develop cognitive and performative strategies in our life worlds (e.g., Rogoff 1990, 2003). Though "cogni-tively motivated," such studies diverge from the main tendencies of the cognitive sciences, both the representationalist strands (which identify cognition with the elaboration of information and symbolic manipula-tion) and the neural network ones (inspired by the model of parallel dis-tributed processing in such networks). The starting point of such studies, instead, is the idea that actors and objects co-organize practices in local

31

contexts. In brief, "cognition" must be here understood not as "computation" (as in the commonsense application to computers), but as embodied, relational, and interactive—hence social. From the foundational work of Michael Cole, Edwin Hutchins, Jean Lave, and Lucy Suchman, one can thus derive a project for an anthropological understanding of cognition as situated action.

As Cole sums up, artifacts are at the same time conceptual and material: they have a modeling function, they are transformative and they orient perception and action according to value (1997). Our systems of activity are in fact saturated with artifacts with which we interact and through which we mediate our interaction with others. Indeed, as recent literature on distributed cognition demonstrates, technological or "cognitive" artifacts and contexts may be instrumental in mediating skill (Hutchins 1995; Cole, Engeström, and Vasquez 1997; Engeström and Middleton 1998). The distributed cognition approach holds that all expert action is situated in an environment whose resources structure and orient it. In other words, all expert action is *mediated*, since external supports guide, describe, and shape it. Cognitive artifacts are one such type of mediators that embody and embed the results of previous expert action. Traffic lights, the arrangement of supermarket rows, and to-do lists are all ways (varying in complexity) to arrange and structure a context of action in which, through the aid of appropriate tools, human action is guided in ways that have been prearranged by previous expert action. The arrangement of the shelf guides my shopping according to a logic, more or less coherent to my own shopping list. I can shop according to my own strict, prearranged list or let myself be guided by an architecture that has been arranged for me beforehand. In order to manage such artifacts we need to align our action with them and continuously coordinate between our plans of action and the interpretation of the resources around us (Hutchins 1986).

The ethnographic research program directed by Lucy Suchman at the Intelligent Systems Laboratory of the Xerox Research Center of Palo Alto (PARC), has focused especially on the role of devices for seeing (diagrams, formulas, models) that simulate scenarios of action on paper, screens, and the like. In an ethnography of an information technology programming team, Suchman and Trigg insist that the team members' interaction can be seen as a *skilled improvisation* woven around the cognitive constraints and possibilities afforded by the material supports of the traces of their brainstorming (1993, 146). Even though IT rests squarely on an idea of knowledge representation, Suchman shows how important aspects of it are highly relational "craftwork," whose main support is the two-dimensional surface of the whiteboard. The whiteboard becomes a space for cognitive, perceptive, performative, and emotional investment. Through it, each programmer can contribute to the team's flowchart as a sharable and manageable object. They draw, cancel, modify, and discuss their inscriptions, which makes them *concrete conceptual objects* (1993, 160).

The visual and situated component of human interaction and communication has been analyzed not only in visual anthropology but in sophisticated studies of linguistics and pragmatics. From the stepping stones represented by the works of Michael Cole, Edwin Hutchins, Lucy Suchman, Jean Lave, and others, ethnographic research on cognition has hence developed as a study of situated action. On yet another versant, actor-network theory has underlined the "metropolitan" and "metrological" nature of technological mediation that is achieved through the dissemination of "mobile inscriptions" (Latour 1991). In this latter perspective, visual inscriptions emerge as powerful carriers of knowledge, sociality, and identity: a successful go-between from the grounded, situated body to the global hierarchies of sociotechnical networks. From this heterogeneous landscape, in the following sections we shall single out some relevant examples.

The Role of Visual Practice in Constructing Reference

Bruno Latour is widely known as a theorist and an ethnographer of scientific practice. His work, like that of many other scholars active in the philosophy and the history of science (see, e.g., Pickering 1992; Miller and Reill 1996; Lenoir 1998; Tufte 1983), starts from an analysis of how we make ourselves visual representations in scientific practices, to show that such representations are in no way spontaneous copies, but are highly constructed. In an essay entitled "The 'Pedofil' of Boa Vista" (1995) he sets out to unpack the notion of *scriptures visuelles*. By "visual inscriptions" he means the media by which we successfully make reference, by way of representation, to the world. Latour is particularly interested in scientists in action (Latour and Woolgar 1979), but his arguments in fact refer—as has become clearer in his latest books on the political effects of the dissemination of scientific objects—to all those cognitive transformations that the world must undergo so that we can make ourselves a picture of it. For instance, the map, as a visual and textual artifact produced in a local context, can be read as a thick inscription of socially constructed knowledge. Different capacities to visualize the landscape correspond to different capacities to contribute to its cartographic representation (depending on personal or professional histories and specializations of practice, e.g., Grasseni 2004b). But a geographer draws a map in such a way as to perform an act of *designation*, and so do we. Latour wishes to pin down exactly what is entailed by such a process of "constructing reference," even though starting from fine-grained, eminently local contexts of knowledge.[6]

What the Latourian approach adds to social constructivism is the thesis that the reliability of our knowledge of the world depends on the dissemination, sharability, and persuasive power of inscriptions. In "The 'Pedofil' of Boa Vista," for instance, Latour investigates pedology as a field science, showing the various stages through which soil from the Amazon forest is progressively transformed and adapted to different kinds of graphic inscriptions. These act as a reliable interface between the actual field, situated at the border between forest and savannah, its raw data, and scientists' theory about how the forest may be advancing into the savannah. Is the forest encroaching on the savannah or is the terrain around the forest slowly degrading into shrubs and grass? One of the "mediating technologies" involved in the inscription process is provided by a page of the Munsell color charts: the coding of samples of soil, according to international standards of color hue, marks a fundamental *mise en forme* of the forest's "raw data." A particular soil sample collected by the research team can thus become a number, that is an index, within a diagrammatic representation of the state of things as they are (see figures 1.3–1.6).

The success of the map and of the overview, or, as Latour would put it, of the technologies of visual "inscription" and technological "mediation," can hardly be explained away as mere Western visualist ideology, nor can they be substituted by "just looking" at something. As other authors in this book authoritatively argue (see Farnell), we should not conflate a critique of visualism with aversion to analytical work on and with vision in anthropology. Indeed we should distinguish generic calls for holistic approaches to embodiment and the senses (Okely 1998, 2001) from actual research on the processes of visual "enskilment," that is, on the apprenticeship of particular skilled visions that are *specific to situated practices*. How much can these tell us about the hegemony of, and resistance to, the "sociotechnical network"? There are several examples of field studies that begin to do just that.

Richard K. Sherwin, Neal Feigenson, and Christina Spiesel, in their study at the frontiers of visual anthropology and cultural legal studies (2007), explain how legal scholars, like anthropologists and many other practitioners of knowledge, have "been struggling to work through a crisis of sorts regarding the nature and communicability of truth." In American

1.3–1.4   A "pedo-comparator," a box devised by pedologists to arrange soil samples in a synoptic manner, as investigated by Bruno Latour in "The 'Pedofil' of Boa Vista: A Photo-Philosophical Montage" (1995). Courtesy of Bruno Latour.

1.5–1.6 Use in the field of Munsell's charts to identify the color of a soil sample. Latour (1995) argues that this is one of the ways in which pedologists practically establish references between their final soil report and the original encounter with the forest. Courtesy of Bruno Latour.

courtrooms, visual artifacts that range from photographs to digital video-recordings and their edited versions, are appropriated and interpreted so as to serve as powerfully effective persuasive devices. In this context, to be highly effective in epistemological terms also means having powerful effects on people's lives and destinies, since "inside the courtroom, the difference between truth and falsity, fact and fantasy, objectivity and subjectivity, may be a matter of life and death" (2007, 144).

In particular, the courtroom treatment of the amateur recordings of the infamous police beatings of Rodney King has been the object of both anthropological and legal analysis. Allen Feldman, in his contribution to Nadia Seremetakis's seminal volume about memory and the body, denounces the "'cultural anaesthesia' that pervades the processes of 'normalizing' and 'silencing' everyday life" (1994, 89). In his words, the video that spurred the Los Angeles riots—an angry popular response to white policemen beating mercilessly an African American driver—was edited by the defense so that King was "montaged into a purely electronic entity with no inwardness or tangibililty" (1994, 98). King's silencing, and the voicing of the policemen's point of view within the courtroom, also by way of video editing, was yet another form of violence, of "sensory privilege."

Similar uses of visual testimony are commonplace in contemporary court cases. The local conditions by which visual authority is actually created, defended, and contested have been authoritatively critiqued (Jasanoff 1998).[7] The King case had also received insightful attention by different scholars and disciplines (see Goodwin 1994). Charles Goodwin has recently contributed many analytical insights on the practice of inscription and has specifically called for an ethnomethodological approach to visual analysis (Goodwin 2000). His analytical treatment of the courtroom recordings of the trial, and of the way edited footage was used in testimony, purposefully argues for a more general thesis, that "coding schemes are a systematic practice used to transform the world into the categories and events that are relevant to the work of a profession" (1994, 608). In other words, "coding," "highlighting," and "producing and demonstrating material representations" of complex phenomenal events are all steps of paramount importance in the construction of a shared perception and interpretation of the world in a given context.

For Goodwin, in general, human interaction and communication also work thanks to visual and situated components, which are provided in ad hoc contexts by different means of inscription. In other words, "the public organization of visual practice within the worklife of a profession" (Goodwin 2000, 164) provides a material and relational setting—something I would call an ecology of practice—without which perception would be abstracted, action would be meaningless, and communication would fail. This is very relevant to a reflection about vision as a highly flexible and structured "way of knowing" (Grasseni 2007b), especially when it is applied to controversial cases—such as the Rodney King beating—involving the structuration of power in and around such settings. Following Goodwin's argument, "professional vision" literally shapes events, by giving them meaning from a point of view that is internal to a community of practice (Wenger 1998). The case of police officers justifying recourse to violence, by way of carefully editing and heavily interpreting a piece of footage, shows how powerful the strategies of professional vision can be when they are coupled with unquestioned hierarchies of expertise, however much one might naively assume that video-recorded evidence would constitute "objective" data.

In this and in several following studies, conducted in diverse working environments using both visual and discourse analysis, Goodwin examines similar yet less controversial processes, such as those in which apprentice archaeologists learn to map a dirt patch, or of laboratory novices learning to discern "the blackness of black" (Goodwin 1996, 1997). As an anthropologist, linguist, and expert of human communication, Goodwin treats vision as a situated negotiation among people who attune their visual capacities both cognitively and socially. Even in the case of a *scientific* gaze (1997, 2000), for instance, he uses ethnographic observation to problematize the idea of a universal color classification. In this latter case study, conducted in a chemical laboratory, an acrylic fiber is subjected to chemical reactions in order to measure the amount of radon in water. The preparation of the fiber entails dipping it in a solution from which it is extracted after about ten minutes, when it has become jet black. The inventor of the process himself is present and teaches young apprentices to recognize when the fiber is black enough. He intervenes in the decisions of the apprentices by exchanging opinions and remarks with them, by making them notice the texture of the fiber as well as the color, and by using comparisons from natural experience (the ink black of the fiber is compared to gorilla fur, while fiber not yet black enough is called "orangutang hair"). On the basis of this ethnography Goodwin argues against a cognitive approach to a universal semantics of color classification (Berlin and Kay 1969; Conklin 1955; but see Wittgenstein 1977). Without contesting its existence, Goodwin simply observes that in order to be put to work, such semantics still needs attuning to local contexts of practice, which provide empirical frameworks of reference for its application.

What has all this got to do with visual anthropology, or with anthropology *tout court*? The apparently elitist practice of the ethnography of science uses the tools of participant observation in professional contexts to answer what is in fact a much more general question, which lies at the core of epistemological debates within visual anthropology: Is it possible to generate automatic visual judgments? How do we agree on a world-image? When we speak of a world-image or a world-view, while it is counterintuitive to speak of a world-smell or a world-taste, does it mean that we are biased toward visualism? (See, e.g., Fabian 1983; Classen 1993; Howes 1991; Feld and Basso 1996.) We expect a uniform perception of what is "under everyone's eyes" but have no such presumption with smells or tastes; where these are concerned, we at least concede that we do not all share the same sensitivity. Is it because we hold a presumption that we can make spontaneous representations—visual copies—of the world?

The case studies and theories that I have briefly reviewed propose a flexible way of approaching this "epistemological problem" by charting actual visual practices in situated contexts. Latour's anthropological study of the pedologists of Boa Vista, for instance, consists in mapping their own acts of mapping the forest. He singles out from their activity the devices thanks to which they "think with eyes and hands" (Latour 1986). Such devices are *artifacts*, endowed with a cognitive and a practical agency at the same time. To look at the empirical ways in which pedologists use the Munsell code pages to itemize samples of Amazonian soil is itself a way to solve on an empirical basis "the epistemological problem." It means putting in brackets "nature," as an ever-distant ontological term to which our representations should adequate themselves, in order to follow instead, and more fruitfully, the actual passages and transformations that allow us to construct and share visual artifacts that are *about* the real world.

Goodwin's and Latour's treatment of Munsell charts share many common observations though leading to somewhat differing conclusions. In both cases, scholars who would not, I think, define themselves as "visual anthropologists" have shared a fascination for the ways in which different communities of practice appropriate the Munsell code. Goodwin analytically highlights all the various phases of adjustment and appropriation that must be put in place around such inscriptions in order to render them operational and functional to contexts: Munsell standard color-coding charts must be made viable in the field and sharable among teachers and pupils. Thus archaeologists make holes in the color samples, single out the relevant pages, use a trowel to be able to look at a soil sample through a peephole in the page, and so on. These professionals are always "highlighting, coding, framing"—all activities that go on around artifacts in order to use them in a coherent way within a common effort. This means that the power of standards is not limitless, or rather that standards must always be adapted to particular material and conversational situations: real contexts in which humans act and speak to each other, exchanging information. Similarly, in his ethnography of a chemistry lab, Goodwin shows how "black" is a shifting category despite the existence of well-established universal color-coding and sampling repertoires. In a laboratory where a chemical process must be stopped when the fabric immersed in a permanganate solution becomes "jet black," the capacity to recognize such jet black is itself subject to training, and to much talk (Goodwin 1997).

For Latour, by contrast, to witness how pedologists adapt pages of the Munsell code to the necessities of their field (exactly as Goodwin's archaeologists do, singling out pages, preparing viewing holes, etc.) is to find a practical solution to the epistemological question in science studies. Namely, it means to shift from structuralism to metrology. The Munsell code is an empirical way to "shift" and "translate" from raw data (soil color) to transportable, treatable, and communicable data (the number of the corresponding colors). A la William James (1981), such passage is not a matter of theorization but of an empirical tradition, of practical expertise. According to Latour, though, far from restating the importance of personal, tacit, and indigenous knowledges (see, e.g., Polanyi 1958), such empirical passages are precisely what allows the construction of reference, by overcoming the strictures of incommensurability, of untranslatability, and of local knowledge. Granted that knowledge is situated, the various and successive operations of inscription, translation, and recombination to which scientists subject their "raw data" serve precisely to transform local contexts of knowledge into manageable, constructed, and sharable settings. In fact, Latour's many-faceted oeuvre illuminates the triumph of metrology.

To put it in Latour's words, "If a picture is worth a thousand words, a map can be worth a whole forest," and "Scientists master the world, but only if the world comes to them in the form of two-dimensional, superposable, combinable inscriptions" (1995, 24, 29). That's why every filing cabinet, grid, graph, or map "is a theory." According to this view, to uphold local and situated knowledge as a paradigm would be unnecessarily polemic. Instead, what is of general interest is to locate and study the operational technologies at work in creating different types of *visual scriptures*, and to highlight their cognitive qualities, as Elisabeth Eisenstein (1979) does with print as an agent of change. According to her reading, for example, the Copernican revolution would not have been achieved if not for the unprecedented dissemination of printed astronomical maps that made available to a synoptic scrutiny the many contradictions and contrivances of the Ptolemaic system (see Latour 1986).

Within this framework, the work of anthropologists, archaeologists, and pedologists alike is that of constructing a passage from one ontological self-contained entity to another (e.g., from soil to color), while maintaining comparative differences, as in geometry. Visual inscriptions are hence any kind of devices that "translate" three-dimensional reality to a two-dimensional "trace" that makes a different kind of data "visible under the same unifying gaze" (Latour 1995, 38). They are mobile, and often they permit new recombinations of traits, thus allowing patterns to emerge, as they literally stand out against new backgrounds. Eventually, "translation" is a matter of creating a synoptic situation in which "oversight" is guaranteed, both in the sense of gaining a vista, an overview, and of forgetting that "the map is not the territory."

To conclude, while Latour underlines the conventional coding of judgments, protocols, tags, logbooks, and all the rites of verification that pedologists, botanists, and anthropologists impose upon themselves in order to guarantee a valid "circulation of reference" between their inscriptions and the world, Goodwin underlines precisely the idiosyncratic aspects of such rites, the fact that they always bring back conventions and standards to the local contexts in which such conventions and standards are applied. Both positions have produced many interesting insights to visual anthropology, starting from the concept of "professional vision" (Goodwin 1994). If the skilled visions approach (Grasseni 2007c) asks how we are trained to see a particular type of object or situation that, for an unskilled onlooker, can be a neutral object, the Latour approach is about how to invent ways of sharing views, or in other words, how to represent a problem by giving it a shape that makes it visible in a new way.[8] Against an intellectual iconoclasm that tends to erase the role of visual scriptures (see Jay 1993), this trend in the ethnography and in the history of science hopes to provide an iconophile description of formalism in its making (Stafford 1996; Galison and Jones 1998; Netz 2004; but see also Bateson and Mead 1942).

I think that a possible convergence of the two approaches can be played on the ground of what Wittgenstein would call *Uebersichtlichkeit* (1956), that is, another way of taking visual inscriptions as constructions, which impose themselves on us as evident but only as a result of training and belonging to specific forms of life. *Uebersichtlichkeit* is the quality of a perspicuous representation of a state of things, a synthetic representation that is achieved in such a way as to be communicable (hence sharable) and manageable (hence operational, often in formal ways, as in mathematics). In other words, Latour's *oversights* and Goodwin's *professional visions* look compellingly plausible only as the result of training, of yielding to the sheer force of repetition that rites of verification and rotas of apprenticeship impose on us. A viable direction for research that can be derived from these insights is to focus visual-anthropological analysis on the disciplined and disciplining aspects of memory and sensibility that are not spontaneous, personal, and subjective but rather embedded in mediating devices, contexts, and routines, taking into consideration the role played by peer-to-peer negotiation, hierarchical relations, and the management of contexts, narratives, and artifacts.

Conclusion

The increasing interest, among the current generation of ethnographers, in the scope and reach of visual research methods (Pink et al., 2004), as well as the intertwining histories of photography, film, and anthropology (Grimshaw 2001; Edwards 2001), can only benefit from the awareness of the many links between science and the visual, as well as from collaborative research and production across the arts and sciences (Schneider and Wright 2006). We are, after all, reminded that the history of film began "as the media and technological variation of a long-term transformation of western epistemology" (Gumbrecht 1998, 362).

Local formations of knowledge are analyzed by the authors and trends reviewed here not as a given but in their making. In particular, the work of ethnographers of science who are sensitive to the importance of visual knowledge highlights the complex relation of a "constructivist" attitude to visual artifacts and the hegemony of the sociotechnical network. We can position these studies at the interface between ethnomethodology, actor-network theory, cultural psychology, discourse analysis, and of course visual anthropology. As we have seen, in fact, the disciplinary literatures evoked by each of these trends are interested, although in different ways and by way of different pathways, in finding and pursuing analytical approaches to visualization and cognition, both in classical scientific contexts and more generally in contexts of communication and cognition. At the intersection of such interests lies a common fascination for the powerful workings of inscriptions (Latour 1986) and for the role of artifacts, to the point that some of these authors have published extensively about precisely the same kind of inscriptions, such as Munsell charts—as variously employed, for instance, by pedologists (Latour 1995) and archaeologists (Goodwin 1994)—or the Rodney King video (Feldman 1994; Goodwin 1994; Sherwin et al. 2007).

Bruno Latour's and Charles Goodwin's works, for instance, provide lucid accounts—however different—of how we do not "grasp an image" of the world but rather construct representations that substitute for the world. I think this is a useful stance from which to approach the epistemological problem of visual anthropology, that is, the ways in which we treat and consider our photographs, film, digital media, and multimedia as "pictures" of the world. In particular, from the point of view of an ecological approach to visual practice, it is important that we consider our visual inscriptions as *artifacts* and that we assess the way in which they contribute to structuring a material, cognitive, and social environment for situated action.

Notes

1. Other authors concerned with the ecology of practice dislike the notion of *habitus* as unduly focused on "unconscious practical logic." See Farnell (2000, and in this volume), who stresses agency over disposition and "the causal and performative power of both action signs and vocal signs as resources for meaningful action in social life."
2. Interdisciplinary discussions around "skilled visions" and situated knowledge were initiated at a preparatory seminar, "Practices of Locality," organized in 2000 at the University of Milan Bicocca with Paola Filippucci. In 2004 I chaired a thematic session titled "Skilled Visions: Between Apprenticeship and Standards" at the Vienna EASA Biennial Meeting and organized a symposium ("Skilled Visions: Educating Attention in the Field") with Mike Bravo and Andreas Roepstorff, hosted by the Centre for Research in the Arts, Social Sciences and Humanities (CRASSH) at Cambridge University. *Skilled Visions*, the editorial project that ensued, gathers selected revised papers of the EASA panel with invited contributions from the Milan and Cambridge workshops. The postgraduate school in Anthropology and Epistemology of Complexity of the University of Bergamo (Italy) provided the basis for a follow-up conference in 2006 whose proceedings were published as *Imparare a Guardare*, ed. C. Grasseni (Milan: Franco Angeli Editore, 2007).
3. Brenda Farnell, in this book, provides a convincing overview and critique of the many links between literature on "the body" in visual culture, the anthropology of the senses, and critiques to visualism.
4. This is also relevant to the debate on indigenous media and to the ways in which different worldviews would be literally a matter of "seeing through" disparate cultural lenses (see Faye Ginsburg's discussion, in this book, of the classic work of Worth and Adair).
5. The emphasis on training vision with reference to naturalistic drawing at an age much earlier than that of photography integrates in interesting ways what Elizabeth Edwards, in this volume, calls "the rhetorics of the disciplinary eye."
6. See, e.g., his analysis of La Pérouse's journey through the Pacific with the explicit mission of bringing back a better map of the Asian coastline for the French king Louis XVI (Latour 1990).
7. Sheila Jasanoff, with reference to the O. J. Simpson murder trial, argues that "scientific evidence must be seen to be believed." Yet, "the judge's uncontested remarks and rulings established at many crucial points whose

vision would be authorized as expert, and in what circumstances lay vision could take precedence over expert sight" (1998, 713).

8. For Latour, "Inscription is a summary for a set of different attitudes of which the visual is still the most crucial, because this is the one that allows the simplification of perceptive judgment that closes disputes down—momentarily of course, as Goodwin nicely shows" (personal communication, September 9, 2006).

TWO

Material Visions: Dress and Textiles

SANDRA DUDLEY

How far can dress and textiles, and anthropological images and texts concerned with them, be said to constitute a visual anthropology? And to what extent do ethnographic photographs and film deal with clothing, fabric, and their production and consumption? This chapter explores these and other questions, in the process assessing both the relation between clothing, textiles, and other visual media and the limitations of the visual lens in this context. Inevitably the chapter is not comprehensive. Much of the writing around dress and textiles does not actually deal with their visual and other sensory dimensions and is thus excluded here. Nor do I cover areas such as the growing literature on secondhand clothing and recycling, factory-produced cloth and garments, or the social analysis of aspects of textile production, such as the religious strictures and prohibitions imposed upon it in particular places and historical periods.[1]

Terminology and Scope

Dress and textiles are often distinguished and treated differently—or at least separately—from each other, in anthropological, art historical, and connoisseurship writing. This separation may, at least in part, be traceable to the distinct genealogies of different material culture studies, originating in social science and in museums respectively (cf. Miller 2005). Yet, while many textiles do not end up being worn as clothing (e.g., carpets, bedding, storage bags), this is precisely the purpose of many others. In those cases, the dress

2.1 Sunlight falls on a partly woven man's skirt-cloth on a frame loom at the Shwe Hintha weaving workshop, Thale, Inle Lake, Shan State, Burma (Myanmar). Photo: Sandra Dudley, 1996.

literature in particular often neglects (and even sometimes explicitly rejects—e.g., Fine and Leopold 1993, cited in Taylor 2002) the significance of the detail and technology of textile (and garment) design, content, composition, and production. Yet choices about color and pattern in particular social and personal settings, and the use of particular fibers and certain weaving, embroidery, and other techniques, may reveal as much if not more than do the cut and context of a garment and the way in which fabric is draped around the human form. Indeed, the potential of textiles is often exploited by clothing designers and producers (figure 2.1). Weavers of Jinghpaw Kachin women's tunics, for example, use dense, continuous and discontinuous supplementary weft patterning with heavy, colored dog—or goat-hair fibers to produce not only decoration but warmth,[2] while those in eighteenth-century Lyon used plaited, flat, stamped, and coiled gold and silver yarns to produce differing shimmering effects in the court costumes for which the cloth was eventually destined (Taylor 2002, 24–25).

The relationship between fiber, technique, and visual and physical effects, on the one hand, and aesthetic and sociocultural purpose, on the other, is hardly surprising for those familiar with the literature in certain areas of dress and textile studies. Some of the literature on Indonesian cloths, for example, while largely ignoring the mundane, everyday use of cloth (Allerton 2007), has nonetheless long examined fabrics in intricate yet deeply socially contextualized detail (e.g., Barnes 1989, 1995; Hoskins 1989).[3] Elsewhere, however, close attention to the material of and techniques by which dress is made—and indeed the way in which it wraps the body that wears it—has often been slight in comparison to the analysis of when and why clothes are worn. Exceptions exist, of course: Tauzin (2007), for example, writing on the female body and its raiments in Mauritania, identifies the importance of palette, density, and material content of the fabric used (specifically, synthetic versus natural fibers). Nonetheless, discussion of such factors within the wider anthropology of dress is still relatively slight. At the same time (and again some of the work on Indonesian textiles is a notable exception), coverage of textiles can be disappointingly limited in its exploration of the social contexts and uses of fabric. It is thus a premise of this chapter that, especially in any approach claiming a visual analytical focus, explorations of textiles and of dress belong together.[4]

With one or two exceptions, I do not consider here textiles not used in or as clothing; equally, I do not discuss dress items not comprised of fabric. Textiles per se are covered in less detail here than is dress as a whole—this reflects the balance in that extant literature which can in some way be termed both visual and anthropological.[5] Nonetheless, parts of this chapter do address fundamental elements of textiles and their production, and later I incorporate those elements into my arguments about appropriate approaches to dress and cloth within visual and wider sensory anthropology.

Dress is defined by Eicher and Roach-Higgins as an "assemblage of body modifications and supplements displayed by a person in communicating with other human beings" (1992, 15). This definition, according to Hansen (although she does not quote it fully), "reckons both with the strategic effects entailed in the material properties of dress and their expressive abilities" (2004, 371). In a later Eicher phrase, this expressive, indeed communicative, aspect of dress is even more evident—it becomes, in fact, what dress is: "a coded sensory system of non-verbal communication that aids human interaction in space and time" (1995b, 1) In perhaps the majority of extant literature on cloth and clothing, the main focus of inquiry is the communicative and often the semiotic and "symbolic."[6]

There are other important approaches to the subject, of course, including exploration of the consumption and exchange of textiles and garments and the part such transactions play in forming and reinforcing social relations (e.g., Brydon and Niessen 1998; Norris 2004). These transactions may take on particular significance during certain rites of passage. Additionally, in certain cultures textiles have themselves become a currency of economic exchange.[7] Furthermore, much can often be gleaned from an examination of the characteristics and consumption of cloth from elsewhere that has come in via trade or other means (e.g., Barnes 1997; Maxwell 1990; Steiner 1985; and Were 2005). Schneider—who cannot be accused of neglecting textile composition and design—also identifies a link between textile production and consumption and "the mobilization of power by . . . units of social action such as classes, dynasties, cities, religious institutions, and ethnic and gender sodalities," a link she argues "is suggested by the relationship of stylistic change to political and economic shifts" (1987, 409; see also Schneider and Weiner 1986) and exemplified in various ethnographies and histories she cites (e.g., Murra 1962; Weiner 1985).[8] In keeping with the main thrust in the extant literature, then, communication, exchange and consumption—in various forms—run as themes through much of this chapter, although, as we shall see, without augmentation these perspectives are all potentially limiting.

Textiles and dress are not always thought of as constituting a core part of visual anthropology; not only are they absent as a main topic from previous reviews of visual anthropology (e.g., Banks and Morphy 1997), but most authors who actually pay attention to the appearance and composition of cloth and clothing as part of a wider anthropological analysis would characterize their approach as material, rather than visual, anthropology (see, e.g., the chapters in Küchler and Miller 2005). Yet clearly part of the intention in the production and wearing of fabric is to make a visual impact—and as such, any attempt to understand the cultural value and meanings of textiles and dress needs to utilize at least some visual approaches (cf. Waterson, this volume, on the built environment).

Visual anthropology has a fundamental "duality of focus," being concerned with (1) "the use of visual material in anthropological research" and (2) "the study of visual systems and visible culture" (Banks and Morphy 1997, 1). This duality structures the early parts of this chapter, in which I first discuss cloth and clothing *in* visual media (in the process reviewing the shifting significance of dress and textiles, and problematizing the notion of "salvage"), and then consider them *as* visual media in their own right (a discussion that encompasses issues of identity, consumption, and the temporality of dress and textiles). As we shall see, however, neither perspective as it has generally been pursued permits us to explore fully the conceptual and ethnographic complexities of dress and textiles, including in their relationship to the human body. Such relationships—and the part they play in multisensory human experience—are intrinsic not only to how clothing is worn, how the body shapes it, and notions of dress as a "social skin" (cf. Turner 1980), but also to how clothing is perceived. Awareness of the importance of corporeality and of the senses, and cultivation of a more phenomenological approach, is current within as well as beyond visual anthropology (e.g., MacDougall 2006; Pink 2006), and it is to such issues in relation to cloth and clothing that the latter parts of this chapter turn.

Of course, other strands have been identified within visual anthropology too. Pink, for example, adds the "activist or applied strand" (this volume; see also 2006, 2007b).[9] I do not deal significantly with this here, but it is an area in which dress may play an important role. Indeed, while it may not be quite the phenomenon Pink has in mind, some early ethnographic photographs can be described as having an activist component. A photograph in the collections of Denison University Art Gallery (Ohio), taken by an American missionary and depicting two traditionally dressed Kayah women, with a handwritten scrawl on the back explaining that after the photograph was taken the women converted to Christianity, changed their style of clothing, and "became clean," is a case in point. While this may be neither contemporary nor the kind of activism in which "anthropologists, local people, and activists" may develop "new forms of collaboration" (Pink, this volume), such images and the interpretive frameworks within which they were placed were important in illustrating and reinforcing a process of deliberately seeking to bring about sociocultural change. A similar example, involving early nineteenth-century missionizing in Bechuanaland, again posits the local wearing of more Western-style or body-encompassing clothes as literally and symbolically bringing about changes in both hygiene practice and moral view (Comaroff and Comaroff 1997; see also Colchester 2005 on Fiji and Dudley 1999 on Karenni refugees). Indeed, the activist strand in visual anthropology is perhaps but an extension of wider cultural practice—and one that is arguably more focused on the body, and by extension the cloths which clothe it, than on any other single, material form. The body as primary subject of—or vehicle for—the disciplining and transforming functions of colonialism, for example, is now well understood (e.g., Anderson 2004; Mills and Sen 2004; Pierce and Rao 2006) and dress has clearly been an important factor within this, though there is not space to discuss it further here (see, e.g., Cohn 1989 and Comaroff and Comaroff 1992, cited in Reischer and Koo 2004, 298).

Dress and Textiles in Visual Media

An obvious relationship between one aspect of visual anthropology and dress/textiles is the use of visual media such as photographs and film to document and analyze clothing, fabric, and objects and processes associated with textile production, consumption, and use. This documentation and analysis may be direct or indirect—that is, it may be the main purpose (or one of the purposes) of the visual record (figure 2.2) or an incidental product of the imaging of something else. Ethnographic photographs of whatever period may prove useful testament to style of cloth, clothing, and modes of wearing, whether or not that was one of the photographer's intentions. For example, the photographs taken of Lan Na royal families in the 1880s and 1890s in what is now northern Thailand, by missionary Samuel Peoples, constitute important historical evidence of dress practices at that time (Conway 2000, cited in Taylor 2002, 152). Equally, the 1930s photographs of dancers in Bali taken by Beryl de Zoete, and the correlative film made by Walter Spies (both film and photographs now residing in the archives of the Horniman Museum), provide an invalu-

2.2 Winding yarn onto a spool, Amarapura, central Burma (Myanmar). Photo: Sandra Dudley, 1996.

able record of how masks and dress items were worn and used (Hitchcock and Norris 1995, cited in Taylor 2002, 153).

Barnes has argued that well before the twentieth century approached, the new, "scientific" methods encouraged by the Royal Anthropological Institute's *Notes and Queries* handbook (from 1874 onward) focused on abstract categories of culture that detracted from a deeper understanding of cloth and clothing (1992, 29–30). This should not be taken as imply-ing that cloth and clothing were absent from or unimportant in early ethnographies, however. In late nineteenth- and early twentieth-century ethnographies and their associated visual material, the textual and visual description of dress, like that of body decoration, was of great impor-tance as evidence of the perceived characteristics of the people in ques-tion. Indeed, the essentializing of identity, and the demonstration of the supposed exotic and bizarre, often hinged upon apparently emblematic styles of dress and ornamentation. In Burma, for example, with its very high degree of ethnic plurality, the use of visual description was a key part of the process of categorizing and separating out all the groups con-cerned.[10] The bewildering array of human diversity encountered by colo-nial officers, missionaries, and travelers in Burma and many other parts of the world, and its intersection with wider "scientific" imperatives to classify and record, was largely based on and reduced to perceived ethnic distinctions. In turn, the focus on ethnicity often relied on the recording of two of its apparently most obvious markers, language and dress. Of those two, and as a visual medium in itself, dress was by far the easier to represent in the published, archival, and museum domains—and as a subject of both visual media and textual analyses it became simultaneously a de rigueur component of ethnographies and a focus of significant attention in its own right.[11] In the process, of course, dress and textiles also became an important component in growing ethnographic museum collections, "as visual evidence of the existence of exotic, mysterious peoples" (Taylor 2004, 67).

Clothing, textiles, and their production and use are thus documented—whether or not as primary subject—in countless archive and private collections of photographs. Sometimes such photographic recording specifically augments the documentation of a collection of actual textile objects—either historically coincidental or assembled simultaneously by the photographer. James Henry Green, for example, a British recruitment officer in the Burma Rifles in the 1920s, made an impressive collection of textile clothing items from Burma's Kachin State at the same time as embarking on an extensive program of photographing the diverse people of the region. The photographs (now, as with most of the clothing items, in the collections of the Green Centre for Non-Western Art at Brighton Museum and Art Gallery in the UK),[12] include some "scientific" typologizing images (Odo 2000; cf. Edwards 1990) but are largely romantic and naturalistic in pose and setting. They are well documented, with text that often names individuals and indicates strong ties of affection between photographer and photographed, and include images of specific clothing items collected by Green. Of course, Green and other photographers were not above manipulating their subjects, for example, by providing suitably "traditional" clothing for them to wear. Willmott, for example, recounts the photographing by John Hillyer of a Paiute woman in 1870s North America, "wearing a White River Ute dress that [John Wesley] Powell had brought into the field from the Smithsonian collections. The accession label is visible in the photograph on the bodice of the dress" (2005, 321, citing Fleming and Luskey 1986).

As the twentieth century was well under way, however, and anthropology's interests and dominant paradigms shifted, dress and textiles became far less important as a subject of study themselves—and thus far less likely to be a primary focus of anthropological visual media. This decrease in focus was compounded by the declining use of photographs generally in published ethnographies (cf. MacDougall 1997, 290). As part of wider moves away from studying material culture, the main theoretical frameworks governing mainstream anthropological research from the

1930s onward meant that clothing in particular was reduced to no more than, as Hansen puts it, "an accessory in symbolic, structural, or semiotic explanations," with the result that "any serious engagement with clothing itself . . . almost vanished" (2004, 370; see also Keane 2005). Indeed, by the 1970s Schwarz went so far as to say, "Descriptions of clothing are so rare in some texts of social anthropology . . . that the casual reader might easily conclude the natives go naked" (1979, 23, quoted in Taylor 2002, 195).

Things have changed again in the last twenty or so years, however. One can hardly agree with Taylor's claim that "assessment of the cultural meanings of textiles, clothing and body decoration" is "central within this [anthropological] discourse today" (2002, 193), but there is certainly a degree of return to ostensibly nineteenth-century interests in material culture, including dress. Today, the focus is of course on the part played by objects in processual, dynamic social life rather than as essential markers of cultural fixity, and in recent material culture studies there has been a shift away from exploring social structure and toward social practice and social agency.[13]

Indeed, this contemporary focus—and the associated discomfort with tying dress to any cultural essence—means that within anthropological visual media dress and textiles are still considerably less likely than they once were to be the primary object that an image seeks to describe. There are, of course, exceptions: the photographs used in books such as Ahmed's richly detailed monograph on weaving among the nomadic pastoralists in Ladakh (2002), or Dell and Dudley's edited volume on historical and contemporary textiles and dress from Burma (2003), are wholly concerned with the textile items and their contexts. Nonetheless, texts such as these are, while anthropological, still specialist in their focus on textiles and dress—hence it is hardly surprising that cloth and clothing should be a principal subject of the images they contain (these and other volumes, however, still rarely if ever discuss how the photographs were taken and how they fit within wider research methodologies, as Taylor [2002, 158] points out). Outside this specialist area, in anthropology more broadly, it remains the case that dress and textiles are less likely than in the relatively distant past to be the main subject of images, except by default.

One visual vehicle for dress and textiles is museum displays. In ethnographic settings in particular, the mode of display varies from the simple use of poles for hanging folded cloths and for inserting through arms of upper garments (e.g., the clothing displays on the ground floor of the University of Oxford's Pitt Rivers Museum), through padded but faceless mannequins, to lifelike waxen-faced figures (Taylor 2002, 41). However, factors such as composition, weight, the decorative exploitation of the play of light on moving fabric, and the way in which clothing fits and moves with the body are notoriously difficult to convey in the tradition-ally static and dimly lit display case. Taylor's example of Japanese Noh theater—and the inability of a fixed display of its costumes to indicate the dramatically important stiffness imposed on the actors' bodies and movement by the multiple, restrictive layers of silk of which the clothes are made—is pertinent here (2002, 26).[14]

Some anthropological visual media depict dress or textiles in films and texts dealing with particular themes, such as cloth and clothing as indicators of social and cultural change. The changes in tastes in, and ap-pearance and uses of, clothing over time, are frequently documented in ethnographic descriptions of wider shifts in the social status of women or other groups.[15] Another theme may be the discussion of clothing, fabric—and persons—as commodities. In Howes's film *Kafi's Story* (1989/2001), for example, Kafi's quest to earn more money so as to be able to buy his prospective second wife the necessary dress turns not only the dress but also himself into a commodity ripe for exploitation in a burgeoning cash economy (Loizos 2006). Globalization and the mass production that is part of it, clearly has significant implications for textile and clothing pro-duction in many areas, effecting not only changes in how things are made and what people wear but also a shift in—or loss of—more local systems of production, in which stages of manufacture (such as weaving, printing, and dyeing) are integrated within, and given meaning by, wider patterns of symbolic and cultural exchange. I do not discuss this further here, but see, for example, Rabine's semiotic analysis of African fashion in west and east Africa and California (2002).

The processes of textile and clothing production, consumption, and wearing may also be a primary focus of anthropological visual media, as they are, for example, in Tiragallo and Da Re's exploration of traditional weaving in Sardinia (1999). Moreover, within the activist strand in visual anthropology it has been argued that filmic representation in a develop-ing world context of women's involvement in such work as traditional textile production can make a convincing case for the importance of such activity to women's status, confidence, and future expectations (Wickett 2007, 128). Film of textile production may also provide a vehicle for the visual examination of a highly (though clearly not solely) visual skill, as Tiragallo explores (2007). Indeed, he purposefully highlights analogies between his own mode of looking as skilled filmmaker and the inten-tional and expert ways of seeing of the weaver, exploring the interaction between the two. He refers to these skilled ways of seeing as "gaze," by which, as Hughes-Freeland et al. (2007) point out, he means an embodied, purposeful way of looking similar to Grasseni's notion of "skilled vision" (see Grasseni 2007c and in this volume).

It is interesting to reflect on the extent to which the visual depiction of dress and textiles can be characterized as "salvage ethnography." For James Henry Green (see above), as for many other anthropological photographers and collectors of his and slightly earlier eras, it is easy to fit both his collecting and his photography (and his later Cambridge dissertation on the same peoples, Green 1934) within such a paradigm, seeing them as primarily driven by an imperative to record ways of life before they disappeared (cf. Odo 2000). Salvage ethnography is an approach that tends to be characterized negatively in postmodern anthropological writing, though rarely with an explanation of why. Certainly, one can see the tensions inherent in salvage ethnography as conducted by the very colonial officers and missionaries whose presence and activities were bringing about rapid social change in the communities their photographs and texts described. Yet visual "salvage," the retention for posterity of something that is perceived to be disappearing or that may already have gone, is arguably an underlying motif in many rather more contemporary collections, as well as in visual documentation of dress and textiles, too (visual salvage is also a clear theme in less academic, "coffee-table" volumes such as Diran 1997). There is an irony here, of course, in that despite the emphasis on social change in some contemporary studies, in many other works, on textiles in particular (especially those aimed at more popular markets), the cloths and the people who produce and wear them are treated as somehow frozen in time, untouched by a changing, globalizing world. Notable exceptions, with explicit discussion of contemporary political and economic challenges, include Dell and Dudley 2003; Lewis and Lewis 1984; and Niessen 1993.

Textiles and people may be "salvaged," however, even without being frozen in time. Among my own field photographs taken in the Karenni refugee camps in northwest Thailand, there is a subset of images of newly arrived Kayah women whom at the time I was conscious of wanting to photograph because of their particularly traditional form of dress (figure 2.3). I did not, when they first arrived in 1996–1997, think that as many women as have now abandoned this form of dress would do so, but I was aware from the outset that many factors—arrival in the heterogeneous refugee camp community, overt pressures from evangelizing longerstaying refugees, and the impossibility of continuing to produce in the camps the handmade textiles of which the clothes were made—would all

2.3   Preparing yarn for resist dyeing, Amarapura, central Burma (Myanmar). In Burmese textile
workshops this is a skilled job, usually undertaken by men. Note the use of a paper pattern.
Photo: Sandra Dudley, 1996.

make the continued wearing of these garments increasingly difficult. My
motivations for wanting to photograph the style of dress while I still could
were complex. In part, I was seeking visually to augment textual discussions of the social tensions (many of which related directly to the female
new arrivals' dress; Dudley 1998, 1999) and processes of cultural reproduction in a diverse refugee population. I wanted too to produce visual
documentation to support my and a local assistance agency's (ultimately
unsuccessful) attempts to enable the women to set up weaving projects
in order to continue production of their preferred clothing. But undoubtedly I also wished to record a traditional form before it disappeared—I
was salvaging, albeit visually rather than materially. Is this necessarily
a bad or uncommon thing? Beyond the fact that this was an unusual
form of dress that I had not encountered before and that was now under
evident pressure, traditional Kayah dress is little documented visually or
textually anywhere (and rarely encountered in museum collections).[16]
Most importantly, the Kayah refugees themselves focused their anxieties
about the future prospects for continuing life as they would like, upon
the problem of women's dress—*they* were the main source of a sense that
this style of clothing was under imminent threat. Nonetheless, at the
time I felt as discomforted by photographing—virtually collecting, as it

felt to me—these newly arrived women and their dress as I did by my later collecting for two museums of contemporary objects from the longer-staying refugee community. It was a personal discomfort, which in this case, I eased by handing my camera to Richard Than Tha, an artistic young student among the preexisting refugee community.

The point of this detour into my own field experiences is not only to problematize and relate to contemporary research some postmodern critiques of "salvage ethnography." It is also to argue that dress and textiles have a particular pertinence in this context. This is so, I suggest, for two main reasons. The first is the visual power of dress and textiles—their functioning as a visual medium in their own right. Certainly, as I shall discuss later, other sensory aspects are important in the impacts of cloth and clothing too; however, the first impact, at least on all those other than the wearer herself, is almost invariably visual. The visual is also usually the most powerful attractor to a collector—and salvage, whether through images, material objects, or ethnographic data, is essentially collection. The second reason is the intimate relationship between clothing, the human body, and identity—there are echoes here of the old essentializing of ethnicity and other forms of identity in styles of dress, but I am claiming that something far more complex and sensitive in the connection between fabric garments and those who wear them is also intrinsic to the value placed on dress by the observer. I will return to the links between textiles, dress and the body later. Suffice it to say here that it is precisely these links, together with visual impact, that give cloth and clothing its power, its collectibility, and its particular salience, in a salvage context or otherwise.

Dress and Textiles as Visual Media

Dress and textiles are not just the subjects of other visual representations, then; they constitute powerful visual media in their own right and, prefigured by the related topic of body decoration (e.g., Strathern and Strathern 1971), in recent decades have been written about as such. Dress and textiles have especial potency—in social practice and in anthropological and museological representations alike—in signifying and mediating identities of various kinds. The relation between identity and dress, in particular, is a subject much written about (e.g., Barnes and Eicher 1992; Eicher 1995a; Gittinger 1979; Kuper 1973; Roach-Higgins and Eicher 1992; Sumberg 1995; Worth and Sibley 1994), including in anthropological analyses of Western contexts (Breward et al. 2002; de Wita 1994). It is a theme I have already touched upon in looking at past, more simplistic approaches to the apparent ability of cloth and clothing to represent an essentialized ethnicity. Now, it is well accepted that "identities," ethnic or otherwise, are not fixed and essential but mutable, constructed, plural, and potentially fragmented (cf. Banks 1996b). As such, they are liable to both deliberate and unconscious manipulation and so, by extension, are the visual and material forms used to signify them. Explorations of shifting linkages between ethnic identities and certain textiles or garments in contexts of nationalist constructions of politically expedient pan-identities, for example, include Arthur's discussion of the Hawai'ian shirt (2006), Dudley's examination of Karenni national dress (2002), and Seng and Wass's study of Palestinian wedding dress (1995). Much of the value of dress and textiles in representing identity in such settings lies in the apparently greater local and cultural specificity of "traditional" dress—a factor that is also exploited in both film and art. Papuan artist Wendi Choulai, for example, has created large-scale "shadow paintings" as commentaries "on the personality split experienced by contemporary Papua New Guineans residing in the city. The person in the painting is the public figure, while her shadow represents the village person . . . the shadow often wears fiber skirts and headdresses, while the public figure might be dressed in a suit or a dress" (Lewis-Harris 2004, 282).

The importance of dress to identity, and the manipulation of it so as to represent, and ultimately inculcate, a new sense of identity, then, can be significant in the production of images. One motivation for this may be the political aspirations of image-makers, or their attempt to resolve tensions between these aspirations and other reasons for the work. Photographs of mixed-ancestry families in the United States in the early twentieth century, for example, taken by Caroline Bond Day (herself of mixed ancestry) as part of her research work for the Harvard eugenicist Ernest Hooton, "collectively provide a visual mediation between Day's political goals [of African American equality], her exclusive focus on mixed-race families and her use of physical anthropology and blood-quantum language" (Ardizzone 2006, 106). Even as she made use of anthropometric techniques in her still controversial fieldwork, Day utilized clothing's function as a marker of identity to convey convincingly the respectability and intelligence of her subjects, through both the general associations between fashionable dress (and grooming) and the middle classes, and the ability of clothes to connote individual identity and achievement—and thus to demonstrate that political demands for equality were appropriate. "A graduate gown," for example, "marked both an individual achievement and a message to white America that excluding Negroes from educational institutions was unjustified" (2006, 117).

Visual media such as ethnographic film may also utilize culturally constituted relations between dress, values, and identity as a narrative device. *Highway Courtesans* (Brabbee 2005), for example, is a documentary about Bachara women who work as prostitutes serving the transitory community of truck drivers and others passing along a busy trunk route in India. In the film's closing scene, its principal character, Guddi, is filmed after the collapse of her relationship with her boyfriend: she wears jeans, clothing to which her now ex-boyfriend had objected, thus demonstrating her newly acquired "independence embodied in consumption" (Feldman and Morarji 2007, 253).

A principal reason why dress and textiles are often of key significance in visual media and analysis thereof, then, is that dress in particular has a central role in how people everywhere signify, visually and with varying degrees of intention, aspects of themselves. In writing about contemporary wedding photographs in Beijing, for example, Constable emphasizes the styles of dress on display in the images (2006). She argues that while the styles of both dress and image superficially suggest similarities with wedding photographs in Taiwan and other parts of contemporary east Asia (cf. Adrian 2003),[17] rather than seeing them "as yet another example of . . . hegemonic global capitalist homogenization" we should understand their "specific meanings of consumption, modernity, nostalgia, gender, and romance that are particular to . . . post-Mao China" (Constable 2006, 40). Indeed, as Hansen argues, the wider anthropological "turn to consumption as a site and process of meaning making is evident also in clothing research" (2004, 369; see also Miller 2005), something that has direct connections too to the notion of fashion. Fashion, as Hansen points out, "is no longer an exclusive property of the West," with contemporary fashion now being produced—and valued and pursued—in quantity in most areas of the globe (2004, 370).[18]

Through fashion and otherwise, dress is frequently and deliberately utilized as a visually direct way to incorporate aspects of aesthetic and other values normally imagined as belonging to a different period or people. One reason for doing so may be an attempt to subvert the mainstream values of the present, or at least superficially to represent such subversion as an integral part of a marketable (and profitable) identity, as may be done by pop musicians. A non-Western example of such behavior is well described by de Kloet, who writes of Chinese rock musicians wearing grey Maoist suits in order to incorporate visual links with "the communist past into [contemporary Chinese] rock aesthetics" (2005,

242). Not dissimilarly, in Japan young people choose "cute" styles in order to rebel against what they perceive as the strictures of the uniforms so ubiquitous in their society (McVeigh 2000; cf. Hethorn and Kaiser 1999 on youth style and cultural anxieties). A different sort of "mixing" of local and other values, one done as deliberate synthesis rather than as subversion, is witnessed in Yoruba handwoven ecclesiastical textiles and the clerical garments made out of them, described by Renne (2000) as expressing Africanness and Roman Catholicism simultaneously. Yet another type of acquisition of the style—or perceived style—of others, happens when one group seeks to fit unnoticed into another: the abandonment of their usual skirt-cloths by displaced Karenni women when they go "into town" in Thailand, so as not to be marked out as "Burmese" and as "refugees," is one example of this (Dudley 2000), as is the adoption of urban dress by rural, Indian villagers working in urban centers in Ecuador (Lentz 1995).

However significant the local specificity of dress in any particular setting, the individual's sense of self and aesthetics also plays a role.[19] Nimis's article on the emergence of female studio photographers in southwest Nigeria, for example, notes the importance for the reputation of women photographers not only of making their studios attractive, but of dressing themselves in a skillful and feminine way (2006, 426). Arguably, the ability of dress to communicate aspects of *individual* identity to others reaches its apotheosis in large cosmopolitan centers in which anonymity is both produced and unfettered. Big cities "allow one to remain a stranger to others in a way that would not be possible in a rural or small town setting. Anonymity further allows for greater creativeness of lifestyle and 'presentation of self,' in which dress becomes a primary mode of communication to others" (Clapp 2005, 6). Of course, self-expression through dress in *private* settings located within and outside cosmopolitan centers may also be important—see Miller (1997) on fantasy dressing and self-expression in the American Midwest.

For Constable's informants on contemporary Chinese wedding photographs, as for many others, the re-creation—and use on certain occasions—of a "traditional" Chinese style of dress is a link to the past (real or imagined). This apparent temporality of clothing is one reason why its visual qualities take on such significance: in the Chinese example, dress provides "[a visual] example of 'nostalgia without memory' [Appadurai 1996, 30], or an attempt to produce an image of a Chinese past and present that seamlessly reconnects pre- and post-Mao China, excising several decades of recent history from memory, in a sense making up for lost time" (Constable 2006, 48). Yet at the same time, the additional production and consumption of wedding photographs in which Western-style bridal clothing is worn "serves as an expression of global modernity" (Constable 2006, 48). Contrasting styles of both clothing and photography are thus used to juxtapose and convey the values and aesthetics of two distinct periods in Chinese history (and sometimes, through the retouching and reshooting of individual images, two distinct periods in the lives of the featured couple too). Similar juxtapositions, uses of multiple forms, and indeed reinventions of tradition—including by different groups (such as age-sets) within one community—are documented elsewhere (e.g., Chapman 1995; Dudley 2002; Eicher 1997; Jirousek 1996; Lynch et al. 1995, 1996; Turner 1954).

Yet in many social contexts, certain forms of cloth and clothing represent not juxtapositions or excisions of particular chronological periods, but visual and material repositories of longitudinal—and often very personal—memory and time. Sampler embroideries in European and North American traditions are an obvious example—and one that often incorporates text that explicitly expresses both the individual maker's identity and the time at which the work was done. Even more complex and personal can be the quilts that are of significance in a number of cultural settings. There is a long tradition of quilting in Europe and, especially, North America—a tradition that is the subject of film (Barret 1976; Bole-Becker and Becker 1997; Ferrero 1980) as well as textual analysis (e.g., Cerny 1992; Forrest and Blincoe 1995; Stalp 2007). Hand-stitched quilts, be they personal and private or part of a public project such as the American AIDS Memorial Quilt (Krouse 1999; http://www .aidsquilt.org), have "lived experiences sewn into" them (Fernandez 1998, 1201). These experiences may be drawn not only from the life of the maker herself but from an intergenerational store of memory, skill, and often quite literally the fabric of history: remnants of old garments, curtains, and clothes that, incorporated into quilts, store, juxtapose, and display vestigial pieces of an individual's and a family's past. Quilts are important in eastern Polynesia too, and Küchler has described the way in which quilts there materially encompass features of women's lives and relationships. Such quilts are made not for display but for keeping and for giving and, ultimately, to wrap a woman's body when it goes to its grave (Küchler 2003; see also Küchler 2005). Other kinds of textile also embody uninterrupted, longitudinal time, often across a number of generations. Duggan writes of textiles on the Indonesian island of Savu as "visual markers of time," for example (2004, 104), and Henare claims that Maori

SANDRA DUDLEY

cloaks "quite literally [provide] continuous threads or pathways between layers of generational time that constitute tangible and substantive links between ancestors and their living descendants" (2005b, 125).

With the exception of quilts, most of the discussion thus far, particularly that pertaining to dress as visual media, has focused on the ability of cloth and clothing to represent and communicate certain values and ideas through what we might call relatively macro-level visual attributes. Style, color, and cut of garments, for example, are all clearly important in signifying wearers' identities and also in such areas as the use of dress as a narrative device in film. But smaller-scale qualities of textiles themselves, including fiber, motif, technique, the mode of transition between colors, material, and design elements, and their juxtaposition in fabric and in the garments made from them, are also important. Thus Perani and Wolff's discussion of clothing and textiles among the Yoruba in Nigeria demonstrates the significance of technological and material innovations in the colonial and postcolonial periods—including the incorporation of Lurex thread in the 1990s (Perani and Wolff 1999; other work on new fibers includes O'Connor 2005). A 1995 exhibition at the Barbican Art Gallery, *The Art of African Textiles: Technology, Tradition and Lurex*, also focused on innovation, change, intercontinental trade, and the continual reinvention of the "traditional"—indeed, in the book that accompanied the exhibition, its curator John Picton claimed that "traditionality was . . . exposed as a fiction" (1995, 11).

In relation to the ubiquitous subject of identity, much has been written on the supposed linkages between particular groups and certain textile styles, designs, and techniques—indeed, as Schneider points out, "scholars have proposed the existence of deeply rooted indexical codes" (1987, 413), especially in relation to textiles from Indonesia and Central and South America (e.g., Fox 1977; Gittinger 1979; Schevill 1985; Wasserman and Hill 1981).[20] Such attempts to concretely link design elements with specific identities and meanings can easily stray into a rigid imposition of fixed cultural categories of the kind now understood to be problematic; it is also an approach that attempts to describe, but fails to explain, cultural diversity and reproduction. In addition, with the exception of analyses of fibers and of weaving and dyeing processes, these sorts of explorations of textiles per se are strongly grounded in the *visual* qualities of the fabric as a whole and of the individual design elements it incorporates, as well as in the supposed mythological and social origins of such patterns (e.g., Morris 1986). Yet textiles go well beyond the visual: color use in dyed, embroidered, or woven patterns, for example, is often elaborately com-

62

plemented by the textures of different fibers and the tactility wrought by the use of techniques such as various float weaves.[21]

The Visual Body

If textiles go well beyond the visual at the relatively small-scale level of the fibers, pigments, designs, and techniques used to produce them, so too do they demonstrate an extensive sensory range in how they are used. This is perhaps especially so when fabric is used for the purposes of dressing the body. Cloth can hide, disguise, or reveal; the way in which it is worn can change how its wearer moves and behaves (see Frembgen 2004); it can be erotic or asexual; and it can absorb, hide, or exude bodily fluids and smells. I will return to extensions beyond the visual below, but first it must be acknowledged that fabric and clothes and their relation to the body, especially in movement and in how the body's flow affects that of the garments and vice versa, themselves constitute a highly visual phenomenon—at least from the perspective of all observers other than the wearer her/himself. Nonetheless, it is as yet a relatively little explored issue in the literature, although some authors do focus on it, sometimes as part of discussions of how clothes are used to make the body appear as if it is of a different shape than it actually is.[22]

One area where the folding of fabric to clothe the body has been more deeply examined is in the case of the sari and other forms of draped cloth (as opposed to cut-and-sewn, constructed garments) in India (Tarlo 1996; Banerjee and Miller 2003). In the colonial period, the tension between draped cloth, on the one hand, and tailored garments, on the other, both mirrored and represented political tension—and fundamental to the opposition between the two forms is the very distinct relationship each produces between clothes and body. Deciding what to wear and the very act of wearing constitute, as these authors demonstrate, not only an individual yet socially, politically, and historically constructed performance, but also a continual process of choice. What is more, folded cloth, such as the sari, demonstrates perhaps more than tailored clothes that clothes and the body are, in most contexts, not fully meaningful without each other. The body gives the sari form and life—and, in a social sense, the reverse is also true. The visual impression made by a dressed body—or a bodily occupied garment—is, while not the only sensorily significant factor, usually the first and most evident way in which clothes and their wearer get noticed.

What is the dressed body noticed *for*? And how much does the body's presence matter in what clothes are deemed to "say"? We have already discussed linkages between dress and notions of identity—dress as deliberate or accidental communicator about the self and belonging. Guddi's jeans at the end of *Highway Courtesans*, for example (Brabbee 2005), are about both contemporary consumerism and doing what she, not her ex-boyfriend, wishes. Some of this would probably have meaning to Guddi even if no one saw her wearing the jeans or, indeed, if they remained in a cupboard, but their very visibility is what allows her to make as much of a statement with them, to herself as well as to others, as she does. Furthermore, the jeans would not have their full meaning and impact consummated if they remained *unworn*, if they did not contain Guddi's *body*. That this seems such an obvious truism may explain why there is still relatively little literature addressing, first, the myriad and complex relationships between fabric, dress, and the body (though see Allerton 2007; Banerjee and Miller 2003; Johnson and Foster 2007) and, second, the importance of cloth and clothing in their own right rather than as simply indicators or communicators of other areas of social experience (a point also made in Colchester 2003). The power of dress (and often textiles too) to communicate identities and values and to stand for itself would, without the body within it, most often be muted at best: clothing is social action; *the impact is in the wearing*. As Hansen states:

In the materialization of value that informs . . . decisions about how to dress and where, needs and wants converge as do ephemerality and continuity. This is the space between the desired and the performed where dress practices become involved in constructing both individual identity and visions about the future. (Hansen 2003, 308)

The draping of fabric around parts of the body is clearly done with different purposes in different contexts. It may be done to accentuate, to modify, or to conceal (see Harvey 2007), and particular forms may be utilized only by specific sex, age, or other groups within a given society. The veil, particularly Islamic forms thereof, is perhaps the example par excellence of cloth used to hide some or all of women's faces and bodies. As Hansen points out, by the 1970s scholarship was already qualifying and nuancing "the connection between veiling and women's subordination" (2004, 382), and ever since, it has continued to enhance understandings of the complexity of the veil's shifting functions and meanings. Brenner (1996), for example, argues that wearing the veil in Java has become increasingly associated with women's and society's hopes for the future rather than with notions of the past, and El Guindi (1999) demonstrates the increasing role of the *hijab* in heightened Islamic consciousness in Egypt (1999).[23] Of course, there is a pointed and important paradox in women's wearing of the veil: it seeks to render all or some of their individual physical features and femininity invisible—yet it is itself a highly visible emblem not only of Islamic identity but of femininity per se. The veil, in other words, makes invisibility very visible—it makes an overt and visual point out of concealment, in the process transforming the private, individual woman into her public representation of generalized womankind. It is in this tension between invisibility and visibility—rooted in both the visual power of the veil and in its intimate (and visually evident) relationship with the body—that all the political, social, and religious potentials of the veil and its uses lie. Such a tension, and its basis in the visual, is hardly unique to the veil; indeed, it is applicable to any use of cloth to clothe the human body: cloth that covers the body and is simultaneously intimately connected with and indicative of it.[24]

Crucially, then, the relation between clothing and the body is double-faced: dress not only faces outward to the world, in ways affected by the shape and movement of the body; it also touches the body. This dual aspect is pointed out by Turner (1980) in his discussion of clothing as "social skin." It allows us, as Hansen puts it, "to explore both the individual and collective identities that the dressed body enables" (2004, 372). Indeed, these identities may often have an uneasy if not downright conflicting relationship, with dress turning into "a flash point of conflicting values" (Hansen 2004, 372). Allerton too uses analogies between clothing and integument, drawing upon Anzieu's approach to skin (Anzieu 1989). She refers to Indonesian sarongs as "super-skins," "artefactual extensions of their wearer's body [that can] absorb substances and intentions, offer comfort at times of upset or illness, and transmit social and emotional messages," and as such have not a specific biography but "a range of possibilities of becoming" (Allerton 2007, 22). The interior of a sarong "acts as a secret container of goods, emotions and body-states" (2007, 37), while the exterior forms part of the visual impression made by the wearer and expresses different messages to those among whom the wearer circulates. Like the visually apparent surfaces of the body about which Schildkrout writes, clothing too becomes an active and multifaceted "interface between the individual and society" (2004, 319).

Of course, one way in which the usually integral relationship between the body and dress is demonstrated is by its very subversion. The removal of clothing and subsequent exposure of the body has its place in certain everyday and ritual activities. It may also be deliberately used to titillate or shock, often in complex ways that rely fundamentally on the *visual*

SANDRA DUDLEY

impact of dress and undress (cf. Martinez 1995). Undress has also been used in particular ways in ethnographic film, both for the titillation of the viewer and for the evocation of certain dominant interpretive frameworks. Thus Alan Marcus, for example, writes that the removal of clothes by Nanook and the women, prior to settling together under their blanket in *Nanook of the North* (Flaherty 1922), is done not only "for our scopophilic pleasure and libidinal desire" (2006, 213) but also as dramatization of Freud's notion of the "primal father" who has rights of sexual access to all women (Freud 1919).

The undressed body, then, has a particular impact. So too does disembodied dress. In representational settings such as museum displays, where people themselves are usually absent, clothing's intimate relation to the person who wore it makes items of dress a powerful tool. Using cloth and clothing in display can enable museums to personalize historical representation, to "make space for private dimensions of historic times . . . [and] ultimately, [to] conceive of history as the historicity of private space" (Bruno 2003, 322). Indeed one might add that through clothing, history becomes the historicity not only of private space but also of private and public aspects of the physical body.

Bruno's article on museums in Havana plays particular attention to the importance of dress in the displays. Clothes, like photographic portraits and shoes (Bruno herself draws a comparison with the shoes displayed in New York's Holocaust Museum), are intimate in their association with those individuals whom they represent. They are "vestiges that metonymically refer to the live body of a departed person . . . corporeally speak of them, connect us back to them . . . traces left behind by people who died . . . matter that allows us to access [the departed's] lives, and process their death" (2003, 319). Using clothing in the way the museums in Havana do is indeed "an intimate way of telling a history" (2003, 320). Through clothes we can see—and tactilely intuit—traces of particular past lives and events. In Havana's Museum of Revolution, for example, the visible bullet holes and bloodstains on some items connect us directly with the experience of those who wore them. Indeed such traces, especially if the garment belonged or is imagined to have belonged to a particularly significant individual, lend further weight to the aura and power that may be attributed to the clothing.[25] But as Bruno points out, there can also be

a loneliness to clothes. As the body that inhabited them departed, they are left hanging. Emptied out. The sole, sparse melancholic trace of a life ended. A sad testimony to that parting, and to the passing of time. (Bruno 2003, 319)

2.4   Kengtung market, Shan State, Burma (Myanmar). While the bales of differently colored
       skirt-cloths on the stall in the foreground present a bright textile array, their flatness and
       their in-bulk anonymity are in stark contrast with the shape and movement of the individu-
       alized cloths worn by each passing shopper. "Clothes are not worn passively but require
       people's active collaboration," as Hansen puts it (2003, 308). Photo: Sandra Dudley, 1996.

Like the undressed body, the unworn piece of clothing is lifeless and incomplete—very different from the dynamic, continually moving fabric
as it is worn in daily life. Indeed, the loneliness and melancholy that can
seem to emanate from clothing such as that in museum collections are
accompanied by more pragmatic concerns with the difficulty in exhibiting dress appropriately and in conveying something of the animation an
item of dress may have had when worn. To an extent, the same can apply
not only to clothes but also to other textile items closely associated with
the animated human form, such as soft furnishings, bedding and bags,
all of which may appear lifeless and somehow incomplete of form without the rumpling and impressions caused by seated bodies or contained
personal objects (figure 2.4).

Beyond the Visual

Yet how much of all this is entirely *visual*? Other sensory qualities are of
course important too. Much recent work on dress within a material culture tradition is said to focus on the efficacy of "materiality as a surface

that constitutes social relations and states of being" (Hansen 2004, 373; see also Johnson and Foster 2007). Work such as that in Küchler and Miller (2005) does, as Hansen summarizes, look at material qualities of clothing and how they impact upon people's use of clothes. This is a perspective in which dress, the body, and social performance together constitute "dress as embodied practice" (Hansen 2004, 373), and in which the visual is important but far from alone. Yet the embodiment being referred to in such approaches is but the beginning of a long story—most of which, one feels, has still to be told.

In representations in museums, film, photography, and text alike, the extravisual qualities of dress and fabric are, like the dynamic relation between body and clothing, difficult to convey. The sense of touch in particular is, theoretically, second only to vision in enabling full perception of textiles and of the three-dimensional, bodily occupied garments that incorporate them—the tactility of fabric, like the shape of bodies, is fully comprehended only when we place our hands upon it. Yet in lived experience as well as in visual and textual representation, such physical touching is often either impossible or forbidden. In daily life, the wearer can stroke the textured metallic brocade decorating her own skirt and a mother can feel the softness of her baby's woolen shawl, but social boundaries prevent observers' having direct tactile access to these characteristics—and of course on film, in a photograph, or behind the glass of a display case, no one has such contact. The smells of a new cotton shirt or an old baby's cloth are likewise unavailable to all but those who are privileged with close and full physical access to the garment. Sound, on the other hand, at least when cloth is worn and thus in movement, like vision, does have public saliency—and indeed often carries notable social meaning and value of its own, as in the literary *swish* of eighteenth- and nineteenth-century European and North American women's long skirts and the notion that the greater and clearer the sound the more luxurious and abundant the fabric used.

Does all this mean that at least some nonvisual attributes of cloth and clothing, such as the texture of fabric or the three-dimensionality of a garment, are generally available only to the maker and wearer and thus somehow tangential to a wider anthropological view? A phenomenological approach would hold that this is not the case, because all aspects are integral to lived experience. Ultimately, the different sensory aspects are inseparable—recall Merleau-Ponty's claim that a color is not simply a color but the color *of* something. That something has physical, material qualities, and thus color too has an intrinsic relation to texture, shape, and so on. The color, in other words, is *felt* as well as seen (1962, 365). Thus, because of the habitual interlinkage we make between vision and the other senses, we can comprehend—or at least imagine we comprehend—texture and other tactile, multidimensional attributes of objects even (as when perusing a museum display that lies behind glass) without actually using our sense of touch.

But it is not only other sensory qualities that extend the perception of dress and textiles beyond the visual. Cloth can acquire religious or other significance not only through past association with particular persons or events—and perhaps the acquisition of visually evident traces thereof—but also through the means of its production or consumption, none of which may be visually or otherwise sensorily apparent at all. That particular taboos were observed during the dyeing or weaving of the fibers, for example, lends power to certain textiles—a power that may be known and understood both by those who see and those who more intimately, physically interact with the cloth. Such power may not be seen or physically felt, yet it can still play an important part in how a cloth is treated, stored, and used—and indeed in how it is seen and felt. Individual well-being is also relevant here. It is a notion that is integrally related to the physical senses but is not detectable by them and goes beyond them into "feeling right," a crucial consideration in the choice of what to wear on a particular day or for a specific event (see Woodward 2005).

Earlier in this chapter I demonstrated that dress and textiles act as visual media in their own right, and I indicated that perhaps the bulk of the literature treats them in this way. Yet there are problems with this common approach, not least of which is that the dominant analytical focus on the visual as signifier results in dress especially being discussed as "representing something else rather than [as] something in its own right" (Hansen 2004, 369). Dress and textiles are, as we have seen, widely explored as standing for and as communicating identities, values, and relationships (often with an emphasis on essentially semiotic modes of interpretation, the objections to which, in a wider art context, are articulated by, e.g., Gell [1998, 14 and *passim*], objections I largely share). Yet dress and textiles are still relatively little examined in their own, material right. Hansen points out that "new efforts to reengage materiality suggest this is changing" (2004, 369), but as yet it remains a small shift.

Decisions made about the clothing one wears and its role in individual daily life and in cultural reproduction, are simultaneously and variously produced by and productive of particular, multiply constituted ideas of who one is, must be, and would like to be. This power of clothing to signify identities, values, and status—the prowess of dress in the processes of subjectivization—appears to be intrinsically visual, relying primarily on the impact of what is seen. Yet, as is now clear, other sensory aspects are important too, not least to the wearer herself. Of course, this renders dress and textiles irrelevant to visual anthropology no more than it might the built environment or the body itself. What is more, it is hardly radical or original now to claim that the visual inevitably extends beyond itself: "Visual representations systems are part of more general cultural processes. They can affect the unseen and the unseeable" (Banks and Morphy 1997, 23).

What is interesting is to consider this in the context of the dynamic between object and viewer, dressed person and observer: the assumption of an absolute dichotomy between the two, where the interpretation of an object with fixed physical attributes depends upon the subjectivity of the viewer, is problematic. If perception and understanding lie not in the viewer's culturally (and otherwise) constituted mind but are continually formed and reformed in the space between object and observer, where both have a degree of agency or influence, then perhaps we can move forward in the study of dress and textiles by approaching them as particular forms of intersubjectivity with an intimate relationship to the human body. As Merleau-Ponty argues, our own bodies are themselves simply another form of material object, an "organism of colours, smells, sounds and tactile appearances" (1962, 275). Our bodies and the physical objects around us, including cloth and clothing, share qualities that determine the nature of our interactions with and perceptions of those other objects. Is this perhaps even more pertinent to bodies and the materials that dress them than to other kinds of object? Certainly, the phenomenological notion that object-human relationships are reciprocal and dialogical (we see and are seen; we touch and are touched) seems especially pointed when considering the relation between a person and the clothes she or he wears. Phenomenological approaches to dress and to cloth may increasingly take over from the earlier, semiotic analyses, which for dress as much as for the body focused on display and on artifactuality (cf. Joyce 2005). Indeed, we might hope that, to paraphrase Joyce (writing on the body but making claims equally applicable here), such future approaches will replace "prior static conceptions" of dress and textiles as "public, legible surface[s]" (2005, 139). As a result, the importance of the visual will not be lost, but it will be more appropriately partnered by other sensory aspects of our lived experience of clothing and textiles, and by a deeper understanding of the relationships between those aspects, social agency, and cultural reproduction.

Notes

I would like to acknowledge the assistance of the Department of Museum Studies, University of Leicester, and Ilaria Benzoni, with some of the research for this chapter.

1. On used and recycled materials see, e.g., Hansen 2000a, 2000b, 2003; Norris 2005; and various chapters in Palmer and Clark 2004. On mass-produced wares, e.g., O'Connor 2005. For social analyses, e.g., Adams 1973; Kent 1983; Messick 1987; Polakoff 1982; Schneider 1988. Other recent reviews of the anthropology of dress that have been particularly useful in research for this chapter, but that range beyond the current visual remit, include Eicher 2000; Hansen 2004; and Taylor 2002, chap. 7.

2. See Maddigan 2003 for an outline of Kachin textiles.

3. Note, however, that much other literature in the same area has decontextualized and effectively dehumanized Indonesian cloth, as Niessen argues (1993).

4. Trying to bring the two together is also at principal intention of Küchler and Miller's edited volume (Miller 2005, 1).

5. See Schneider 1987 for an extensive review of the anthropology of textiles more broadly.

6. See, e.g., Bridgwood 1995; Calefato 2004; Hamilton 1989; Kaiser 1989; Sharma 1978; Wariboko 2002; and, on Western fashion, Barthes 1972, 2006; Hebdige 1979.

7. On textile exchange and rites of passage see, e.g., Bloch 1971; Darish 1989; Feely-Harnik 1989; Gittinger 1979; Kahlenberg 1979; Kendall 1985; Schneider 1980; Weiner 1976. On textiles as currency, e.g., Dorward 1976 and Douglas 1967, both cited in Schneider 1987.

8. For more on links between usage and socioeconomic shifts see Edwards 2005.

9. Pink also adds another, pedagogical strand (this volume), but this is not of central concern here.

10. E.g., Carey and Tuck 1896; Colquhoun 1885; Enriquez 1923; Lowis 1906; MacMahon 1876; Marshall 1922/1997; Mason 1868. For more on clothing and the categorization of identities in colonial Burma, see Dudley 2003a. Although early ethnographic descriptions placed significant emphasis on dress and its apparent associations with group identities, they did not *solely* describe clothing. Many museum publications, on the other hand, confined themselves entirely to visual and technical description of the cloth and garments of different ethnic groups (e.g., Hansen 1960; Innes 1957; Start 1917).

11. E.g., Emmons 1907; Linton 1933; O'Neale 1945; Roth 1934. See also critical discussions in Scott 1911; Trevor-Roper 1983.

12. The University of Oxford's Pitt Rivers Museum also holds objects field collected by Green. Green's photograph collection is explored and illustrated in Dell 2000, and the textile collection in Dell and Dudley 2003.

13. While it is not a primary topic for discussion here, it is interesting to note that in anthropology, as in art history, social history, and beyond, the majority of contemporary writing on dress and textiles is still produced by women. See Taylor 2002 and the references she cites—Gaines 1990; Vickery 1998; Wilson 1985—on feminist critique of the gendered nature of both scholarship and its subjects in this area.

14. Taylor's book includes a full chapter on problems in displaying dress. One way in which museums may seek to augment the visual—if not other sensory—limitations of static display, of course, is through the accompanying use of additional visual forms, including video and photographic stills.

15. Eicher 1997; Jirousek 1996; Joshi 1992; Lowe and Lowe 1982; Michelman and Eicher 1995; Park et al. 1993; Renne 1995; Tauzin 2007.

16. See Dudley 2003b for more general outline of Burmese textiles in museums.

17. For more on Chinese wedding photographs, see also Cheung 2006; Eric 2006; Lozada 2006.

18. On fashion beyond the West and globally see, e.g., Hopkins 2005; Khan 1992; Niessen et al. 2003.

19. On older women's sense of their appearance and its relationship to how they dressed see Jackson and O'Neal 1994.

20. The conviction in much—mostly earlier—scholarship that non-Western textile designs invariably had complex symbolic explanations constitutes an extended version of these sorts of analyses. I do not discuss this further in this chapter. Suffice it to say that, as Schneider (1987) points out, it is problematic in both its interpretation and in its own arguable claims that the inability of informants to convey such explanations themselves must be due either to reticence or the loss of cultural memory (e.g., Gittinger 1979; Wasserman and Hill 1981). Contrast the distinctions between cloth valued for ceremonial purposes and that valued for artistic merit alone, in Fox 1977, and see also writing on the differences between items produced for internal use and those intended for purchase by outsiders, including tourists (e.g., Graburn 1982; Steiner 1985; Waterbury 1989).

21. Useful sources on the many possible techniques and their effects are numerous. See, e.g., Gillow and Sentence 1999; Schneider 1987.

22. See Tauzin 2007. On dress and the body more generally see Entwistle 2000; Entwistle and Wilson 2001; Summers 2001; Warwick and Cavallaro 1998.

23. For other works touching on aspects of Islamic forms of the veil and other head coverings, see Abu-Lughod 1990; Ong 1990; Rasmussen 1991; Sandıkı and Ger 2005; Shirazi 2001; White 1999.

24. One topic identified by Hansen (2004) within this area that I will not explore here but in which there is an expanding literature (e.g., Behrman 1995; Besnier 2002; various in Cohen et al. 1996) is dress and the body in the context of beauty pageants in different parts of the world. As Hansen outlines, beauty pageants involve "complicated negotiations between local and global norms of beauty, gender and sexuality" (2004, 383, citing

Cohen et al. 1996) and, as such, comprise "a rich site for dress research on representation, gender construction, performance, and politics" (2004, 383).

25. Examples include Nelson's coat, in the UK National Maritime Museum (http://www.nmm.ac.uk/collections/nelson/), and the Turin shroud. The power of a garment because of its association with particular individuals can of course be important even without the existence of specific physical traces such as blood and damage (cf. Weiner 1985).

THREE

Visual Anthropology and the Built Environment: Interpenetrations of the Visible and the Invisible

ROXANA WATERSON

Some aspects of culture are designed to have visual impact and cannot be studied effectively without the incorporation of visual methods. Architecture is one such aspect; at the same time, being lived in, it is more than simply visual, offering a particularly meaningful point of entry into cultures and their ideas. The communicative power of architecture has, however, received very uneven attention from anthropologists until quite recently. Lewis Henry Morgan made a useful beginning with his *Houses and House Life of the American Aborigines* (1881/1965), but his example was not systematically emulated. This chapter will review the shifting focus of architectural studies in anthropology over time, and the revelations they offer about relations with the environment, cosmology, kinship structure, gender roles and symbolism, politics, ritual, memory, and life processes. It will sketch out the rapid development of the field within the last twenty years and argue for the still untapped potential of cross-disciplinary research, which can unite the special skills of both architects and anthropologists.

Some aspects of culture are intended to make a visual impression, and can hardly be effectively understood or described without the use of visual methods. Architecture provides perhaps the most obvious example. Yet beyond this quality of high visibility, the built environment typically gives expression simultaneously to less tangible dimensions of culture. Many features that are integral to a community's sense of itself and its well-being in the world—ideas of cosmology, kinship, fertility, growth, political power and status, the articulation of gendered spaces, relationships between the living and the dead, and more besides—find their expression or are even summoned into being by the house and other built forms.

Place-making, whether or not it involves architecture, is a universal cultural impulse, and humans have been at home in the landscape since long before they built any permanent structures in it.[1] For those hunter-gatherer groups who traditionally have kept built structures to a minimum, the imposition of meaning on the landscape itself is vital to their sense of dwelling, being "implicated," in it, as Peter Gow puts it. "Implication depends on actively moving around in the landscape, and leaving traces in it," he writes (1995, 51). Place-making, and narratives of places that help to bind people together in relationships, are thus integral to social life everywhere. They require the ability to read and understand visible traces, architectural or otherwise.[2] Whether buildings are designed to be monumental and ostentatious, conveniently portable (like the no-mad tent), or discreet to the point of near invisibility (like Punan leaf shelters in the Borneo forests),[3] they all tell stories about the human lives for which they provide the settings. Structures may be made to endure for hundreds of years, like the massive stone temples of past civilizations, or be deliberately temporary, springing up for the occasion of a ritual, for instance, then rapidly decaying, thus finding their immortality in repetition rather than solidity.[4] In my own fieldwork in Tana Toraja, Sulawesi (Indonesia), I became aware that houses create networks that are at once spatially and temporally linked, providing both a sort of geographical map of settlement, embedded in the landscape, and a historical frame of reference, linked to genealogical memory. One might almost say that the remembering of important origin houses, and the branch houses founded by descendants who spread out to establish themselves in new locations, creates a genealogy of the houses themselves, their life spans surpassing those of any of their individual inhabitants (Waterson 1995b, 2003, 2009).

How buildings become points of reference in an inhabited landscape is thus an integral part of the creation of cultural meanings in most societies, and thus must be of obvious concern to anthropologists. But have we paid sufficient attention to the visual dimensions of such studies? That is the question I shall review in this chapter.

Vernacular Architecture as an Interdisciplinary Field of Study

The professionalization of architecture is far from universal, and still to-day, as Paul Oliver (1987, 7) pointed out twenty years ago, the vast majority of the world's buildings are constructed by the users themselves. Exact figures are impossible to ascertain, but by Oliver's calculation in the 1980s, of a total of up to nine hundred million dwellings, perhaps 5 percent had been built with any professional or official involvement, while those actually designed by architects were still fewer, probably less than 1 percent. Though these figures are by now somewhat outdated, there is no reason to suppose that the proportion of the built environment being produced by nonprofessionals has changed, or indeed is likely to change in the near future. The vernacular building traditions of non-industrialized societies thus involve the transmission of knowledge not just between a few highly trained specialists but much more broadly within the community. Women are still the main producers of architecture in a wide range of African societies where mud or plant materials are used for house-building. Among the nomadic herding peoples of the Sahara and the Sahel, and the numerous West African peoples who have ingeniously exploited the potentials of mud as an architectural resource, women typically work together to erect and maintain household structures. Their artistry is celebrated in Courtney-Clark (1990) and Prussin (1995); see also the film *Building Season in Tiébélé*, directed by Beate Engelbrecht (1999), to which I shall refer again below. By contrast, in most Southeast Asian cultures, adult men are all generally skilled in the cutting and working of bamboo and wood. They have sufficient carpentry skills to build their own houses and a range of other structures, calling on communal help where needed (figure 3.1).

The specialist in such societies may be needed as much, or more, for his ritual or divinatory knowledge as his practical skills in construction (Waterson 2009, 122–29). It is these nonprofessional traditions with which I am chiefly concerned here, and I shall be concentrating my attention on vernacular architectures, broadly defined. For the anthropologist these must always be of interest, since they represent a more direct reflection of the customs, intentions, and desires of the users than do professionally designed buildings. There is of course nothing to stop anthropologists from studying life in architect-designed environments either (see, e.g., Rapoport 1982; Cieraad 1999). But in these contexts we find differing degrees of tension between the designer's desire to impose his or her

3.1 Toraja villagers often use their carpentry skills in communal labor to build the temporary structures used in rituals. Here villagers are preparing for a funeral by constructing, in front of the deceased's house of origin, a tower to hold the corpse during the final days of the mortuary rites. Hundreds of guests will be housed in temporary two-story shelters built around the house yard. Tana Toraja, Sulawesi, Indonesia, 1996. Photo: Roxana Waterson.

personal style on a building and the need users feel to adapt the spaces created in order to suit their own needs and express their own meanings.

As Bechhoefer and Bovill (1994, 2) observe, "Vernacular architecture presents a complex cascade of rhythm patterns and detail. There is a clustered randomness to the pattern. A similar clustered randomness is displayed in almost all natural shapes, from trees to the clouds and stars in the sky." No doubt there are ethological reasons why humans tend to respond strongly to these organic qualities, but as these authors propose, it takes a different kind of geometry, fractal in place of Euclidean, to come close to analyzing them. The "vernacular" is at the same time a term that has tended to be defined negatively—as nonmonumental, non-Western, nonprofessional, even nonmodern (or at any rate, nonmodernist, in architectural terms—those architects who have been driven to study it have often been in rebellion precisely against the tenets of architectural modernism). Such definitions carry the risk of a problematic assumption that this category essentially belongs to the past—either as an "authentic" expression that cannot be changed without decline and loss, or as something "backward" and therefore irrelevant, doomed to disappearance in the face of globalization.[5] "Tradition" is an even more vexed term, so I must stress at the outset that where I use the word "traditions," I am talking about practices that are living and changing. They are not frozen in time or immune to the adoption of new techniques, materials, or elements of design but are constantly being renegotiated in the present. I concur with writers such as Oliver (2006b) and Vellinga (2006) who argue that vernacular traditions around the world should be seen as dynamic and, though vulnerable, far from dead, and that they should be studied with an emphasis on the processual. Vernacular and modern traditions, Vellinga argues, are nowadays merging in unexpected new ways, producing what he terms a "vernacularization of modernity" (2006, 94). The concept of the vernacular ought thus to be widened to include "all those buildings that are distinctive cultural expressions of people who live in or feel attached to a particular place or locality" (Asquith and Vellinga 2006, 10). But when the new nomadisms of our time can unsettle even the most familiar, comforting categories of "attachment" and "locality," we should no doubt be alert to the need for even more fluid definitons than this. The discussions in a recent volume, *Drifting: Architecture and Migrancy* (Cairns 2004), are less about concrete structures than they are about exploring the architectures of belonging, which in diasporic lives may at times be best traced in the imagination.

On the other hand, the anthropologist, wherever engaged in fieldwork in an unfamiliar culture, is guaranteed a very direct experience of the built environment in which social life is being carried on. One can hardly fail to be aware of it, while learning by trial and error how to adapt oneself to its often invisible rules. In many instances this involves for the Westerner a surrender—more or less graceless but never painless—of the privacy to which she or he may be accustomed. Where life is lived in a more intensely face-to-face setting the desire to be alone may be practically impossible to achieve, and may anyway be viewed as abnormal, giving one's hosts cause for concern. Considering, then, how the anthropologist must be affected in a very personal manner by this experience of an unfamiliar built environment, one might expect that the resulting ethnographic monographs would have more to say on the subject. Yet strangely, anthropological attention to architecture has been intermittent and, until recently, often lacking. In asking why for so long architecture remained a neglected subject among anthropologists, one answer seems to have been a tendency within the discipline as it developed in the early twentieth century to separate off "material culture" as something for museum curators to study, or as being somehow less worthy of attention than the abstractions of social structure, kinship, or mythology.[6] This trend was perhaps a reaction to nineteenth-century tendencies to document material culture obsessively, sometimes at the expense of providing a dynamic picture of social institutions and relations. Even Lévi-Strauss (1983), whose reanalysis of earlier ethnographic accounts of the societies of North America's northwest coast led to his thought-provoking conceptualization of "house societies," insisted that it was not the material structures of houses in themselves that interested him. He thus chose to ignore, in what he judged to be a kinship problem, the possibility of investigating a most impressive building tradition. This demotion of architecture on account of its materiality must now strike us as mistaken. In the case of Indonesian cultures, for instance, it is easy to show that aspects of material culture—whether houses, textiles, boats, daggers, or gold heirloom jewelry—all provide a "way in" to the immaterial world of ideas, cosmologies, kinship patterns, marriage arrangements, and so forth, and it is in fact impossible to understand one without the other.

Lewis Henry Morgan set a fine early precedent for the anthropological study of architecture with the publication of his *Houses and House Life of the American Aborigines* (1881/1965). This represented an original attempt to understand house forms in terms of social organization and kinship structures. But few followed Morgan's example until the rise of structuralism, in the 1960s and 1970s, stimulated a resurgence of interest in how the built environment might be shaping social life. It was not only French theoreticians such as Durkheim and Mauss who inspired this trend, but also Dutch writers on Indonesian societies, such as van Ossen-bruggen (1918), van Wouden (see P. E. de Josselin de Jong 1977), and J. P. B. de Josselin de Jong, to whom Lévi-Strauss paid tribute in his influential paper of 1963 on the analysis of settlement patterns. After this, there was a gradual increase in anthropological analyses of spatial organiza-tion, some well-known examples being Cunningham (1964) and Schulte Nordholt (1971) on the Atoni of Timor, Griaule (1965) on the house as microcosm among the Dogon of Mali, Ortiz (1969) on the Tewa of New Mexico, Douglas (1972) on the symbolic uses of domestic space in British homes, Bourdieu (1973, 1977) on the Kabyle Berbers of Algeria, Tambiah (1973) on the shaping of space in the villages of North Thailand, and Humphrey (1974) on the Mongolian tent.

These studies have retained their classic status in the discipline of an-thropology. But richly informative as they were conceptually, in terms of providing a visual record they are mostly nonstarters, and any ar-chitect would doubtless judge them to be hopeless failures. Pictorially they hardly even begin to document the buildings they are describing; photographs and measured drawings are largely absent, and in many of them the odd sketch of the exterior or floor plan provides the only visual material. There has been a tendency also, until recently, to give a single representation of an "ideal" type rather than documenting the actual diversity of structures, which may depart to different degrees from the ideal or express it variably. (To be fair, anthropologists have more often been prevented by thrifty publishers than by their own inclinations from illustrating their work at all abundantly.) Hugh-Jones's article (1985) on the social and cosmological significance of the *maloca* (communal dwell-ings of the Barasana and other Amazonian peoples) was an exception because it was commissioned as part of an exhibition at the Museum of Mankind in London. This centered on the partial reconstruction of an actual *maloca*, furnished with the objects of daily use that would be found within such a structure. This context, and the production of a book to accompany the exhibition, provided an opportunity to bring the subject to life through the use of plentiful visual materials (figure 3.2).

In recent years, publishers have relented a little on the question of il-lustrations, though it has to be said that the quality of the images is often poor. Thus a recent monograph on the Kholagaun Chhetris of Nepal by John Gray (2006) contains a relatively generous complement of thirty diagrams and photographs. Gray provides a multifaceted analysis of the house as an embodiment of Hindu cosmology. He focuses on the pro-cessual and performative aspects of everyday life, notably the often tacit

3.2 Maloca, or communal house, Aiary river, northwest Amazon. From T. Koch-Grünberg, *Zwei Jahre unter den Indianern: Reisen in Nordwest-Brasilien, 1903–05* (Berlin, 1909–1910).

and embodied enactment of ideas about purity and impurity, inclusion and exclusion, in the domestic setting.

Over the past two decades, a number of anthropologists have been inspired by Lévi-Strauss's (1983, 1987) idea of house societies to explore its application to Southeast Asia, especially Indonesia, as well as to South America (Macdonald 1987; Waterson 1986, 2009; Carsten and Hugh-Jones 1995). The concept has also provided archaeologists with new angles for interpreting their data. Joyce and Gillespie (2000) is a good example of cross-disciplinary fertilization and collaboration between archaeologists, ethnohistorians, and anthropologists, especially in geographical regions such as Polynesia and Central America where there are potential continuities between the data of all three disciplines. Most of these are not very generously illustrated either, and even a very recent volume, such as Low and Lawrence-Zúñiga's *The Anthropology of Space and Place: Locating Culture* (2003), has hardly any visual element. Out of this collection of twenty papers, only one includes photographs, while two have diagrams or floor plans. Although admittedly several of these papers are theoretical essays dealing with issues of space and locality in the broadest sense, the idea that such a theme needs visual illustration is clearly still far from automatic.

By contrast, architects have been drawn to the vernacular primarily by its visual and aesthetic qualities, sometimes producing works that are almost entirely pictorial (Rudofsky 1964, 1977; Guidoni 1978). These wide-ranging studies are visually impressive but lack the depth of ethnographic insight that anthropologists may be able to provide about how built forms are lived in. Rather than concentrating on any single culture, they have tended to take the form of global photographic surveys.[7] They have, in any case, helped to awaken the attention of a generation of architects to the almost forgotten visual and sensory pleasures of "anonymous" architectures. They praise especially its organic forms and textures and its power to evoke a feeling of authenticity, judged to reside in the fact that these architectures have evolved over time, as an ingenious response to a particular ecology and way of life, and manifest the functional and environmental appropriateness of the resulting designs for living. All of this stands in sharp contrast to the hard lines, impoverished textures, and inhuman scale of modernist architecture, as well as to the extreme egotism of what has become a high-profile profession in industrialized societies. But the focus remains principally on the idea of design itself, and ethnographic detail in such studies has usually been lacking.

How to give due regard to architecture as a visual study is an issue that anthropologists ought in their practice to address. We often have great opportunities to study and record indigenous architectural traditions, but these are often wasted either because the opportunity is ignored or because for the most part we are not adequately trained in the techniques that architects use to document and represent buildings. Anthropologists are good at analyzing the social significances of architecture but rarely know all the technical terms for the parts of a structure; most, moreover, have no training in how to do measured drawings, to analyze what makes a building stay up, or to choose the axis for a cross-section of a building that will best allow the viewer to understand its construction. The best architects, on the other hand, are usually talented artists who have developed a fine hand for architectural drawing and painting over a lifetime of constant practice. They have wonderful skills for looking at buildings but may be less sensitive to the possibilities for social analysis. In presenting their own work, architects prize good photography but are notorious for excluding any sign of human presence. In many architectural photographs, human figures, if they are present at all, appear in the middle distance, walking away from camera, or are included solely as generic figures to give a sense of scale. In situating the study of the built environment as a specifically visual form of anthropology, then, I must state right away that anthropologists still have much to accomplish in this field. And in looking at what has already been achieved, I shall very often be referring to the work of architects as much as anthropologists.

Since the cross-cultural study of the built environment is by its very nature an exercise that crosses disciplinary boundaries, it is not hard to see that great advantages could be gained from combining the skills and insights to be had from both architectural and anthropological training. One solution would be to offer anthropologists a basic training in architectural drawing and photography before they start their fieldwork. This would be very useful, but it is not realistic to suppose that all anthropologists, even if they have the inclination, will have the talent to take this to a high level. Another solution, which in my view has not so far received the attention it deserves, is for architects and anthropologists to work *together* to provide fuller documentation and analysis of indigenous architectures. However, such collaboration is not as straightforward as it sounds. For it to work well there must be genuinely equal relationships and some obvious benefit to both parties. If anthropologists expect to find architects who are happy merely to contribute the hard work of making measured drawings in the field, leaving all of the interpretation to the anthropologist, they are likely to be disappointed. Most architects are too ambitious for that, though it is possible that architecture students might sometimes be willing to do it as part of their training. Architects who are seriously interested in studying the social history of vernacular buildings may just as well choose to do so independently, following the traditions developed within their own discipline. Perhaps this is why there are still relatively few studies that exemplify this transdisciplinary approach, though I shall mention some that do and make reference to researchers who have aimed in their own work to combine both approaches.

Among architects who have developed a keen sense of the social meanings of the built environment, Amos Rapoport (1969, 1982), Spiro Kostof (1985), and Henry Glassie (1975, 1982, 1993, 1997, 1999, 2000) have been particularly influential. Other cross-cultural surveys have included those by Fraser (1968) and Crouch and Johnson (2001). As a geographer with a strong interest in vernacular architecture, Ronald Knapp (1989, 1999, 2000a, 2000b, 2003; Knapp and Lo 2005) has produced a sizable body of work on China and has recently launched, with Xing Ruan, a book series with Hawai'i University Press, entitled "Spatial Habitus: Making and Meaning in Asia's Architecture." Very substantial contributions to the field have come also from Jean-Paul Bourdier and Nezar Alsayyad, who founded the International Association for the Study of Traditional Environments (IASTE) at Berkeley in 1988, as an international cross-disciplinary forum where scholars could exchange ideas, findings, and research methods in the study of cultural aspects of design. Selected papers from the conference at which this organization was founded were published in Bourdier and Alsayyad (1989). The group has gone on to organize a series of biennial conferences and publishes the biennial *Traditional Dwellings and Settlements Review*, as well as a working paper series, which by now represents an impressive body of well-illustrated work in the comparative study of environments that can be variously defined as vernacular, traditional, or indigenous.[8]

No single individual better exemplifies the embrace of both disciplines, architecture and anthropology, than Paul Oliver (1969, 1971, 1975, 1987, 1997, 2003, 2006a). No one has done more to promote the serious study and documentation of vernacular architecture, or to raise awareness of the enormously valuable human resource it represents. Not only has he nurtured a whole generation of student researchers in this field, he has also pioneered studies in the field of disaster response, attempting to ensure that emergency shelter provided for those who have suffered disasters such as earthquakes should be culturally appropriate (which in the past it has often not been, leading to its rejection by the recipients). Oliver (2006a), a collected volume of the author's papers dating from the 1970s to the present, well illustrates the scope of his contribution. He has been instrumental in developing the Centre for Vernacular Studies, in the School of the Built Environment at Oxford Brookes University, where since 1997 one can pursue a master's degree course on International Studies in Vernacular Architecture. That course welcomes anyone with a concern for the world's built environment, whether their first degree was in architecture, anthropology, geography, conservation, or social development work; it is very comprehensive in its approach and the subjects covered reflect a keen concern for issues of sustainability. No account of Oliver's work would be complete, moreover, without special mention of his monumental achievement in conceiving and editing the massive, three-volume *Encyclopedia of Vernacular Architecture of the World* (1997), which includes entries by hundreds of contributors (a good number of them anthropologists) from around the world. This work represents easily the most extensive effort to date to lay out theoretical approaches and to document built environments in all their cultural diversity; it was widely acknowledged upon its appearance as an "instant classic" in the field. From the point of view of practice, Oliver has urged a closer study of how vernacular building traditions are actually transmitted; as he notes, out of all the accumulated studies of vernacular buildings, those that examine the many physical and mnemonic processes involved and how they are learned are still "exceptionally rare" (Oliver 2006a, 161). This also

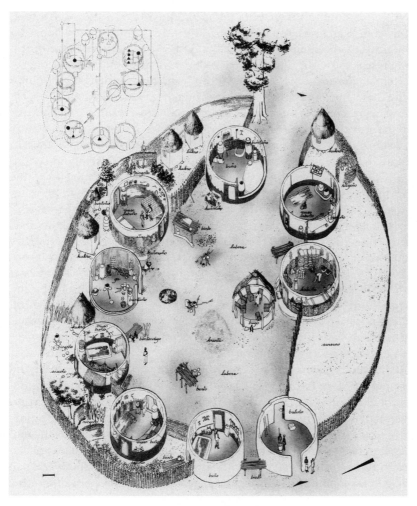

3.3   Cutaway drawing of a Jaxanke homestead in Diakha Madina, Senegal. Drawing by Jean-Paul Bourdier, from Bourdier and Trinh (1996, 174).

raises the question of whether they *are* currently being effectively trans-mitted, or whether (as can so easily be the case in rapidly changing soci-eties) they are at risk of being extinguished by a breach in transmission. Young people may no longer be interested in learning old skills, and "vernacular know-how" (Oliver 2006a, 109) is in danger of being lost.[9]

The 1980s and 1990s saw the publication of a growing number of stud-ies combining lavish illustration with substantial text, and an interest in both visual and ethnographic understandings. Often these have been the work of architects or architectural historians who have developed an interest in ethnography.[10] Occasionally they are the work of photographers, such as Courtney-Clarke (1990), whose stunning, vibrant images celebrate the creativity of West African women as architects and interior designers and provide a simply breathtaking example of what we are missing when we ignore the visual dimensions of our subject. In Bourdier and Trinh's *Drawn from African Dwellings* (1996), too, the superb quality of Bourdier's photography, the beauty of his sketches and complex cutaway drawings, and even the creativity of the book design and layout, for which he is also responsible, may all give pause for thought to the anthropologist thinking of embarking on a study of the built environment (figure 3.3).

Labelle Prussin, who describes herself as "an architect and architectural historian," is another scholar whose efforts to cross disciplinary boundaries should be humbling to anthropologists. Her magnificent *African Nomadic Architecture: Space, Place and Gender* (1995) documents the transportable structures of desert peoples from across the continent, combining a rich display of drawings and photographs with an insightful and informative ethnographic discussion.[11] Among nomadic pastoralists in modern Africa, women are the architects, though few scholars have paid attention to their achievements. This architecture comes into being in the context of marriage rituals, when a tent is erected for the bride and groom. The tent is the "moving center" of nomadic life, providing a constant element of spatial organization in an otherwise transient lifestyle. Permanence is achieved here through repetition; in each new location, the same tightly ordered space is continually being re-created as the tent is repitched. A Rendille elder's account of nomadic movements over a seventy-one-year period (1903–1974) produced a route map covering an area of over a hundred thousand square miles with journeys amounting to twelve thousand miles, during which his family camp with its tents had been pitched, struck, loaded, and unloaded almost twelve hundred times. Materials typically consist of poles or artificially curved branches, covered with mats, animal skins, woven hair fabrics, cloth, grasses, or other vegetal materials. This work depends on the memories and skills of women; dimensions and proportions, even the distribution of furniture, are a direct extension of their own bodily proportions. Aesthetically, the tent mediates relations with the environment rather than cutting people off from it, while providing a sense of security in otherwise limitless and relatively undifferentiated spaces. In an environment that is often harsh and unforgiving, the superfluity of brilliant color and decoration lavished

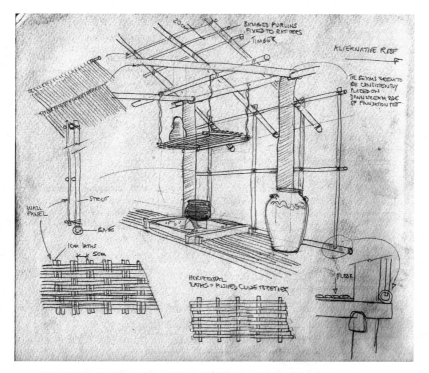

3.4 Field sketches by Julian Davison of a Jarai kitchen interior, Cambodia.

on specific elements of the structure and its interior furnishings can create, as the photographs testify, a surprising sense of comfort and sensual luxury within the space of the tent. This study should serve as a reminder to anthropologists of how much goes missing in our ethnographies if visual illustration is neglected, for aesthetics are a deep and integral part of the expression of any way of life.

Packing the house onto a camel in such a way as to ensure a stable load is itself a considerable skill, which earlier explorers might have admired more readily had they tried it themselves. The houses then transform themselves into shaded palanquins, within which the women and children ride when on the move. Building and transport technologies thus intersect; Prussin (1995, 63) remarks that "playing house for young nomadic girls involves the skills of tent building as well as tent transport." Playing with miniature models is one way in which they familiarize themselves with the technology. Economy of design is everywhere: everything has a dual purpose, like the camel litter that, when turned

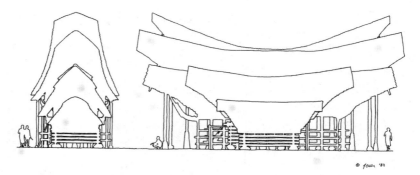

3.5 Silhouettes of five Toraja houses of different ages compared, displaying the historical development in form and shape. Longitudinal study of this kind remains something of a rarity in the study of vernacular architectures. Drawing: Jowa Imre Kis-Jovak.

upside down inside the tent, becomes a useful shelf on which to place or hang food supplies, out of reach of ants and poisonous insects on the ground (figure 3.4).

Perhaps less often, studies with a substantial visual content have been produced by anthropologists who discover an interest in architecture (Hauser-Schäublin 1989; Waterson 2009) or who have had the benefits of dual training (Davison and Granquist 1999). These studies have attempted to combine the visual communication of the subject matter with the close consideration of social structures and processes that has always been a chief concern of anthropology. Yet works that combine the skills of these intersecting disciplines remain surprisingly, and regrettably, few and far between. *Banua Toraja: Changing Patterns in Architecture and Symbolism among the Sa'dan Toraja, Sulawesi, Indonesia,* by Jowa Imre Kis-Jovak, Reimar Schefold, Hetty Nooy-Palm and Ursula Schultz-Dornburg (1988)—an architect, two anthropologists, and a photographer, respectively—remains a rare example and attests to the rich results that can be obtained by collaboration (figure 3.5).[12]

In Leiden, an ambitious tridisciplinary project led by Reimar Schefold (anthropology), Gaudenz Domenig (architecture), and Peter Nas (sociology) has served to nurture a new generation of researchers in vernacular architectures who have focused their attentions on less well documented areas of western Indonesia. *Indonesian Houses*, an outcome of this project, comprises two volumes. The first, *Tradition and Transformation in Vernacular Architecture* (Schefold, Domenig, and Nas 2004), includes an excellent glossary of technical terms, with diagrams by Domenig, that should be required reading for any anthropologist setting out to study timber architectures. Volume 2, *Survey on the Traditional House in Western Indonesia* (Schefold et al. 2009), is even more generously illustrated by the normal standards of anthropological publishing. One can only hope that this example will be copied more widely, since it is an obvious way to capitalize on multiple skills in what is so clearly by nature a multidisciplinary area.[13]

Current Directions in the Anthropological Study of the Built Environment

The papers in this latest volume (Schefold et al. 2009) are indicative of some of the directions now being pursued in the anthropology of architecture. As a valuable contribution to Indonesian studies in particular, there has been a concerted effort to cover lesser-known areas for which documentation has been poor, but the better-known areas have also been readdressed in order to go beyond the simplifications or stereotypes with which earlier works tended to be satisfied. Full attention is paid to variations within a given area, avoiding the mistake of distilling actual variety into a single, supposedly "ideal" type, a common distortion in earlier studies. There is a stress on change, some chapters including the analysis of urban as well as rural types of vernacular architecture, and not neglecting even modern concrete bungalows as a potential object of study. There is a concern also with how life-cycle changes affect how and in what structures people live at different stages of life or marriage. Previously overlooked categories, such as forest lean-tos and boat dwellings—actually rather significant structures in the Southeast Asian region—are included. There is a even a discussion of "haunted" houses and of the subject of memory and emotional attachment to places.

Architectural Anthropology, edited by Mari-Jose Amerlinck (2001), is another welcome addition to the growing literature in this area and one that, commendably, aims to build bridges in several directions—between architecture and anthropology, between the possible contributions of both biological and social anthropology to our understanding of the built environment, and between Spanish-speaking and English-speaking academics in this field. Amerlinck, a professor of anthropology at the University of Guadalajara, has already published in Spanish on this topic (Amerlinck 1995; Amerlinck and Bontempo 1994). In her introduction, she too expresses the hope that a more fully interdisciplinary relationship can be developed through collaborative research projects that would utilize more effectively the skills of both disciplines. Two distinguished researchers on the built environment—Amos Rapoport and Nold Egenter—contribute theoretical papers to this volume. The rest of the papers are by anthropologists, covering a diverse range of case studies. It must be said that, again, this is a predominantly textual, rather than visual, presentation, though for a publication of its type it is comparatively well illustrated, with drawings, diagrams, and some photographs.

In general, recent anthropological writings have moved away from the rather static and synchronic emphasis that tended to result from structural analysis of spatial layouts, taking instead a more diachronic and processual approach to understanding the built environment. According to this perspective, architectures, far from being merely inert physical structures that passively reflect cultural or symbolic concerns, actively help to constitute social life, cosmology, and the transitions of personal biographical experience. Structuralism's fundamental insights can thus be enhanced by a more dynamic and close-grained analysis of the interactions between buildings and their inhabitants over time, or during the specially marked times of ritual. The mundane social spaces of an Iban longhouse, for instance, in ritual become the stage for the acting out of cosmic dramas. In healing rituals the journeys of souls and spirits are articulated with the physical and symbolic features of the longhouse itself in a most intricate way, and even items of furniture may be used as props to signify landmarks of the spirit world—a rice mortar becomes a mountain, or a door stands for the "Violently Shutting Rock" that bars the river to the Otherworld. The shaman in his chanted soul journey thus aims to work upon the social and intrasubjective experiences of both the patient and the audience. At the final secondary rites for the dead, the great Gawai Antu celebrations, when the gathered bards sing to summon the shades of the ancestors, again the longhouse becomes the symbolically organized terrain through which they travel and, in a merging of social and spiritual space, the threshold between human and spirit worlds (Sather 1993) (figure 3.6).

The Sakuddei of Siberut island (off the west coast of Sumatra) also build impressive longhouses, though instead of being divided into nuclear family apartments giving on to a communal veranda, as among the Iban, theirs are divided into two main sections. The larger front compartment is the more public and masculine in its associations; the rear or inner compartment, more associated with the female and with birth, is reserved as a sleeping place for women at night. But Sakuddei couples live only part of the time in the longhouse, preferring to spend periods

3.6 Women serving the warriors ritual wine (*ai jalong*) toward the climax of the Gawai Antu celebration in an Iban longhouse. Throughout the night of the ceremony, the spirits of the dead, gods, and spirit-heroes, summoned by the recitation of ritual poetry, are believed to throng the gallery along with the living. Behind the warriors stands a group of bards, two of whom hold bowls of wine. Photo: Clifford Sather.

together in the more relaxed and private atmosphere of their field houses. In the longhouse, life is intensely communal; very different patterns of behavior are required, and there are numerous taboos to be observed. These articulate human relations with the unseen, the simultaneously natural and spiritual world of the surrounding forest. The social life of the longhouse, Schefold suggests, reflects a sense of multiple vulnerabilities in Sakuddei life: to external conflicts, internal tensions, and the danger of disease, attributed to the anger of spirits at the neglect of taboos. The longhouse is also the site of ceremonies and the frequent entertaining of guests till late into the night; yet another reason for retiring to the field houses is to catch up on sleep (Schefold 2009). Life is thus lived with a certain fluidity of movement between the two types of structures. For the Zafimanary of Madagascar, the house embodies and makes visible the progress of a marriage; starting from a simple, permeable, and unadorned structure built of perishable materials, a couple gradually adds more and more hardwood posts and beams, ornamented with carving, as they have children and their relationship is seen to be stable and fertile. This "beautifies" the house and "hardens it with bones," so that over time, after the original owners have passed away and their children formed new households, it will become a "holy house" where descendants come to obtain blessing from the ancestors. Thus, "the aesthetics and architecture of house building become the objectification and fetishization of a social relation" (Bloch 1995, 79). The idea of the house as having a biography of its own is not unique to Madagascar but is a predominant feature of Austronesian cultures generally. If the house is typically treated as if it were in some sense alive, this means that it also has a life history, intertwined with and extending beyond the lifespans of individual inhabitants. This idea of the house as offering a sort of immortality to its descendants is comparatively explored in Waterson (2003).

Vellinga (2004) provides a further example of a more dynamic and diachronic approach to the study of architecture. Observing that although the Minangkabau of West Sumatra are renowned for their elegant architecture, surprisingly few detailed studies of it had ever been carried out, Vellinga chose as the site for his fieldwork the village of Abai Sangir in the little-studied southern borderland district of Solok. In the past, the Minangkabau "great house" (*rumah gadang*) often accommodated a number of matrilineally related nuclear families under one roof, and there were many that achieved impressive sizes. Disasters of war and accidental fires have taken their toll over the years, however, and today's generation often prefer the privacy of smaller dwellings. The inhabitants of Abai can claim the achievement of having constructed the longest houses in the whole of West Sumatra. The village includes eight such houses (known as *rumah barih*), reaching lengths of over seventy meters. The longest comprises twenty-one bays or family compartments. Their construction appears to have started in the early twentieth century, developing a competitive element from the 1950s onward that caused them to become even longer. When Vellinga started his fieldwork in 1993, out of thirty-two houses in the village eight had been built within the past forty-five years, and twenty-two (or two-thirds) were still under construction or in process of improvement. The village would thus appear to be in a permanent state of becoming. What could account for such vigorous investment in these extraordinary houses?

For the inhabitants of Abai the house (*rumah*) is the most salient category, more crucial even than the groups linked by matrilineal descent that make up its core, since it includes both men of the descent group (mothers' brothers, or *ninik mamak*) and in-marrying husbands (*urang sumando*). To have a house, as a physical structure, is absolutely vital to the existence of the *rumah* as a group. House and kin group thus are seen to constitute each other. According to *adat* regulations, the group can neither hold ceremonies nor receive guests from another *rumah* in the proper manner without a house to provide the setting. This is especially crucial for weddings, lavishly celebrated, by means of which the *rumah* perpetuates itself by entering into a relationship with another *rumah*. Guests at any ceremony have to be seated in the correct locations within the house, and if no house is available, they cannot be invited in the first place. Furthermore, the interior spaces of the house are needed in order to conduct the ceremonial appointment of the house's own representatives, who perform the role of honored guests at other houses' celebrations. Hence, when a longhouse starts to fall down (after a period of about seventy years), a new house must be built before it can be demolished.

Nowadays, most people do not wish to reside in the longhouse, but make smaller houses for their families alongside it. Still, for ritual purposes, they must have their own space within the longhouse in order to participate. Thus it is felt that if, at the moment of demolition, no new house had yet been built, the group would socially cease to exist. Old houses are often simply left to fall down after they have been replaced. The cooperation needed to achieve these architectural feats is formidable. Each *kaum* or subgroup is responsible for maintaining its own compartment and may improve the walls over time as they can afford it, giving houses a somewhat uneven visual appearance. But house construction also provides a means of expressing difference. Roof spires, floor levels, ornaments, and other details of construction, as well as the uses of space

3.7   Raising the framework of small posts, Bakah Dalam, 1996. Photo: Marcel Vellinga.

in daily life and on ritual occasions—all of these visual elements can be telling means of accentuating or acting out hierarchical relationships, and they are exploited in different ways depending on context. House construction provides a socially approved project by means of which a wealthy contributor can raise his own status and that of his *kaum* within the *rumah* and come to have a greater say in its ongoing affairs. Even if this involves some manipulation of history, it can be presented as a demonstration of respect for tradition. Conversely, not to contribute would be tantamount to surrendering one's place in the social organization and finding oneself excluded from future social activities. Thus Vellinga argues that, far from being, in a passive sense, merely a "microcosm" or reflection of the wider social structure, the house plays a very active role in bringing the social group into being and enabling it to perpetuate itself. This confirms, in my view, that Lévi-Strauss was quite mistaken in concentrating his attention on the idea of the house as a group, at the expense of the actual architecture. We cannot fully understand the one without taking into account the vital material presence of the other, so closely is the life history of the house intertwined with that of its inhabitants (figure 3.7).

Other recent studies likewise demonstrate a sensitivity to diachronic perspectives and issues of change and transformation. Winzeler (1998, 2004), an anthropologist with architectural leanings, has produced well-illustrated studies of the built environment in Borneo, paying special attention to the differential effects of government policies toward indigenous religion and the preference for longhouse dwelling, which have produced very different patterns of architectural change on either side of the Malaysian-Indonesian border. Conversely Ruan (2006), an architect with ethnographic leanings, is the author of a well-illustrated and also ethnographically rich portrait of the little-known architecture of the Dong of Yunnan in southern China. Dong architecture shows some distinctively Austronesian features (notably building on piles), as well as unique structures, such as the ritually important Drum Towers, and the dramatically cantilevered covered bridges known poetically as "Wind and Rain Bridges." Rather than viewing architecture as static "text," Xing focuses on the image of "inhabiting" as a dynamic social process, the architecture providing the shell within which the Dong continually renew and reinvent their myths and cultural practices (figure 3.8).

Having survived various historical pressures to conform to Han culture or to abandon aspects of its underlying culture, Dong architecture is currently undergoing something of a revival, and some related rituals have also been newly invented. Having shown how intimately Dong architecture is bound up with ritual and identity, Ruan wryly notes some of the tensions and ambiguities involved in this relation:

Considering the newly invented ritual for the farewell of the drum and the many thousands of years' contact with the Han, the Dong could not possibly have maintained an "unbroken and stable" tradition that we now see as Dong ethnicity. But ethnicity for a minority group in the majority Han context is, historically as well as contemporarily, a necessity both for the warmth of their own home and a legitimate position in the Han world. Yet the desire for ethnicity comes from outsiders as well, for the majority population seems always to expect minority groups to be exotic. Romanticism does, however, help minority groups imagine an "authenticity" in the name of tradition, though the whole thing could be an invention. (2006, 168)

Some of the most important factors sustaining indigenous architectures are precisely the less tangible ones of ritual, cosmology, and kinship patterns. In my own research I have found that for the Toraja people of Sulawesi, the house as origin-site is such an important focus of ritual that migrants will return at great expense, and over long distances, in order to be present at ceremonies. For a family to allow an origin-house to fall into decay is a matter of shame; here, compared to almost anywhere else in Indonesia, the requirements of a ceremonial economy, however much

3.8   Drum tower in Zengchong village, Congjiang region of Guizhou province, 1993.
Photo: Xing Ruan.

this has been adapted to Christianity, remain a driving force behind the maintenance and renewal of traditional houses (Waterson 2009, 236–39). Nathalie Lancret (1997), too, has analyzed in detail how Bali's urban dwellers, in towns like Denpasar, seek to adapt their living spaces in order to provide appropriate locations for the holding of household rituals. These cannot be performed in an enclosed room but must be carried out in a traditional, open pavilion. If this is not available in the town house, the occupants feel compelled to return to their ancestral home in order to be able to stage rites in the proper setting.

Lancret's diachronic study shows how cultural requirements continue to play a significant role in determining the form even of urban dwellings. She is concerned with what is involved in the *transmission of an idea* of "tradition," which obliges actors to make strategic choices of continuities, changes, and erasures, in the process of which built form itself becomes "an instrument of transmission" (1997, 3). This more open and fluid approach to the understanding of "tradition," as well as the willingness to investigate urban contexts, deserves our closer attention. Living in the city presents a number of constraints to the traditional Balinese style of dwelling. The population of Denpasar quintupled in the space of thirty years (1960–1990), while land prices soared. Space constraints restrict the traditional Balinese courtyard arrangement with its dispersed pavilions, which simply takes up too much room to survive the translation to an urban context. At the same time, new housing projects (often based on "international" models) fail hopelessly to conform to Balinese cultural requirements. In their efforts to create more suitable dwellings, Balinese therefore resort to a pragmatic application of traditional principles according to the limitations of place, time, and circumstances. Newcomers in the city will be expected to maintain allegiances to the *banjar* (or village association) of their original community as well as that of their new city ward. The idea of the "house" as a kin group (the *dadia*), forming branch houses and temples over time, also remains important. In the rural context, the extended family builds new houses on adjoining or nearby land as required; in the city, lack of space forces the owners to subdivide the original plot and squeeze extra structures into it. Architectural transformations are thus a response, in part, to a cultural rationale (the requirements of the kinship system), and not just to the exigencies of the urban situation.

Houses of "mixed" or "transitional" style often seek to maintain important elements of·the traditional house yard, even if in altered form or new materials—an enclosed room or *meten* (now perhaps with added windows for ventilation), an open pavilion or *bale* (now sometimes partially walled), altars, and a house temple (now occupying a much reduced area). Cosmological rules of organization such as the oppositions between high and low, mountains and sea, the sacred and the profane, have to be reinterpreted to deal with vertical space in buildings of more than one story. Common innovations in the use of internal space include a higher degree of subdivision into rooms with separate functions, such as bedrooms. A continuing belief that defects in construction (including its ritual aspects) may cause harm to the occupants of a building is one factor that acts as a brake on architectural change. Ancestral spirits may refuse to return to visit the family temple if the dwelling departs too far from the rules that have traditionally governed construction. The overall picture, then, is one of continual adaptation rather than a complete rupture with traditional models. No doubt more and more studies of the built environment will have to deal with such changing, urbanized contexts.

Visual Methods and the Study of the Built Environment

I believe there are still ways in which we as anthropologists are neglecting the potentials of visual media to enhance our studies. Not only photography but film, video, and hypermedia deserve to be utilized more fully. Visual anthropologists working with video, for instance, should consider more closely the potentials of film to record the processes of house-building.[14] A very informative example is the film *Building Season in Tiébélé: A Royal Compound in Change, Kasena, Burkina Faso,* directed by Beate Engelbrecht (1999). The film has won a number of awards, and it well illustrates the advantages of visual presentation. The anthropologist involved in this film, AnneMarie Fiedermutz-Laun, had already contributed to the literature a substantial book about Kasena architecture, yet, aware of the limitations of textual form, sought to make a film as well. The result is a document of great visual and ethnographic richness. A sense of intimacy is achieved partly due to the anthropologist's already established close relations with the compound's inhabitants and the effective use of local interviewers, and partly through the fluid camera work of Manfred Krüger, which carries us on a winding journey through the narrow alleys and into the countless courtyards of this remarkable, vigorously decorated, and endlessly renewable mud-built architecture (figure 3.9).

What film can show us, in a way that a book cannot, is the processes that go in to the endless cycle of maintenance and renewal of such an architecture. During each dry season, houses, granaries, and staircases are

3.9   Woman of Tiebele decorating a mud wall with incised and painted patterns. Photo: Beate Engelbrecht.

built and restored. The necessary material is available underfoot; earth can be dug directly on the site of a new compound and mixed with water, or a worn-out structure can be demolished and reduced again to mud for reuse. The film documents the rhythms of work: men dig with hoes, while women bring water; groups of men and women sing back and forth to each other to make the work easier; football-size lumps of mud are passed from hand to hand in a human chain to lay the base of a new house, squeezed in between already existing structures. There are rhythms of clapping and pounding, of working and resting. Meanwhile, children play at house-building in miniature. There is a strong focus on women in the film; we see them painting houses, discussing designs, restoring granaries, feeding the workers, performing ritual tasks to ensure the well-being of a building's inhabitants, and talking about their work. As the camera brings us from one courtyard to another, we encounter many small incidents of daily life—fixing a calabash, brewing beer, grinding millet—and engage in many interesting fragments of conversation. We gain a picture of the whole process of construction—how doors are cut after the walls are finished, how flat roofs are built up on a structure of crossed branches, supported by forked trunks placed against the interior walls, how a broken pot may provide the smoke-hole for a kitchen. The house itself is revealed as a symbolically female domain: the main room is its "womb," the kitchen is made by the women into a work of sculpture with its sensuously molded patterns, the stove symbolizes a woman with her two knees drawn up. There are ironic comments too: when the filmmaker asks a group of women engaged in painting a house whether the purpose of the designs is "to honor the mother of the house," they reply, "We are doing this because the whites are coming," referring to the impending visit of a tour group.

The film also provides reflections about change. Although traditional structures are round and made with hand-kneaded lumps of clay, another increasingly common style is to build square houses with prefabricated, sun-dried mud bricks held together with a mud mortar. Such houses are quicker to build but cannot be used for the performance of traditional rites. The inhabitants of this royal compound were formerly able to live on the tribute rendered by their followers but now face economic difficulties. An old man comments on the problem of land shortages, which cause young people to emigrate to the towns to look for work. Or they lose interest in farming, and go to Ougadougou "to sell ice." Thus the film offers a vivid sense of physical spaces and textures as well as insights into social relationships, the organization of work, the rhythms of everyday life, and the pressures of change. This film is an excellent example of how different media can be used to complement each other to provide a fuller, richer ethnography.

The inclusion of video clips and photographs in multimedia presentations also opens up many exciting new potentials for archiving and interactive display of research materials. Although the vast amount of data input required may require the help of computer specialists, there is also the possibility of using hypermedia to create "walk-through" online environments. Researchers at the University of Kansas School of Architecture and Urban Design began experimenting with this more than a decade ago, creating an online version of Al Mu'izz li-Din, the most famous street in the medieval quarter of Cairo (Sanchez del Valle and Abdel-Kawi 1994). The street contains a number of historic monuments, studies of which have often drawn or presented them as if in isolation from the dense urban environment that flourishes around them. Given that the fabric of the old city is severely strained by modern developments, and many Islamic monuments have already been damaged or destroyed, the idea was to create the fullest possible portrait, one that would include ruins or now-vanished buildings as well as the surviving ones, and that would pay attention to "human activities, attitudes and fictions." "We work on the assumption," the authors state, "that any intended development of this area, particularly any that involves the preservation of the antiquities within it, shall invariably depend on the cooperation of the users and effective owners of the area. Therefore, for any description to be of significance, it needs to incorporate the perspective of the inhabitants" (1994, 52). In this site one can navigate up and down the street, getting a full impression of the architectural setting and some of the social activities carried on there. Or one can "parachute" in to pick out the famous buildings (still receiving a visual impression of their settings) or can click on certain features for further links and information. By clicking on a door, for instance, one might be able to see details of its construction or ornamentation, and also to pass through it to enter the interior of a building. Additional links allow one to access maps, survey data, architectural drawings, photographs, and paintings, as well as historical accounts of particular buildings, on-site interviews, or fictional narratives for which this street provides the setting. A first attempt led the authors to reflect on the shortcomings of rendering in two dimensions what is really a three-dimensional, sensory experience: a true sense of the location requires that the viewer have an impression not only of vertical surfaces, but also, for instance, of "the ceiling of the street clogged with tent-like coverings and clothes for sale; the uneven texture of the floor surface covered with dust, mud, and overflowed sewage water; the arrangement of the store fronts that were not photographed for the sake of simplicity; and the people conducting their everyday affairs" (1994, 53). "Sensuous scholarship" (Stoller 1997) may yet have a way to go before it can be convincingly rendered in virtual habitats! But still, this example should suffice to show that it is possible to create a fairly complex interactive resource that need not neglect either the visual dimensions or the features of social life that are intrinsic to a particular built environment. Second-generation web page technology will make such projects increasingly easier to produce.

An innovative way of using visual media in an ethnography of shantytown life is currently being explored by Gauri Bharat, a graduate student of architecture at the National University of Singapore, who participated in a course I teach for students of the social sciences called "The Practice of Visual Ethnography." Her doctoral research investigates architecture and life in a *basti*, or slum area, on the fringes of Jamshedpur in eastern India. Having decided to use video as a research tool, she went one step further by handing the camera to her informants and asking them to film what is significant to them about their lived environment, while providing their own running commentary. The results so far (in the form of a video work in progress, *Banter in the Basti*) are very revealing of the inhabitants' priorities and values, subtly gendered domains and movement patterns, different individuals' personal pathways through the neighborhood, aspects of community organization, and the problems faced by the inhabitants in securing and maintaining infrastructural features. With this technique, Ghauri has accumulated a diverse collection of filmic narratives representing different points of view on the community. A key feature of these narratives, she notes, is that rather than representing spaces in the form of abstract diagrams, as is customary in architectural research, they are composed of "sequences of interpersonal events" involving the informant and the people, settings, and events that they encounter or seek out to become a part of their narrative—or which conversely, they may choose not to record. They thus provide a rich and nuanced source of data from which to learn what people really think and feel about their neighborhood. Digital video is so easy to use today that one can quickly acquire a reasonable degree of competence with it. Departments should introduce basic training for graduate students before they go to the field, for in the future the video camera will become as much a taken-for-granted piece of equipment for fieldworkers as the more traditional notebook and camera.

Conclusion: Future Directions and the Practical Relevance of the Anthropology of Architecture

Ann Cline (1997), herself an architect, writes of the pleasures of inhabitation and of building for oneself in a poetic celebration of a type of structure that exists, even in industrialized societies, outside the realm of the professional architect—namely, the hut of the individual eccentric or recluse. She suggests that hut dwellers of this type (among whom she counts herself), out of step as they often are with the architecture of their own era, have not just been seeking a romantic return to the "primitive" or to the hut of childhood play and fantasy, which Bachelard (1969, 32) sees as still more elemental. Their lives, she notes, "may instead have been ahead of their time, as if their very inability to march in step raised exactly those cultural issues that later on become helpful." Seeking "to overturn Architecture's victory over Individual Experience" (1997, ix), she therefore proposes that from the kind of life lived in the hut, important messages may still be learned for the future. The same is undoubtedly true of vernacular architectures generally. While indigenous architectural traditions can indeed be very vulnerable (Waterson 2002), to pay attention to them is not a mere surrender to nostalgia, focusing attention on a category that is doomed to eclipse in the onward rush of modernization or globalization. Nothing could be further from the truth, for there is still an urgent need for study and practical application of the lessons they can offer us.

Apart from recovering a philosophy of how to live more lightly on the earth, there is much still to be learned and appreciated in what Oliver (1969) termed "vernacular know-how," in the very practical sense of building solutions to climatic and other issues. How to make our buildings "greener" is an increasingly serious topic of debate. We need the study of the vernacular for this reason; but there is also the possibility of innovating new forms and techniques from out of a vernacular heritage. In many parts of the world, a key problem for sustainability of indigenous architectures themselves is the growing shortage of timber, and other less "authentic" materials have long been accepted as alternatives. Corrugated zinc has in many areas tended to replace vegetal materials and has become part of the picture of evolving traditions. In parts of Indonesia it has been in use for over a hundred years already—quite long enough to count as traditional! Bamboo, on the other hand, is a material indigenous to tropical regions that has always been an integral part of vernacular traditions.

Bamboo has the advantage of being both very fast-growing, and marvelously light and strong; its potentials for sustainability have still not been fully explored, though one radical architect who has been most creative in this direction is the Colombian Simón Vélez. In the book *Grow Your Own House* (Kries and Vegesack 2000), he documents how he has explored and experimented with bamboo from every possible angle. Seeing that its properties make it in his view "inherently a high-tech material" (2000, 64), he has found ways to construct even very large buildings of this material, including the ZERI pavilion at Expo 2000 in Hanover (figure 3.10).

And why should the vernacular not find its way back, at the same time, into high-tech contemporary architectural design? There are signs, here and there, that it is doing so. Krinsky (1996), for example, analyzes the application of indigenous conceptions to new buildings designed by and for Native American communities in the United States, which she perceives as expressive of a resurgent self-confidence and desire for self-determination, while Richardson (2001) reviews the work of international architects inspired by the vernacular in a variety of geographical locations and settings (figure 3.11).

The collection brought together by Asquith and Vellinga (2006) provides a concise overview of fresh directions in the study of vernacular

3.10 Factory hall under construction in Pensilvania (Colombia), an experimental large-scale design in bamboo by Colombian architect Simón Vélez, 1993. Photo: Günter Pauli, ZERI Foundation.

architectures. They urge a processual and forward-looking approach to the subject—one that would more thoroughly document what is involved in the enactment and transmission of skills; that sees vernacular architectures as living traditions to be learned from; and that would educate architects to be more sensitive to the tremendous and continuing scope of nonprofessional contributions to the world of architecture. If this is still, as Oliver (2006b, 268) laments in the conclusion to this volume, "a field without a 'discipline,'" that is also a problem that could be addressed by the establishment of more interdisciplinary courses and departments. Here anthropologists would be able to work together with participants from other specializations to produce graduates with professionally acknowledged qualifications, equipped to work on settlement issues at national, international, NGO, or community levels. Vellinga, Oliver, and Bridge have recently collaborated to produce a more intensely visual presentation of global vernacular traditions today in their *Atlas of Vernacular Architecture of the World* (2007).

Oliver (2006a, 417) urges us to be aware of the resource represented by the capabilities of nonprofessionals, deployed as they are as much in an urban as a rural context. In the vast areas of "illegal" squatter settlement that surround most cities of the developing world, as much as in rural areas, millions of people still make their own dwellings. In the face of global population growth, which is predicted to raise the world's population by 50 percent within the next half century, how are these extra three billion people to be provided with shelter? Official solutions for "low cost" housing designed by professionals all too often disdain to inquire into the needs, desires, and cultural heritage of the "masses" for whom they are intended and end up being too expensive for the proposed users anyway. That kind of approach is never going to be sufficient to respond to the inevitable global housing crisis that lies ahead. Oliver contends that it is precisely the capabilities of local communities, and the vernacular traditions that they have continued to sustain, that should be taken most seriously as the only realistic possibility of addressing this problem. While cities grow exponentially and the overwhelming focus of most planning reports and conferences is on urban areas, Oliver reminds us that all the same, half of the world's population continues to live in rural areas in

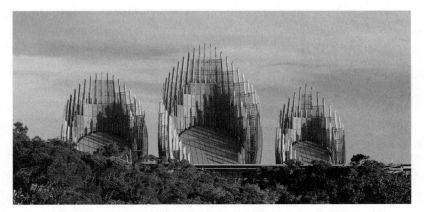

3.11 Tjibao Cultural Centre, Nouméa, New Caledonia, designed by Italian architect Renzo Piano in consultation with Albert Bensa, an anthropologist and specialist in South Pacific culture. The design draws creative inspiration from the architecture of Kanak huts, made from intertwined plant fibers, but transcends the danger of kitsch in its startling originality. A total of ten structures, made from timber ribs and joists held together with steel rods, provide spaces for different kinds of cultural exhibitions and performances; the exterior spaces between them form a ritual pathway, the "pathway of history," in which Kanak themes of death, rebirth, and nature are metaphorically expressed. The structures exploit trade winds from the sea for natural ventilation, moving and vibrating in the wind together with the surrounding trees. The tallest is 28 meters high, forming a landmark visible from far away. Photo: Jon Gollings.

what he terms "sustained traditional environments" (2006a, 420). Supporting the continuity of these and the human resource they represent will be a far cheaper and more viable alternative for governments and planners than more formal planning solutions. Anthropologists, attuned as they are to inquiring into how people make meaning in the places and practices they create, ought to have a great deal to contribute to such planning.

The study of vernacular architectures, then, is valuable for its own sake in documenting human "designs for living" across the widest possible range of contexts. Often neglected in the past, it deserves to be seen as an integral part of the anthropological project. New approaches need to move beyond older, more static accounts, to consider diachronic processes, methods of transmission, and the lived experiences of a building's creators and inhabitants. There is no doubt that, to do justice to its subject matter, the study of vernacular architectures needs to make the best use of visual media and techniques for documentation, and in this regard I have suggested that much still remains to be achieved by anthropologists and architects working in collaboration. But as Oliver has demonstrated, these are not just academic concerns. The lessons to be learned from a study of the world's vernacular heritage can help us to address the urgent practical problems of human habitat today and for the future.

Notes

I am grateful to Gaudenz Domenig for his insightful comments on an earlier version of this paper.

1. Heidegger's (1965) philosophical insight that dwelling precedes building can just as easily be arrived at by a consideration of comparative ethnography and the recognition that at least 90 percent of human history is a hunter-gatherer history. Peter Wilson (1988) has argued for an architectural watershed in human relations, when sedentism, and the building of permanent structures, first transformed the open society of hunters and gatherers and began the long progress of our alienation from nature and from each other.
2. See Basso (1996) for a fascinating example of the imposition of narrative meanings on a landscape among the Western Apache of Arizona.
3. Tillema's photograph of such shelters, taken in the 1930s, is reproduced in Waterson (2009, 92). He suggests that the occupants at one time preferred to blend into the forest because they feared being raided by the headhunting Iban.

4. See Zerner (1983) for a discussion of temporary architecture among the Toraja of Indonesia.
5. For fuller discussions of what constitutes the "vernacular" and of what alternative terms might be appropriate, see Highlands 1990; Asquith and Vellinga 2006; Oliver 1997, 2006a.
6. This impulse is discussed by other authors in the present volume; see in particular the chapters by Farnell, Dudley, and Schneider.
7. Duly (1978) is also a fine pictorial survey, by an anthropologist rather than an architect.
8. Other cross-disciplinary volumes include Kent (1990) and Blanton (1994). Both of these authors are archaeologists concerned with developing an interdisciplinary understanding of factors affecting the house and household formation, so as to provide a sounder basis for the interpretation of archaeological evidence. Turan (1990) and Benjamin, Stea, and Saile (1995) include contributions from architects, anthropologists, archaeologists, geographers, ecologists, and urban planners.
9. The social contexts of transmission may change as a result of globalization or of régime change. For instance, the fine old Buddhist *wats* of Luang Prabang, a UNESCO World Heritage Site, used to be maintained by the monks themselves, who were trained in the various crafts involved. Under socialism, as enrollment in monasteries has declined, so have the crafts. To ensure the future of the buildings, UNESCO identified as a matter of urgency the training of a new generation of young monks in the necessary skills (Somsanouk et al. 2004).
10. See, e.g., Domenig 1980; Kawashima 1986; Cinatti 1987; Morgan 1988; Prussin 1995; Blier 1987; Nabokov and Easton 1989; Boulay 1990; Maas and Mommersteeg 1992; Bourdier and Trinh 1996.
11. Of the several contributors to her book, it is not clear whether the others are architects or anthropologists by training, but their contributions certainly indicate an intimate knowledge of social life in the groups depicted.
12. On aspects of Toraja architecture, see also Waterson (1988, 1989) and Nooy-Palm (2001).
13. Anthropologists and architects have also collaborated in the production of special volumes on architecture in the *Encyclopedia of Indonesian Heritage* (Davison and Goh 1998) and *Encyclopedia of Malaysia* (Chen 1998).
14. See also Dudley's chapter in this volume for a discussion of the potential of film to document processes involved in the making and wearing of textiles.

FOUR

Unfinished Dialogues: Notes toward an Alternative History of Art and Anthropology

ARND SCHNEIDER

Rather than providing a survey history of the anthropology of art, this chapter will chart the relationship between the disciplines of art (visual arts in the widest sense), art criticism and art history, and anthropology, with a particular emphasis on these disciplines' practices of appropriation of other cultures, as well as their relationship with each other. Paradigmatic figures whose work has crossed boundaries and gone beyond accepted frames will be explored. Examples include Aby Warburg's interpretation of snake rituals observed among Native Americans in the southwestern United States, Alfred Court Haddon's early film recordings, Robert and Margaret Park Redfield's collaboration with the journal *Mexican Folkways* and the photographer Tina Modotti, Michel Leiris's participation in the surrealist movement, Julius Lips's early work on representation of the West in non-Western art, and Maya Deren's ethnographic and film work in Haiti, as well as classic innovators of the subject in anthropology, such as Franz Boas and, more recently, Alfred Gell.

Preamble

Any narrative not owing exclusively to the vantage point of anthropology, supposing a relational understanding of the subject of art and not starting from an a priori meaning of the term, must take into consideration disciplinary varieties and consider a multiplicity of approaches. In this essay, I shall explore a number of border crossings between disciplines (or fields), especially those of art practice, anthropology, and art history. My aim is not to privilege any one point of view; rather, the relationships among historical actors and between disciplines will be in the foreground.

I review in this essay a number of paradigmatic cases, each of which stands for a set of specific issues that, I contend, continue to have relevance. In my interpretation of the "past," then, I am deliberately guided by how I see the relationship between art and anthropology in the present. In this sense, a narrative, historical exploration of anthropology-art entanglements becomes meaningful only as an account of the fulfilled and, equally, the unfulfilled, or short-cut, destinies of past experiments, which present and future generations can mine. Like veins of quartz in a rock, such past experiments are arrested in time, yet the contemporary work of narration and interpretation can retrieve and illuminate their meaning and potential. Hence, in terms of the underlying *Erkenntnisinteresse* (i.e., cognitive interest, or in a broader sense, epistemological interest; Habermas 1971), I take my lead from a philosophical hermeneutics of history. I am especially indebted to philosophers of history such as Ernst Bloch (1986) and Reinhart Koselleck (2004), who view the present and events of the past-present against a foil of projected, future-oriented event horizons or destinies (of human social and cultural aspirations). Of these projections only a small number will be realized, whereas the vast majority will acquire the status of unfulfilled and ultimately utopian projects.

From the vantage point of the present, then, my principle, and perhaps too crude, question is What can contemporary practitioners in anthropology and art do with the past? Or more precisely, How can they retrieve the explicit and implicit experimental potential of past projects, even if this entails conjecture or hypothesis regarding paths not crossed, encounters missed, dialogues not developed, exhibitions not held, and performances not staged? The present narrative will be one of juxtaposition, bringing together what are many times separate, parallel histories in order to forge a common synergy for future border crossings and projects. Eventually, and beyond the scope of this essay, such explorations of the parallel and multiple histories of art practice and theory and of anthropology could chart a matrix for future collaborations.

At present, I contend that the options and possibilities are clearly laid out by recent writings and theorizing in art and anthropology, namely the new or renewed emphasis on practices and collaborations (Grimshaw and Ravetz 2005; Schneider and Wright 2006, 2010; Schneider 2006, 2008), and on the senses (Jones 2006; Classen 2005; Howes 2004; Stoller 1989, 1997)—in both cases art is seen as a participating subject, not a passive object. These new directions will also impact on studies, where art, though embedded in social relations, is seen as the "object" of inquiry: explorations of global art worlds (Plattner 1996; Colloredo-Mansfeld 1999), the social agency of art objects (Gell 1998; Pinney and Thomas 2001; Knappet 2005; Henare, Holbrand, and Wastell 2007), combined with reflective museum practices (Henare 2005a), and changing production sites and practices of art (Svašek 2007), both Western and non-Western, as well as. ultimately, the fundamental issue of the recognition of otherness through art historical (Kubler 1991; Pasztory 2005) and anthropological writing (e.g., Taussig 1993).[1]

Most of the examples in the following sections are not part of the canon of anthropological writing (including the anthropology of art), and one could ask why this would be the case when some of the figures discussed, such as Franz Boas or Robert Redfield, clearly occupy a prominent role in the mainstream. The approach, as will become apparent, is deliberately anticanonical, bringing into juxtaposition different approaches and fields of inquiry.

Embodiment, Camouflage, and Performance: Boas, Warburg, Haddon

The role of practical experiment in anthropology usually goes unacknowledged. While theoretical writings are routinely saturated with thought experiments, it is the embodied or bodily form of experiment that will be addressed in this first section, as well as the hermeticism that prevented dialogue beyond disciplinary borders. My three examples are Franz Boas's demonstration of a Kwakiutl Hamatsa dance in 1895, Aby Warburg's wearing of a Hemis kachina mask among the Hopi in 1896, and Alfred Court Haddon's staging and reenactment of a myth on the Torre Strait Islands in 1898.

At the end of the nineteenth century, a variety of approaches in anthropology coexisted and the discipline had not yet standardized a methodology for empirical inquiry. Fieldwork was often of the expeditionary type, involving a combination of ethnological and physical anthropology researches, interviews, and questionnaires. Longer, participant observation in situ would only later be introduced and sytematized, in different ways, by Franz Boas and Bronislaw Malinowski (Stocking 1983, 1996). It is in this atmosphere of methodological unruliness that I wish to consider three examples of dealing with art in the wider sense of visual research and representation.

Over the last few decades there has been a resurgent interest in Boas, focusing especially on his fieldwork methods and epistemology. While for some he has become a precursor to postmodern projects (Krupat 1990), for most others he clearly shows the imprint of the natural scientist (trained in physics), and even the classificatory abstraction of pre-evolutionary eighteenth-century natural science (e.g., Verdon 2007). The performative aspect of his fieldwork and exhibition practices has only more recently been addressed in relation to his writings on art (Jacknis 1984, 1996; Jonaitis 1995; also Ruby 1980b, 2000b; Edwards 2004).

In the field of the anthropology of art, the great innovator of American anthropology is best known for his mature work *Primitive Art* (Boas 1927), as well as numerous other studies, primarily of the art of North American indigenous peoples (a representative collection of texts appeared in Jonaitis 1995). Yet here I want to turn to an early incident, which shows the anthropologist physically and bodily enmeshed in the visual interpretation of previously observed reality. In 1895 Boas posed for the museum technicians at the American Museum of Natural History, who were going to build a diorama illustrating the Hamatsa ceremony of the Kwakiutl (Hinsley and Holm 1976) (figure 4.1a, b).[2]

This case is perhaps best understood as an example of "imitative experiment," a term coined by Robert Ascher to describe experiments by archaeologists (Ascher 1961; also, on the experimental and multimedia side of Boas's methodologies, Jacknis 1996, 186, 189). More than writings or even photographs, these postures are embodied representations, showing very clearly the interpretive work of anthropology, and here providing the bodily "model" for the museum display. Boas's reenactment was intended not for consumption by a wider audience but as a "demonstration" for the museum sculptors, in the image of which the diorama was to be fabricated.[3] Yet we get a distinct sense of performance. The postures themselves, even fixed in photographs, retain the liveliness and expressiveness of the original episode. As a reenactment of a religious performance that Boas had observed in the course of his fieldwork, they are, at the same time, also an appropriation of another culture, while as a performative reenactment they recall an earlier instance, where Boas had posed in full Eskimo dress after his return from Baffinland in 1884 (Bunzl 1996, 54). A later, though undated, photograph of Boas demonstrating an Inuit harpoon, again in full dress, is reproduced by Griffiths

4.1a, b Franz Boas demonstrating the pose of the Kwakiutl Hamatsa dancer for model makers at the United States National Museum, February 1895. A life group depicting the dance was subsequently installed in the museum. Courtesy of the National Anthropological Archives, Smithsonian Institution (negative nos. 8304 and 9539).

(2002, 304). A history of anthropologists literally wearing and posing in the clothes of their research subjects still needs to be written. After all, through the second skin of the Other, so to speak, this is one of the most physical-material and sensual ways of cultural appropriation and interpretation through artifacts.[4] I am eerily reminded here of *Wearing Somebody's Jacket* (1986–1991), the poignant artwork by Nikolaus Lang based on his artistic fieldwork stay in Southern Australia.

The point here is that Boas's demonstrations for the museum sculptors are not just the "copy" of what he had seen. Implicit in them are his reading and memorial reenactment, which will result in a further translation or mimesis, that of museum display. Mimesis, in the sense Taussig (1993), following Benjamin, has used this term, is the most apt way of thinking about these images, endemic in the early scientific anthropological enterprise.[5] A further context is provided by late nineteenth-century popular culture which presented reenactments and stagings of indigenous people, using indigenous actors, a practice that Boas was aware of and participated in (Hinsley and Holm 1976; Kirshenblatt-Gimblett 1998; Griffiths 2002) and one that distinctly contributed to the shaping of an American identity (Trachtenberg 2004).

The next example is that of art historian Aby Warburg. Warburg is known primarily as a historian of Western, especially Italian Renaissance, art, and through his "Mnemosyne Atlas" of pictures as one of the predecessors of modern iconology in art history. His travel to the American Southwest in 1895 to 1896, and his essay on the Hopi snake ritual, based on a lecture he gave in 1923, when he was recovering in a psychiatric institution (published for the first time in 1939),[6] have been much written about. Yet he remains less known to anthropologists than to art historians (see Freedberg 2004, 2005, and the extensive bibliography therein). In his famous essay, Warburg interpreted the Hopi snake ritual using much the same categories as he had in analyzing the Italian Renaissance, in fact establishing a link between the two, by way of the "demonic that lies at the roots of the classical, or the irrational at the base of the rational" (Freedberg 2005, 4), and surmising universal features of pagan religions, such as cults of trees and souls (Warburg 1988, 36). The sometimes ethically risky and cavalier conduct of his trip (in profiting from a ruthless ethnographer, the Reverend Voth) has been criticized recently by Freedberg (2004, 2005), but it is for Warburg scholars, and beyond the scope of this essay, to further examine these concerns. Warburg entertained personal contacts with more professional and eminent anthropologists than Voth and met Frank Hamilton Cushing and James Mooney before his travel. Meeting Franz Boas, though, did not seem to

4.2   Aby Warburg wearing a Hemis Kachina mask, Oraibi, Arizona, May 1896. Unknown photographer. Photo: Warburg Institute Archive, London.

have affected his interpretation (Freedberg 2004, 2). For instance, he did
not apparently interrogate his basic assumptions about the evolutionary
development of religions and cultures (see Warburg 1988, 12). In the
context of my discussion, however, he is of interest in terms of the appropriation and embodiment of indigenous culture, epitomized in his
posing for a photographer with a Hemis kachina mask (figure 4.2).

Freedberg characterizes Warburg's pose as insulting, since he did not
wear the mask fully. He even suggests that Warburg might have seen the
dance with different eyes had he worn the mask fully, as required by the
dance (Freedberg 2004, 16, and n.65). But then, do we know that he had
not merely pulled it halfway up for the photo? After all, this particular
photo is evidence only for the act depicted, not for what preceded or followed it.[7] In any case, it is clear that embodiment here stopped short of

proper understanding, and it is only through later exegesis that Warburg was able to achieve an interpretation of the snake ritual, one that supported his own theories rather than being built on emic notions of the Hopi (Freedberg 2005, 9). Warburg and Boas were contemporaries, both were influenced by Adolf Bastian in Berlin (see Glenn Penny 2003), and, as mentioned above, Warburg saw Boas during his travel, yet there is no evidence of this in his essay. Although Warburg did consult personally with anthropological scholars of the Southwest (such as Cushing and Mooney), he did not engage with the contemporary situation of the Hopi, then engulfed in tense social conflict between Friendlies and Hostiles, one faction favoring "modernization" and contact with whites, the other the retention of traditional ways of life (Freedberg 2005, 13). Warburg's case, then, is not only one of insensibility toward the native Other, but also one of a missed opportunity for art history and anthropology to engage more fully in direct dialogue. Like the half-raised mask, Warburg's attempt remains one of intellectual camouflage obscuring the distinctions between himself and his surroundings, rather than acknowledging cultural difference and engaging fully with other disciplinary traditions (especially Boas's criticism of evolution in anthropology).

The final example is Alfred Court Haddon's staging of the death of the culture hero Kwoiam, on Mabuiag in the Torres Straits Islands in 1898, which has been interpreted in the context of early, pre-Malinowskian visual strategies of fieldwork (Edwards 2004; Grimshaw 2001). I have deliberately chosen an example from visual anthropology, conceived of here as a field larger than ethnographic film and video, and encompassing the visual both as practice and object of study, with implications for a renewed emphasis on practice in the anthropology of art. Haddon trained as a biologist and experimented with the staging and reenactment of events for both still and movie cameras, using theatrical techniques (also Edwards 2004). The death of Kwoiam was reenacted by a native of Mabuiag, and Haddon also drew a sketch for the event, as well as making the Malu Bomai masks, from cardboard and children's crayon, before filming the sequence (Herle and Philp 1998, 36; Edwards 1999, 18) (figure 4.3).

Edwards has characterized this reenactment in terms of both the turn-of-the-century frame of natural sciences laboratory practices, where experimental "evidence" was reenacted for scientific observation (2004, 157–59), and the subjective agency of the fieldworker and reenacting islanders, which together show the theatrical possibilities of history (2004, 161, 177).

In the context of visual anthropology, a creative development was

4.3   Man imitating the death of culture hero Kowoiam, Mabuiag, 1898. Photograph taken on the Cambridge anthropological expedition to Torres Straits. Reproduced by permission of the University of Cambridge Museum of Archaeology and Anthropology (N.23033.ACH2).

here cut short because of the later positivist emphasis of Malinowskian functionalism (although Malinowski used reenactment occasionally in a very restricted sense, not to interfere with the ethnographic present; cf. Edwards 2004, 158) and because images where henceforth relegated to support functions, as illustrations in text, rather than retaining their own interpretative and analytic value (a point argued by MacDougall 1998, 2006; and Grimshaw 2001).

Relevance for Art and Anthropology Practices

At first sight, Boas appears as the methodical scientist in the Hamatsa demonstration, which serves the clear purpose of facilitating an ethno-graphically "correct" display in the museum, truthful to his fieldwork data. This has been the standard interpretation of the event, and we could leave the matter here. However, I suggest that with his embodied involvement he took certain risks in the epistemology of representation. He could very well have drawn a sketch, or asked an assistant to strike the poses, but instead he decided to personally perform the demonstration (something other anthropologists of the time were also doing; Glass 2006). Boas here gives an example of the nature of practical and creative experiment in the anthropology of art—which in later twentieth-century traditions is rarely acknowledged. Warburg, although his attempt as an art historian to encroach into anthropological territory remains noteworthy, seems (according to Freedberg 2005) to have made inappropriate incursions into native territory, revealing himself as an imposter in his wearing of the mask rather than offering an understanding. It is then Haddon's reenactment that most clearly shows the role and potential of experiment in early anthropology. Yet another point needs emphasis here. Because it is inevitably posterior to the events it is supposed to represent, and despite the inherent dangers of fictionalizing, reenactment stands in opposition to and overcomes the diachrony-synchrony opposition that would characterize later, Malinowskian approaches to fieldwork. Put simply, this doctrine posits that as a fieldworker you can only observe (and participate) contemporaneously with your subjects of study, and must rely on other methods to investigate their past. This is perhaps the reason why experiments such as staging and reenactments were excised from the repertoire of ethnographic method by functionalists, with their heavy emphasis on the ethnographic present and strong aversion to history.

Warburg, on the other hand, reminds us of the implicit dangers of cultural appropriation, which continue to characterize anthropological and artistic projects with the Other till the present (see also Schneider 2006, 2008).

These three early examples also clearly demonstrate that disciplinary traditions occupied with the study and construction of the visual do not talk to each other, that discourses remain unmitigated and self-enclosed, prohibiting fuller understanding—to say nothing of the paradigmatic framing of this research in colonial situations (for Haddon, despite some indigenous influence on the research situation; see Edwards 2004) or as a primitive survival (for Warburg) or salvage anthropology (for Boas). This is certainly the case for Warburg, who could have engaged more fully with the anthropology of his day, especially with those, like Boas, who were starting to criticize evolutionary approaches. But Boas and Haddon, too, in their visual representations—despite implicit creativity when compared to later early twentieth-century paradigms—did not make use of then current artistic techniques or discourses. To my knowledge neither the Torres Strait expedition nor Boas's expeditions included any contemporary visual artists (although Boas was later involved with Edward Curtis's reconstructions in films such as *In the Land of the Head Hunters*

[1914; rereleased as *In the Land of the War Canoes*], and in the mid-1930s asked the painter Stuyvesant Van Veen to make drawings from his own film footage, shot in 1930; see Ruby 1980b, 7). In any case, it is doubtful that the inclusion even of accomplished artists would in itself have substantially changed the noncommunication between disciplines. For when artists did accompany expeditions (a frequent occurrence since the age of exploration, exemplified in the early twentieth-century by the participation of expressionist painters Emil Nolde and Max Pechstein in German expeditions), the different modes of inquiry and representation associated with the science, anthropology, and art remained substantially separate, producing different sets of works which did not speak to each other (Brugger 2001; Moeller and Dahlmanns 2002).

Collaborations: *Documents* (1929–1930) and *Mexican Folkways* (1925–1937)

Whereas the first three examples involved single representatives of disciplinary traditions, I turn now to the question of what is at stake in collaborations between disciplines. While this could be done as a thought experiment, establishing the criteria for potential collaborations in terms of their heuristic and epistemological costs and benefits, I want instead to examine two of the few historically documented examples, the journals *Documents* and *Mexican Folkways*, published in the 1920s and 30s, respectively in Paris and in Mexico City. *Documents* is by now a well-researched case of different disciplines coming together in unexpected and experimental ways, in the milieu of surrealist writers, artists, and anthropologists in late 1920s Paris.

Appropriation from non-Western cultures was, of course, not a new phenomenon for artists in the 1920s; there had been important precedents of "primitivism" with Gauguin, the Fauves, and cubism (see Goldwater 1986). It is now widely accepted that Picasso's stylistic innovation of cubism with his painting *Les Demoiselles d'Avignon* (1907) was inspired by so-called primitive art, both non-European (African and Oceanian) and European (ancient Iberian) (Goldwater 1986; Rubin 1984; Clifford 1988; Rhodes 1994). The anthropologist of art, art historian, and poet Carl Einstein had made explicit in print the connection that Picasso had expressed pictorially with his short treatise *Negerplastik* (1915), which included reproductions of a large number of African sculptures (and deliberately avoided captions) and appreciated African art through the principles of cubism. The significant turning point for the journal *Documents* (published 1929–1930 under the editorship of Georges Bataille, with the cooperation of Einstein, who had left Berlin for Paris in 1928) was that now a number artists, writers, and anthropologists were connected to a truly transdisciplinary, boundary-crossing project, whereas on other occasions such efforts had been limited to individual artists (or groups of artists) and were not explicitly connected to professional anthropology. The outcome was one of the most fascinating of art-anthropology collaborations, wherein different artistic genres and anthropological approaches were mixed and juxtaposed in both formal and theoretical terms. Intellectual montage and collage became the norm: artists were appreciated through an ethnographic lens, and the subjects of anthropology and archaeology were reworked artistically, often with surrealist devices.[8] Significantly, as Clifford put it (characterizing the relationship between Alfred Métraux and Georges Bataille), "French ethnography [was] on *speaking terms* with the avant-garde" (1988, 126; my italics).

The *Documents* project, then, has to be seen in the context of a period of unparalleled fertility in experimentation and creativity across disciplinary *and* institutional boundaries, involving, for example, the Institut d'Ethnologie, founded by Marcel Mauss in 1925, the Musée du Trocadero, succeeded in 1938 by the Musée de l'homme, and Bataille's short-lived Collège de Sociologie, 1937–1939 (Clifford 1988). Although late nineteenth-century art, as well as early twentieth-century modernism, were punctuated with those who appropriated from the non-Western cultures, there were few concerted efforts of transdisiciplinary cooperation prior to the *Documents* enterprise.

In pre-1933 Germany and Austria expressionist artists visited ethnographic museums and, as I noted earlier, went on ethnographic expeditions, and in early and mid-twentieth-century Britain, for instance, Jacob Epstein and Henry Moore knew William Fagg, Keeper of Ethnology at the British Museum. But in contrast to France, such contacts and mutual interests did not lead to more sustained collaborations between artists and anthropologists, going beyond the confines of each discipline.[9] This despite the fact that Fagg took the unusual step of inviting Moore to comment, in an interview in the journal *Man*, on the exhibition *Traditional Art from the Colonies*, held at the Imperial Institute in London (Moore 1951). Fagg later also published a catalog on Epstein's collection of African art (Fagg 1960), but there is little in his own writing on the art of contemporaries. The reason is perhaps a misunderstanding of contemporary artists' intentions in relation to non-European art, which is somewhat evident in the interview with Moore. On other occasions he found modern art lacking in comparison with "primitive" art. For example, in a review of the exhibition *40,000 Years of Modern Art* at the Institute of Contemporary Arts, in London (Archer and Melville 1949), he advised:

Readers of MAN will not look here for a critique of the modern paintings in the exhibition, but an anthropologist's impression may perhaps be recorded (though it is hardly a new one) to the effect that the experimental art of the modern schools suffers severely in comparison with Negro or Melanesian art by reason of the apparent lack of any informing conviction comparable to the religious sanctions behind the primitive sculptures. This is clearly seen, for example, in a characteristic painting by the doyen of surrealists, Giorgio de Chirico, in the foreground of which appears an unmistakable derivative of a ritual mask of the Dogon tribe in the Niger bend;[10] these masks (for the study of which there are unequalled facilities in Griaule's great work, *Masques Dogon*, Institut d'Ethnologie, Paris, 1938) are among the most awe-inspiring of African carvings, but little or nothing of that awe is communicated by the painting (reproduced in the catalogue, but not exhibited), though it may well move one in other ways. If the modern work imparts a sense of experiment, of trial and error, the primitive sculptures are remarkable for their extraordinary stability, for the sense of evolutionary development through the thousands of years which one must postulate to explain their extreme diversification. (Fagg 1949, 9) (figure 4.4)

Fagg obviously prefers non-European, primitive art over modern art, and his understanding of modern art is traditional in that it presupposes a kind of spiritual center. Moreover, Fagg sees De Chirico as the doyen of the surrealists (which he perhaps was in terms of seniority), yet although he had preceded surrealism in some ways, he was clearly not at its *experimental* center; if anything, he represented the mystical and metaphysical side of surrealism. How else would one not capture the implicit, but completely unintended irony of Fagg mentioning in the same sentence the great ethnographer of the Dogon, Marcel Griaule, who contributed to *Documents* and whose famous Dakar-Djibouti expedition was in fact accompanied by surrealist writer and anthropologist Michel Leiris, who not only was a principal collaborator of the journal but is also listed in the acknowledgments of the same London exhibition Fagg mentions in his review (Fagg 1949, 5). Although in another part of the review Fagg recognizes Paris's world leadership in modern art (compared with Britain, where "quasi-photographic naturalism is still the official religion"; 1949, 9), the specific combination of anthropological and artistic overlap in the cultural climate of the French capital seems to have eluded him—another indication of disciplinary boundaries and lopsided preferences, despite his observation

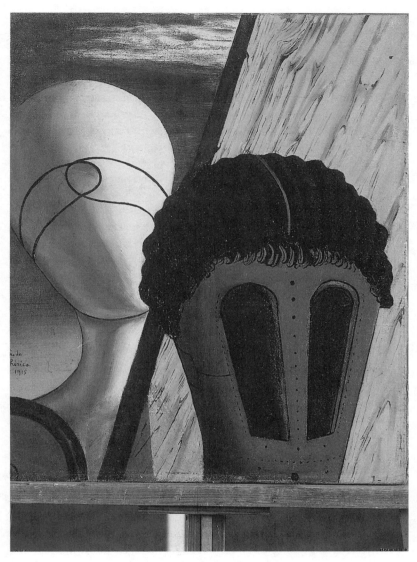

4.4   Giorgio De Chirico, *The Jewish Angel I*, 1915, oil. From Archer and Melville (1949, 33).

that in Britain "there are few artists yet who pay much attention to primitive art" (1949, 9). Among the "few" Fagg acknowledges would have been, of course, Epstein and Moore, both of whom he knew personally.

Similarly, anthropologist Leonhard Adam, in his *Primitive Art* for the Penguin paperback series, wrote two short chapters on the relation between European and primitive art.[11] There he discussed Gaugin, Pechstein, Picasso, and Epstein, among others. However, like Fagg, Adam did not do full justice to the contemporary arts, when he apodictically prescribed their task as follows:

Modern art can learn from primitive plastic art, particularly from African culture, a refreshing naïvité, a wholesome concentration on essentials, and a spontaneous approach to both man and beast, without arbitrarily adopting its obvious imperfections. The aim should be not to introduce another kind of 'ism', but to get rid of certain modern 'isms' by recovering the spontaneity which European artists have largely lost. The artist of to-day, however, even when he captures that original naïvité, will never produce really primitive works. . . . Imitating the mere primitiveness of primitive art is like rejecting all modern comforts and acquisitions, and going back to caves and skins. It is not only against the rules of logic, but utterly untrue to our own nature. (Adam 1949, 230)

One reason, then, for the lack of communication between artists and anthropologists, and by the same token between art discourses and anthropological reasoning, might have been that in Britain (as in the German-speaking countries before 1933) truly transdisciplinary go-betweens were lacking.[12] This was in clear contrast with figures such as Michel Leiris and Carl Einstein, who would move between the disciplines of art and anthropology and who were themselves accomplished writer-poets. Einstein fulfilled the role of the go-between more in Paris than in Berlin (see Joyce 2002; Zeidler 2004; Ades and Baker 2006). Although he had contacts to the Berlin anthropological museum and its curators, Alfred Schatzabel (Einstein 1921, 32) and August Eichhorn (Fleckner 2006, 305), and wrote a critically constructive review of its newly reopened collections in 1926 (Fleckner 2006, 293–307), reciprocal interest by museum anthropologists was rather muted and his suggestions for reform not fully appreciated (Fleckner 2006, 302–3). Furthermore, in terms of "contemporary" visual art, Einstein was more interested in French cubists and the Russian avant-garde (including Russian visitors and exiles in Berlin) than, for example, in the earlier movement of German expressionists (this is despite his own literary production, which was influenced by expressionism). There is also an unveiled attack against primitivism in

Afrikanische Plastik [African Sculpture], which opens with the words "Exoticism is often unproductive romanticism . . ." (Einstein 1921, 5). This charge was directed especially against expressionist painters such as Max Pechstein and Emil Nolde, the latter's exoticism characterized as "cheap romanticism" by Einstein in his important *Kunst des 20. Jahrhunderts*, the first monograph dedicated to the "Art of the 20th Century" (Einstein 1926/1931, 29–30). However, given Einstein's cubist leanings, Picasso's own primitivism is not further interrogated, and he just repeats Picasso's famous reply to the insinuation that he had been influenced by African sculpture: "*J'en connais pas*" (1926/1931, 90).

Mexican Folkways, produced on a different continent and driven by different artistic, ideological, and not least commercial agendas, has received much less scholarly attention, and as yet none beyond specialist Latin Americanist circles. Like *Documents*, *Mexican Folkways* straddled the decades of the 1920s and 1930s and brought together practitioners from art, art history, and anthropology (including archaeology). It was not, however, indebted to one artistic movement, as *Documents* was to dissident surrealism, but to a broad ideology of *indigenismo*, the idealization of past and present indigenous and peasant cultures in postrevolutionary Mexico, rekindled as folkloric exoticism by North Americans. I contend that it can nonetheless be usefully compared to *Documents*, if only for the purpose of pointing out important differences in scope and relevance.

Mexican Folkways was published from 1925 to 1937 (Boggs 1945), in Mexico City, by the American Frances Toor, who had trained in anthropology at the University of California (Delpar 1992, 36). The journal assembled an array of famous artists, writers, exhibition curators, and anthropologists, working in and on Mexico, among them the muralist Diego Rivera, the photographer Tina Modotti, anthropologists Robert Redfield and his wife, Margaret Park Redfield, Anita Brenner (who got her PhD under the supervision of Franz Boas), Manuel Gamio (who also studied with Boas, and occupied important posts in Mexican archaeology and anthropology),the exhibition curator and art writer René d'Harnoncourt (who organized a famous touring exhibition of Mexican art to the United States in 1930, and later served as director of the Museum of Modern Art, New York, 1949–1968), the anthropologist Elsie Clews Parsons, and the writer Carleton Beals, as well as his anthropologist brother, Ralph Beals.

In the wake of the Mexican Revolution (1917), the country's capital city had become something of a hub for young, often wealthy American intellectuals who projected onto Mexico their own fantasies of a supposedly uncontaminated, archaic folk peasantry. Depending on political inclination, this might be coupled with enthusiasm for the revolutionary changes, devised as *indigenismo* by the new Mexican elites in the cultural and social fields, including muralism, land reform, and the promotion of folk art. Such romantic projections not only affected the intellectual enterprise but were linked, in many cases, to substantial commercial interests in folkloric arts and crafts, catering to large-scale American tourism and demand in the United States for Mexican culture, and folk art in particular (Delpar 1992; Oles 1993). Figures like Frances Toor, through the journal *Mexican Folkways*, and also Anita Brenner, with her book *Idols behind Altars* (1929, 1967), for which Edward Weston and Tina Modotti took the photographs (see Noble 2001), promoted this trend and were vital to shaping an idealized and folkloric image of Mexico, both in the United States and among Mexican intellectuals, linked to the ideology of *indigenismo* and to state policies of homogenizing the nation and its diverse ethnic heritage (Brading 1988; Knight 1990). In more prosaic ways, *Mexican Folkways* also served as an advertising outlet for commercial enterprises: American-owned curio shops, art dealers in Mexico city catering to a clientele of American and European tourists, as well as its own mail order services, which offered, for example, Modotti's photographs of frescoes by Diego Rivera for 50 cents each.[13]

Yet there were also artistic contributions that can be read as subversive to the hegemonic discourse of the overall ideological framework of idealized folk arts, peasants, and Mexican indigenism. This was arguably the case when Modotti's photographs *Aztec Mother* and *Aztec Baby* were juxtaposed with anthropologist Margaret Park Redfield's article "A Child Is Born in Tepotztlan" (Park Redfield 1928). As Andrea Noble has pointed out, these particular photographs differ from totalizing anthropological photographs, in that they focus, close up, on the bodily, tactile, sensual relationship between mother and child.[14] They do not just illustrate Redfield's article but, with their decentered gaze, assume their own agency and can be understood as voicing a feminist critique (Noble 2001, 125–39) (figure 4.5).

Relevance for Art and Anthropology Practices

Notwithstanding some initial work by scholars, *Mexican Folkways* still awaits its full appraisal. The journal is useful to consider, both in its historical context and for the present, as it fostered transdisciplinary discourse and practice (even if this was not explicitly acknowledged and overall couched in the ideology of *indigenismo*) and opened up unforeseen critiques—internally, by Modotti and Redfield, and externally, by the eminent muralist José Clemente Orozco.

4.5 Tina Modotti, *An Aztec Baby*, ca. 1926–1927, gelatin-silver print, 8 by 7 inches. Courtesy of Throckmorton Fine Art, New York.

Certainly, *Mexican Folkways* was less radical, in both formal and theo-retical terms, than *Documents*, and more limited in its range of experi-mentation across genres and disciplines. This was due, not least, to the different class background of its contributors and its being tied to the postrevolutionary Mexican cultural elite. Rather than being subversive, as *Documents* was in the European context, *Mexican Folkways* was linked to a state-induced project, albeit one with revolutionary rhetoric. *Mexican Folkways* did not, in a more critical and counterhegemonic sense, fully ex-ploit the potential arising from collaboration, or rather the juxtaposition of artistic and anthropological work, and it remained, with few exceptions (such as a critical rejoinder by Orozco, who questioned the folklorization of the Mexican peasant; Orozco 1929; also Braun 1993, 190), tied to the elite and commercial interests of its editors and contributors. Despite these shortcomings some more subversive positions were expressed, and the journal showed some potentially interesting art-anthropology assemblages (mainly by way of juxtapositions of articles and illustrations by different contributors). The example of *Mexican Folkways* clearly puts into relief the dangers and possibilities of any cultural project conceived in proximity to ideologically framed political and institutional power, as well as the appropriation and idealization of a cultural other (here: the indigenous peoples in Mexico). While there are few occasions in the present, at least for art-anthropology collaborations, where the framework would be similar, one might also think, by comparison, of the contemporary state and its agencies—research councils, institutions of higher education—as well as the agendas of private foundations that ultimately set limits and conditions for freedom of research and creativity.

Epistemological Transgressions: Maya Deren

Not all artists feel that they belong to larger ideological movements (even if art historians later assign them to such) or to explicit collaborative projects, but rather pursue individual agendas. On this individual level, Maya Deren is perhaps one of the best examples for the challenges posed by artistic-anthropological border crossings.[15] Deren had been an experimental filmmaker especially occupied with bodily movement, dance, and rhythm. After a series of short films that highlight also feminine issues, Japanese dance, and ritual, such as *Meshes of the Afternoon* (1943), she intended to compile in one film, as a comparative essay, studies of dance from various parts of world, as well as children's games in New York.[16]

Deren contacted Gregory Bateson to obtain material from the enormous footage from his Balinese research with Margaret Mead (from which the two had edited films, such as *Trance and Dance in Bali*, for the Character Formation in Different Cultures Series, 1952; see De Brigard 1995). The footage she received stimulated her to undertake a comparative dance study. However, Bateson warned her against making just a filmic comparison of widely disparate cultures, urging her instead to concentrate on only two cultures from a "single culture area," such as the Caribbean (Bateson to Deren, December 12, 1946; in Deren and Bateson 1980, 18–19).

Deren did not relent on her plan completely. She applied for, and obtained, a Guggenheim grant for a filmic study of Haitian Voudon in 1949, which she later wanted to compare with Bateson's material. (She had also consulted with mythology scholar Joseph Campbell, who would later write a preface to her book *Divine Horsemen*.)

Once in Haiti, however, Deren changed her mind. She continued to film, and the substantial footage was posthumously edited into a film by Cheryl Ito (1985). Her principle aim was now ethnographic documentary investigation, as she understood it. In *The Divine Horsemen* (1953) she explained the change of media thus:

I had begun as an artist, as one who would manipulate the elements of reality into a work of art in the image of my creative integrity; I end by recording, as humbly and accurately as I can, the logics of a reality which had forced me to recognize its integrity, and to abandon my manipulations. . . . I feel that the fact that I was defeated in my original intention assures, to a considerable degree, that what I have here recorded reflects not my own integrity. But that of the reality that mastered it. It is this which encouraged me to undertake this book, for I was well aware of the fact that it is un-orthodox for a non-professional to speak of matters that are normally the province of trained anthropologists. (Deren 1953/1983, 6).

Bateson and Mead supported her project initially (and cofunded it through their Institute of Intercultural Studies; Neimann 1980, 9). After reading the finished book, however, Mead, a more mainstream voice in anthropology, was critical. She wrote to Deren that the book was "beautifully written, but methodologically, it's utterly unadmissable" (Mead to Deren, November 22, 1953; quoted in Jackson 2002, 153).

Deren was aware of the ethical implications inherent in fieldwork, whether anthropological *or* artistic, and voiced self-critically her reservations in her unpublished diary:

If I insisted . . . that ethnography was a parasitic exploitation of culture, then was my esthetics less so? And if, as I added to myself later, such exploitation was particularly detestable when it was brought to a culture which was full of human misery (unlike Bali) and pursued in the face of that misery, then I ought to give myself a good, swift kick and get out." (Maya Deren, Haiti Journal, October 11, 1947, quoted in Jackson 2002, 146).

The artist-ethnographer nevertheless stayed on and produced an intimate portrait of Voudon culture that transgresses the art-anthropology border, while affirmatively trying to be "objective." Yet it was precisely Deren's training as an artist that, to some degree, unreflectively and also naïvely, allowed her to capture the ethnographic material with "disinterested receptivity" and to "permit the myth to emerge gradually in its own terms and its own form" (Deren 1953/1983, 7). Deren could not betray or hide her own professional socialization and practice as an artist, and despite her seemingly objectivist aims, her book turned out to be a highly subjective and expressive record of her fieldwork experience.

Relevance for Art and Anthropology Practices

Deren's Haitian work (book, diary, and film) throws up at once a host of issues for contemporary art-anthropology relations. First, there is the supposedly perceived, but in effect constructed, border between "objective" anthropology and "subjective" art practices. In the present, too, Deren's stance toward anthropology is not unfamiliar, as many artists perceive anthropology as "science" rather than as a discursive or hermeneutic social science (see Schneider and Wright 2006, 9).

Second, her project shows the complexity and challenge for any comparison of cultures or cross-cultural visual record. Deren's initial approach is somewhat similar to that of contemporary artists who work with different cultural situations, moving quickly in and out of cultural contexts, although she wanted to base her comparison on formal principles of dance, ritual, and film. Third, Deren's project highlights the ethical implications of fieldwork, and the potentially exploitative nature inherent to such work as a technology of cultural appropriation of the Other. Fourth, her project shows the epistemological limits of participant "observation," in her case "going native" to the point of becoming possessed, as she did in the Voudon rituals.[17] The dilemma of representing, or not, possession as personal experience, in film or text, has been well expressed by Catherine Russell, when she writes on Deren:

Writing, no less than filming, is only a means of representing possession, which is itself a form of representation. She [Deren] found film to be an inadequate means of penetrating the layers of signification set up by ritual performance, and so she wrote the book as an interpretation of the performances she witnessed. The characters of the *loas* (gods who mount the possessed dancers) are not perceptible on film because those who are seen are not those who are present. The *loas* remain invisible to the film spectator, and since the purpose of the rituals is to prove the existence of the *loas*, the film fails as a document of reality." (Russell 1999, 211–12)

Maya Deren, then, highlights the epistemological implications of crossing borders between disciplines (art/anthropology), media (writing/film), and research roles (detached observer/involved participant).

Any border crossings from art into anthropology, or vice versa, will have to assess the epistemological risks such excursions into uncharted territory imply—in cruder terms, the costs and benefits. The aim should not be to reify borders between art and anthropology practices, but rather to think of larger, overarching practices of knowledge appropriation such as "fieldwork," which characterize direct engagement with others, as well as conceiving a field of the "visual" for both research practices and objects of study that comprises more than the parts related to it, in this case, art and anthropology (e.g., Banks and Morphy 1997; Thomas 1997; Schneider and Wright 2006, 2010).

Artificial Boundaries: Western versus Non-Western Arts

The previous sections have charted the success and failure of experiment in individual and collaborative border crossing projects between art and anthropology in the first part of the twentieth century. Other historically contingent examples, both individual and collaborative, could be added for the next fifty years. Individual cases include the work of Edmund Carpenter and Pierre Verger. Among the collaborative endeavors are the journal *Alcheringa* (published by representatives of the ethnopoetry movement, such as Jerome Rothenberg and Dennis Tedlock, in the 1970s), the collaboration between photographer Leonore Mau and writer Hubert Fichte (e.g., Mau 1976),[18] and later projects by Rainer Wittenborn and Claus Biegert (1981) and George Marcus, Abdel Hernandez, and Fernando Calzadilla (Marcus 1998; Calzadilla and Marcus 2006). A more fundamental issue, already highlighted in the discussion on *Documents* and *Mexican Folkways*, and one which decisively impacts on the possibilities of collaborations, has to do with the artificial distinction, in terms of research disciplines, between the arts of Western and non-Western societies.

For a long time the anthropology of art upheld an artificial distinction between the art of non-Western ("primitive," "exotic") peoples, and the art of the West, the former the subject of anthropology and the latter the domain of art history. Most classic general texts in the anthropology of art (starting with Boas 1927) do not address Western art, past or present. There have, however, been exceptions. Einstein (1915, 1921), for example, looks at non-Western art through the lens of Western contemporary art, Lips (1937/1966) considers the appropriation of the West by non-Western artists, and Kubler (1991) examines Pre-Columbian art in terms of art historical categories, rather than solely archaeological or anthropological ones—all thus establishing precedents for disciplinary border crossings, and eventually a more unified approach to art and art worlds of the West and non-West.[19]

As noted in a previous section, the art historian Carl Einstein in 1915 delivered the first work in which African sculpture was appreciated in contemporary artistic terms, not only as the primitive work of less-developed peoples. In both *Negerplastik* (1915) and *Afrikanische Plastik* (1921) Einstein clearly recognized the value of sub-Saharan African art as artistic achievements *sui generis*, with relevance for the "modern" art of his contemporaries, especially Picasso and Braque. In fact, cubist principles were perceived by Einstein to be inherent in African art. In *Negerplastik* he writes, for instance, under the heading "Cubic Vision of Space":

We saw how the African condenses sculptural forces into visible resultants. Even the masks resonate with the power of a cubic vision that makes the planes thrust against one another, which gathers up the entire significance of the foremost parts of the face into few sculptural forms, and which deploys the three-dimensional directional vectors, minor as they may be, in their resultants. (Einstein 1915/2004, 138)

Julius Lips, too (1937/1966), demanded the study of Western art in relation to the arts of non-Western societies. His suggestion was not taken up by anthropologists, though it was adopted by the art historian Robert Goldwater (1986).[20] Lips's own book was a study in reverse appropriation, examining how non-European peoples perceived Europeans and appropriated from them in their art and artifacts.[21]

Lips's work was exceptional, clearly ahead of its time, but did not find immediate followers. Western artists, of course, had always appropriated from non-European cultures, and the modernist period's primitivism was paramount in this respect, as exemplified in the journal *Documents*. A later example is the exhibition *Lost Magic Kingdoms*, in which artist Eduardo Paolozzi juxtaposed his own appropriations of non-European art with art and artifacts from the Museum of Mankind in London, including pieces that in turn appropriated from Europeans, such as Ghanaian tin lamps (Paolozzi 1985). However, only relatively recently has the anthropology of art occupied itself with the mimetic process in the encounter of Western and non-Western art and cultures (Jahn 1983; Kramer 1993; Taussig 1993; Thomas 1991).

Also, only in recent decades has the anthropology of art addressed the long-standing fragmentation of art among various disciplines, and started to reestablish art as a potentially unitary subject, across civilizations and cultures. More specifically, it has addressed relations between Western and non-Western art, the contemporary art of postindustrial societies and that of the so-called third world or less complex societies, including critical interrogation of the art/artifact divide in institutional display settings. Starting with Graburn on tourist art (1976), the literature has become prolific.[22] Scholars have questioned the validity of the Western/non-Western distinction and called for a "symmetrical anthropology" of art worlds (Wolbert 1998). I concur with Thomas when he states, "The distinction between 'Western' and 'non-Western' needs to be rejected as an instrument of disciplinary framing because it has ceased to correspond with any real divisions of cultural domains or practices" (Thomas 1997, 264).

Relevance for Art and Anthropology Practice

The anthropology of art cannot, as it did for most of the twentieth century, sustain an artificial distinction between Western and non-Western art and deal only with the latter as its objects of study. It must also critically engage with theory and practice from contemporary artists, art criticism, and art history (Westermann 2005; Schneider and Wright 2006, 2010). This engagement should include the "iconic turn" (Mitchell 1986), as well as the *Bildwissenschaft* ("image science") and *Bildanthropologie* ("icon-anthropologie") approaches promoted by scholars such as Hans Belting (2005), and Horst Bredekamp (2003), which could provide fruitful avenues for anthropologists, if complemented with the stress on social agency of material objects.[23] It is curious and intriguing that new theorizing in the fields of art criticism and curatorial practices has stressed that much of contemporary art is about *artificially* establishing "social relation," both within and without the art world (Bourriaud 1999/2002), creating an interesting point of connection to Gell's work.[24] This emphasis on the construction of social relations by artists, and through the art world more generally, would offer another possibility of critical dialogue with anthropological approaches of social agency. In relation to global "World Art" a more unified view is now also being slowly addressed (see Morphy and Perkins 2006). Anthropologists are realizing that West/non-West ascriptions are becoming obsolete (while regional and local specificities are not) since artists during their lifetimes pass through art educational establishments located in different parts of the world, have often nomadic lifestyles, and work both from "home" and abroad. However, as yet there are few who also engage with contemporary art production and its practitioners and theoreticians (exceptions include Thomas 1999; Schneider 2006, 2008; Schneider and Wright 2006, 2010).

Outlook

We have seen that the development of experiment in the anthropology of art, as well as crossings from art historical into anthropological terrain, after early attempts by Boas, Warburg, and Haddon, could have been more productive had there been more cross-disciplinary dialogue.

To the extent that there were, as with *Documents* (and to a more limited degree *Mexican Folkways*), such dialogues, with anthropologists on "speaking terms" with the contemporary arts and artists (such as Maya Deren) with anthropology, these border crossings also cut across the artificial divide between "primitive," "non-Western" art and "Western" art, and potentially established a common subject of art or visual culture.

Those "speaking terms" (Clifford 1988, 126), although historically contingent, need now to be recovered and filled with contemporary content, if dialogues ("speaking") and theoretical engagements ("terms") between the disciplines are to be effective in the present and future.

At the end of this essay we can ask, then, hypothetically, what conditions must be met, in order for "speaking terms" and, eventually, collaborations to develop. As I have suggested, apart from historically favorable conditions (in a broad sense), this will require go-betweens, transdisciplinary subjects who can fulfill a mediating and brokering role, one that historically has been occupied, in admittedly disparate fashion, by people such as Carl Einstein, Michel Leiris, Francis Toor, and Anita Brenner.

Go-betweens in anthropology, art, or art history are in some ways comparable to "culture" brokers in the societies anthropologists have habitually studied.[25] Yet there is no need, in invoking this analogy, to revive surpassed concepts of bounded cultures. From the present vantage point, it is evident that there can be no normative demands, no catalog of qualities to be fulfilled. Rather, everything depends on concrete and historically contingent situations that will allow the successes and failures of mediating personalities to operate. The question of what makes such border crossings possible and what prevents them, which in this essay has been posed with hindsight to the historical events, is also one that could be asked for the present predicament of the disciplinary practices involved, whether they remain silent to each other or develop a dialogue.

Notes

I am grateful to Sarah Lund for helpful comments on an earlier draft. I am also grateful to Victoria Walters and the participants in our panel at the SIEFF congress in Derry in 2008, to Jay Ruby, and to the audience at our panel at the AAA meeting in Philadelphia, December 2009, for stimulating discussions when first presenting this material.

1. My aim here is to go beyond a mere historical account of the anthropology of art. For this the reader is advised to turn to useful encyclopedia and review articles (e.g., Morphy 1994; Silver 1979), in addition to recent overviews and introductory treatments (e.g., Layton 1991; Morphy and Perkins 2006; Svašek 2007) and the comprehensive bibliographies contained therein.

2. On the history of panoramas and dioramas as precursors to 3D technology, see Griffiths (2004).

3. Broader publication would only happen after the photographs were rediscovered in the mid-1970s in the archives of the Smithsonian Institution (Hinsley and Holm 1976). Since then the images have been widely circulated and written about (e.g., Jacknis 2002, 74, 97; Glass 2006).

4. See Banerjee and Miller (2004) for an example (of Banerjee wearing the sari). On the more general sensory experience of wearing clothing, see the section "Beyond the Visual" in Dudley's chapter in this volume.

5. See also Edwards (2004, 157–65), who speaks of double mimesis in the context of Haddon's reenactments (which are discussed further on).

6. See Warburg 1938–1939, 1988.

7. This is not the place to dwell on the "before" and "after" of the photographic moment, intrinsic to the constructed and temporal nature of photography. See also Waterson's essay in this volume for a discussion of temporal-spatial construction in virtual, computer-generated architectural models.

8. See Clifford 1988; Ades and Baker 2006. This latter catalog gives a good indication of the range of media and approaches employed.

9. More research needs to be done on possible links between artists and contemporary anthropology (both in university departments and at museums) in 1920s and 1930s Britain. As a piece of purely anecdotal evidence, I remember a conversation at an informal lunch in the early 1990s, attended by the late Sir Raymond Firth, on the premises of the Royal Anthropological Institute (London). Asked about cultural life in 1920s and 1930s London, Sir Raymond mentioned visits by Josephine Baker and other celebrities but gave no indication that contemporary artistic production in dance, art, or film was in any way connected to the anthropological avant-garde, clearly represented by his teacher Malinowski. To paraphrase Clifford, in Britain certainly the arts and anthropology were not on "speaking

terms" but represented two very different endeavors of creative knowledge pursuit.

10. The painting Fagg refers to is *The Jewish Angel I*, a 1915 oil by Georgio de Chirico (erroneously identified in the catalog as André Chirico); see Archer and Melville (1949, 33). The painting is also known as *The Two Sisters (The Jewish Angel)*.

11. Adam had emigrated in 1938 from Berlin to England. He was interned during the war and later stayed on in Australia.

12. More comparative research needs to be done also for other areas of the world concerning the relationships between artists and anthropologists. One thinks, for instance, of the friendship of the young Malinowski in Poland with the artist Ignacy Witkiewicz (e.g., Skalník 1995), and of Kandinsky's interest in ethnography (e.g., Weiss 1995).

13. One shop, called Tlaquepaque (after the city in the state of Jalisco), advertised for "Mexican Curios. Just the things you want to take back home. We specialize in furnishing Mexican rooms. We invite you cordially to visit our rooms" (*Mexican Folkways* 6, no. 1 [1930]: 1).

14. Modotti contributed forty-five photographs altogether to *Mexican Folkways*, and from 1927 was a member of the editorial board.

15. See also Kathrin Ramey's discussion of Deren in this volume. Other examples are the folklorist, filmmaker, and theater producer Zora Neale Hurston, who trained with Boas, and the anthropologist, dancer, and choreographer Katherine Dunham, who studied with Melville Herskovits (Rony 1996, 203–11).

16. Initially, Deren wanted also to include the Navajo, but she dropped the idea on the advice of Margaret Mead, who told her there was no contemporary anthropological film material; Mead was apparently not aware of film footage from 1938 by John Adair (Neimann 1980, 4, 8).

17. In anthropology, of course, there is a long tradition considering the benefits and costs of participating (and believing) in supernatural beliefs and practices. Famous examples are E. Evans-Pritchard's *Witchcraft, Oracles, and Magic among the Azande* (1937), Hans-Peter Duerr's *Dreamtime*, or even more controversially, the writings of Carlos Castañeda.

18. The literature on Fichte is extensive, and this is not the place to review it. He crossed fields of literature, ethnopoetry, and anthropology and collaborated with the photographer Leonore Mau. Little of his own work is as yet available in English, and there are very few critical studies in English that specifically interrogate his relation to ethnography and anthropology (but see, e.g., Neumann 1991). Fichte's collaboration with Leonore Mau has been researched by Braun (1997) and was the subject of a recent exhibition at the photography center of the Deichtorhallen in Hamburg (Schoeller 2005).

19. An area which is now starting to be addressed by some art historians (e.g., Zijlmans and Van Damme 2008), opening up a new field of world art studies.

20. The two men knew each other in New York; Goldwater reports a verbal communication from Lips (1986, 14). Lips (1937/1966, 38) makes reference to a discussion with art historians at a museum exhibition in New York at the beginning of 1935, likely the Museum of Modern Art exhibition *African Negro Art* (March 18–May 19, 1935), which may be where he and Goldwater met.

21. How original Lips's approach really was, further research will have to establish. Pützstück (1995, 240) argues that Lips might have been inspired by an early article by Berlin anthropologist Hermann Baumann "Der Schwarze karikiert den Weißen" [The black caricatures the white], *Die Woche 29*, no. 25 (1927): 722–24. There is no reference to this short popular science article in Lips's work (see also Centlivres 1997, n1).

22. E.g., Price 1989; Vogel 1989; Karp and Levine 1991; Michaels 1994; Steiner 1994; Marcus and Myers 1995; Phillips and Steiner 1999. See also Morphy and Perkins 2006; Price 2007.

23. Gell 1998; Henare 2005a; Pinney and Thomas 2001. For applications in art history, see Osborne and Tanner 2007; for positions critical to Gell see, e.g., Layton 2003; Morphy 2009.

24. The worlds of art theory/art criticism and anthropology still remain largely separate. For a few recent examples of anthropologists who have started to connect Gell's and Bourriaud' theorizing see, e.g., Born (2005) and Sansi (2005).

25. This concept has a long genealogy and is used for people who "mediate" between different levels of social and cultural distinction and identity groups, or "cultures." See Press 1969.

FIVE

Theorizing "the Body" in Visual Culture

BRENDA FARNELL

This article provides a historical overview of attempts within anthropological inquiry to theorize "the body" as a component of visual culture. It charts a paradigm shift from an observationist view of behavior to a conception of the body as a somatic and sensory resource for dynamically embodied action in cultural space/time. I argue that to understand the human body as a biocultural resource for the dynamic construction of self, personhood, and identity, and as a means for creative expression as well as more mundane skilled embodied practices, requires theorizing across the usual disciplinary boundaries between biological and social being.

Introduction

The explosion of academic literature on "the body" in the humanities and social sciences that began in the late 1970s was such that by 1986 sociologist J. M. Berthelot remarked, "The body would appear to be everywhere" (1986, 155). The scope of this literature has been broad, multidisciplinary as well as interdisciplinary, and largely postmodern or poststructuralist in its theoretical orientation. Stimulated especially by the work of Michel Foucault, Pierre Bourdieu, a range of feminist theorists,[1] and a postmodern, phenomenological valorization of the sensuous, we find a number of social theorists working on "the problem of embodiment."

In the social sciences, this move to "bring the body back in" (Frank 1990) was an acknowledgment of how fundamentally *disembodied* earlier social theory had been.[2] Scholars suggest the historical and cultural reasons for this relative neglect stem from a long-standing bias against the body in the philosophical and religious traditions we call Western (i.e., European and European-derived).[3] This precluded social theorists from attending to physical being and bodily practices in their definitions of social action. In brief, the Platonic legacy, together with Descartes's radical separation of mind and body during the rise of science in the seventeenth century, provided a set of unexamined assumptions about "personhood" that permeated all the social sciences. With its now familiar dualisms of mind/body, mental/behavioral, reason/emotion, subjective/objective, inner/outer, and nonmaterial/material, Platonic-Cartesian metaphysics produced discourses in which these various oppositional dimensions are mapped onto each other.

Although recent studies of the body include attention to visual aspects of corporeality, it is beyond the scope of this paper to review this voluminous literature. I shall focus, instead, upon a selective historical overview of attempts within anthropological inquiry to theorize "the body" as a component of visual culture and in relation to the use of visual material in anthropological research (Banks and Morphy 1997, 1). I also point to domains of critical inquiry within the history of the discipline that are usefully encompassed within a critical visual anthropology of the body, broadly conceived.[4]

Although certainly theoretically disembodied along Cartesian lines, the body has been less excluded from anthropology than is sometimes represented. Visual representations of the body can be said to have permeated anthropology since its inception, and to have been prevalent in visual anthropology since its emergence as a potential subfield in American anthropology around the 1940s. However, not all investigators can be said to have problematized or theorized the body as such, and it is to these contributions that I will confine my inquiry. The paper charts broadly a series of paradigm shifts from an observationist view of "the body" as biological or cultural object, which perhaps emits "behavior," to a conception of the body as a somatic and sensory resource for dynamically embodied action in cultural space/time.

I divide the paper into three main sections according to different theoretical foci. The kinds of studies in which the body is positioned as a biological, cultural, or social object, I will call "discourses *about* the body." In these, "it" is observed, classified, written about, and represented visually. The second section, "Discourses *of* the Body," charts the "first somatic revolution" of the 1980s and 1990s, a theoretical shift away from disembodied social science and toward a "paradigm of embodiment" (Csordas

BRENDA FARNELL

1989; Farnell and Varela 2008). Influenced primarily by the existential phenomenology of Merleau-Ponty, the focus here is on "I feel/experience" the subjective, lived body. This approach to embodiment stimulated an "anthropology of the senses," which, accompanied by a broader critique of "visualism" in anthropology, may have discouraged investigators from also examining visual aspects of embodied experience and cultural practices.

The third section, "Discourses *from* the Body," describes a "second somatic revolution," which moves toward a post-Cartesian conception of dynamic embodiment (Farnell and Varela 2008). This brings into studies of visual culture not "the body," as object, but *dynamically embodied persons in action*. To understand the human body as a biocultural resource for the dynamic construction of self, personhood, and identity, and as a means for creative expression as well as more mundane skilled embodied practices, requires theorizing across the usual disciplinary boundaries between biological and social being to articulate an adequate account of human agency as a causal power. In positioning dynamically embodied persons as components of visual culture, however, there is a somewhat ironic proviso—analysis and interpretations must be grounded in the multiple and complex *invisible* forms of cultural knowledge that make that which is visible meaningful to its practitioners (Farnell 1995b).

Discourses about "the Body"

The Body as Cultural Object

In sociocultural anthropology, recent academic interest in the body also represents renewed interest in a long-standing, if relatively minor, anthropological tradition. From the earliest descriptions of exotic cultures, and prior to the discipline's inception, we find representations and studies of the often racialized bodies of non-Western Others, viewed as cultural objects. Through photographs, drawings, and written descriptions, early anthropologists and ethnologists often drew attention to visual phenomena such as masking, clothing, costuming, body ornaments and decoration, and notions of beauty, alongside art and material objects (see Schildkrout 2004 for a review). Interpretations and significance were, of course, influenced, if not determined by, the evolutionary and, later, functionalist explanatory paradigms of the time. However, while evidence certainly supports this claim (see Edwards 1988, 1990, 1992), and photography was often naively assumed to be an objective recording practice, Banks and Morphy (1997, 8) suggest that the photographs themselves often "fundamentally contradicted the theoretical positions [anthropologists] endorsed and revealed a world of far greater complexity than their evolutionary framework allowed."

Anthropologists have also focused on inscriptions on the *surface* of the body itself, in the form of tattooing, scarification, and body paint, as markers of social identity in terms of gender, age, and political status. Reischer and Koo (2004) identify the broad anthropological rationale for such studies: "Our capacity for self modification and adornment is a central and essential feature of our humanity, though the particular ways in which we alter our bodies are clearly a cultural phenomenon" (2004, 297). Such studies, on the whole, document and classify the decorated body as a social phenomenon and note its symbolic functions as a vehicle for collective and personal identities. This tradition continues,[5] but recently has been supplemented by studies of bodies closer to anthropological selves.[6]

As part of a broader, reflexive approach to the history of the discipline, critical museum studies and other critiques of the representation of non-Western Others offer deeper understandings of the "colonizing gaze" at work in the colonial and racial contexts in which early anthropologists were embroiled and, as such, constitute an important part of a critical visual anthropology of the body (e.g., Pinney 1990; MacDougall 1997).[7]

The Body as Biological Object

As a result of the pervasive mind/body, material/nonmaterial, and nature/culture dualisms in Western thought, in anthropology "the individual body has usually been conceptualized as a universal biological base upon which culture plays its infinite variety" (Lock 1993, 134). The body as a biological/physical object was of central importance to the general anthropology of the nineteenth and early twentieth centuries, in both Britain and the United States. Its practitioners theorized the physical body as a marker of a biological determinism, however, and not as a social phenomenon or a component of visual culture.

Within the paradigm of a descriptive, empirically focused, positivist natural science, the recording of new facts about human physical variation that could be interpreted according to a racializing evolutionary theory was predicated upon describing, classifying and distinguishing

human beings by their visible physical characteristics. Critical investigations of taxonomies of the body in eighteenth- and nineteenth-century
natural history and early physical anthropology are instructive in this
regard (e.g., Gould 1981/1996).

Early physical anthropology made unsupportable generalizations
about human "races," often marked by the tendency to conflate cultural
and biological characteristics. This is most evident, perhaps, in the physical anthropology of Carl Linnaeus (1758), who proposed a classification
of seven races, each with associated "characteristics": the white *Europaeus*
was "sanguine" and "muscular"; the sallow *Asiaticus*, "melancholy" and
"stiff"; the red *Americanus*, "choleric" and "upright"; the black *Afer*,
"phlegmatic" and "relaxed." Completing the list were the wild and hir-
sute *Ferus*, which ran about on all fours; the *Troglodyte*; and, to accommodate what could not be classified otherwise (such as giants and genetic
mutants), the *Monstrous*. In 1776 Blumenbach's emphasis on anatomy
rather than cultural characteristics caused him to differ from his teacher
on these questions: he rejected Linnaeus's *Ferus* and *Troglodyte* but added
a *Malayan* race for the inhabitants of Southeast Asia. His revised system
consisted of *Caucasoid* (White), *Mongoloid* (Yellow), *American* (Red), *Ethio-
pian* (Black), and *Malayan* (Brown). The ranking of the races according to
their "excellence" was, however, as explicit in Blumenbach's work as in
Linnaeus's. For example, he considered a skull from the Caucasus Mountains in Central Europe to be the perfect form and regarded the other
four races as examples of degeneration from European perfection (Blumenbach 1776; Gould 1994). Clearly, such "scientific" taxonomies were
not only conflations of cultural and biological factors but also frequently
laden with ethnocentricity.

Lock (1993, 134) claims that because human variation and evolution
among human populations have always been a part of the anthropological bailiwick, anthropologists have proved a good deal more alert to the
challenge posed by the body than have other social scientists. I respect-
fully disagree. All the social sciences in the late nineteenth and early twentieth centuries started with the Darwinian paradigm and had to come
to terms with it—anthropology was no exception. Since Darwin's theories positioned animals (including humans) as members of species in
dynamical adaptation to their environment, the *biological organism* was
at the center of social scientific theorizing. Conceived as a deterministic system, however, the body was reduced to a biological mechanism,
the machinery of which was energy (e.g., Lesley A. White), instinct, and
reflex (Varela 2006). Behaviorists in psychology and sociology, as well
as in anthropology, having rejected "mind" as unavailable to scientific

inquiry because unobservable, were especially focused on bodily "behavior" (Harre and Gillett 1994).[8] It is certainly also the case, however, that mainstream anthropological paradigms—structural-functionalism, structuralism, and symbolic as well as semiotic anthropologies—were on the whole disembodied because primarily idealist in orientation given their focus on kinship systems and social organization, structures of the mind, symbolic classification, and semiotic/linguistic models.

The Body as Moving Object

In addition to the body's *surface* as a cultural palette for decoration and modification, the *moving* bodies of non-Western peoples have also long been subject to anthropological attention. Expressions of curiosity and disgust over alien bodily practices, such as unfamiliar domestic activities, "excesses" of gesticulation, "exotic" rituals, and "wild" dancing, frequent the accounts of early explorers, missionaries, and nineteenth-century amateur ethnologists. Such accounts provided a rationale for labeling non-Western peoples as "primitive." On the whole, the greater the variation from acceptable European norms of physical behavior, the more primitive a society was judged to be. This line of reasoning provided justification for widespread colonial efforts to "civilize the savages" through the radical control of bodily practices (clothing, hairstyles, eating habits, sexual liaisons, social manners, work ethic and ritual activities). For example, in North America, American Indian children sent to Indian boarding schools were transformed in appearance to conform to European norms and subjected to all-pervasive, often harsh, militarized daily regimens designed to "kill the Indian and save the man" (Child 1998; Lomawaima 1994). Likewise, the US Office of Indian Affairs book of regulations for 1904 listed participation in Native American religious rituals and dancing as a punishable offense because they stirred the passions of the blood and hindered progress toward "civilization" (that is, assimilation).

Although the radical separation of mind and body in Western culture remained constant at a metatheoretical level until the aforementioned poststructuralist and postmodern challenges in the late twentieth century, theoretical perspectives arose in US cultural anthropology and British social anthropology that viewed human body movement in contrasting ways.

While studies of "gesture" can be traced back as far as Greek interests in rhetorical performance, it was during the discipline's formative period that the evolutionist search for the origins of language motivated a brief but significant flurry of interest in the subject. The English anthropologist E. B. Tylor (1865) regarded sign languages and gesture as components of a universal "gesture language" more primitive than speech or writing, and he expected the elements to be universally recognizable. Reflecting upper-class Victorian attitudes toward gesticulation as "natural" and therefore "rude," meaning raw and unformed, Tylor believed he was close to discovering the original sign-making faculty in humans that once led to the emergence of spoken language (Farnell 1995a). He did not, however, go so far as to suggest that "the gesture language" represented an earlier *stage* of evolution through which humankind had passed before speech developed. Not entirely the armchair anthropologist, Tylor collected data from the sign systems of German and English deaf communities and compared them with data from North American sources. These interests in gesture and language origins were shared by the nineteenth-century German psychologist Wilhelm Wundt, who thought that human language could have originated in innate expressive actions characteristic of emotional states.

Meanwhile, in the United States, Tylor's work provided theoretical support for Garrick A. Mallery's extensive collection of data on sign languages and gestural systems. Mallery (1881) compared Native American signing systems with deaf sign languages and provided accounts of the use of gesture in classical times, in Naples, and among contemporary actors. The first publications of the newly established Bureau of American Ethnology in Washington, DC, were entirely devoted to accounts of Mallery's research on the subject (1880a, 1880b, 1881). On both sides of the Atlantic, however, this focus quickly disappeared once social evolutionism and the fascination with "origins" waned (Farnell 1995a).[9]

In addition, between the latter half of the nineteenth century and the 1960s there was considerable interest from popular writers, anthropologists, and historians on the subject of dancing. Williams's survey of writing in English on the subject of "dance" during this period uncovers a fascinating array of interpretations and explanations accounting for "why people dance" in terms of emotional, psychologistic, biological, intellectualist, literary, religious, and quasi-religious theories, as well as evolutionary and functional ones (Williams 1991/2004, 19–117).

In typical contrast to the universalist theories of gesture espoused by the evolutionists, American anthropologist Franz Boas stressed the learned, culture-specific nature of body movement. He recognized that artistic form and cultural patterning were present not only in Native American dances, but also in the complex hand gestures and other body movements that accompanied song, oratory, and the performance of oral literature (Boas 1888, 1890, 1927; see also Kaeppler 1978, 33; Williams 1991/2004, 88–89).[10] Despite this, Boas chose to exclude "gesture-language" from his influential introduction to the *Handbook of American Indian Languages* (1911). Aligning body movement with "musical means of communication," he limited his consideration to "communication by groups of sounds produced by the articulating organs [of mouth and tongue]" (1911, 10). Boas thus inadvertently set the pattern for the exclusion of body movement from future research in American linguistic anthropology and subsequent research became focused on a rather narrow conception of spoken language structure. Although Boas's student Edward Sapir recognized that manual gestures interplay constantly with speech in communicative situations, the linguistic and social significance of what he referred to as an "elaborate and secret code" were left unexplored (Sapir 1949, 556). Likewise, Whorf (1956) made programmatic suggestions about spatialized metaphors in speech and gesture but his statements appear to have gone unnoticed (but see Farnell 1996a).

Ruby documents how, in 1930, when Boas was seventy years old, he returned to the site of his earlier studies among the Kwakiutl with a motion picture camera and wax-cylinder sound recording machine. He used the camera to generate data in natural settings (as opposed to a laboratory) in order to study gestures, dances, games, and methods of manufacturing as manifestations of culture (Ruby 1980b, 1).[11] Much earlier than this, in *Primitive Art* (1927), Boas articulated a theory of dance as emotional and symbolic expression as part of his theory of rhythm in art and culture. Ruby suggests that Boas was trying to overcome the prejudice of some scholars that dance and other arts of body movement were not fit subjects for scientific investigation since they were so "emotional" in content. Although Boas certainly saw dances as emotional and aesthetic outlets for the dancers, his interest was not in the individual so much as the social—in the dance as an expression of culture. For Boas, Ruby suggests, body movement of any kind was a means of signifying one's cultural identity and, as such, should be amenable to ethnographic description and analysis (Ruby 1980b).

Historical evidence suggests that Boas was interested in using the films and sound recordings for a study of rhythm but that he could find no suitable method of analysis. Two letters written in the field to Ruth Benedict in 1930 are particularly revealing and are relevant here: on November 13 he wrote that "Julia [his field assistant] danced last night with the crowd and had her first formal dancing lesson tonight . . . the dance problem is difficult. I hope that the films will give us adequate material for making a real study." On November 24 he wrote to Benedict, "I already have a good deal of materials for this style-motor question." On the same day he wrote to his son, Ernst, "Julia is learning the dance, but I believe it is too difficult to learn quickly. At any rate, *through the criticism she receives I learn what it is all about.*" (Rohner 1969, 293–94, cited in Ruby 1980b; italics added). Clearly, Boas understood two criteria that today we take for granted as necessary to good field research in the anthropology of human movement: First, that learning the "action sign system" (Williams 1975, 1979) under investigation from local skilled practitioners is essential, and just as important as learning the spoken language of a community. Second, that critical remarks from such practitioners provide important means for understanding those things that cannot be observed, such as indigenous concepts of the body, space, and time, as well as criteria for adequate performance.

Since Boas had gathered written descriptive data on Kwakiutl dances since 1888, it is interesting to ask why he thought the new filmed data could provide him with "adequate material for making a real study." Ruby notes that Franziska Boas provides us with a tantalizing possibility. In a personal communication she suggested that Boas filmed because he had heard of Laban's work and "wanted to know whether Laban Notation was being expanded for wider use than just for [Western theatrical] dance, but I did not know enough about it to make use of it myself. His pattern was to investigate any new channels that might be fruitful. He very probably would have used Laban Notation had he lived later into the 1940's." If her conjecture is accurate, Boas was not only among the earliest researchers to use a camera with a view to using filmed data for detailed analysis, he also recognized the analytic possibilities that a transcription system like Labanotation offered the anthropological study of body movement.[12]

Although Sapir, like other Boasians, regarded culture as symbolic patterns of behavior, investigation of the symbolic patterning of human body movement in space as constitutive of that behavior remained absent from investigations. Consistent with the high status of US psychology, interest in the psychological (mental) took precedence over the bodily at this time, as witnessed by the rise in studies of "culture and personality."

As is well known, Boas was a fervent opponent of the popular misuse of race as an explanatory device for human social differences and sought to establish the primacy of culture over race as a means of understand-

THEORIZING "THE BODY" IN VISUAL CULTURE

ing social behavior.[13] He combined this with his interest in gesture and "motor habits" in the work he directed by one of his last students, David Efron. Efron's contrastive analysis of the gestures of Italian and southeastern Jewish immigrants in New York illustrated the cultural specificity of gestural codes and documented how subsequent generations either lost or preserved their parents' gestural repertoires according to personal commitments to assimilate or preserve traditions. His conclusion that different ways of gesturing depend upon the cultural environment discredited biological and racial explanations (Efron 1942).

Boas had also encouraged earlier students to pay attention to body movement. While in the field, Margaret Mead wrote to Boas on March 29, 1938, saying, "When I said I was going to Bali, you said: 'If I were going to Bali I would study gesture'" (Mead 1977, 212; cited in Ruby 1980b). Mead and Bateson's subsequent use of photography as a method of data collection was central to their psychologically oriented study of Balinese character, an attempt to identify and analyze "culturally standardized behavior" through visual means (Bateson and Mead 1942).[14]

Boas's students contributed to a functionalist view of human movement systems. Mead's earlier study, for example, regarded the dances of Samoan adolescents as a vehicle for psychological adjustment (1928/1959); for Benedict (1934) the function of the entire Kwakiutl Winter Ceremonial (a series of religious rites) was to rehabilitate the individual back into secular society.[15] Actual body movement is epiphenomenal in such descriptions, however, because ritual actions and dancing are described in terms of adaptive responses either to the social, the psychological, or the physical environment (Williams 1991/2004, 119). Similar descriptions appear in the work of many British functionalist anthropologists (e.g., Firth 1965; Malinowski 1922; Radcliffe-Brown 1913/1964).[16]

The unprecedented, seminal essay of French anthropologist Marcel Mauss (first published in 1935) prefigured the interests of Benedict, Mead, and others in noting how each society imposes on the individual a rigorously determined use of the body during the training of a child's bodily needs and activities. Mauss's essay clearly illustrated how seemingly "natural" bodily activities were (Durkheimian) social facts that were simultaneously sociological, historical, and physio-psychological.

It is at this historical juncture that Ray Birdwhistell emerged as a pioneer, coining the term "kinesics" to describe his microanalytic approach. In addition to being influenced by the work of Bateson (1956) and Goffman (1963, 1969), Birdwhistell was inspired by what he viewed as Sapir's anticipation of the interdependence of linguistic and kinesic research (Sapir 1949), and by attempts on the part of H. L. Smith and G. L. Trager to apply the methods of structural linguistics to nonsegmentable aspects of vocalization ("paralinguistics").

Birdwhistell envisioned a discipline that would parallel linguistics but deal with the analysis of visible bodily motion. Using filmed data, he applied a linguistic model, attempting to identify movement units based on contrastive analysis in a manner similar to that established by structural linguists for establishing the phonemes and morphemes of a spoken language. His descriptions frequently lapse into functional anatomical language, however, and the status of movements as meaningful actions becomes lost in the endeavor to divide up the "kinesic stream." Unfortunately, without the theoretical means to specify how bodily movements could be made finite for analytic purposes, and minus the concepts of "action" and "sign system" that would provide suitable units of movement and a concept of structured system (Williams 1975), Birdwhistell's analyses tended to dissolve into microanalytical minutia from which he seemed unable to emerge.

Davis (2001) illuminates some reasons for this, given the influence of behavioral psychologists such as Shelfen on Birdwhistell's analytic attempts. Behavioral microanalysis in laboratory and experimental settings asks different questions than those posed by anthropological investigations in ethnographic contexts. Birdwhistell was clearly aware of this, given his criticism of experimental controls and his call for "naturalistic observations" more in line with anthropological principles. However, Davis tells us that Ekman and the experimental psychologists managed to win control of the funding source from Birdwhistell when kinesics couldn't defend having spent four years on the microanalysis of one film (Davis 2001)!

Birdwhistell (like sociologist Erving Goffman) limited his research to interaction contexts, usually in clinical settings, and he considered more formalized idioms such as dancing, drama, mime, and religious ritual to be beyond the interests of kinesics (1970, 181). This was unfortunate as it narrowed the scope of the potential field, separating kinesics from much that was of interest to mainstream anthropology.[17]

Whereas Birdwhistell's kinesics focused on body motion, Edward T. Hall's "proxemics" (1980) drew attention to the role that space plays in human relations, although again, one must draw attention to two prior contributions: A. Irving Hallowell's "Cultural Factors in Spatial Orientation" (1955) and Haugan's "The Semantics of Icelandic Orientation" (1957/1969). Hall postulated that there are socially established zones of space surrounding individuals that are generally out of awareness but that influence, and may even determine, daily interactions (Hall 1966, 1959/1980); his writings include many thought-provoking ethnographic observations about the uses of space in different contexts, including situations of cultural contact. As Collier (2001) notes, Hall's applied interests and desire to engage a wider audience frequently led to overgeneralization, but his work was widely known and appreciated, sensitizing many nonspecialists to the cultural construction of space. Hall has been criticized for failing to clarify his theoretical position on the relation between proxemics and ethological notions of territoriality in animals. However, many ethologists as well as psychologists who specialize in nonverbal communication continue this behaviorist, Darwinian universalist agenda. Objectivist views of movement as "behavior"—as raw physical data of some kind, the result of biologically triggered impulses or survivals of an animal past—have been of little interest to sociocultural anthropologists because cultural and symbolic dimensions are excluded (but see Prost 1996 and the critiques in Williams 1996b).

"Kinesics" and "proxemics" provided important sensitizing constructs in the 1960s and 1970s. They raised new questions, suggesting frameworks that could be advanced by later investigators. Problems arise in the two approaches, however, from the separation of body motion and space. Kinesic motions of the body exist in a spatial vacuum, while proxemic zones of space are empty of the dynamically embodied action that structure their meaning. Today, we recognize that it is dynamically embodied action within structured semantic spaces that we wish to account for. In retrospect we can see that this separation was possible because both approaches take an observationist rather than an agentic perspective on action.

Alan Lomax's "choreometrics" joins this literature as a somewhat extreme and late example at a time when the functionalist approach had been largely abandoned as a viable paradigm within mainstream sociocultural anthropology (Williams 1991/2004, 19–117). Laden with unexamined presuppositions and pseudo-theories that suppose cause-effect relations for which there is little or no evidence, this approach has been met with grave objections presented in painful detail by well-qualified critics, including Keali'inohomoku (1976, 1979), Hanna (1979), and Williams (1972, and esp. 1991/2004, 139–50).

Choreometrics represents the worst kind of abuse of statistical models. Its primary data are arbitrary fragments of filmed body movements torn out of the social contexts that provide them with meaning. We know nothing of the danced events from which the stretches of movement are taken, nor what the movements might mean to the people dancing. On the contrary, we are told the intent is explicitly "not to translate" (Lomax 1968, 228). In choreometric explanations, a misguided notion of objectivity assigns the dancers only physical identities, and the dances (whatever they were) are reduced to raw movements bereft of any semantic content or significance whatsoever. Completely unjustifiable assumptions follow, such as: "When we find analogous bits occurring with notable frequency in life activity outside the dance, we assume that the bit in the dance and the bit in life stand for each other" (Lomax 1971). Statistical correlations are conflated with causation when motor complexity in one set of work activities connected with agricultural technology is assumed to be a constant factor in danced activities. Overblown claims are made that the resultant movement profiles can capture "the characteristic stances and modes of using energy that underlie *all* social interaction, *all* work, *all* activity in a particular culture" (italics added) and that these will map out nothing less than movement-style families on a continental scale.[18]

Transitional in the move from behaviorism to an agentist standpoint (discussed in the section "Discourses *from* the Body") are Erving Goffman and Adam Kendon. By the 1960s Goffman's influential microsociological studies of social interaction included attention to the agentic management of bodily performances in the presentation of self, thereby prefiguring the shift from "behavior" to "action" (Ardener 1970). Goffman introduced the term "body idiom" to describe the socially constructed knowledge found in conventionalized vocabularies of gestures and postures as well as the corporeal rules important to understanding behavior in public. He did not, however, systematically explore this notion, nor was he concerned with providing an explicit theory of the body in society (Goffman 1963, 1969; Shilling 1993, 74, 85–88).

Kendon, moving in an interdisciplinary sphere between anthropology, linguistics, nonverbal communication, psychology, and semiotics, has been a most active researcher of gesture and signed languages. His work remains empirically driven while affiliated with a variety of approaches. His earliest work on face-to-face interaction was grounded in psychological behaviorism (e.g., 1972) but he later shifted his orientation to a view more compatible with that of semiotics and symbolic anthropology, producing a definitive work on Australian Aboriginal sign languages (1988). Although he has yet to clarify a theoretical position, Kendon has, since the 1980s, written extensively on gesture and its connections to speech, insisting that "the gestural modality is as fundamental as the verbal mobility as an instrument for the representation of meaning" (1983, 2004).[19]

Discourses of the Body

In the 1980s and 1990s studies inspired by Foucault centered primarily on the physical body as cultural construct, on its regulation and restraint, as metaphor and machine, and on biopower and discursive formations. Attention was also paid to phenomena such as the "medical body," the "sexual body," the "decorated body," the "political body," and "the body as social text." Terence Turner (1994) attributes this shift to a virtual cult of the body in contemporary late capitalism, with fetishes ranging from fitness to fat control and the self as a "project."

At about the same time, the social sciences were undergoing a number of complementary developments. In anthropology, sociology, and psychology it became commonplace to understand that human activity in everyday life is best conceived as *action*, not behavior (Taylor 1964; Harre and Secord 1972; Ardener 1970; Crick 1976; Williams 1991/2004; Varela 1996). In anthropology there was a further understanding that human action is best framed in accordance with the ideas of *practice, discourse,* and *embodiment* (see Ortner 1984; Bourdieu 1977; Hymes 1971; Jackson 1989). By the 1990s the third component, embodiment, was captured in part by Csordas's call for the adoption of a "paradigm of embodiment" (1989, 5–47). The special feature of the new paradigm was that human action was seen as centered in, and constituted by, human *physical being.*

For anthropologists such as Csordas and Jackson (1989), following the existential phenomenology of Merleau-Ponty, "physical being," refers explicitly to the subjective (lived) body, in contrast to the objective (mechanical) body. The "lived body" means the body as human beings themselves perceive it—*felt, experienced, and sensed.* The thread tying these three perceptual processes together is the *feeling of doing.* In sociology, Shilling (1993) and Turner (1984) embraced this paradigm and its special features, as did Harré (1984, 1986a, 1991, 1998) and Shotter (1993) in psychology. Varela and Farnell (2008) consider the paradigm articulated by these anthropologists, sociologists, and psychologists to represent a first somatic revolution. This was an important challenge to disembodied theories of human action, whether idealist (as in the case of classic Levi-Straussian structuralist anthropology and early cognitive anthropology), or reductionist (as in the "unconscious" in Freud's structural model of id, ego, and superego as a deterministic system of bio-psycho-social forces and in behaviorism).

Jackson (1989) rejected semiotic processes as *necessarily* representational, (formally) cognitive, and linguistic, in favor of a phenomenologically inspired radical empiricism wherein sensory experience and perception are thought to afford a pre- or nonlinguistic, precultural mode of experiencing the world.[20] Farnell (1994) and Varela (1995) argue that such a formulation does not transcend the problem of Cartesian body/mind dualism; it merely entrenches the bifurcation, by swinging the pendulum over to "the body."

Csordas (1989) moderates Jackson's position with the important corrective that Merleau-Ponty's concept of the "pre-objective" does not mean "precultural" or "prelinguistic," but rather "prereflective"—not thought *about*. In Gilbert Ryle's terms this would be "knowing how" rather than "knowing that." However, Csordas likewise limits the concept of the semiotic to representational signs and symbols, which, he maintains, reduces embodied experience to language, or discourse, or representation (Csordas 1989, 183). He proposes that we embrace Merleau-Ponty's pre-objective being-in-the world as a dialogical partner to representation: "The equation is that semiotics gives us textuality in order to understand representation, phenomenology gives us embodiment in order to understand being-in-the-world" (1999, 184). In so doing, Csordas seems to accept the dualism on which the separation of a representational mind from an experiential body is predicated. Csordas's work thus remains rooted in the spirit of the Cartesian tradition, although that is certainly not his intent.[21]

Ironically for visual anthropology, this theoretical interest in embodiment in the 1980s and 1990s led away from the visual and toward other sensory modalities: the postmodern turn to the sensuous was accompanied by a broader critique of "visualism." Fabian (1983) and Jackson, among others, accused anthropology of being intellectualist and rationalist, with an overemphasis on vision and observation as metaphors of ethnographic production (Fabian 1983) that was related to the impact of perspective and literacy (Jackson 1989, 6; Tyler 1987).

Conflating science with positivism, Jackson in anthropology and Bryan Turner (1984) in sociology position observation as necessarily objectifying, locating people as things or objects rather than sensory beings-in-the-world. However, this critique is based upon accepting an empiricist interpretation of what observation means in science. Already in the 1940s cultural philosopher Suzanne Langer, following Cassirer, had revolted against the tradition of positivist views of science, understanding that observation is always mediated by symbolic languages that require interpretation (Langer 1942; Cassirer 1944/1953). Nevertheless, the visualist critique may have discouraged investigators from examining visual aspects of embodied experience and cultural practices, despite recognition of the terror of visual power in the policing of bodies, as in Foucault's discussion of Bentham's "panopticon" (1977), and modern modes of power that still rely predominantly on the power of the visualist language of statistics and surveying (Pels 1996).

Discourse *from* the Body

Interesting and important as these studies were, their focus was largely upon the body as *a static object*—albeit a social and cultural one rather than a biological or mechanistic entity. Little or no attention was paid to the human body as *a moving agent in a spatially organized world of meanings* (Farnell 1994). Absent, on the whole, are accounts of persons *enacting* the body, that is, using physical actions—actions that may be out of awareness through habit or highly deliberate choreographies—in the agentive production of meaning.

An enrichment of the first somatic revolution has been articulated in the approach to embodiment taken by Drid Williams, developed in the theoretical and ethnographic contributions of Brenda Farnell, and articulated further in a series of papers in the philosophy of the social sciences by Charles Varela. Williams, Farnell, and Varela contribute the idea that human action is best understood as a *dynamically* embodied discursive practice, a move that Farnell and Varela (2008) regard as a *second somatic revolution*.[22] In contrast to the theoretical approach championed by the earlier paradigm, their interest is in the *moving* body, the doing itself (which may, of course, also be felt). Here we have with greater precision a distinction between the first and second somatic revolutions: a difference between the *feeling* of the body (moving or not) and the *movement* of the body itself.

The paradigmatic shift, from an empiricist and observationist view of movement to an agent-centered perspective, is encapsulated in the preference for the term "action" over the term "behavior" (see Williams 1991/2004, 244–76; Ardener 1970). At the heart of theories that define body movement as "culturally and semantically laden actions couched in indigenous models of organization and meaning" (Williams 1982, 15) lies an entirely different definition of what it means to be human from that implicit in theories that define movement as "physical behavior" or "motor movements."

Farnell, Varela, and Williams argue that to make the actions of a moving agent central to a definition of embodiment (and therefore to social action) requires a postpositivist "new realist" philosophy of science (Aronson 1984; Bhaskar 1975; Manicus 2006) rather than the existential philosophy of Merleau-Ponty. As Varela (1994a) has shown, only when grounded in Harré's new realist notion of human agency (as a generative but not deterministic "causal power") do Merleau-Ponty's suggestions for embodiment remain fruitful. Williams discovered Harré's work on causal powers theory in the 1970s and used it to ground a semiotic approach to the embodied, signifying, moving person known as "semasiology" (Williams 1982).

A semasiological persective explicitly theorizes the new realist perspective that is required to ground human agency adequately as a causal power in the natural world. This is significant because it connects the biological with the sociocultural and offers a post-Cartesian concept of "person" (Varela and Harré 1996). I have utilized the new realist approach and semasiology to argue that the invention of an analytic construct like "the *habitus*" is necessary to Bourdieu's theory of practice (1977) because he does not have an adequate conception of the nature and location of human agency or of the nature of human powers and capacities (Farnell 2000). I maintain that, as a result, Bourdieu's theory gives us an essentially ungrounded and mindless notion of human action that is restricted to habituated practices and separated from language. Without any deeper understanding of the performative power of both action signs and vocal signs as resources for meaningful action in social life, I suggest that Bourdieu is stuck on the twin banks of objectivism and subjectivism despite his desire to transcend this and other conceptual dualisms.

I have also employed the anti-Cartesian position inherent in new realist causal-powers theory and semasiology to reexamine Lakoff's (1987) and Johnson's (1987) concept of "kinesthetic image schema" (Farnell 1996a). This construct posits a basic level of preconceptual physical experience out of which concepts are structured, thereby compromising Lakoff's and Johnson's important moves toward embodiment by restricting body movement to the role of an experiential, preconceptual *precursor* to spoken concepts. Once transformed into "mental images," such experience assists in the building of a conceptual system from which physical action is subsequently excluded. From this perspective, bodily experience provides only the ground upon which that which really counts—spoken language concepts and categories—can be built into metaphorical schemas. Physical being and bodily actions have thus been denied the status of signifying acts and forms of knowledge. In contrast, using semasiology, supported with ethnographic examples, I argue that action signs (signifying movements) provide a medium other than speech that shares the conceptual stage and systematically employs metaphoric and metonymic conceptions realized in space. This implies that our imaginative capacity is not merely indirectly embodied, as Lakoff and Johnson suggest, but directly embodied because *action signs themselves can be imaginative tropes* (Farnell 1996a).

Interest in the moving body by some linguistic anthropologists, facilitated by video technology, has resulted in renewed attention to gestural systems and signed languages. For example, Goodwin, Havilland, Kendon (see McNeill 2000), Farnell (2001), and others, challenge the persistent verbal/nonverbal dualism in mainstream linguistic thought, suggesting that traditional approaches to language have failed to see the vocal/visual integration at work in the performance of communicative acts. However, despite these important exceptions, and despite the "breakthrough to performance" in the ethnography of speaking tradition of the 1960s and 1970s, the dominant disembodied-language ideology within linguistics and linguistic anthropology continues to segregate spoken signs from visual-kinetic action signs.

In Conclusion: Bodily Discourses

The enrichment that constitutes the second somatic revolution proposed here stems from a theoretical principle that unifies the aforementioned concepts of action, discourse, and embodiment: *the primacy of the signifying moving person.* Starting with the premise that all human action is the discursive practice of persons, Farnell (1994) and Varela (1995) have proposed a way of interconnecting three kinds of social theoretical discourse that the Csordas-Jackson paradigm of the first somatic revolution presupposes to be separate and perhaps even incommensurable approaches to embodying social scientific theory. We can observe the following:

1. In traditional disembodied social theory there are *discourses about the observed body* (visual representations, talk, writing) from an objectivist, intellectualist standpoint (e.g., classic evolutionary and functionalist anthropologies, psychoanalysis, Durkheimian sociology).
2. In the predominant dissenting tradition of embodied social theory that comprises the first somatic revolution, there are *discourses of the experienced body* from a subjectivist, lived standpoint (e.g., the Jackson-Csordas paradigm).

3. Finally, in dynamically embodied social theory there are *discourses from the moving body*—an agentist, enactment standpoint that constitutes a second somatic revolution (Farnell and Varela 2008).

Here we have a basis from which we can better identify the first somatic revolution in social science theory. The Csordas-Jackson paradigm was a revolt against the deterministic reduction of the human body to a mechanical system: behaviorism, psychoanalysis, and naturalistic sociology were different ways of theorizing that reified conception of human somatics. Farnell and Varela (2008) propose instead that we conceptualize the three forms of body-referenced discourse as *complementary* moments of everyday social-symbolic interaction. Each of the three moments can now be regarded as a situated option that persons may take up in reference to themselves or others as they contextually see fit, according to their ordinary or professional interests.

Central here is the idea that *the way human agency works is in terms of the signifying enactments of moving persons*. This position is commensurate with Ingold's dwelling perspective (2000) and his use of Gibson's environmental theory of perception (1966, 1979). The varied discursive practices of semiosis are performatively grounded in, and conventionally a structuring of, a suitable region of the body that serves the purposes of meaning-centered sociocultural living—such regions as the mouth and lips in speech, the hands in sign languages, and the whole body in forms of dance, ceremony, or practical skills of various kinds (Farnell 1999). The human actions that constitute speech-act systems, action-sign systems, and any other form of semiosis are the creative outcome of a primary generative act—signifying enactments *from* the body (Farnell 1999, Williams 1991/2004).

While Csordas proposed a paradigm of the *experienced* body for the 1990s, Williams, Farnell, and Varela are proposing a paradigm of the *moving* body for the beginning of the twenty-first century.

In this paper, I have sought to provide a selective historical overview of attempts within anthropological inquiry to theorize "the body" as a component of visual culture and in relation to the use of visual material in anthropological research. Ironically perhaps, understanding "the body" as a component of visual culture from this perspective requires equal attention to a range of *invisible* systems of knowledge and ensuing practices and processes—cultural, perceptual, and cognitive—that provide the visible with meaning (Williams 1995, Banks 1997, Farnell 1995b). But this is also the case with visual media, such as film and photography, that have constituted the heart of visual anthropological inquiry (see MacDougall

2006). In the case of dynamically embodied movement, these knowledge systems and practices can range from widely shared or system-specific concepts of the body, space/time, and personhood to indexical and deictic features of specific events and interactions in performance. It must also be acknowledged that the visual is only one sensory modality employed in dynamically embodied events; equally important is kinesthesia. Indeed, one of the lessons to be learned from the phenomenological turn to the senses and the critique of visualism is that a multisensory semiosis is at work in human lives, and for that reason many investigators of human movement do not consider themselves visual anthropologists as such.

During the postmodern interlude, we have seen theorizing—as a means of unifying disparate studies, interests, and problems—largely dismissed in light of a taboo on "grand theorizing," conceived as an antihumanist, positivist, and determinist agenda. Now that we understand science as a realist practice rather than a positivist one, there is reasonable promise that theorizing can once again provide the kind of centripetal intellectual energy that will encourage greater theoretical coherency, in tension with the centrifugal impulse of postmodernism, with its fragmentation of disciplinary knowledge and concomitant moves toward interdisciplinarity. I like to think that the concept of dynamic embodiment offers such theoretical promise for future studies of the body and human movement as visual culture.

Notes

1. E.g., Foucault 1973, 1977, 1978. Influential feminist theorists of the body include Allen and Grosz 1987; Bordo 1993; Butler 1993; Grosz 1991, 1994, 1995; Jagger and Bordo 1989; Martin 1998; Suleiman 1986. See also the essays in Fehar et al. 1989.
2. See also Csordas 1989, 1994; Frank 1991; Featherstone et al. 1991; Shilling 1993; Turner 1984, 1991; Varela 1994a, 1994b, 1995.
3. Barish 1981; Best 1974, 1978; Farnell 1994, 1995b; Harré 1986a; Ingold 1993a, 1993b; Streeck 1993; Turner 1984; Varela 1995 discuss the pervasive influence of the Platonic-Cartesian notion of person.
4. This story of entanglements with "the body" presents just one theme in the history of anthropology, one that most disciplinary historians would probably consider relatively minor. Annual review articles that usefully summarize work on the body and embodiment in sociocultural anthropology are Lock 1993; Farnell 1999; Reischer and Koo 2004; and Schildkrout 2004. See also Kendon 1997, on gesture, and Kaeppler 1978 and Reed 1998, on dance.

5. E.g., Burton 2001; Gell 1993; Gaines and Herzog 1990; Groning 1998; Mageo 1994.
6. E.g., Burroughs and Ehrenreich 1993; Lock 1993; Mascia-Lees and Sharpe 1992; Scheper Hughes and Lock 1987; Demello 1993; Winkler 1994; Winkler and Cole 1994; Halperin 1999.
7. E.g., Karp and Lavine 1991.
8. In classical psychoanalysis also, Freud, as a biologist of the mind, built his theory of personality around the premise that "in the beginning is the body," as illustrated in his final model of personality—*id* as the organism, *ego* as the brain (become mind) of the organism, and *superego* as the internalization of culture.
9. Interest in tool use and gesture continued to play a significant role in accounts of the evolution of human intelligence, however; see Gibson and Ingold 1993. Renewed interest in gesture and the evolution of language is found in Armstrong, Stokoe, and Wilcox 1995; on the evolution of gesture, tool use, and language see Ambrose 2001.
10. In the first volume of the *Journal of American Folklore*, which appeared in 1888, Boas published an article, "On Certain Songs and Dances of the Kwakiutl of British Columbia," and his interest in Kwakiutl dance continued throughout his life.
11. Boas asked his daughter Franziska to study the Kwakiutl dance footage, and she did so, supplementing her observations from the film with ethnographic material from her father's earlier work (Boas 1897). Part of this material was published as a discussion following the article by Franz Boas in a volume entitled *The Function of Dance in Human Society*, edited by Franziska Boas (1944). Lock (1993, 149) mistakenly attributes this book to the father, Franz Boas.
12. Labanotation is a script for writing body movement well suited to anthropological research. Pioneered in anthropological contexts by Williams in 1975, it is also used by Kaeppler, myself, and others for transcribing movement data of all kinds. It is quite distinct from Laban's effort/shape analysis, a largely ethnocentric classification of dynamic movement qualities that was used in Lomax's choreometrics project. Movement literacy via Labanotation is an important means of data documentation and an analytic resource in the anthropology of human movement (see Farnell 1994, 1996c; Page 1996).
13. This interest took on a particular urgency in the 1930s, when racism in America and Nazism in Europe were powerful forces. When Nazi social scientists began to publish their allegedly scientific explanations for the racial inferiority of non-Aryans, Boas gained an additional reason for advocating the primacy of culture for understanding human differences.
14. Additional contributions in the 1940s and 1950s were La Barre's essay on the cultural basis of emotions and gestures (1947) and a paper on the cross-cultural comparison of "postural habits" by Hewes (1955).

15. In addition to the essay by her father, Franziska Boas's edited collection contained essays on the functions of dance in Haiti, Bali, and "primitive" African communities.

16. Alan Lomax's brand of functionalism differs from this in the sense that he did at least attempt to deal with the movement itself. The problem was that he removed arbitrary fragments of movement from the social and linguistic contexts that gave them meaning.

17. Adam Kendon has suggested that the program of work Birdwhistell proposed might have gotten under way had the interest of many people in linguistics and related disciplines not been redirected in the 1960s by the work of Noam Chomsky. Chomsky's generative linguistics was exclusively concerned with the formal analysis of linguistic competence and proposed "structures of the mind" that generate language per se. Actual acts of speaking were consigned to what Kendon called "the wastebasket of performance" (1982). Only when linguistic anthropology embraced an "ethnography" of speaking/communication" in explicit contrast to the Chomskian agenda did attention return to pragmatics, ethnopoetics and verbal art as performance. This provided a theoretical climate in the 1980s and 1990s in which gesture, spatial orientation, and deixis (the spoken and gestural organization of persons and of space/time) and indexicality (connections to the communicative context) became of interest to some linguistic anthropologists (Farnell 1995b).

18. Williams cautions us that choreometrics provides an important example of how *not* to handle the subject of dancing and notes that this project has contributed (perhaps more than anyone is aware) to the stultification of further subsidized research on dance and other structured movement systems. Policy makers and those who exercise control over research monies now seem to believe, owing to these failures to produce a viable "measure of dance" or a reliable "theory of dance as the measure of culture," that there are simply too many variables and that dance therefore cannot be studied in a "scientific manner" or in any manner that would make a further contribution to knowledge (1991/2004, 141).

19. See Farnell (1999, 352–53) for a summary of research on gesture, signed languages, and studies of space in cognitive anthropology. Within linguistic anthropology and conversation analysis, the focus is on understanding language rather than the visual per se, although some attention is given to spatial orientation, spatial deixis, and spatial contexts of performance. Signed-language research offers important challenges to the disembodied ideology of traditional linguistics.

20. The problem is, if there is a way of knowing that is precultural and prelinguistic that is somehow provided by the body in some sense, what could be the mechanism or mechanisms by which it is accomplished? Unless one resorts to some form of instinctivism or genetic determinism, what biological mediator is conceivable? The only logical next step is back to

a Cartesian formulation of mind as a nonmaterial entity, because such a formulation would have to bypass the central nervous system as a mediator of all sensory experience.

21. Since the theoretical emphasis in both anthropological and sociological versions of the first somatic revolution is on the *feeling* of the doing and not the *doing itself*, Varela and Farnell (2008) remain skeptical of the extent to which the Csordas-Jackson paradigm faithfully employs the existential phenomenology of Merleau-Ponty (Varela 1995, 1996). While it is certainly true that Merleau-Ponty's key idea of the perceived-body or embodied consciousness has been a major source of the somatic turn in social scientific theory, it is important to recall that the central principle that underwrites his concepts of the "lived body," "intercorporeity," and "flesh" is the "self of movement" (Merleau-Ponty 1962, 257).

22. Ironically perhaps, the second somatic revolution predates the first, having been initiated by Williams's doctoral dissertation in 1975.

SIX

Tracing Photography

ELIZABETH EDWARDS

Setting the Focus

This essay explores the uneasy history of photography in anthropological practice as a series of cross-cultural interactions, agencies, reengagements, and evidential potentials. I shall present three thematic "snapshots" of moments of entanglement, which chart the shifting anthropological relationship with the medium. For as Pinney has argued (1992a), there is an historical confluence of the parallel yet intersecting and mutually supporting histories of anthropology and photography in a complex matrix of mechanical inscription, desire, power, authority, and agency. My "snapshots" might be summarized as questions of evidence, questions of power, and questions of agency. They are not mutually exclusive—they both overlap and merge at various points—but they do constitute moments of focus. Further, although there is a broad chronological drift—circa 1890–1970s, mid-1970s–late 1990s, mid-1990s to present—that doubles back on itself too often to constitute a linear history. Reflecting anthropology's multifaceted histories, I consider photographs with which anthropologists have engaged, not only those that they have made.

There is necessarily much that is left out. I am concentrating here on the historical record and research responses to it rather than presenting a history of methodology, although again, the two are far from mutually exclusive. Contemporary developments in the latter can be tracked in volumes such as Pink (2001) and Banks (2001) and in the pages of the subdiscipline's journals. I shall also, given the limitations of a short essay, restrict myself largely to the English-speaking world, although such a history and commentary could be written equally, with overlaps on one hand and specific inflections on the other, to imaging practices in the anthropologies produced by, for instance, the French-, German-, or Dutch-speaking worlds (see, e.g., Dias 1994, 1997; Blanchard et al. 1995; Theye 1989; Schindlbeck 1989; Zimmerman 2001; Roodenberg 2002) and elsewhere in the application of anthropological method in many parts of the world.

In the first snapshot, on questions of evidence, I address the ways in which photography and photographs have been used to establish anthropological fact. I shall track the shifting responses to realism and truth values of photography through the set of socio-aesthetic propositions that cluster around the discourse of "pose," with all its implications for the nonnatural, the unreal, and anthropological "naturalism."[1] These questions are integrally associated with ideas of observation, evidence, truth, and cultural integrity, the moral weight of which are at the core of the anthropological project.

Second, I look at the way in which the representational practices of photography become a forceful presence in the cultural politics of representation within the discipline and without. Photography, especially its role in the production of the colonial body as an anthropological object, became a key site of cultural critique in the "crisis of representation" that began in the 1970s. Haunted by anthropology's colonial past and uncertain of its role in a postcolonial and increasingly global environment, the discipline found in the visual legacy of its past a rich prism through which to explore the construction of anthropological knowledge.

Finally, I shall explore the revitalized and reimagined role of photography within anthropology, namely the emergence of ethnographies of photographic practices, on one hand, and historical reengagement with anthropology's visual legacy, on the other. Such studies have not only opened up the possibility of agency in the cultural historical domain but also destabilized the authority of both anthropology and its photographic production. This has enabled the emergence of critical, reflexive, and collaborative microhistories of visual, cross-cultural encounters and photography's relation with the material and sensory. These studies reveal complex orders of photography, but more significantly, they use photography not only to record according to the best practice of the moment but as a prism through which to think through other areas of anthropological endeavor.

Thus, overall, this essay looks at how photography might be positioned, not only in visual anthropology, but in the discipline more broadly. Through the fluid circulation of images and representational strategies across the shifting boundaries of disciplinary practice, through the multivalency and recodability of the photograph itself, is constituted a complex web of influences, ideologies, and theoretical and methodological approaches to photographs, to the extent that disciplinary contemporary practices and the visual legacies of anthropology's past cannot necessarily be disentangled. Implicit in such a history is the shifting dynamic of how anthropology makes its evidence, how it arrives at its truths, and how it positions its objectivity, handles its subjectivities, and understands its intersubjectivities (Pink 2001, 19–21).

Evidential Strategies

The mechanical and indexical nature of photographs as apparently unmediated inscriptions made them central to the establishment and articulation of objective method and desire across a wide range of disciplines. However, while the photograph might be the realist tool par excellence, evidential validity has, for over a century, been vested in the quality of observation. This was increasingly embodied in fieldworkers' presence, to the extent that the body became a sort of camera, absorbing data through scientifically controlled observation of the trained analytical eye (Grimshaw 2001, 53; Grasseni, this volume). Thus the source of the photograph, the anthropologically creating eye, became as significant as the mechanically inscribed content, encompassing therefore both empirical reliability and procedural correctness (Daston and Galison 1992, 82) in order to create an authoritative anthropological realism.

Of course realism, and its empiricism as politically complicit, hegemonic, and appropriating, has come under particular scrutiny in film and photography over the last thirty years or so (for instance Krauss 1982; Nichols 1991; Roberts 1998), and this is not the place to revisit those arguments. What is significant here is the way in which photography's forceful realist effect and transparency gave authority to the ethnographic account, at least until the 1960s, and gave concrete form to the illusionism of anthropological representation, proclaiming, "This is what you would see had you been there with me—observing" and "You are there . . . because I was there" (Clifford 1988, 22). Thus photographs become privileged sites for communicating a feeling of cultural immersion, a sort of substitute for the personal experience of fieldwork, presenting authoritatively what could have been seen.

It was for precisely these reasons that the statement of the parameters of the image became so important. Photography had to not only record but to preserve evidential authority and illusion. The photographic act itself had to be inconspicuous and transparent: as late as 1951 the handbook *Notes and Queries on Anthropology* advised against the use of the 35-millimeter camera, held to the eye and thus masking the face, as "undesirably obtrusive" (RAI 1951, 354), and throughout the twentieth century the same handbook urged the sense of the spontaneous and the invisible camera, for "many photographs . . . are spoiled because the subject is looking at the photographer" (BAAS 1912, 271), advice repeated in the 1929 edition. Looking into the camera, in self-conscious representation, marks the presence of the subject, the author, and the viewer, challenging the authority of the anthropologist as it disrupts the sense of immediacy, spontaneity, and naturalism on which observational validity and illusionistic re-presentation is grounded.

Pose is thus presumed to be "unnatural," whereas anthropology is concerned with the natural flow of culture, unmediated and direct. These values are clearly articulated by Margaret Mead and Gregory Bateson, whose seminal work on child development, socialization, and personality in Bali between 1936 and 1938, resulted in a tour de force of observational translation in the social sciences as they attempted to use the camera as a new systematic methodology of precision and integrity.[2] Over 750 of the photographs were published as *Balinese Character: A Photographic Analysis* (1942), arranged as a series of scientific "photo-essays" that demonstrate their thesis, under such rubrics as "Stages of Childhood," "Autocosmic Play," and "Boys' Tantrums" (Jacknis 1988, 168–70).

It is worth considering Mead and Bateson's method because it articulates a culmination of a specific set of relations between field anthropology, photography, and the construction of its object, especially in relation to the pose and the "natural." Could pose, intervention, or reenactment constitute an anthropological truth? They state, "We tried to shoot what happened normally and spontaneously rather than to decide upon norms and then get the Balinese to go through these behaviors in suitable lighting" (Bateson and Mead 1942, 49). In other words the dominant values of the immediate translation of vision and experience shaped both the photographic methodology and subsequent analysis (figure 6.1).

However, the situation is not clear-cut. Despite their concern for "the normal" in "natural space and time," they write, "In a great many instances, we created the *context* in which the notes and photographs were

6.1   Men Karma breastfeeding one of her children, August 19, 1937. Photo: Margaret Mead
       and Gregory Bateson. Margaret Mead Papers, Manuscript Division, Library of Congress,
       Washington, DC (container P39, negative #LC-MSS-32441-559-33, digital ID #10961).

taken for example, by paying for the dance or asking the mother to delay bathing of her child until the sun was high," but, they stress, "this is very different from posing photographs" (1942, 50). The interventionist creation of contexts was justified as an extension of the accepted parameters of participation, and thus disciplinary truth, in that payment was indeed the economic basis for theatrical performance or that a delayed bath served to focus a natural attention on the baby, diminishing the problematic awareness of being photographed that might destabilize the key concept of disciplinary validation—the normal and spontaneous.

But at the same time Bateson and Mead locate anthropological truth in the unmediated chemical inscription on the negative. Bateson is at pains to stress that any intervention in the photographs was within "scrupulously respected . . . scientific conventions" (1942, 51), that nothing was added to the photographs, and that any darkroom manipulation of the negative/print translation served merely to "mak[e] it possible for the paper to give a more complete rendering of what is present in the negative" (1942, 52). In negatives that were enhanced, the process was carefully recorded, making the parameters of the statement clear. Equally the parameters of the selection and presentation of the photographs in the book were made clear, again articulating the quality and form of evidential value: "Each single photograph may be regarded as almost purely objective, but juxtaposition of two different or contrasting photographs is already a step toward scientific generalization" (Bateson and Mead 1942, 53). In this one sees the moral values around the articulation of an anthropological truth emerge, premised not merely on truth to nature (the normal and spontaneous) but on the morality of scientific self-restraint. This excluded the destabilizing potential of "the pose" and created a scientific framework in which subjectivities might be controlled.

If one can see in Bateson and Mead's work an anticipation of later debates on photography and the making of anthropological authority, one can also find resonances of those concerns much earlier. The values that clustered around photography, and the crystallization of observational truth as articulated through the camera, emerge from the beginning of the twentieth century. As the practices of fieldwork became more strongly articulated, so the truth values around photography shifted. Again we can see this reflected in attitudes toward pose. Despite Malinowski's uneasy relationship with the medium and its implications (1935, 461–62; Young 1998, 5–6), he was an active and competent photographer. He used photographs extensively, with careful placement and cross-referencing, throughout his publications (Samian 1995). His attention to the nature of his photographic evidence belies his overt stance. However, Malinowski, like Mead and Bateson, was careful to position his photographs in current practices of realism and ethnographic authority. This is most marked in the caption to plate 100 in *Coral Gardens and Their Magic*, where he is careful to stress the observational basis of the fieldworker's authority: "This picture is not posed, it was taken during the actual *gibuviyake* rite, and shows the concentration of the magician at work" (1935, opposite 280). That is, it may look posed but it is not. Nonetheless, despite his stress on immediate observation, he was not averse to using carefully controlled pose or reenactment to make images that could not be obtained "naturally," such as war magic or sexual intercourse (Malinowski 1935, 461–62; Young 1998, 17). In drawing attention to the parameters of the photograph, Malinowski is also defining the parameters of participant field observation and thus the anthropological validity of his evidence and the role of the photograph within this.

Similarly, in his classic ethnography *Witchcraft Oracles and Magic* (1937), Evans-Pritchard specifically draws attention to the parameters of plate 13, "Kamanga Blowing a Magic Whistle (Posed)." He is mindful of exactly the same questions of evidential status and authority as Malinowski. However, Evans-Pritchard's photograph carries a visual mark of its status. Not only do Kamanga's lips not actually touch the whistle (the low camera angle shows this clearly), the close framing of the uncropped photograph is stylistically different from the "no-style style" and the embodied immediacy of observation that informs most of his photographs (Morton 2005).[3] It is as if he is stating visually that evidentially this photography is of another order (figure 6.2).

It can, of course, be argued that the need for pose or reconstruction is dependent on the technologies available. Certainly this is part of the equation. Technical possibilities shift the social expectations that cluster around photography, as what was technically possible is integrally entangled with what is thinkable at a given historical moment (Winston 1998, 120–23). However, we cannot reduce the relations between the natural and the posed, the real and the "untrue," to technologically determined absolutes; rather, as I have suggested, we must consider shifting parameters of objectivity and their associated visual statements.[4]

In the early period, pose and reenactment have to be understood as a form of scientific demonstration in which replication is itself part of the evidential system. For instance, responding to the first edition of *Notes and Queries* (1874), E. H. Man inscribed on one photographic plate a cultural tableau, "Andamanese Shooting, Dancing, Sleeping and Greeting," which was reproduced as demonstrational evidence in the pages of the *Journal of the Anthropological Institute* (figure 6.3).

6.2 Kamanga blowing a magic whistle, reenacted for Evans-Pritchard's camera. Photo: E. Evans-Pritchard. Pitt Rivers Museum, University of Oxford (PRM 1998.341.282.2).

6.3   Cultural tableau: hunting, sleeping, greeting and dancing, Andaman Island, ca. 1874.
      Photo: E. H. Man. Pitt Rivers Museum, University of Oxford (PRM 1998.230.4.1).

The concept of the scientific demonstration of method and evidence, and its associated concept of "virtual witnessing," resonates through the work of many scientifically trained anthropologists of the late nineteenth and early twentieth centuries. Haddon, for instance, uses pose and re-enactment to verify and clarify his data to demonstrate a scientific point (Edwards 1998). In a similar vein, Boas not only produced "posed photographs" to demonstrate his data (Jacknis 1984) but himself posed for photographs in order to demonstrate the exact form of the Hamat'sa ceremony to make scientifically accurate representations for the American Museum of Natural History (Glass 2006).

The concept of demonstration in the sense of the performative statement of evidence and scienticity, while coming from nineteenth-century science, arguably remained central to the establishment of anthropological authority through publication; Bateson and Mead, for instance, "intended us to view the photographs as a *demonstration* of how the various habits of the Balinese form their character" (Sullivan 1992, 29; emphasis added).

The relation between anthropology and photography was haunted, however, by the impossibility of containing the medium's random inclusivity. All evidential strategies are attempting, in their different ways, to control the excess of meaning in photographs (Pinney 1992b, 27; Poole 2005), for their inherent instability threatened to destabilize not only anthropological data but anthropological authority itself. Scientific intervention and pose constituted a way of controlling photographic excess by arranging data and focusing attention. However, if photographs could not be contained at the inscriptive level they could be so contained through the rhetorics of the disciplinary eye. In the nineteenth century it was argued that a scientifically trained "eye" would suppress some categories of visual information while privileging others, creating scientific evidence. This was crucial given that in the period little "anthropological photography" was made with specific scientific intent but, rather, became "anthropological" through categories of consumption as images were often negotiated between the competing scopic regimes of popular voyeurism and science (Edwards 2001, 27–50; Zimmerman 2001, 174–75).

However, the appropriation of images into science became increasingly problematic for anthropologists by the end of the nineteenth century. Concepts of scientific rigor and objectivity could no longer be vested in the recoding of the indexical trace alone, but through, as I have suggested, the quality of observation. Modes of visual evidence production that presumed a level of intervention sat uncomfortably with the "naturalistic" mode of anthropology as it emerged in the early twentieth century. That naturalism, as we have seen, privileged the direct experience of the fieldworker rather than the development of scientific data skills (Grimshaw 2001, 52). Not only did pose and intervention have uncomfortable resonances with the photographic mapping of race and material culture of the previous generation (which Malinowski described as "scientifically sterile"; 1935, 460). It was also understood as lacking the intellectual and moral values of immediacy, closeness, and observation. Indeed, by the time Collier published *Visual Anthropology* in 1967, questions of pose were not discussed—unmediated realism translating the experience of participant observation for the interrelated purposes of recording, photo-interviewing, synthesis, and analysis had became the assumed value of photography.

We cannot, however, see this process of evidential refinement in disciplinary isolation. Grimshaw has pointed to the fluid boundaries between anthropology and other visualizing practices, and if excesses made photography difficult to control within anthropology itself, they also connected anthropology to other photographic practices and discourses (Ruby 1976; Becker 1981; Edwards 1997; Grimshaw 2001). Anthropology had always been mindful of its "photographic other"—a more creative inscription of actuality of arts and documentary practices.[5] I turn now to explore briefly evidential status on that boundary.

Becker defined the difference between social sciences and photography, casting "one as the discovery of the truth about the world and the other as the aesthetic expression of someone's unique vision," but he also suggested that the two strands were inextricably entangled (1981, 9). Connections can be made, for instance, between Malinowski's arrangement of photographs in *Coral Gardens and Their Magic* and Bateson and Mead's sequencing in *Balinese Character* and the emergent photo-essay form in magazines such as *Life* and *Picture Post*. And there are clear stylistic parallels between unmediated verisimilitude of anthropological field photography and other amateur snapshot practices.

A good example of this cross-fertilization between anthropology and documentary photography is the work of Tim Asch at Cape Breton, Nova Scotia, a project of rural documentation that ran for a number of years starting in 1952 (Harper 1994). Although the importance of the project was not recognized by anthropologists at the time, it is interesting because it dates from the period after World War II, when visual anthropology as a fully articulated subdiscipline emerged from a number of different visualizing skills and experiences, notably studies in visual communication, while at the same time drawing on a self-consciously photographic style to create a sense of immediacy and solidity of observation rather than an anthropological "no-style style."

Although better known as an ethnographic filmmaker, Asch had a photographic background that was rich and eclectic. He had worked with modernist photographers such as Minor White, Edward Weston, and Ansel Adams and been influenced by others such as Eugene Smith (Nordström 1994, 97). On the Cape Breton project Asch worked closely with John Collier, who at this period was shaping his ideas about photography as a research method in anthropology. Yet Collier's own inspiration came not only from anthropology but also from Roy Stryker and the work of the Farm Security Administration. [6] Stryker had employed photographers such as Dorothea Lange and Walker Evans, whose photographs of agrarian distress in the 1930s United States have become classics of the humanist and progressivist documentary canon.[7] Consequently, while the Cape Breton photographs are grounded in observational tenets of anthropology—"the little things of life" (Harper 1994, 13), which resonates with Malinowski's "imponderabilia"—they nonetheless demonstrate the classic modernist articulation of the character of the medium. The impact of ostensibly ethnographic detail rests for its effect on compositional elements (Nordström 1994).

Nevertheless, despite the potential for an extended base for photographic work in anthropology, the emergence of increasingly focused methodological volumes such as Collier's *Visual Anthropology* (1967), and continuing concerns about evidential method (Ruby 1976; Harper 1987; Larson 1981; Caldarola 1998; Grady 1991; Pauwels 1993; Simoni 1996), there appears to have been a simultaneous systemic denial of the potential of photographs to add to anthropological understanding. This systemic iconophobia is demonstrated by another book on the boundaries of anthropology and photographic practice. *Death Rituals of Rural Greece* (1982) was half ethnography, half photo-essay, and featured anthropologist Loring Danforth responding to a set of photographs by Alexander Tsiaras. The narratives of each section, interspersed with verse from funeral laments, effectively mirror one another. The authors' intention was precisely to "communicate both an intellectual and emotional response" and to "collapse the distance between Self and Other" (1982, 7). Tsiaras's photographs, in a humanistic documentary tradition, supply a sense of emotion and affect through a strong sense of personal engagement.

However, when the volume was reviewed in the anthropological journals, it was as a text. Danforth's routes through Van Gennep, Hertz, and Geertz in relationship to ritual, death, and the everyday were dissected with little or no reference to the photographs.[8] Was it that the photographs, with their strong visual geometry and humanistic documentary credentials, could not constitute an anthropological authority? That their evidential force engaged emotional responses to the subject matter rather than rational description? Or that the image itself was simply "invisible," marginalized in the intellectual debate? Maybe Geddes summed up the dilemma when reviewing another photographic book, Robert Gardner's *Gardens of War* (1968), in *American Anthropologist*: while it could be seen as "unduly subjective," he wrote, "cross-cultural interpretations however, must necessarily go beyond fact. The final test as to whether they should be regarded as merely subjective or truly insightful must be the degree of conviction they carry for the individual reader, viewer and listener" (1971, 347). We are back with questions of too many meanings and the control of evidential possibility.

The result appears to be a photography that, despite methodological struggles, was effectively marginalized, at least intellectually, in anthropological debate. Indeed, photographs had all but disappeared from serious anthropological texts by the 1960s (de Heusch quoted in Poole 2005, 690), apart from the authentication of fieldworkers' observations and scene-setting. Further, the advent of easier and more accessible film technologies offered ways of recording that appeared more fitting to the anthropological project. More importantly, the continuing distrust of academic anthropology in the visual, especially the fragmenting and reifying qualities of the still photograph, made it not merely problematic but intellectually sterile, a tool perhaps of an old anthropology that remained the delineator of surfaces, not the revealer of the deep truths of human experience.

The Power of Representation

Mead's preface to Hocking's *Principles of Visual Anthropology* (1975), lamenting the condition of the visual in the discipline of words, effectively constitutes a final statement of realist confidence and salvage concern before a radical shift in the profile of photography burst on the scene. As in other disciplines in the social sciences and humanities, the poststructuralist turn in anthropology looked at the construction of disciplinary knowledge and its associated representational practices and institutions, from fieldwork to the museum.[9] Despite the iconophobia of the discipline, debates about photography entangled with broader critiques of anthropology's occularcentrism and anxieties about vision, especially in the contexts of anthropology's collapsing scientific paradigm (Grimshaw 2001, 6–7). Photography became central in the shift from the visual as field methodology for data gathering and analysis (albeit an increasingly reflexive one) to an anthropology of visual systems. This latter, especially in attending to the socially and politically constructivist nature of imaging practices, has perhaps been photography's most signficant contribution to anthropological thinking more broadly. For concepts of abstract anthropological concern, such as ethnicity, gender, and identity, as well as the discipline's own history of colonial entanglement and self-definition, came to be explored increasingly through the prism of photography. This moment, when photography effectively became a metaphor for anthropological knowledge and its power structures, constitutes my second snapshot.

Photography and its signifying practices were the focus of an analysis of increasing theoretical sophistication and complexity in the context of a ferment of cultural and identity politics that challenged Western hegemony. Following Foucault's work on the framings of power, discipline, surveillance, and the complex politics of knowledge, it became integral to discursive regimes of truth that defined, appropriated, constructed, and objectified the subject of anthropology. While the arguments and their theoretical tools were strongly informed by literary theory, postcolonial theory, and cultural studies, the theory of photography itself provided the specific critical tools. Anthropologists engaged with not only Foucault but with a range of poststructuralist and Marxist-inspired debates. Especially influential were Tagg's constructivist approaches to photography (1988); Burgin's semiotic and psychoanalytical account (1986); photographic applications of the semiotics of Charles Peirce and the linguistic models of Saussure, most notably in the work of Roland Barthes (1977); Sekula's Foucauldian analysis of the archive and taxonomic desire (1989); and new readings of Walter Benjamin. It was the very nature of the photograph, as the mechanical and chemical trace of the body of the subject, that made it so powerful a metaphor and rhetorical force. Objectification was understood as inherent in the very stillness and fragmentation of the medium, allowing the gaze to linger, to desire, and to appropriate the subject, constructing categories of race, class, and gender, which were normalized through the transparency and discursive practices of photography itself and legitimated through anthropological concepts of race and hierarchy (Green 1984; Alloula 1986; Corbey 1988; Lalvani 1996).

The spatial and temporal ambiguities of the medium and its reifying propensities sat alongside critiques in anthropology. For instance, Fabian's (1983, 32) analysis of the visualist metaphors of anthropology and his critique of the construction of the atemporal anthropological object, resonates with Barthes's famous description of photography as the "there-then becoming here-now," reproducing to infinity that which could not be reproduced existentially (1977, 44; 1984, 4) and reinforcing the different temporalities involved in the "fleeting immediacy of the encounter and the stabilising permanency of fact" (Poole 2005, 172).

These features of photography also mapped onto theories of the gaze and of the construction of stereotype through the semiotic structure of images, especially dichotomous models of white/black, clothed/unclothed, civilized/primitive, dominant/dominated, and their associated hierarchical significations. The instability of the signifier and the infinite recodability of photographs enabled the reproduction and performance of such tropes even in the face of the inherent ambiguity of forms. Ideas such as Sontag's violent metaphors for the camera's voracious visual appropriations—hunting, shooting, taking (1979, 14–15)—became metaphors of colonial oppression, the Western gaze, and the disempowerment of the subject. The combination of capture and trace in the contexts of a specifically focused cultural politics become symbolic of the space between the collector and the collected, the photographer and the photographed, the community and the institutional structures of anthropology—the asymmetries of power and the spaces in which indigenous communities are locked, dispossessed, disenfranchised, silenced, marginalized, and appropriated (Harlan 1995, 20).

Photographs thus presented a mine of a century of disciplinary assumptions and asymmetrical power relations to be excavated. In this pose in particular, the arranged and manipulated body stood as a signifier of the power relations between "white science and black bodies" (Wallis 1995), over a wide range of material: Zealy's slave daguerreotypes, made for Louis Agassiz (Wallis 1995); the anthropometric work of Lamprey, Huxley, or, in France, Broca and Topinard; or the removal of clothing to expose the body, especially women's bodies (Peterson 2003, 124–25; Edwards 2001, 145). The racialized and sometimes pathologized body was thus made visible, laid out for somatic mapping, mathematicized for the gaze (Pinney 1992a; Green 1984, 1986; Dias 1994).[10]

It is significant that much of this debate focused on nineteenth-century and colonial imaging that had been absorbed, and indeed legitimated, as scientific data in the nineteenth century, rather than the mass of photographs produced within anthropology after about 1910. Such early images assumed the character of a political and ideological marker of the colonialized body, controlled under the appropriating gaze of the camera. Alloula, for instance, writes: "The model is a figure of the symbolic appropriation of the body (of the Algerian woman), the studio is a figure of the symbolic appropriation of space. . . . This double movement of appropriation is nothing more than the expression of violence conveyed by the colonial postcard" (1986, 21).

The concept of the ideological instrumentality of the archive was an important part of this critique. Influenced by Foucauldian works such as Alan Sekula's "The Body and the Archive" (1989) and Tagg's analysis of the instrumentality of photography (1988), the anthropological archive became a double trope of postmodern fixation, photography, and taxonomy, through which the objectified body of "the Other" was produced. The archive was analyzed as an articulation of encyclopaedic desire, knowledge production, and taxonomic certainty, reproducing dominant hierarchical values (e.g., Green 1984, 1985).

This can only be a summary of a labyrinthine and far-reaching set of interconnecting arguments. However, the strands and nuances of this position became increasingly conflated, while within the discipline the possibility of photographic representation became increasingly paralyzed. For, while they addressed the broader ideological frameworks that made certain kinds of photographic practices thinkable at any given historical moment, such critiques nonetheless slipped almost too comfortably into a series of overdetermined, reductionist, ahistorical, and reifying inter-pretations (Spyer 2001, 182).

While much of this debate was happening outside of anthropology itself, there were similar critiques from within the discipline as anthropologists engaged increasingly with the concept of the "archive," as in Corbey's exploration of African postcards (1988). Photographs were also part of the wider debates on the politics of the production of ethnographic text and ethnographic authority. For instance, both Hutnyk (1994) and Wolpert (2000) analyze Evans-Pritchard's photographs as integral to appropriating discourse practices of fieldwork and its dissemination of observation, raising more general questions about the nature of that observation and the relations for which it stood. Perhaps the most extensive and unforgiving is Faris's discussion of the cultures of imaging and imagining the Navajo people. In *The Navajo and Photography* he explores the systemic and "predatory success" (1996, 301) of the politics of appropriation that render the Navajo powerless and passive before the camera as an instrument of Western oppression.[11]

While this process, and its articulation of power structures, is indisputable and its political impact equally so, it was also a critique that denied anthropological photography, and indeed anthropology, its own shifting and critical dynamic.[12] It reductively posited all anthropological photographs and all cross-cultural photographic encounters as operating "immovably within a 'truth' that simplistically reflects a set of cultural and political dispositions held by the makers of those images" (Pinney and Peterson 2003, 2). One of the first volumes to explore this was *Anthropology and Photography* (Edwards 1992). Perhaps I am not the right person to be discussing the legacy of this volume, aimed at anthropological and non-anthropological readers alike, which attempted to give a critical framing of practice, history, and institutional structures articulated through short case studies of specific images as historical statements, framed by a series of methodological and theoretical essays. While not unproblematic (I now feel some of the argument was overdetermined in the manner I have just outlined), the volume nonetheless opened up a range of debate about the imaging history of anthropology, its strategies, and its relevance to contemporary anthropological concerns.

While profoundly informed by the debates outlined here, anthropologists working on photography increasingly challenged the reductive and often presentist readings and instead explored photographs as "a productive site for rethinking the particular forms of presence, uncertainty and contingency that characterizes both ethnographic and visual accounts of the world" (Poole 2005, 159). They approached the subject matter as a culture of imaging that itself could be explored anthropologically, complicating the asymmetries of power, the processes of stereotyping, objectification, and appropriation (see, e.g., Poignant 1992a, 1992b; Pinney 1997; Edwards 2001; Jacknis 1984; Scherer 1988), to "create whole new arenas of inquiry" (Scherer 1995, 201).[13]

A further concern about reductive analyses was their denial of agency to the Other. There was a very real sense in which homogenizing models of overt power relations, while recognizing these tropes and ideological formations, did not destabilize or displace them but merely reproduced the power relations they were intended to critique.[14] The Other, the photographic subject rendered as Object, remained powerless, passive, voiceless, and objectified. Such an analytical position allowed little space for an indigenous voice, for while it undoubtedly forwarded a form of radical politics, it also "disempower[ed] tribal people who see their ancestors in these photographs, oversimplifying specific and often complex human relations, or simply shutting down discussion" (Dubin 1999, 71).

By the mid-1990s Foucaultian approaches to anthropological photography were looking "hopelessly bleak, a vision of total social control in which a mysterious force, 'power,' holds absolute sway" (Banks 2001, 112). To counter this, anthropologists engaged in a trenchant critique and reappraisal that embraced the potential of the new critical reflexivity and multivocality in order to excavate the complex historical relations from which were constituted photographic encounters (Poole 1997; Pinney 1997). Such positions had begun to emerge in *Anthropology and Photography*, especially the essays by Salmond, Binney, and Hamouda (1992), and in work on indigenous responses to photographs, such as, *Partial Recall* (Lippard 1992), which presented a series of Native American readings of photographs.

The late 1980s and 1990s, in particular, saw the maturing of a range of ethnographies. There were detailed studies of the image worlds and work of specific anthropologists, for instance, Boas (Jacknis 1984), Baldwin Spencer (Walker and Vanderwal 1982),[15] Mooney (Jacknis 1992), Malinowski (Young 1998), Haddon and the Torres Strait expedition (Edwards 1998), and Mead and Bateson (Jackinis 1988; Sullivan 1992). Expeditions such as the 1927 Denver African expedition to Namibia (Gordon 1997) and the Jesup North Pacific expedition of 1897–1902 (Kendall, Ross-Miller, and Mathé 1997) were explored as cultures entities. There were also regional studies such as Pinney's *Camera Indica* (1997), which explored continuities, contestations, and dreamworlds around photography in India; an examination a wide range of colonial imaging and its legacy in Namibia (Hartmann, Silvester, and Hayes 1998); and detailed analysis of the complex cross-cultural photographic dynamics between missionaries and local elites in the Cameroon Grassfields (Geary 1988). These were supplemented by studies of institutional and collecting practices, both generally (Edwards 2001) and in specific institutions, such as the Peabody Museum, Harvard (Banta and Hinsley1986), the Royal Anthropological Institute, London (Poignant 1992a), and the Musée de l'Homme (Dias 1994).[16]

What emerged was a more complex reading of photographic dynamics in cross-cultural encounters. Power was certainly a central element, but its workings emerged as discursively complex. Photographs were not merely the overt instruments of surveillance, discipline, and political control but sites of intersecting and contested histories, intentions, and inscriptions. Even the production of the most overtly oppressive of images, anthropometric photographs, revealed points of fracture and resistance, which worked to restore the humanity of the subject (Edwards 2001, 144–47). In closing the distance between the viewer and the objectified body, the oppressive nature of such imaging practice was brought into even sharper focus.

These studies constituted a dense, critical, theoretically weighted base of historical ethnographies that addressed the question "What vision of the anthropological project animates the work of particular individuals?" (Grimshaw 2001, 7). Collectively they not only mapped the contexts of the photograph in detail but complicated the dominant models of power relations between observer and observed, self and other, subject and object, and thus the problematics of transparency and truth, which had characterized much of the postcolonial and poststructuralist writing on photography.

An influential model to emerge from this was Deborah Poole's "visual economy," developed in relation to the imaging traditions, assumptions, and performances of photographs of and in the Peruvian Andes. Poole argued that photographs operate in political, economic, and social matrices that are not reducible to semiotic codes alone; rather, one must consider the whole pattern of their production, circulation, consumption, possession, and preservation, encompassing both the broad modes of production and the microlevels of individual usage (1997, 9–13). While still working within a broad Foucauldian frame, of the "mundane practices of inscription, registration and inspection" and their "representational machineries" (Poole 1997, 15), the model pointed to the fluidity of images and the social relations that gave them meaning.

Such an approach was linked conceptually with work in material culture studies on the sociability of objects, especially that of Appadurai

(1986) and Kopytoff (1986) on the social biography of objects. This work argued that objects could not be understood as having stable identities and meanings but rather that they assumed and accrued meaning as they moved through different interpretative spaces. Whatever its constraints, this model has proved especially relevant for photography, with its multiple originals, various performances, and unstable, context-dependent signifiers. For instance, Morton (2005) discusses the transformation of Evans-Pritchard's photographs from field to publication, complicating ideas of field relations and authority. While this model resonates with the recodability of the image, it also displays a concern for the possibility of materially generated meaning. Pinney's *Camera Indica* (1997), for instance, tracked photography across the intersecting cultural and historical landscapes of India. Linking historical and contemporary practices in terms of both continuity and contestation, he argues for the transformation of the medium through three different historical moments: the colonial, the establishment of the modern nation-state of India, and the contemporary everyday practices of imaginative engagement with photography. While coming from a strong and eclectic theoretical base, these studies overall increasingly characterized photography not as an abstract discourse but as situated in real, materially constituted encounters between people in space and time.

The density, and sometimes nearly paralyzing nature, of debate on the politics of representation and the symbolic status of photography in cross-cultural relations has, it can be argued, enabled it to make a substantial contribution to theoretical thinking within anthropology. Emerging from the refigured politics of knowledge as it affected the relationship between anthropology and photography, it is part of a larger shift in the production of knowledge that is "simultaneously collaborative, critical, and interventionist" (Poole 2005, 170). The way in which photographs have become very real sites of contestation and symbols of the yawning void in power relations, of the control of history and voice and thus of power in the world, particularly among peoples subjected to settler colonialism, is a register of their significance beyond the merely representational. Anthropological responses to this constitute some of the most significant current work in visual anthropology.

Reexperiencing and Repositioning

My third "snapshot" is therefore of two contemporary strands that have their roots in the debates just discussed. First, I look at refigured questions

6.4   Cambridge Torres Strait expedition members. Reproduced by permission of University of Cambridge Museum of Archaeology and Anthropology (N.23035.ACH2).

and methodologies that reengaged with anthropology's historical deposits and made them the focus of contemporary field research.[17] Second, I explore the ethnography of photographic practice as it has recently emerged within visual anthropology. The two strands are linked conceptually in that not only are both concerned with voice and agency, but both address culturally specific usages of photographs in everyday life.

First, I am going to consider the reassessment of colonial practices, cross-cultural relations, and multiple agencies as they are played out through photographs and photography. In detailed analyses of cross-cultural encounters, some of the visual deposits of anthropology's history begin to take on a different complexion (figure 6.4).

While there is a danger that a simplistic overvalorization of this approach elides the very real asymmetries of power relations and the power of interpretation and re-presentation, nevertheless the intellectual and political frameworks of such research stress the multivalency of photographs and the histories inscribed within them. Poignant, for instance, demonstrated how, even in a situation of political appropriation and economic control, the arrangement of Aboriginal subjects in a group photograph from the 1880s, taken to publicize their music hall act, reflects their kin relations, not an order imposed by the photographer (1992a, 58). Scherer (2006) has explored the cross-cultural relations of a photographic studio in Idaho that was frequented by people from the local Shoshone-Bannock reservation at Fort Hall.

While the resulting images might be read as stereotypes, and have been used as such, they also reveal the extent to which active commissioning of images was integral to the negotiation of local indigenous identities. Lydon, in examining the imaging of Coranderrk station in Victoria, Australia, demonstrates how, through an understanding of the role of images in colonial society, Aboriginal people attempted to exert influence on representational practice within the complex and shifting relations of the colonial situation (2005). What all these studies demonstrate is the possibility of excavating the dialogic space of photography and thus complicating the view of cross-cultural relations, indigenous agency, and the density of photographic inscription.

Much of this work is now happening collaboratively and involves both the reengagement with historical material in contemporary situations and the production of new material in collaborative and community projects (e.g., Hubbard 1994; Rohde 1998; Kratz 2002). Importantly, indigenous communities have reappropriated, reengaged with, and effectively reauthored anthropological photographs, as photographs themselves have become symptomatic and symbolic of people's desire to control their own histories and their own destinies (e.g., Harlan 1995, 1998; Rickard 1995; Tsinhnahjinnie 1998; Hill 1998; Vizenor 1998; Chaat Smith 1992; Aird 1993, 2003):

It was a beautiful day when the scales fell from my eyes and I first encountered photographic sovereignty. A beautiful day when I decided that I would take responsibility to reinterpret images of Native peoples. My mind was ready, primed with stories of survival. My views of these images are aboriginally based—an indigenous perspective—not a scientific Godly order, but philosophically Native. (Tsinhnahjinnie 1998, 42)

"Photographic sovereignty" is a concept that has been developed, especially in the Native American context, to define the right to reclaim photographs and to tell one's own history (Rickard 1995; Tsinnahjinnie 1998). It is in these contexts that the random inclusiveness of photographs, and their recodability, provides alternative routes for making meaning. Visual reappropriation and reengagement is, in many ways, about finding a present for historical photographs, realizing their "potential to seed a number of narratives" (Poignant 1994–1995, 55) through which to make sense of that past and make it fulfill the needs of the present.

As Binney and Chaplin (1991) have demonstrated in writing about the response to photographs in the Tuhoe Maori community at Urewera, photographs confirmed and cohered a reality that lived in individual experience but had been suppressed in colonial historiography, thus enabling the active articulation of those histories.

Thus "looking past" the colonial and scientific surface of the photograph could allow the articulation of multiple pasts (Pinney and Peterson 2003, 4–5; Aird 2003, 25). "The dehumanizing aspect of portrait photographs as mere inventory is undermined by the irreducible presence of a self" (Lippard 1992, 16). Photographs that started as anthropological or colonial documents become family or clan histories. However painful those histories may be,

images intended to refer to issues of race and acculturation, with all the implications of colonial control these interests implied, could be used today to address not only the nature of revisionist history but also the need . . . to articulate to themselves their experiences of the past and, ultimately, to speak to their children about the strength of their community. (Brown and Peers 2006, 5–6)

The term "visual repatriation" has been used increasingly for such collaborative and restitutive agendas involving anthropologists (Fienup-Riordan 1998; Brown and Peers 2006, 101–3). Perhaps the fullest working out by to date is by Peers and Brown (2006), who worked with Kainai Nation (Alberta, Canada) to facilitate access and historical reengagement with photographs taken by anthropologist Beatrice Blackwood in the 1920s. The project was set up as a collaboration with a wide range of people, from tribal elders to schoolchildren, the anthropologists working under the community's guidance and toward its goals, "reorient[ing] their work to facilitate and allow community input into research design and the research process itself" (Brown and Peers 2006, 101) (figure 6.5).

While such research relations increasingly typify anthropological work, they take the relation between anthropology and photography beyond the merely reflexive into a new collaborative order. This has substantial methodological implications, not only reshaping the negotiation of field access and the establishment of joint research protocols but, in visual anthropology, refiguring of the idea of photo-elicitation. Collier, in his classic methodological account, acknowledged a dialogic quality to the photographic encounter—it afforded a "gratifying sense of self-expression" (1967, 48). However, it was constituted as a one-way flow of information, from the subject to the ethnographer, with the aim of enhancing the latter's understanding (see Edwards 2004, 87–88). Refig-

6.5　Rosie Red Crow, Kainai Nation, Alberta, Canada, looking at photographs. Photo: Alison
Brown, November 21, 2001.

ured, the process of "elicitation" constitutes a shift in power relations
and anthropological authority, wherein the anthropologist lets go of
photographic meanings in the traditional forensic, or even structured
semiotic, sense. The anthropological focus becomes, instead, the way in
which the photographs assume their own dynamics of sociability within
communities. For as Niessen has argued, such a position also challenges
ethnographic authority in the way I discussed in the first snapshot, for
this expectation of photographic control "is an aspect of our own mythology about who we are in relation to 'the other.' Photographs do not
perpetuate this relationship but are manipulated in its service and as such
act as an extension of ethnographic authority" (1991, 429). Conversely
work on the sociability of photographs has raised questions about the
photograph as an historical or cultural source within an environment of
intersecting historical forms and traditions. What, for instance, is the link

between the visual and the oral? What is the role of photographs in the processes through which history, memory, and identity are reproduced and transmitted?

Nonetheless, these are not uncontested practices. They constitute complex and sometimes contradictory contexts within communities, as narratives inflected with age, gender, or lineage, for instance, are woven with and around photographs. As Niessen found, using photographs of museum textiles in photo-elicitation in Sumatra, photographs brought into focus the gendered relations of history telling (1991, 421), as well as tensions between the community and the anthropologist. Similarly, Bell (2004, 115) and Poignant (1992b, 73) report on how photographs became absorbed and controlled through local social structures, reflecting the right to "tell stories."

Yet in such cases, it is precisely the shape of such social dynamics and the flow of images within them that is anthropologically revealing. This reflexive turn, and questions of voice and the politics of representational practices, have also had an impact on field practice, especially in relation to image ethics. Ethical issues are central not only in the making of images, around culturally specific ideas of private and public space, for instance (Michaels 1991; Kratz 2002; Gross, Katz, and Ruby 1988, 2003), but in the institutional practices around images. The realization that the family photographs of many peoples are effectively locked away in anthropology's institutions (Dubin 1999, 72) has had a profound effect on practices about ownership of and access to images, on rights regarding knowledge, and on ideas of evidence and value (Holman 1996; Powers 1996; Isaac 2007; Peterson 2003; Brown 2003; Edwards 2004). This has been perhaps most marked in North America and Australia, where indigenous and traditionally "subject" people of anthropology have reclaimed images of anthropology's past as their own history and demanded an institutional voice in their control, management, and dissemination. Images that anthropologists forty years ago would have assumed a right to use with impunity to demonstrate their ethnography, are now restricted, requiring negotiation and permissions from the communities involved, as they reclaim the cultural knowledge inscribed in photographs (Peterson 2003). For instance, the Hopi "feel they have to adopt a political position against photography" to protect their privacy (Fredericks, quoted in Lippard 1992, 22) but also as a local position expressing disquiet about the broader disposition of cultural heritage (Brown 2003, 15).

Brown and Peers's project, for one, necessitated a shift in museum policy to enable Kaiani people to use collected images free of legalistic encumbrances (2006, 175–94). In New Zealand in 2001, a group of Maori activists blocked the sale of three hundred rare nineteenth-century photographs of Maori people, claiming them as *taonga* (cultural treasure). Their concern was not simply with the images, but with the *mauri* (life force) materially invested within the photographic trace, which was threatened with dissipation through the use and reproduction of the photographs (Dudding 2003).

In Australia, reparations for the Stolen Generation have included a radical shift in the accessibility of archives and in the way anthropological photographs can be engaged with by both indigenous peoples and anthropologists (Fourmile 1990; Smallacombe 1999; Peterson 2003; Stanton 2004). These shifts respond not only to the sensitivities of Aboriginal people over access to their images but to debates around photography as a tool to substantiate and communicate cultural claims on issues such as land rights, housing, and education, as well as to revive and maintain cultural practices (Stanton 2004, 150).

This brings us to my second strand, the ethnography of photographic practices. If engagement with the refigured historical image suggests that the Western theoretical circumscriptions of visual history are too narrow to accommodate what is actually emerging from field studies, ethnographies of photographic practice in relation to images made by and for people in Kenya, Peru, or Malaysia, for instance, are pointing the same way. Pinney and Peterson's volume *Photography's Other Histories* (2003), as its title suggests, attempts to move the critical debate on photography away from the dominant Euro-American model to look at the way in which the understanding of photographic practices in other cultural spaces might illuminate and rebalance understanding of the medium. It includes essays on photography and memory practices by Dreissens and Aird, and reprints Sprague's foundational 1978 paper "How the Yoruba See Themselves." Although still entrenched in two key framings of Western analysis, the "vernacular" (in relation to what, one might ask?) and the "modern," the book reveals as profoundly ethnocentric the canons of photographic theory and its classic tropes, which were so influential in the 1970s and 1980s. It argues also that global and local photographic practices have necessarily been understood in terms of simplistic models of the absorption of a technology and advocates instead an understanding that embraces not only culturally specific articulations of the nature of the photograph but its connection with the specifics of emotion, imagination, history, and politics.

It raises questions, for example, about the nature of the indexical trace and, for instance, material intervention and additive practices at the surface of the image in relation to concepts of realistic representation in

6.6   Studio interior, New Millennium Image Hunters, Brikama. Photo: Liam Buckley, 2000.

India (Pinney 1997, 2004). It raises questions too about photography's relation with other cultural practices, such as Gambian studio photography, that relate directly to the aesthetic discourse of the social surface and particularly the molding and tailoring, specifically cutting, of that surface: "the sound of the shutter making its slice sounds . . . like the snip of scissors, cutting out people, clarifying their edges, and making them cutting edge. Cameras, in The Gambia, are scissors for seeing" (Buckley 2000–2001, 72) (figure 6.6).

There are studies of the relations between migrant identities and the fleeting world of the photographic studio on the Mombassa dockside in Kenya (Behrend 2000), in middle-class Senegal (Mustafa 2002), in the Fijian Indian diaspora (Chandra 2000), in the memorializing albums of AIDS victims in Uganda (Vokes 2008); of photography, materiality, and the coeval ancestor in Papua New Guinea (Halvaksz 2008) or, in that same country, photography and disco culture (Hirsch 2004). Other studies have looked specifically at the interpenetration of photography, materiality, and memory in the Solomon Islands, (Wright 2004) or the use of historical and contemporary photographs in Australian Aboriginal communities (Poignant 1992b, 1996; MacDonald 2003; Smith 2003). *Visual Anthropology* devoted a whole issue to studio practices in Africa, including case studies from Côte d'Ivoire, Ghana, and Uganda (Behrend and Werner 2001); another issue was dedicated to changing practices of wedding photography in Southeast Asia (Cheung 2005), and yet another explored interrelated and affective practices of photography and the spirit cross-culturally (Smith and Vokes 2008).[18]

What these detailed ethnographies of photographic practice have in common is an explication of local photographic practices, specific social expectations of the medium, and the exploration of indigenously generated aesthetic and social categories in and of themselves, which cannot be reduced to a mimicking of Western practice or an asymmetrical absorption of Western technologies. While the social functions to which photographs are put may be similar in most parts of the world—expression, identity, remembrance—the cultural premises upon which these functions are built are profoundly different. They require new sets of analytical and conceptual tools to liberate photographic thinking from the demands of a Western canon, and at the same time to allow practices their own identities. They raise questions about what a photograph, as an image and as a material object, actually *is*, challenging assumptions about the nature of realism, the perception of the value of the indexicality, authorship, pose, and "portrait"; the role of photographs in negotiating identities and presentation of the self to the camera; the material affects of photographs; and the social expectation of the medium and the kinds of relations with the past for which it stands—concerns that cannot necessarily be accommodated within a Benjaminesque configuration of photography/past/memory (Poignant 1992b; Wright 2007).

An important strand of these reformulations is the recent emergence of a more material and sensory approach to thinking about photographs in anthropology—a phenomenological turn that privileges the experiential rather than the semiotic (Pinney 2004; Wright 2004; Edwards 2006). For instance, working with photographs in an Aborignal community in Queensland, Smith has argued that through their indexicality and reproducible form, photographs can appear as "distributed objects," which in turn can be seen as initiating and acting on social relations. Photographs are a form of extended personhood in that they constitute a sum of relations over time. In this, "the effect of images is not simply symbolic or the result of social relations"; rather, images "can themselves imitate and act in social relations" (Smith 2003, 11). While the specifics of such relations are profoundly cultural, Smith's argument appears indicative of a broader pattern that is emerging through detailed ethnographies.

Also concerned with materiality and "affect," Pinney has coined the term "corpothetics" to refer to "the sensory embrace of images, the bodily engagement that most people . . . have with artworks" (2001, 158). His intent is to offer "a critique of conventional approaches to aesthetics and argue for a notion of corpothetics—embodied corporeal aesthetics—as opposed to 'disinterested' representation which over-cerebralises and textualizes the image" (2004, 8). But his argument can also stand as a critique of an approach couched solely in the visual semiotics or technological determinates of the photograph or the film, an approach that separates visual anthropology from its correlates, such as material culture studies and anthropology of the senses. Such ideas are having a profound effect on the way anthropologists write about visual systems and photography. For instance, Harris (2004) has demonstrated the way in which the bodily engagement with photographs in Tibet is used as a form of political resistance under Chinese rule. Buckley (2006, 62) has explored the relation between body and photograph, not in terms of gaze and surveillance, but as a form of embrace, a visceral sense of being "cherished" and a sense of "elegance" that can be linked to civic and political identities in the modern nation-state of the Gambia.

The anthropological attention given to different cultural parameters of the production and use of photographs has revealed again the inadequacy of the dominant Western models of photographic analyses, with their stress on semiotic structures and their linguistic translation (Pinney 2001; Edwards 2006; Wright 2007). These new critical approaches emerge not only from the concerns with the occularcentricism that have haunted anthropology but from an increasingly strongly articulated sense, coming out of material culture studies, that even as an anthropologically informed understanding of photographic practices expands, photographic meaning cannot necessarily be explained through the visual alone.

A Tentative Conclusion

The examples I have cited, and there a many others, demonstrate the claim that I made at the beginning of this essay, that work with photographs is becoming a fruitful route through which to explore other areas of theoretical disciplinary concerns. As such it can be said to be making a substantive and conscious contribution to the production of anthropological knowledge in a way that has not, perhaps, been experienced since the positivist certainties of the late nineteenth century. The potential for an expanded theory of photography that extends or even destabilizes the theoretical canon, and at the same time connects to major anthropological concerns such as memory, identity, ethnicity, nationalism, and globalization, is one of the most exciting possibilities for visual anthropology today.

This must not be read as a triumphalist progress toward an enlightened reading of images, a march toward some representational nirvana, or a teleological unfolding of visual anthropological method. Elements of modern practice with photographs—the sharing of images, collaborations between anthropologists and local people, the use of photography in establishing social relations in the field[19]—are evident already in the late nineteenth century, just as there remain traces of nineteenth-century attitudes in today's institutional structures. Further, in many ways, while the publication of photographs as integral to ethnographic analysis remains more limited than it should be, work on photography is becoming more diffuse and dispersed across the anthropological field, no longer confined within visual anthropology. It is becoming one methodological and theoretical strand or one element of social practice, informing and informed by a broader ethnography. One finds, for instance, the use of photographs to excavate the relations between Dutch colonialists and local servants in Dutch East Indies (Stoler and Strassler 2000), a detailed forensic analysis of missionary photographs as integral to a study of ritual change in northern Cameroon (Fardon 2006), and a radical phenomenological analysis of photographs in a cult of Buddhist meditation on corporeal decay in Thailand (Klima 2002). Such work indicates not the disintegrating focus of photography within visual anthropology but rather its centrality as a theoretical and discursive prism. It is the sheer ubiquity of photography and photographs, their global reach, their mass circulation and explosion into the blanket visuality of the digital age, yet their quiet, largely unremarked, banal qualities in terms of everyday experience and material practices that makes them so potent as a focus of anthropological investigation (Spyer 2001, 181).

Further, while new political emphases might emerge highlighting different readings of photographs and different dynamic foci in anthropology, the problematic of the uncontrollable semiotic energy and institutionalized power relations that embed photographs and their historical deposits remain a contested space. The shifts that I have presented— rather than being absolute or irreversible paradigm shifts in a Kuhnian sense—should be seen as the opening up of layered meanings, a process that will surely continue. Photographs will always be used to great effect as field records, as sites of cross-cultural social interaction, as sources for analysis, as objects of study, and as visual and sensory systems that raise key anthropological questions. Yet photography and photographs will also remain problematic in anthropology. In many ways this is precisely why they can contribute to the debate. Maybe they are the sand in the anthropological oyster—they become a metaphor for the whole project, standing in for the fluid, dynamic, unpredictable confusion and creativity of human relations.

Notes

1. I do this to keep some sort of frame on this part of the story—a massive, messy, and sprawling domain of the emerging discipline. Other grids, such as intentionality, subjectivity, or selectivity, could equally well have been used.
2. Mead and Bateson shot over twenty-five thousand still photographs and twenty-two thousand feet of film. Despite Mead's photographic experience in her earlier fieldwork in Samoa, Bateson took most of the pictures, devised the documentation methods for them, and undertook most of the analysis (Jacknis 1988, 161–62).
3. I am grateful to Chris Morton for discussing this image with me. I term the image's style "no-style" because whatever the parameters of objectivity, stylistic nullity is, of course, impossible; the articulation of a lack of mediation and stylistic suppression are unavoidably styles in themselves.
4. This is admirably demonstrated in two key papers on anthropological photography that appeared in the pages of the *Journal of the Anthropological Institute* in 1893 and 1896, respectively. Im Thurn, drawing on his experience of British Guiana, argued that in addition to the photographs for anthropometric reference, more naturalistic or spontaneous photographs of people "as living beings" should be taken (1893, 184; Tayler 1992). Conversely, M. V. Portman, a colonial administrator and ethnographer in the Andaman Islands, argued that scientific knowledge could be controlled only when carefully posed photographs that demonstrated observed fact (for instance, the making of an adze) provided primary evidence (1896, 76).
5. The boundary between anthropology and arts practice is beyond the scope of this paper, but see, e.g., Schneider and Wright (2006) and Schneider (this volume).
6. Collier dedicated *Visual Anthropology* (1967) to Stryker.
7. Significantly, the work of the Farm Security Administration started at precisely the same time as Mead and Bateson were in working in Bali (Larson 1993, 15).
8. For instance James M. Redfield *American Ethnologist* 1984 (1193): 617–18; Ruth Gruber Fredman in *Anthropological Quarterly* 1983 56 (4): 119–200, who described the "touching photos" and a "coda to the text." Only Peter

Metcalf in *American Anthropologist* 1984 88(1):208 engages with the photographs which "upstage the text."

9. For a useful summary of the broader politics of representation in relation to photographs see Kratz 2002, 219–23.

10. Particular analytical focus was given to the anthropometric images produced in early anthropology, the most extreme and dehumanizing form of pose and scientific control. Outside anthropology in particular, anthropometric photography came to stand for all forms of anthropological imaging regardless of the specific historicities of the photographic encounter. The photographs made to demonstrate John Lamprey's anthropometric system, published in the *Journal of the Ethnological Society* (1869), for instance, have become signature images for all anthropological photography over a hundred-year period in visual culture studies and have been reproduced endlessly (see, e.g., Green 1984, 34; Sturken and Cartwright 2001, 285; Ryan 1997, 150; S. Edwards 2006, 25).

11. For a review that highlights the methodological problems in this approach see Jay Ruby, *Journal of the Royal Anthropological Institute* 4, no. 2 (1998): 369–70.

12. As Pink has pointed out, many of these discussions of anthropological imaging entail a "disregard [for] any work that has been done since 1942" (the date of Mead and Bateson's publication) (2003, 185) and hence a failure to situate anthropological work either historically or theoretically, or to engage with much of the critical work coming out of anthropology itself.

13. The significance of this departure is marked by the inclusion of a review essay on the subject by Scherer in the second edition of *Principles of Visual Anthropology* (Hockings 1995).

14. See, e.g., Mieke Bal's critique of Corbey (1996, 195–96).

15. A new edition, with greatly extended analytical content, appeared as Batty, Allen, and Morton 2005.

16. High-profile exhibitions such as *From Site to Sight* (Banta and Hinsley 1986), *Observers of Man* (Poignant 1990), and *Der Geraubte Schatten* (Theye 1989) also raised critical awareness of anthropology's photographic legacy.

17. It should be noted that research increasingly brought together the archive and the field. See, e.g., Pinney 1997; Wright 2004; Bell 2004; and Geismar, 2010.

18. There are three notable ethnographic films on the social practices of photography: David MacDougall's *Photowallahs* (1991) explores the many layers of photographic engagement in a north Indian hill town (see also MacDougall 1992b), Tobias Wendl and Nancy de Plessis's *Future Remembrance* (1998) examines photographic studio practice in Ghana in relation to other memorializing graphic practices, and Judith MacDougall's *The Art of Regret* (2006) focuses on photographic practices in China.

19. For instance, the complex cross-cultural social relations of photography in the Cambridge Torres Strait expedition, 1898 (see Edwards 1998).

SEVEN

Ethnographic Film

MATTHEW DURINGTON AND JAY RUBY

This essay will take a historical and critical approach to ethnographic film, ethnographic filmmakers, and the relevant literature. As some people regard visual
anthropology as nothing more than ethnographic film, it is essential to place
this genre of film within its proper context. Questions of definition, the place of
professional filmmakers who are not anthropologists, and the relation of ethnographic film to sociocultural anthropology must all be discussed. In addition to
reviewing the major films that have evolved into the established canon, a critical
discussion of the literature will be undertaken.

This essay is an attempt to provide a condensed critical overview of the field. We discuss a select number of films and
their makers, examine the relevant literature, grapple with
questions associated with defining ethnographic film, and
discuss the institutional support that has evolved. We conclude by challenging the popular assumption that anthropological uses of film are confined to its being a research
tool or a teaching aid and speculate on what the future of
ethnographic film might look like.

For some, visual anthropology is simply a fancy term for
ethnographic film. Indeed, writers from Hockings (1975/
2003) to Fadwa El Guindi (2004) hold that position. As can
be seen in the introduction to this book, we regard visual anthropology as an umbrella concept that encompasses all aspects of visible and pictorial culture, with ethnographic film
as merely one part of a larger whole. (In this essay we shall
use the term "film" to stand for all varieties of motion picture media—16-millimeter film, videotape, etc.)

Scholarly literature in anthropology that addresses ethnographic film is predominantly concerned with the assumed dilemmas in balancing science and art; questions of accuracy, fairness, and objectivity; the appropriateness of the conventions of documentary realism; the relation between texts and ethnographic film; films as an adjunct to teaching; and collaborations between filmmakers and anthropologists. Particular ethnographic films have also become touchstones to engage theory (Taylor 1994).

Film scholars such as Trinh T. Minh-ha (1986), Rony (1996), and Nichols (1993) have been critical of ethnographic films and cultural anthropology in general as having a sordid past and being associated with colonialism. Their criticism has had an impact on postmodernists and cultural studies scholars while providing entrée for a number of films to be positioned as "ethnographic" despite having no anthropological intent. As their critiques suffer from a serious lack of knowledge of both ethnographic film and cultural anthropology, few anthropologists take them seriously (Ruby 2000b).

While acknowledging the importance of film to archaeology and biological anthropology (particularly primate studies), we only explore the materials that are most germane to the understanding of the role film has played in cultural anthropology (social anthropology, ethnology, and ethnography). While recognizing that ethnographic films are being made all over the world, our emphasis here is on films produced in the United States, United Kingdom, France, Australia (Bryson 2002), and Germany. We look forward to the publication of articles and books about activities in Latin America, Asia, and other places.

The Conundrum of a Definition

It is probably best not to try to define ethnographic films. In the broadest sense, most films are ethnographic—that is, if we take "ethnographic" to mean "about people." And even those that are about, say, clouds or lizards or gravity are made by people and therefore say something about the culture of the individuals who made them (and use them). (Heider 1976/2006, 6)

As scholars tend to nitpick about the parameters of a field, the exact boundaries of what constitutes an ethnographic film have been argued about for as long as the genre has been recognized. An examination of which films are included in Heider's foundational *Films for Anthropological Teaching* (Heider and Hermer 1995), which are selected for review in scholarly journals like the *American Anthropologist*, and which are screened at the many "ethnographic film" festivals, such as that sponsored by the Royal Anthropological Institute, suggests that traditionally an ethnographic film is regarded as a documentary that explores some aspect of a culture, most commonly a non-Western one. "Ethnographic" is used in a very broad sense, as a generalized term for exotic cultures, and not in the way that anthropologists tend to use it. Anthropologists have long ago abandoned the notion that they must confine themselves to the "exotic other." Some ethnographic filmmakers have not made that adjustment, perhaps due to the fact that many lack formal training in anthropology. In fact, many of the films found in the abovementioned sources are produced without the benefit of any professional anthropologist at all. Moreover, it is frequently assumed that the sole purpose of these films is as audiovisual aids to teaching that need to be accompanied with text to be fully effective (Heider 1976/2006; Asch 1972) or as television films designed to popularize anthropology. In addition, there seems to be some confusion about whether or not any film, fiction or nonfiction, that is used in a course about cultural anthropology should be considered an ethnographic film, as suggested by the Heider quotation above. While we argue that film may have the potential to become a powerful tool for anthropological expression, the majority of the literature seems to dwell solely on its potential for research and teaching.

The definition employed in this essay is one based upon usage. It is not without some debate. There is a continuum of opinion, from the arguments of scholars like Heider (1976/2006) that all films can be considered ethnographic to Ruby's contention that only films made by professional anthropologists about their field research should be called ethnographic (2000b). While the former relies on content as the defining characteristic, the latter uses production, intention, or method to define a film as ethnographic. The tension between these two extremes has marked an active and productive debate about the concept for some time. As this essay is designed to examine the field as broadly defined, we will take no position in this debate but rather seek to review the corpus of work that is most commonly understood as being an ethnographic film.

Research film

In October 1897 Messter's first German cinema catalogue appeared, illustrated with no less than 115 pages. . . . By its means historical events can henceforth be preserved just as they happen and brought to view again not only now but also for the benefit of future generations . . . [revealing] the lives and customs of the most distant primitives and tribes of savages. (Ceram 1965, 250)

Since the invention of a technology that records images, there has been a belief that such recordings make it possible for scholars to obtain researchable evidence that can be taken back to their labs for analysis and shared with other scholars who were not in the field with them. First it was still photography that held an attraction (Serres 1845), then, a half century later, the motion picture. Insofar as the assumed goal of social science research was then to obtain "objective data," these media appeared to offer unimpeachable evidence. In 1955 Michaelis outlined the idea and need for research film and an archive to preserve it and make it accessible to scholars.

The first attempt to record researchable human behavior was accomplished by French anthropologist Félix-Louis Regnault at a Paris exposition in 1896 (Regnault 1900; Rony 1996), followed in 1897 by Haddon's Torres Straits expedition (Griffiths 1998). Many others followed, including Austrian anthropologist Rudolf Poch, who shot research footage during his 1904–1906 expedition to German, British, and Dutch New Guinea and to New South Wales (Poch 1907; Griffiths 1998, 366). Franz Boas, a father figure in US anthropology and mentor to Margaret Mead, took film footage of dance and body movement in Alaska in the 1930s but died before completing his analysis (Ruby 1980b). Margaret Mead and Gregory Bateson's well-known Balinese research in the 1930s resulted in a series of films, such as *Karba's First Years*, that were released for others to study—the goal of all research film projects but one that has seldom been accomplished (Jacknis 1987). Influenced by Mead, Ray Birdwhistell, in the 1950s, developed kinesics, a method for exploring the cultural basis of body movement that was dependent upon filmed records (1970). Similarly, Edward Hall's study of the social uses of space—proxemics—required filmed behavior for analysis (Hall 1980). E. Richard Sorenson (1967), another student of Mead, produced footage of a New Guinea group that was the basis of his dissertation. He later worked with D. Carlton Gajdusek at the National Institutes of Neurological Diseases and Blindness to establish the first archive devoted to ethnographic film in the United States. It was later moved to the Smithsonian Institution, where Sorenson became the leading advocate in the US for research film before he left scholarly studies (see Edwards and Farnell, this volume).

For researchable footage to fulfill its potential it has to be accessible to other scholars, hence the development of archives was essential. The oldest and most extensive is found at the *Encyclopedia Cinematographica* at the Institute for Scientific Film (Insitut für den Wissenschäftlichen Film; IWF) (Fuchs 1988; Taureg 1983). IWF, which not only constructed an extensive research archive but regularly allowed its staff go into the field to acquire more footage, closed in 2009. Founded in 1975, the Smithsonian's Human Studies Film Archive serves a function similar to that of IWF.[1] Similar film archives exist in a number of European countries, primarily for the preservation of "folk cultural habits" such as dances and handicrafts. Many of these archives are now utilized by members of the groups filmed historically to access the forms of traditional culture documented in the past, as depicted in Glass's *In Search of the Hamat'sa: A Tale of Headhunting* (2004).

The concept of research film was originally based upon the positivist notion that film can objectively record human behavior and will thus aid the historic goal of anthropology—the objective study of humankind. Regnault articulated this approach as early as 1900:

Only cinema provides objective documents in abundance; thanks to cinema, the anthropologist can, today, collect the life of all peoples; he will possess in his drawers all the special acts of different races. He will be able to thus have contact at the same time with a great number of peoples. He will study, when it pleases him, the series of movements that man executes for squatting, climbing trees, seizing and handling objects with his feet, etc. He will be present at feasts, at battles, at religious and civil ceremonies, at different ways of trading, eating, relaxing. (Regnault 1923, 680–81; translated by Rony 1996, 48)

There have, however, been few publications based upon the analysis of filmed behavior. Sorenson's 1967 Fore studies and Allison Jablonko's 1968 dissertation, which was accompanied by the film *Marings in Motion*, are among the few exceptions.[2] Social psychologists appear to have more success studying human behavior with film than do anthropologists (e.g., Eckman, Friesen, and Taussig 1969).

Alan Lomax's study of dance and culture, labeled choreometrics (1968, 1971), did involve the use of filmed data. He was able to use footage shot by numerous people, even including some materials derived from fiction films such as *King Solomon's Mines*. Many dance analysts have been extremely critical of Lomax's data collection methods, mode of analysis, and conclusions (Williams 2007). It is ironic that the only large research effort to utilize research footage should be so controversial.

Needless to say, since the era of postmodernism many have challenged the validity of objectivity when applied to the study of human behavior. The idea that film is objective and that anthropology's purpose is to produce objective studies has also been seriously questioned. In addition, Feld and Williams (1975) have made a convincing case about the almost insurmountable technical problems associated with obtaining reliable data using the motion picture camera. This lack of faith in objectivity seriously undermines the notion of film as an objective medium and thus raises the difficult question as to what the camera actually records. Perhaps because of this dilemma few scholars have been able to publish research based upon their analysis of their own footage or that of others (see Grasseni, this volume). It is possible to conclude that, like the still photograph, research footage is best understood as aides-de-memoires that cause the scholar to relive field experiences—a useful device when writing an ethnography.

Important Ethnographic Films and Their Makers

Creating a canon of ethnographic film that would be universally accepted is virtually impossible. Often what films are used is more a result of what films are accessible. The Royal Anthropological Institute's film library is dominated by British films, the Nordic Anthropological Film Association's archive is predominantly Scandinavian, and so on. Translating and subtitling was, prior to videotapes, a costly operation that further limited accessibility. Bouman (1954) and Luc de Heusch (1962) were among the first to offer listings of ethnographic films. Most of those films are no longer available. Englebrecht (2007) has edited a volume devoted to the history of ethnographic film from 1960 to 1980. Loizos in his 1993 book discusses a number of ethnographic films he considers innovative. The most extensive listing of ethnographic films is Karl Heider's *Film for Anthropological Teaching*, started in 1967 and currently in its eighth edition (Heider and Hermer 1995), which focuses on films available in English and in distribution within the United States. We will use it to assist us in discussing those films that people have found useful in the teaching of anthropology and those transmitted via television and the Internet. There are no up-to-date histories of ethnographic film.

If it is assumed that an ethnographic film is a documentary that illuminates some aspect of a culture, then the earliest ethnographic films are the Lumiére brothers' "actualities"—one-reel, single-take episodes of human behavior, such as *Leaving the Lumière Factory* (1895). Scholars, explorers, missionaries, and colonial administrators often made footage for public display (Ceram 1965). Ethnographic film designed for the public began with a general-educational film movement in the 1920s. Films of "exotic" peoples were produced commercially, sometimes with the assistance of anthropologists, and screened as "Selected Short Subjects." For example, Pathé employed members of Harvard's Department of Anthropology when producing *People and Customs of the World* in 1928. The only venues for any film at this time were, of course, theaters and occasionally museums. Few of these films still exist, and there is no evidence that they were ever used in teaching.

There were a number of early attempts to represent native life in feature-length theatrical films. Edward Curtis's *In the Land of the Head Hunters* (1914) (now retitled *In the Land of the War Canoes*), a romantic epic of the Kwakiutl of British Columbia, was a box-office failure. Interestingly enough, Curtis called his film a "documentary" a decade before Grierson used the term in discussing Flaherty's *Moana*.

Robert Flaherty's *Nanook of the North* (1922) is a film frequently described as the first documentary and ethnographic film. Some, though, question whether it was either (Ruby 2000). *Nanook* was ignored by anthropologists, including Franz Boas, who Flaherty invited to collaborate with him (Ruby 2000b). Flaherty did consult with Edward Curtis prior to making *Nanook* (Ruby 1981). Few documentary or ethnographic filmmakers sought to emulate Flaherty. No one claimed to be influenced by him until Jean Rouch in the 1950s, in his development of a "shared" anthropology, declared Flaherty as a major influence, alongside Dziga Vertov (Feld 2003).

Nanook's international box-office success prompted Paramount (then called Famous Players) to finance Flaherty's Samoan film, *Moana* (1926), and to distribute Meriam Cooper and Ernest Scheodsack's *Grass* (1925/1992), a study of the annual migration of the Iranian Bakhtari (Cooper 1925). These films had more impact on Hollywood than on subsequent ethnographic films. The movie industry developed its own traditions of Native American, Asian, African, and South Sea Island adventure drama. In *The Silent Enemy: An Epic of the American Indian* (1930), director H. P. Carver employed an all-native cast to tell the tale of an Ojibway warrior. We can find no evidence that anthropologists considered these films relevant.

For forty years, movie audiences learned about the "exotic other" from back-lot Tarzan films and cowboy and Indian movies. A belief in the rapid disappearance of native peoples as well as Western culture's folk customs caused salvage ethnographic film projects to be undertaken. The Heye Foundation supported a series of films on Native Americans between 1912 and 1927, produced by Owen Cattell and Frederick Hodge. However, it was not until after World War II that substantial activity is noted in the United States.

As discussed above, Margaret Mead and Gregory Bateson extended Regnault's ideas and "published" fieldwork films like *Bathing Babies in*

7.1   Jean Rouch and Edgar Morin in the Musee L'Homme, from *Chronicle of a Summer* (1961), Icarus Films.

Three Cultures (1941). Mead was mentor to both Sorenson and Jablonko and a forceful advocate for research film and the development of a visual anthropology.

The development of French ethnology and film were closely associated with Marcel Griaule, a father figure in ethnology who produced films about the Dogon of West Africa in the 1930s, a group later visited by a number of French filmmaker/ethnologists. One of Griaule's students, anthropologist/filmmaker Jean Rouch, has gained the attention of both academics and filmmakers, initially with his films about Africa (Brink 2007). In the early 1960s technical advances made it possible for small crews to produce synchronous-sound location films. Rouch's *Chronique d'un été* (*Chronicle of a Summer*, 1961) was produced with sociologist Edgar Morin, who called the film cinema vérité, as it combined the ideas of Soviet avant-garde filmmaker Dziga Vertov and Robert Flaherty (figure 7.1). Rouch took cameras into Paris streets for impromptu encounters in which the filmmaking process was often a part of the film. Those filmed became collaborators, even to the extent of participating in discussions of the footage, which was in turn incorporated into the final version of the film.

Rouch initiated his collaborative approach in a number of early films made with West Africans, such as *Les maîtres fous* (*The Mad Masters*, 1955), which was criticized by some because of an assumed ethnocentric emphasis on the bizarre. At the same time, others considered it among the best surrealist films (Adamowicz 1993). Rouch sought a "shared anthropology" with his "ethnographic science fiction" films, such as *Jaguar* (1965) and *Petit á petit* (*Little by Little*, 1971), and worked with his African collaborators for over forty years. The impact of his work was immediately evident in the films of French New Wave directors such as Chris Marker and Jean-Luc Godard. During his long career Rouch produced over 150 films; he died in Africa in 2004 on his way to a film festival. He also trained a number of African filmmakers and helped to found an African film school. Feld (2003) has produced a book of Rouch's writings and a filmography, and Stoller (1992b) has explored Rouch's films from the point of view of their place in French anthropology. Rouch may be the only person to be recognized for his accomplishments both as an anthropologist and as an important filmmaker.

Rouch's attempt to allow us to see the world through the eyes of those traditionally in front of the camera was taken a step further in the Navajo Film Project by Sol Worth and John Adair (1973), when some Navajos were taught the technology of filmmaking without the Western ideology usually attached to it (Worth 1981). Since the 1970s Sarah Elder and Leonard Kamerling, through the University of Alaska's Alaska Native Heritage Film Project, produced more than fifteen community-collaborative films, such as *Uksuum Cauyai: The Drums of Winter* (1988), in which the people filmed played an active role in the film from conceptualization to realization (Elder and Kamerling 1995). In the 1990s and beyond "indigenous media" have been produced by people who had traditionally been the subject of ethnographic films (Ginsburg, this volume; Ginsburg et al. 2002). Through the efforts of such people as Vincente Carelli in Brazil (1988), Eric Michaels in Australia (1986), and Terence Turner in Brazil (1992a, 1992b), many indigenous people have been enabled to produce their own media.

The Hunters (1957) is the first North American ethnographic film to gain the worldwide attention of both the film world and anthropologists (figure 7.2). It is part of John Marshall's almost fifty-year-long film study of the Ju/'hoansi (also known as the San or Bushman) of southern Africa. Marshall devoted a considerable amount of his life to the San, both as a filmmaker and advocate (Ruby 1992). He started as a teenager with his family—a mother who was an ethnographer (L. Marshall 1965) and a sister who was a nonfiction writer (Thomas 1989). In a lifelong venture, Marshall amassed the largest body of film work ever produced about an indigenous group. Together with Timothy Asch, Marshall founded Docu-

7.2   John Marshall filming *The Hunters* (1957). Courtesy Documentary Educational Resources, Watertown, MA.

mentary Educational Resources, the largest distributor of ethnographic film in the United States, through which their films are made available. The San footage currently resides at the Smithsonian Institution, where several San people have been able to view it. Marshall subsequently produced dozens of African and North American films, including *N'ai* (1980), a life history of a San woman, broadcast on *Odyssey*, US public television's only series about anthropology. His final film, a comprehensive review of his film work among the Ju/'hoansi, *A Kalahari Family* (Durington 2004), was completed shortly before his death in 2005.

Robert Gardner, a former associate of Marshall and editor of *The Hunters*, released *Dead Birds*, a study of symbolic warfare among the Dani of New Guinea in 1964 (Heider, in Englebrecht 2007; Barbash and Taylor 2008; Ruby 1989a; Gardner 2007a; Kapfer, Petermann, and Thoms 1989). The film grew out of a project in which ethnographers (among them Karl Heider), a novelist, and a filmmaker all described the same culture. Gardner was instrumental in the creation of the Program in Ethnographic Film and early attempts to get anthropologists interested in film. He later produced several films in East Africa and India. Gardner's relationship with his anthropological collaborators has not always been productive. Ivo Strecker (1988) was highly critical of his portrayal of the Hamar in *Rivers of Sand* (1973), but Ákos Östör remains a strong advocate of Gardner's

7.3 Timothy Asch, *The Ax Fight* (1975). Courtesy Documentary Educational Resources, Watertown, MA.

Indian films, particularly *Forest of Bliss* (1986) (Gardner and Akos Oster 2002).

Timothy Asch, a colleague of Marshall, worked collaboratively with anthropologist Napoleon Chagnon, creating a series of films on the Yanomamo of Venezuela, among them *The Feast* (1968) and *The Ax Fight* (1975) (figure 7.3). These films, accompanied by written ethnographies and study guides, were designed to teach college undergraduates cultural anthropology. In addition, Asch worked collaboratively with anthropologists in Bali and Indochina. He was one of the few ethnographic filmmakers whose goal was exclusively to produce effective teaching tools. Asch was the director of the ethnographic film program at the University of Southern California until his death in 1994 (Lewis 2003; Ruby 1995a).

The Educational Development Corporation developed curriculum for what became an infamous multimedia work titled "Man: A Course of Study." Produced by Canadian anthropologist Asen Balikci and filmmakers such as Robert Young, the films on Netsilik Eskimo life were originally designed for use in a grammar-school course and later repackaged for college-level courses, a commercial television special (*The Eskimo Fight for Life*), and a Canadian preschool children's series (Balikci and Brown 1966). Like *Nanook* and several other ethnographic films, the Netisilik films were "authentic reproductions" of these people's lives prior to contact with the West. The series became a political hot potato when some US congressmen objected to the films' culturally relative position and purported anti-Americanism (Dow 1991). *Through These Eyes* (Laird 2004) is a recent filmic attempt to review this project and the controversy that followed it.

Australian indigenous Aborgines have been filmed since the turn of the century, beginning with the UK-sponsored Torres Straits expedition in 1898 (Bryson 2002). The Australian government has provided a consistent source of funding to continue this tradition. The Australian Commonwealth Film Unit (Film Australia) made it possible for Ian Dunlop to undertake long-term filming projects such as the "Peoples of the Western Australian Desert" series, in particular, *The Desert People* (1966). The Australian Institute of Aboriginal Studies has employed staff ethnographic filmmakers. In that capacity, Roger Sandall produced films on the ceremonial life of Australian Aboriginal peoples, including *The Mulga Seed Ceremony* (1969). Sandall has the somewhat dubious distinction of being one of the only ethnographic filmmakers to have his films officially banned by the Australian government because of the secret nature of some ceremonial acts portrayed. While at one time only initiated men were permitted to see these films, many are being opened to viewing today.

David and Judith MacDougall followed Sandall as the Institute's resident filmmakers. They are most noted for their African films, such as *Lorang's Way* (1979) and *The Wedding Camels* (1980), shot in a distinctive reflexive observational style that caught the attention of cinéastes as well as anthropologists. David MacDougall, while lacking any formal training in anthropology, has become an impressive autodidact and authored a number of books of essays (1998, 2006) and taught at several European universities. He is currently a Professorial Fellow at the Centre for Cross-Cultural Research at the Australian National University. His recent work has been about the Doon school in India (*Doon School Chronicles*, 2000). MacDougall has a singular identity in ethnographic film as someone who makes ethnographic films and also writes about the subject theoretically.

The Institute for Papuan New Guinea Studies has carried on the tradition begun by their Australian colleagues and sponsored a number of films on native life. Of particular interest is *First Contact* (1983) by Bob Connolly and Robin Anderson, which combines footage from 1930 of the forays of three Australian miners into remote sections of the New Guinea highlands with contemporary interviews with the surviving miners and Papuan natives as they recall their first encounters. The film is part of a trilogy that follows the fate of the miners and the native New

Guineans who became involved in their exploits. Les McLaren and An-nie Stiven's 1996 film *Taking Pictures* reviews several of these New Guinea filmmakers and their films.

Television networks have become a significant outlet for ethnographic film and an opportunity to popularize anthropology. In Britain, Grana-da's long running series *Disappearing World* (1970–1977) established a fruitful tradition of collaboration between field ethnographers and pro-ducers, resulting in films like Brian Moser's *Last of the Cuiva* (1971) (Loizos 1980). BBC-TV ethnographic projects have included the series *Face Val-ues*, produced in cooperation with the Royal Anthropological Institute, and *Worlds Apart*, in which producers Chris Curling and Melissa Llewlyn-Davies explored the impact of Leni Riefenstal's photography in *The Southeast Nuba* (1983). In addition, there is Andre Singer's series *Strangers Abroad* for the UK's Central Television (1986), and more recently BBC 4's *Anthropology* series in 2007. There were few ethnographic films produced before television in the UK. Granada TV was later to sponsor the Univer-sity of Manchester's Center for Visual Anthropology.

A similar series was maintained by Japan's Nippon TV under the title *Man*, produced by Junichi Ushiyama, the founder of documentary and ethnographic film in Japan. NAV producers had the luxury of being able to be in the field/location for six months out of the year and were respon-sible for only two thirty-minute films per year. When Ushiyama died in 1997, the series was discontinued.

In the United States, the Public Broadcasting Service aired *Odyssey*, a series that covered all aspects of anthropology (1980–1981). Documen-tary Educational Resources (DER), discussed below, currently distributes fifteen of the programs, some reedited versions of *Disappearing World* productions. *Odyssey* lasted only two seasons and was, by and large, ig-nored by the anthropological world, expect perhaps for John Marshall's *N'Ai* (1980). In the United States no one else has tried before or since to produce a television series about anthropology (O'Donnell 1980).

Since the mid-1990s some ethnographic filmmakers have become increasingly interested in the potential of new digital technologies and multimedia productions in which video is combined with still photo-graphs and text, resulting in an interactive experience for the viewer that is more often viewed on a computer screen than projected. In addition, the Internet and the web are being explored as new production and dis-tribution outlets. Among the first to produce multimedia works was Peter Biella with his *Yanomamo Interactive* (Biella, Chagnon, and Seaman 1997). Biella was also the first to suggest that combinations of text and image within one work might enhance the ability of films to communicate anthropological knowledge. More recently, a number of these hybrids have appeared—Sarah Pink's CD-ROM *The Bullfighter's Braid* (1998), Rod Coover's *Cultures in Web* (2003), and Jay Ruby's CD-ROM *Oak Park Stories* (2004–2006). It is fairly certain many more will follow as this technology becomes more accessible and more accepted in academia (see Pink, this volume). Strictly speaking these multimedia projects go beyond film/video and could be considered as something other than "ethnographic film." Indeed, hypermedia ethnography projects may provide an altogether "different way of knowing" (MacDougall 1998) as they break with traditional linear forms.

Venues, Publications, Organizations, Training, and Festivals

By the end of World War II, interest in ethnographic film was sufficient to warrant the development of the institutions and support systems necessary if this growing field was to be taken seriously in the academic world. In the 1950s French anthropologist/cinéaste Jean Rouch, together with Luc De Heusch, founded UNESCO's International Committee on Ethnographic and Sociological Film (Gardner 1970; de Heusch 2007). With the assistance of several Neorealist filmmakers, the committee was also instrumental in establishing the Festival Del Popoli in Florence, Italy, in 1959—the oldest continuously running nonfiction film festival. Recently, the emphasis of the festival has been upon documentary to the virtual exclusion of ethnographic films.

By 1966 the US Program in Ethnographic Film (PIEF), analogous to the UNESCO committee, was founded by Robert Gardner, Asen Balicki, and Karl Heider. Organized with a grant from the Wenner-Gren Foundation—a longtime supporter of ethnographic film because of the early leadership of Hungarian anthropologist/filmmaker Paul Fejos, who was in charge of its research program for several years (Dodds 1973)—PIEF was originally housed in the Film Study Center, the visual arm of Harvard's Peabody Museum of Archaeology and Ethnography (http://www.filmstudycenter.org). The Film Study Center was in turn funded by Lawrence Marshall, the father of John, as a place for him and Robert Gardner to edit *The Hunters*. From these foundational efforts all organizations and screening venues have flowed.

PIEF made several subsequent moves: to the Carpenter Center at Harvard, then to Temple University in the 1970s, and eventually to the University of Southern California. It also reorganized, becoming, in the early 1970s, the Society for the Anthropology of Visual Communication (SAVICOM),

MATTHEW DURINGTON AND JAY RUBY

founded by Sol Worth, Margaret Mead, and Jay Ruby. In 1984 SAVICOM morphed into the Society for Visual Anthropology (http://www.society forvisualanthropology.org/ svawelcome.html), a section of the American Anthropological Association that publishes a journal—first titled *Studies in Visual Communication* and now *Visual Anthropology Review*. SVA organizes an annual film festival at the American Anthropological Association meetings. These screenings are symbolically significant in that the films are regarded as being as important as the scientific papers.

The International Ethnographic Film Festival of the Royal Anthropological Institute of the UK convenes biennially and is combined with a conference of scholarly papers. Other national and regional organizations have followed suit, like the Nordic Anthropological Film Association, which sponsors a film festival, maintains a rental archive, and publishes a web newsletter (*NAFA-Network*). Pekka Silvennoinen, the founder and director of Finland's Visual Culture Festival has started CAFFE (coordinating anthropological film festivals in Europe), with which he plans to compile an archive of films shown at these events. Viscult broadcasts its entire program online. The Taiwan Visual Anthropology Association, which sponsors the Taiwan Ethnographic Film Festival, has a film library available to its members. Keyan Tomaselli and the University of KwaZulu-Natal have developed the South African Film and Video Project, a collaboration of seven institutions in South Africa and Michigan State University. SAFVP is creating a definitive multinational database of film and videotape about South Africa. The list of film festivals and libraries is so vast that it is impossible to summarize here. Colette Piault has attempted such a list in her article "Festivals, Conferences, Seminars and Networks in Visual Anthropology in Europe" (in Englebrecht 2007).

Access to ethnographic film was difficult and expensive when they were mainly 16-millimeter films. At one time a number of US universities functioned as distributors, offering films for rent and sale; the University of California Media Center and Pennsylvania State University's Media Center were among the largest. As 16-millimeter films started to be replaced by videotape and DVD and university budgets tightened, these centers closed down. Today in the United States Documentary Educational Resources (DER) in Watertown, Massachusetts (http://www.der .org), is the primary source of ethnographic films. Founded in 1971, it was originally an outlet for the films of John Marshall and Timothy Asch. DER's catalog has since expanded to include hundreds of films, mainly in DVD format. According to executive director Cynthia Close, DER sells its DVDs in Canada, Australia, New Zealand, Asia ("Taiwan, Singapore primarily. We also sell films by Chinese filmmakers and are doing some promotion in China"), and Europe. Both the Royal Anthropological Institute in the UK and the Nordic Anthropological Film Association maintain film lending libraries available to their members. We assume such arrangements are also available in other parts of the world.

The National Film Registry, a prestigious registry of films selected by the US National Film Preservation Board for preservation in the Library of Congress, has to date recognized eight ethnographic films: Edward Curtis's *In the Land of the Head Hunters*, Robert Flaherty's *Nanook of the North* and *Louisiana Story*, Mead and Bateson's *Trance and Dance in Bali*, John Marshall's *The Hunters*, Robert Gardner's *Dead Birds*, Worth and Adair's *Through Navaho Eyes*, and Sarah Elder and Leonard Kamerling's *The Drums of Winter*.

Opportunities for training in all forms of nonfiction filmmaking have always been limited. In the United States training has benefited from the comparatively large numbers of film schools associated with universities. The MacDougalls are graduates of the short-lived course of studies in ethnographic film organized by Colin Young at the University of California, Los Angeles in the 1960s. Young went on to set up a similar program at the UK's National Film and Television School, where visual anthropologists Paul Henley, Felicia Hughes-Freeland, and Marcus Banks were trained.

As a consequence of Barbara Myerhoff's successful collaboration with filmmaker Lynn Littman (which resulted in the Academy Award–winning film *Number Our Days*), the University of Southern California hired Ira Abrams to develop an MA program in ethnographic film that utilized the facilities and faculties of its film school. In 1982 Timothy Asch assumed the leadership of the program, which blossomed until his untimely death in 1994.

Because Temple University was host to the Conference on Visual Anthropology (1968–1980) and then housed PIEF, it obtained funds from the National Science Foundation in 1972 to sponsor a Summer Institute in Visual Anthropology (SIVA) with Sol Worth, Karl Heider, Carroll Williams, and Jay Ruby as organizers. SIVA had two consequences: the creation of the Society for the Anthropology of Visual Communication and a partnership between Carroll William's independent Anthropology Film Center and the anthropology department of Temple University. The relationship ended in the 1990s, but William's center continued until his death in 2005. Temple's program was enlarged to offer a PhD in the anthropology of visual communication with some opportunities for students to take production courses in the film school.

Under the direction of Faye Ginsburg, the anthropology department at New York University, together with the NYU film school, offers a one-year certificate in ethnographic filmmaking. NYU has also been instrumental in the development of the Margaret Mead Film and Video Festival, founded in 1977 and held at New York's American Museum of Natural History. NYU's certificate program is the only remaining training program in ethnographic filmmaking in the United States.

In the United Kingdom the Granada Center for Visual Anthropology has existed since 1987 and enables Manchester University to offer an MPhil in ethnographic documentary as part of its graduate program of studies in visual anthropology.[3] Other UK universities, including Oxford, Kent, and Goldsmith, offer courses of study in visual anthropology but without an emphasis on film production. We look forward to future productions from those that have moved on into academic posts; many graduates of these training programs, however, have ended up with careers in the media and not as academic anthropologists. If the purpose of the training is to produce anthropologists who can make films as an expression of their scholarly work, then these programs are not working. This is not an opinion held by everyone.

Like the number of ethnographic film festivals, training opportunities in ethnographic film production have mushroomed in the past decade. They are found all over Scandinavia (Tromso), Europe, China, Korea, and Japan. Unfortunately, no one has documented this expansion. *Visual Anthropology.net*, an Italian periodical delivered via email and the web, offers a listing of some of these courses and other relevant events.

Conclusions—A Digital Future?

We are in a different experiential world—one not necessarily inferior to reading a text, but to be understood differently. (MacDougall 2006, 270)

It is always dangerous to predict the future of something like ethnographic film, as it involves both technological and conceptual changes. The public's fascination with the exotic has always been a factor in the market for ethnographic film. However, with the impact of globalization on even the most remote corners of the globe, there is a gradual "graying out" of exotica. At the same time indigenous people are demanding their own voice and producing their own films (see Ginsburg, this volume), thus further eroding the market for traditional ethnographic films about the other and causing some ethnographic filmmakers to look closer to home for their subjects.

There is a tendency for some to believe in what we call "technosalvation," that is, the notion that the next technological innovation will solve problems. The days of 16-millimeter film production are clearly over. Some form of video will undoubtedly dominate the production of motion picture images into the near future. As three-chip HD cameras improve and become less expensive, more anthropologists will likely try their hand at producing an ethnographic film. With DVD and the web becoming more common as distribution tools, anthropologists can, if they so choose, self-distribute. With that said the question remains, will the new ethnographic films be subject to less marginalization and more acceptance from the mainstream of cultural anthropology as a serious means of anthropological expression, or will they remain merely an audiovisual aid to teaching?

A number of scholars have questioned whether or not a film is capable of conveying anthropological concepts to an audience (see Pink, this volume). Others have questioned the capacity of ethnographic film to overcome students' stereotypical if not racist understanding of the "exotic other" (Martinez 1992). Heider (1976/2006) and Asch (1972) have both argued that a film is an "incomplete utterance" and must be accompanied by written materials—preferably a study guide. This is, of course, an assumption about the nature of film, that it lacks the capacity to present complex ideas. There is no empirical evidence to support or refute this assumption, and few have been bold enough to try to make a film that is a "complete utterance." Underlying this notion is the assumption that ethnographic films will only be screened in classrooms where students are required to read the study guide. An alternative to this solution to the problem of conveying anthropological knowledge in visual form is the development of multimedia ethnographies that combine images and text in a nonlinear fashion. These new ethnographies can be delivered via the web or on CD-ROM disks. These experiments, first proposed by Biella in 1994, are now being produced by a growing number of ethnographic filmmakers (e.g., Pink 1998; Ruby 2004–2006; Coover 2003). When contemplating the future of ethnographic film perhaps the most productive exercise is to focus on exploring the capacity of digital, multimedia, nonlineal work to engage the ethnographic project as it is conceived in the twenty-first century in ways that ethnographic film has never achieved. It is not an impossibility that in the near future, ethnographic film will be fundamentally altered by media that combine film, text, and still images in an interactive way, creating ever-exciting means for anthropologists to utilize media as a form both of anthropological research and of dissemination.

Notes

1. See http://www.nmnh.si.edu/naa/.
2. Jablonko's analysis of Maring dance was later published in 1991.
3. See http://www.socialsciences.manchester.ac.uk/disciplines/ socialanthropology/visualanthropology.

EIGHT

Digital Visual Anthropology: Potentials and Challenges

SARAH PINK

This chapter examines the relationship between visual anthropology and digital media. Historically this discussion starts in the 1980s, when the precursors of contemporary digital visual anthropology were emerging as laser discs. It explores how digital media have become increasingly accessible to visual anthropologists and are not only used by those with "anthropology and computing" expertise but have become integral to three areas of visual anthropology: as a component of research methods; as a form of "visual culture" for analysis; and as a means of representing and disseminating (audio)visual knowledge. Suggesting that digital media pose the first real challenge to the dominance of ethnographic film as a means of representation in visual anthropology, the chapter concludes by imagining a future visual anthropology where diverse digital representations are in circulation.

In early 2007 the cultural anthropologist Michael Wesch posted a five-minute digital video, *The Machine Is Us/ing Us*, on the YouTube website.[1] The video, "set to techno music[,] . . . helps explain Web 2.0—the so-called second wave of Web-based services that enables people to network and aggregate information online" (Powers 2007). Wesch's video fast became what he has called a "viral video"—"within three days it was the #1 video in the blogosphere, outranking Super Bowl commercials by almost ten to one. Within two weeks it had been linked by over 6,000 blogs, had over 1 million views, was in the Top 100 Favorites of all time on YouTube, and was gaining international 'big media' attention" (Wesch 2007). This news was posted around e-mail lists, including VISCOM and the EASA Media Anthropology Network,[2] from which I learned of it. Wesch produced the video as part of an article published in the first electronic issue of *Visual Anthropology Review*,[3] about which he remarked: "I was trying to explain this stuff in the traditional paper format, and I thought, 'This is ironic' . . . 'I can illustrate this much better in a video'" (Wesch, quoted in Powers 2007). *The Machine Is Us/ing Us* uses visualizations of text on computer screens to represent behaviors generated through human-computer relations. It is not an observational ethnographic documentary of the type that dominates anthropological film festivals. Nevertheless it was informed by and represents anthropological principles, as Wesch outlined: "For me, cultural anthropology is a continuous exercise in expanding my mind and my empathy, building primarily from one simple principle: everything is connected. . . . As I tried to illustrate in the video, this means that a change in one area (such as the way we communicate) can have a profound effect on everything else, including family, love, and our sense of being itself."[4] In his *VAR* article Wesch describes how after posting the video on YouTube he posted it on a second site, Mojiti, which offers a collaborative environment in which users can add annotations and graphics to video. There the video became dotted with comments and graphics; most were helpful, but some, Wesch notes, were inappropriate (2007).

The case demonstrates both the enormous potential and some of the limitations of digital media for the representation of other people's experiences and anthropological knowledge. For example, Wesch made an anthropological point through an audiovisual narrative that employed computer interfaces, digital video, and techno sound. Because the subject of *The Machine Is Us/ing Us* was digital text as viewed on screen, he could represent written words as both language and hypertext symbols. Other scholars working at the interface between anthropology and media also publish anthropological video online, using various strategies to alert others to their new projects, including announcements on e-mail discussion lists. These practices are especially pertinent to visual anthropology because they present possibilities for a future subdiscipline that is multimedia, collaborative, activist, and corporeally engaged (see Ginsburg, this volume, for a discussion of activism).

Yet Wesch's experience also raises some warnings. As a viral video, *The Machine Is Us/ing Us* reached a number of viewers that most anthropologists who aspire to getting their ideas across to mass audiences could only fantasize about. Simultaneously, it left the domain in which its maker could maintain control over it. In Wesch's words: "Just one week after I released it on YouTube it had been placed on <u>over 1,000</u> blogs and contextualized in a multitude of ways beyond my control" (2007; underline is a hyperlink in original). While there are relatively few ethical issues when one represents computer-generated words and links, this loss of control raises serious questions concerning the desirability of using "snapshot" documentary videos as a form of public anthropology. As Wesch himself points out, "In the context of this video, such actions [as those of his Mojiti collaborators] were relatively harmless, but it is not hard to imagine the kinds of comments and graphics that might be added to ethnographic film that could not only degrade the quality of the work, but also violate the dignity of those portrayed in the video" (2007).

If ethnographic video clips are to communicate anthropological issues and ideas outside academia, how should they be contextualized? Some visual anthropologists have argued that ethnographic film screenings should be accompanied by at least a presentation given by the film-maker/anthropologist. Similar conditions would pertain for digital clips (see also Biella 2008). How could we ensure that the "aberrant readings" Wilton Martinez claims even students taking anthropology courses give to carefully crafted, full-length ethnographic documentaries (1995, 2004) would not be applied to online video shorts? Other existing visual anthropology uses of digital media attempt to surmount some of these problems—in particular through the publication of interactive, multimedia or hypermedia projects on CD-ROM and DVD (see Pink 2006, chap. 6; Biella 2008). In this chapter I explore how an emergent digital visual anthropology is using collaborative methods, interactive hypermedia, and the Internet to produce ethically responsible texts that engage with the corporeality of vision, have activist ambitions, and might bridge the gap between written and visual academic anthropology.

Although it might seem clichéd to start this chapter with proclamations about the *potential* of digital media for future visual anthropology, a discussion of the relation of visual anthropology to rapidly changing media needs involves recognizing past imaginings and current possibilities and fantasizing about what will be next. This is a complex task, as the scenarios we imagine for the future are sometimes more ambitious and far-reaching than the practices that actually emerge. In a sense, my project is foiled before I begin—technological changes in this field are so rapid that it would be impossible for this chapter ever to be up to date. Therefore, it is more sensible to see the cases discussed here as examples of how changes in visual anthropology practice emerge in relation to digital technologies. Since these tend to be characterized by continuities with and sometimes recourse to past practices and ideas, it is unlikely that there will be any enormous rupture from past anthropological practices in the wake of a new digital technology. To date, shifts created in digital visual anthropology practice are largely represented in the creative practice of a handful of (influential) pioneers. Through their actual practical work and reflective writing about it, they are producing a series of innovations and models with the promise of extending this field.

Extending Visual Anthropology

I take visual anthropology to involve a five-strand set of interdependent practices. This definition has its roots in the three components delineated early in the history of visual anthropology by Jay Ruby and Richard Chalfen: "(1) the study of human nonlinguistic forms of communication which typically involves some visual technology for data collecting and analysis, (2) the study of visual products, such as films, as communicative activity and as a datum of culture amenable to ethnographic analysis, and (3) the use of visual media for the presentation of data and research findings—data and findings that otherwise remain verbally unrealized" (Ruby and Chalfen 1974). To these points, reiterated by Howard Morphy and Marcus Banks (1997), I add two strands that are especially relevant to a digital visual anthropology, though also embedded elsewhere in the history of visual anthropology. A fourth component, I have argued, is the activist or applied strand of visual anthropology (see Pink 2006, 2007b). This is not unrelated to Jean Rouch's notion of a "shared anthropology" (e.g., Rouch 1975) and implies visual anthropology's potential role as a public anthropology.[5] Finally, some of the best-known works in digital visual anthropology are pedagogical projects (e.g., Biella, Chagnon, and Seaman 1997). This represents a fifth strand of the subdiscipline.

This essay explores how aspects of these strands might be realized in a digital era, and how they generate practices that contribute to the production of a digital visual anthropology. Visual anthropology does not exist in a vacuum, however, but in relation to wider anthropological theories and agendas. Therefore my analysis also situates a digital visual anthropology in relation to a focus on human place-making practices, emplacement, and the multisensoriality of human experience, which cuts across not only social and cultural anthropology but the social sciences and humanities. This approach connects to issues already current in the subdiscipline, such as the corporeality of anthropological film

(McDougall 2006) and the need for visual anthropology to engage with multisensory experience (Pink 2006). The idea of place-making as a sensory phenomenological practice (e.g., Casey 1996; Feld and Basso 1996) can be applied to visual anthropology practice as we see visual anthropologists themselves as emplaced and place-making human agents (Pink 2009). This also requires focusing on human practice and agency, both as we examine other people's lives and to account for shifts in visual anthropology practice and the emergence of a digital visual anthropology.

Digital Visual Anthropology: Computers, Media, and Principles

Historically the relationship between visual anthropology and mainstream social and cultural anthropology has been a problematic site (see Grimshaw 2001; Pink 2006, chap. 1). In recent years, however, certain shifts in approach and technological developments have served to narrow, albeit not to close, this divide. First, what has come to be known as the "writing culture" debate of the 1980s brought about a recognition that films and other visual representations might be no more subjective than written anthropological texts. Second, although in the past still cameras and later camcorders have often been used by anthropologists, as both hardware and software related to visual media have become more sophisticated, user-friendly, and affordable, photography and video have become increasingly standard tools for anthropological fieldwork (see Durington and Ruby, this volume, for a discussion of changing technologies' implications for visual anthropology). One should not assume, though, that digital visual anthropology and mainstream anthropology are now more closely aligned simply because their practitioners use similar equipment: it is what is done with the equipment rather than the simple fact of its use that identifies a practice as "visual anthropology." Still, the existence of digital media research practices within mainstream anthropology, along with anthropological study of digital media, indicates increasing potential for an anthropology that is appreciative of the visual and questions about vision, and thus more likely to draw on principles already developed by visual anthropologists. In this section I discuss some existing contact points between digital visual anthropology and other areas of anthropological practice to establish where both the (false) boundaries and the interconnections and interdependencies lie.

While visual anthropologists are increasingly interested in digital media, practitioners of "digital anthropology" increasingly use (audio)visual media in their work. Digital anthropology involves, broadly, the use of digital resources and technologies in anthropological research, representation, teaching, collaboration, and public anthropology. It has its roots partly in what has been called "anthropology and computing," which includes the development and use of a range of software tools for anthropological research, representation, and teaching and learning. Some earlier work in this area involved visual symbols (e.g., in kinship software)[6] and visualization, and by the 1990s had become increasingly relevant to visual anthropologists. One early innovator in anthropology and computing was Alan MacFarlane, who describes (2004) how his own work evolved from the 1970s, when data had to be input via punch cards or paper, through the 1980s, when it became possible to work with video discs, Windows systems came into use in computers, and analog video became available for use in fieldwork, to the 1990s, when he was already using a laptop computer with a Windows system and a digital video camera, and finally into the twenty-first century, where he uses the Internet to disseminate his multimedia work.[7] Other leaders in this field include Michael Fisher and David Zeitlyn at the Centre for Anthropology and Computing (CSAC) at the University of Kent (UK). Anthropology and computing involves much more than simply using digital visual materials and includes various forms of data management and representation (see Fisher 1994). However, the work of CSAC is highly relevant to visual anthropology. By the 1990s this included the production of pedagogic projects that make extensive use of digitized video and photography, and in the 2000s Fisher and Zeitlyn are creating software for visual ethnography that can be used in photo-elicitation and video logging, annotation, and analysis. Similar pedagogic projects have been produced through the Digital Anthropology Resources for Teaching project (DART), developed between the London School of Economics and Columbia University. These developments lead to some convergences between visual and digital anthropologies, although as I discuss below, the extent to which this involves the mutual engagement of these subdisciplines with each other's principles varies.

Simultaneously, a convergence of the interests of visual anthropology and media anthropology has developed in a number of spheres, notably over questions relating to indigenous media and indigenous media production (e.g., Ginsburg 2002). Particularly salient are recent convergences between media and visual anthropologies in their analyses and practical uses of digital visual media. Calling for a departure from the recent past, where (drawing from the work of Georgina Born) "in most cases new media have been embraced by anthropology as an upgrade of methodological tools," Hart Cohen and Juan Salazar (2005) argue for a new approach to Digital Anthropology that

is concerned with the visualisation and digitisation of knowledge; with the cultural construction of audiovisual information and communication technologies, or identity formation within new media architectures; with the relationship between cultural identity and knowledge and the technological contexts in which they are formed; with the crafting of experience and participation in digital, virtual and online contexts—in brief, with the cultural underpinning of information society. (2005, 6)

For Cohen and Salazar this digital anthropology has an added role as a political tool for participation in public debate, as a way of critically appraising new cultural subjectivities and social formations in an era of increased technologization (2005, 7). Their aspirations for a digital anthropology run parallel with those I suggested for the future of visual anthropology in a digital age—as a public anthropology capable of making critical interventions (Pink 2006, chap. 7). The anthropology of digital media is inescapably partly a visual anthropology since it is a multimedia anthropology that necessitates engagements with (audio)visual media—whether this involves simply its analysis or also its coproduction. Thus a relationship between visual anthropology and the anthropology of digital media seems inevitable. It also offers two essential points of exchange: first, anthropologists of digital media benefit from engaging with principles of visual anthropology to inform their approaches to visual media; second (as I argue in detail in Pink 2006), visual anthropologists benefit from recognizing that visual practices in anthropology should be situated in relation to multiple other media.

To sum up, digital visual anthropology is not simply a digital version of what visual anthropologists have already been doing for the last fifty or so years—that is, predominantly making ethnographic films and showing them at anthropological film festivals (there are of course exceptions, several of whom I discuss here). Rather, it is developing in relation to other subdisciplines and has a series of potentials in academic anthropology, as a public anthropology, and in other academic disciplines that visual anthropology, marginalized as it was in the last century, never had.

The (Recent) Historical Context: An Overview

During the 1990s initial discussions of a digital visual anthropology focused on practical innovations in anthropological hypermedia and written reflections on this. The idea that hypermedia would bring to academic texts ways of communicating that were both innovative and familiar to the existing practices of readers has been a theme in much writing on the topic. In 1988 Alan Howard stressed how because reading tends actually to be a nonlinear practice, hypertext in fact "articulates better with actual modes of thinking far better that lineally written materials" (1988, 306), a point often reiterated by advocates of a hypermedia visual anthropology.

In 1992 Gary Seaman and Homer Williams published a fascinatingly futuristic essay in which they discuss contemporary technologies in terms of what ethnographers might do in a future about ten years on (1992, 303), effectively the time we are living as I write. In the early 1990s video, audio, and photographic technologies already allowed ethnographers to produce data using multiple media, but the problem was "how to process, analyze and integrate it into a generally accessible presentation format" (Seaman and Williams 1992, 303). At the time such integration of multiple media could be achieved by "close control of external machines like video disc or video tape players," but the authors predicted that "in the next decade it [the computer] will become powerful enough to store all cognitive media except three-dimensional artefacts on a single storage medium; portable enough to use in almost any fieldwork situation; inexpensive enough to be widely used; and capable of linking multimedia field data by means of hypermedia or interactive multimedia programmes" (1992, 303). These changes were indeed rapid, and as the history of digital visual anthropology progressed Seaman participated in the production of the *Yanomamö Interactive* CD-ROM project (Biella, Chagnon, and Seaman 1997), which followed along the lines described above (Biella 2004, 2008).

To offer a sense of how these changing technological possibilities became interwoven with visual anthropology practices, I describe my own experiences from 1990, when I completed my MA in visual anthropology at the University of Manchester using VHS and SVHS cameras, the latter so heavy that I had to train to carry both the camera and the weighty battery belt needed to power it. I began my PhD about women and bullfighting[8] in 1991, and in 1992 (the year that Seaman and Williams's chapter was published) left to do my fieldwork in Spain. I took with me a traditional analogue camera, having my photos printed locally during fieldwork. I wrote field notes on A4 sheets that I sorted into thematic sets on a large table. It did not occur to me to take a laptop computer with me (although some anthropologists were already using them). By 1994 I was starting to write up my thesis on a secondhand PC using an early word-processing program. I was, by anthropology and computing standards, a bit "behind" in my uses of technology. By now more established visual anthropologists were debating the possibilities for anthropological hypermedia that had opened up in the wake of new computing systems.

In 1994 a discussion about interactive multimedia was published online, initiated in a conference paper by Marcus Banks in which he "*deliberately overstated the anti-multimedia case in my talk to provoke discussion and comment*" (emphasis in original)[9] and followed by Peter Biella's response.[10] As Biella notes, the electronic publication of these articles itself provides a "nonlinear juxtaposition of ideas [that] is particularly useful for emphasizing points of scholarly agreement and disagreement." The wider context in which Banks and Biella were debating was one where initial developments in digital visual anthropology often took the form of pedagogical projects. In the 1990s this work emerged as new technology made hypermedia projects possible and, simultaneously, higher education institutions and funding bodies became interested in supporting online and interactive electronic learning developments. These currents were accompanied by various concerns, including (now seemingly unfounded) fears about a decline in face-to-face teaching and the potential redundancy of the lecturer role. In retrospect, the 1990s can be seen as a period of experimentation and development in anthropological hypermedia. This created a base of experience and knowledge about the potential of hypermedia that has informed the more research-orientated narratives of some later anthropological hypermedia texts published since 2000.

In 1994 the discussion between Banks and Biella expressed some of the key issues. In his "sceptical view," Banks suggested that interactive multimedia was not viable on several counts: first, he predicted that it would, "like ethnographic film . . . find its major use in undergraduate teaching rather than professional research"; second, he deemed it problematic in that "it calls on the twin rhetorics of 'freedom' and 'choice' to disguise its control and command of authority"; and third, he argued for the centrality of linear processes in scholarly work, stating, "Most—probably all—intellectual analysis proceeds along a linear path, where pieces of data need to be assessed alongside each other in the right arrangement in order for the analysis to work." Biella's reaction to this critique drew from his own practice to set an agenda for anthropological hypermedia that continues to inform his written and practical work (e.g., Biella 2004, 2008; Biella, Chagnon, and Seaman 1997).

Biella, who at the time was already developing what would be his *Maasai Interactive* DVD project (Biella, forthcoming) countered Banks by arguing for the pedagogical validity of anthropological hypermedia, contingent on good design and on its projects maintaining a relationship between research and teaching. He insisted on departing from the idea of linear analysis to reflect on alternative ideas, arguing that "the interjection of nonlinear critique into time-based, linear media adds an important new element to the educational struggle. Nonlinear interruptions guide viewers to rewind and reflect not only on the ethnographic material they have seen, but also on the assumptions, prejudices and anxieties that they bring to their interpretation." This form of interruption, he suggested, also contributed to the role of visual anthropology in combating racism and stereotyping. Biella's discussions were informed by, and continue to be represented in, his own anthropological hypermedia practice. He continued this discussion in 1997 in an article that reflected on *Maasai Interactive*, in 2004 in a discussion of a similar project, *Yanomamö Interactive*, and most recently in arguing for the potential of anthropological hypermedia in countering racism (Biella 2008). I return to Biella's work in later sections to discuss the potential of digital visual anthropology as social intervention and as pedagogic device.

By this point in the mid-1990s few other visual anthropologists were using new media similarly. In 1995 I submitted a word-processed thesis, inserting my photographic prints on photocopied pages. Three years later my photographs were digitized at the University of Derby, where I was working on a pedagogic CD-ROM, *The Bullfighter's Braid* (1998), intended to teach photographic methods in ethnography. Within this 1990s context, which encouraged developments in pedagogical hypermedia, I was able to experiment with hypermedia narrative and digital images. I collaborated with multimedia developers who created a design I had visualized in diagrammatic form and inserted materials I provided. The result was an interconnected set of written narratives that led to hyperlinked images and captions. I later saw several flaws in my work and realized that this production method did not allow me to adapt the project later. However, this, along with a training course provided by the Experience Rich Anthropology (ERA) project at the University of Kent, prepared and inspired me to explore how such projects might be more visually led in the future.

Although ethical concerns prevented me from publishing online the project I developed at the ERA workshop (Wesch 2007 describes a similar experience), by 2000 I was producing my own CD-ROMs, *Gender at Home* (2000) and *Women's Worlds* (unfinished, but see Pink 2004 for a discussion), based on a later research project about domestic life and the sensory home (Pink 2004).[11] I used clips from digitized video clips and combined this with written text and still images to represent gendered experiences and practices in the sensory home. Simultaneously, Jay Ruby was writing and speaking at conferences about his visual ethnography of Oak Park (USA). Ruby had initially planned to represent this work through a "video essay" but, realizing that he wanted the viewers of his work to interact with the text, instead published the research as a series of multimedia CD-ROMs in the early 2000s. Other research-based anthropological CD-ROMs emerged at the same time, for example, Joanna Kirkpatrick's *Rickshas of Delight* (2003). While these publications have been designed with differing architectures and purposes, in common they combine video, photographs, and written texts (see Pink 2006, chap. 6, and Pink 2007a, chap. 8, for detailed analysis and discussion of these works).

By 2007 I could download digital materials from my video camera, still camera, and audiorecorder directly onto my laptop and store them in an archive kept on an external hard drive. I shared these materials with the people who participated in my current research (about the development of the Cittàslow [Slow City] movement in the UK)[12] by e-mail and on CD and DVD. These options are now available to most anthropologists. However, as I emphasize below, their realization needs to be informed by knowledge of the ethical and technological potentials and limitations of digital media.

Anthropological Hypermedia: Digital Visual Anthropology as Representation

Digital media have opened up various points of innovation in visual anthropology representation, the most obvious being the potential for new anthropological film forms and the production of anthropological hypermedia projects published on the Internet, DVD, or CD-ROM. David MacDougall has commented on how his practices of shooting and editing video changed once he had access to digital video. He comments how, when starting his Doon School project in 1996,

we were at the beginning of the digital video revolution. I realized that I did not have to use film, that I did not even have to make a "film" as it was understood in any conventional sense. Instead I began to think about a long-term study of the school using a video camera as my means of inquiry. What would emerge from this I did not know, and therein lay one of its attractions. (2006, 122)

This freedom from the constrictions of working with television companies allowed MacDougall to produce a series of five films that were not organized in the "linear way" that usually guides documentary series: "In fact they are tied together according to several different kinds of logic" (MacDougall 2006, 122). These factors will have affected the practices of most anthropological filmmakers working with contemporary digital video and editing software. However, my interest in digital documentary-making here is less about how anthropological documentary styles themselves are shifting than how digital anthropological video might be resituated further through its incorporation into anthropological hypermedia representations. Hypermedia gives visual anthropologists opportunities to situate documentary in relation to other materials and knowledge that are absent from ethnographic film. I argue not for the obsolescence of ethnographic film but for enhancing the capacity of audiovisual media to communicate in academic and public contexts through its insertion into multimedia hypermedia narratives. In such texts digitized film/video can be a situated component within a body of interlinked representations of knowledge and experience, rather than the isolated event that anthropological/ethnographic documentary viewing too often becomes. I will discuss in this section some of the qualities of and arguments for the use of hypermedia in visual anthropology representation and in later sections, the way this has developed in practice and theory in terms of research text, pedagogy, and social interventions.

Several scholars have argued that hypermedia offers a form of anthropological representation that better reflects both how people think and read. Above I noted Howard's (1988) suggestion that the nonlinear potential of hypermedia runs parallel to how we think. Michael Fisher and David Zeitlyn stress how conventional academic text is itself often treated multilineally, even if its structure is not presented as such, observing that "it is difficult to imagine much more freedom than is afforded by a book! Although there is a linear order to the pages, the reader is free to look at the pages in any order, and parts of pages at will. Most books come with a device called an index which facilitates non-linear use" (2003). Others propose that hypermedia better represents the interconnectedness of the forms of cultural knowledge they encountered when doing their fieldwork. For example, Barbara Glowczewski found that Australian Aboriginal people's "survival knowledge is not encyclopaedic but reticular" and can be better represented using the forms of connectedness that can be implied through hypermedia. She describes how in Warlpiri:

Thousands of stories and songlines stage separate entities (a Dreaming, an ancestor, a group, a person, an animal, a plant), but they criss-cross one another and the meeting points produce singularities. . . . Non-linear or reticular thinking mostly stresses the fact that here is no centrality to the whole, but a multipolar view from each recomposed network within each singularity—for example, a person, a place, a Dreaming—allowing the mergence of meanings and performances, encounters, creations as new original autonomous flows. (2005, 28)

Glowczewski sought to represent this using multimedia in the CD-ROM *Dream Trackers* (2000), in which "a virtual map—made up of 14 layers of connections—became the interactive gateway to some 14 hours of audiovisual data. The user can click on any of the sites or lines to enter into the relevant constellation of Dreamings and explore them from the point of view of hundreds of proposed hyperlinks." She reflects that "multimedia allows the experience of reticular travelling as a learning process" (2005, 28–29).

Peter Biella has looked at this form of nonlinearity in terms of its relationship to interactivity. He suggests that "interactive ethnographies can be designed to help readers discover new evidence of cultural coherence" (2007). Using the concepts of the labyrinth and the maze, he presents the possibilities available to users in interacting with his multimedia project *Maasai Interactive*, which is based on eleven minutes of sync-sound film, fifteen hours of audio, and six hundred photographs. The project has forty-four interlinked scenes, which with "photographs, audio recordings, transcriptions, translations and annotations are all electronically indexed" (Biella 2008). Biella suggests that "the simplest way to work through *Maasai Interactive* is to treat it as a *unicursal* path or route, from Transcript to Annotation, [which] would trace a labyrinth: one would follow each node of evidence to its analysis, then return back to the next." However, because the design also allows users, using hyperlinks, to move between layers and levels of multimedia data that are included in project, it also enables "readers to exit the labyrinth of my [Biella's] knowledge and enter a maze of their own design. There they may find golden nuggets previously undiscovered" (Biella 2007).

When ethnographic video recordings are included within these sorts of hypermedia architectures they have been authorially situated in relation to other sets of knowledge through potentially multiple interconnections. David MacDougall suggests that film is both "well suited to expressing the unique individuality of human beings through their faces, gestures, postures, speech and interactions with others" and to "communicat[ing] the forms, textures, intricacies, and sensory qualities of physical objects and their culturally complex configurations" (2006, 272). However, there are limits to which individual emotions and the cultural meanings of sensory experiences can be communicated cross-culturally through film (Pink 2006). Hypermedia architectures can work toward resolving this by situating sensory and corporeal experiences in terms of cultural knowledge. Such connections between video representations of experience and written explanations might invite users to question stereotypes (Biella 2008). Viewers' empathetic responses to what they perceive as being common (or precultural) embodied experiences are themselves unavoidably culturally and biographically informed, and ethnographic film narratives may not always bring these differences to the fore. In contrast, hypermedia links can create possibilities for users to be involved in more academic, situated, and reflexive forms of corporeal engagement with other people's embodied experience, knowledge, and practice as represented in hyperlinked digital video clips or longer sequences.

These possibilities for anthropologists' representation of and users' engagement with visual images in visual anthropology are inextricable from approaches to pedagogy, theory, and activism in anthropology.

The Pedagogical Strand

Ethnographic documentary films have long been used in teaching social anthropology. Indeed, in 1994 Marcus Banks suggested that "the major use of ethnographic film . . . [was] in classroom teaching, not in research" and stated, "From all the current signs it seems that IMM [interactive multimedia]—like ethnographic film—will find its major use in undergraduate teaching." The classroom use of film has been criticized as a "babysitting device," deployed when the lecturer cannot be present. Moreover, doubts have been raised regarding whether the pedagogic messages of ethnographic films are interpreted as intended by the filmmakers (Martinez 1996, 2004). This is not to say that ethnographic film showings cannot play a useful role in teaching and learning anthropology (see Ruby 2000b); in my experience students, when appropriately guided, make good use of film screenings. However, ethnographic documentaries are infrequently designed for the teaching and learning of anthropology. A notable exception is Tim Asch and Napoleon Chagnon's *The Ax Fight* (1975), which uses an explanatory structure in place of the expository narrative that ethnographic documentary tends toward (Nichols 2004, 231–32). Significantly, *The Ax Fight* is the first anthropological film to be digitized for republication, along with a set of supplementary materials (photographs, interview data, written anthropology, biographical data on the people in the film, kinship diagrams, charts), on CD-ROM.

An equally important example is *Yanomamö Interactive: The Ax Fight* (Biella, Seaman, and Chagnon 1997), which, accompanied by a short printed text, was the first anthropological multimedia, hypermedia CD-ROM project to be published and distributed commercially. *Yanomamö Interactive* had two precursors: the didactic film *The Ax Fight* (along with Chagnon's written ethnography) was the basis for the CD; and *Maasai Interactive*, an ongoing anthropological hypermedia project that Biella was developing throughout the 1990s (see Biella 1993, 2008), served as a template. The CD contains an encyclopaedic database of interlinked resources: photographs; historical, descriptive, and analytical texts; the biographical details of fifty-one people; kinship diagrams; and maps, figures, and charts. The additional visual and written materials afford a new perspective on *The Ax Fight* and the questions originally posed in the film (Biella, Seaman, and Chagnon 1997, 37).

While *Yanomamö Interactive* was distributed on CD-ROM, other recent pedagogic projects in digital anthropology have used the Internet for their dissemination. These include the Experience Rich Anthropology (ERA) Project at the University of Kent (UK), which ran from 1996 to 1999 (see Zeitlyn 2000), and Digital Anthropology Resources for Teaching (DART), developed by the London School of Economics and the Columbia University, which commenced in 2003.[13] The ERA project, led by David Zeitlyn and Mike Fischer, was "designed to enhance the teaching and learning of anthropology by encouraging teachers to help students explore the relationships between field data and analysis as reported in monographs and journal articles" and aimed to "disseminate elements, methods and sample teaching materials based on existing field data (field notes, film or photographic or other types of data) suitable for incorporation into current and new courses." Several pedagogic projects developed within ERA used digitized video clips and photographs. The project marks a significant innovation in the production of online resources for teaching and learning in anthropology. Importantly, and in tune with the emphasis on reflexivity, the project stressed the possibilities that using visual media offer to bring the experiential elements of doing anthropology to the fore. More recently, the DART project declared its aim "to explore the potential of digital resources for the teaching of undergraduate anthropology" and to "investigate digital-library technologies that will allow for the flexible delivery and customized use of these resources." The resources developed by DART include digital photographs, digitized video clips, and simulations, although some are more distant from visual anthropology (e.g., its "Criterion" resource uses grids and written texts to teach students about complex anthropological concepts). DART is a good example of how visual resources are becoming more central, alongside other digital technologies.

Yanomamö Interactive, ERA, and DART all involve students with visual materials in ways that would have been unlikely were they simply viewing a sixty-minute ethnographic documentaries in a lecture theater. However, the level of engagement with visual anthropology varies. While *Yanomamö Interactive* invites its users to explore how knowledge is produced thorough ethnographic film, the use of film in DART's "What's Going On?" video interpretation tool is aimed at students working "as if they were an anthropologist trying to make sense of the situation."[14] That is, *Yanomamö Interactive* asks students to engage with the involvement of the filmmakers and anthropologists who made the film in knowledge production, while "What's Going On?" attempts to emulate the long-term fieldwork process by providing students with varying degrees of knowledge and skills required to interpret the content of a video clip. While projects like DART are oriented toward pedagogic goals rather than the development of innovations in visual anthropology, both sorts of projects signify an increasing use of the visual in mainstream anthropology teaching and the potential for using existing visual anthropology resources (films, photographic archives), once digitized, in teaching and learning in new ways. Stacy Lathrop (2004), writing in *Anthropology News*, has also made an important point about such projects: "In integrating digital resources, the anthropologists are not replacing such teaching, but they are questioning conventional pedagogy." She writes that, "in thinking about how the DART project can improve anthropology teaching, the LSE fellows note: 'The majority of digital applications exploit the storage and retrieval potential of digital media.' Going beyond this, they are focusing 'on developing an approach to teaching which enables the incorporation of a whole range of interactive strategies of which digital tools are just one. The long-term outcome of the project is the promotion of the idea that a wide range of digital media can be harnessed as a means of supporting embodied, experiential learning.'"[15] Seeing DART as an attempt to emphasize the embodied and experiential elements of learning brings to the fore the role of the visual in creating sensorial, embodied reactions in viewers, empathetic responses to the embodied emotions and experiences that are portrayed in video and photography. It additionally promotes the idea that visual representations might be able to give viewers a stronger notion of the phenomenological "sense of place" that others inhabit and of their social relationships. The notion of experiential and embodied learning links to the idea of a corporeal visual anthropology that foregrounds the senses and experience (MacDougall 1998, 2006; Pink 2006). It is at this point of convergence that the potential for applying the practice and theory of visual anthropology in the context of creating digital teaching and learning environments might be realized.

Digital Ethnography: Digital Visual Anthropology as a Research Method

In recent years the idea of taking a visual approach to ethnography has become increasingly popular across the social sciences (Pink 2007a; Pink et al. 2004; Banks 2001). The use of digital media in the process of exploring other people's experiences and environments has facilitated various developments in the research practices involved in the production of print, film, and hypermedia ethnographies. When working on the second edition of my book *Doing Visual Ethnography* (Pink 2007a), which outlines a visual ethnographic process, I found myself rewriting it for readers who would be most likely to be using digital media. In some cases this required little alteration: we tend to use new media technologies in ways that are very similar to how we used the old ones. For example, both conventional ethnographic documentary filmmaking and contemporary video ethnography use the technique of following or accompanying research/film subjects as they walk (discussed in full in Pink 2009). Digital media, however, extend the possibilities and offer new and exciting opportunities to innovate. This has inspired the development of new forms of collaborative and participatory visual research method (covered in more detail in the next section). Moreover, such developments in software, hardware, and practice mean that digital media can support the development of phenomenological approaches to visual ethnographic research in anthropology.

In the 1970s Jean Rouch wrote about his idea of a "shared anthropology," part of which involved screening his films for his "first audience"— the films' subjects (1975, 43). This method, he wrote, enabled him to generate anthropological knowledge much more efficiently, noting that by screening one of his films in this way, "I was able to gather more information in two weeks than I could get in three months of direct observation and interview" (1975, 44). Laptop computers (sometimes using alternative energy sources), digital cameras, editing software, and portable projectors can make this process much faster, more interactive and participatory, and, of course, less cumbersome than it was with conventional filmmaking equipment. Documentary-making along these lines is already being practiced by visual anthropologists (e.g., Durington 2007).

Digital media also have implications for how visual anthropologists treat and share their materials with other researchers. A concomitant effect of digital production is the fact that anthropologists are now archiving, logging, and annotating visual research materials electronically. Developing a digital archive using folders and inventing categories does not require any specialist software. However, possessing digital materials also implies the possibility of using new digital forms of categorization and analysis. Some computer-assisted qualitative data analysis software (CAQDAS) already accommodates visual materials and is popular among some social scientists (e.g., Dicks et al. 2005), although it is not, to my knowledge, commonly used among visual anthropologists. I review these cross-disciplinary developments elsewhere (Pink 2007a). Here I focus on two examples of computer applications that have more parallels with and specific implications for visual anthropology practice.

One strand of current developments is the reproduction in digital form of already established visual anthropology methods. A good example is photo-elicitation, initially written about by John Collier Jr. in 1967 and now a key visual ethnography method used across the social sciences and advocated in particular by the visual sociologist Douglas Harper (e.g., Harper 2002). As part of the AnthroMethods project, Zeitlyn and Fischer and their colleagues have developed a series of software tools to be used in anthropological research, some of which are specifically appropriate to working with (audio)visual media.[16] One of these—Image Interviewer—is a photo-elicitation tool developed by Janet Bagg that allows an interviewer to upload digital photographs, diagrams, or other images and to record for each both audio commentary and sequences of mouse movements that indicate relevant areas of the image. Image Interviewer thus goes further than CAQDAS applications and actually participates with researcher and informant in the production of knowledge. It allows for a more collaborative photo-elicitation process in that interview files can be reviewed as part of the research process and multiply annotated in the light of informants' comments on their own comments.

Another program, VideoGrok, authored by Fischer, has been designed for working with digital video materials. It "is a set of applications for relating metadata to segments of video, and then locating and analysing these."[17] The tool is very useful for transcribing but also for annotating segments of digital video footage, enabling researchers to situate footage in relation to other knowledge. Significantly, tools like Image Interviewer and VideoGrok are open-source, free software, not commercial packages. The implications of the use of digital media for the production of knowledge during both anthropological research and analysis go beyond the idea of the lone anthropologist being better able to archive, access, organize, and annotate her or his digital video, still images, and audiorecordings. Projects like the Image Interviewer make explicit the ways in which visual images and conversation are part of the same context in photo-elicitation interviews. They provide a record of the research process in which an intersubjective relationship between researcher, informant, and image forms the basis for the production of anthropological knowledge. Digital media also facilitate the development of collaborative research methods—involving the sharing of research materials and ideas with participants in the research or with coresearchers, who might be other academics or collaborators/clients in applied research. Although data sharing and teamwork has not been unknown in visual anthropology research, historically it has been used more often in applied visual anthropology (e.g., Collier 1973; Chalfen and Rich 2007; Martinez Perez 2007).

The Anthropology of Digital Visual Forms and Practices

For those visual anthropologists whose focus of attention has been material visual culture, photography and other visual practices, or the idea of vision of looking/seeing itself as a practice, digital media present new substantive, theoretical, and methodological opportunities. They also create interesting connections between other disciplines and subdisciplines with common interests, for instance, the study of digital video and how it is contextualized. One example is Wesch, who discusses the idea of doing an ethnographic study of YouTube.[18] However, it is difficult to isolate the research to simply *visual* representations, in that digital representations tend to be multimedia in some aspect; one is likely to be dealing with written text too. For example, working with Ana Martinez Perez, I developed an analysis of a Spanish website, www.telemadre.com (Pink and Martinez Perez 2006). The analysis, based on our existing visual ethnographic and anthropological studies of Spanish gender, focused on the photographs, visualizations, and written text that made up the site. Essentially we were exploring how digital visual representations created meanings in relation to written texts.

Digital Media Anthropology: Application, Activism, Sharing, and Collaboration

This area of a digital visual anthropology creates crossovers with other subdisciplines, in particular linkages between digital visual anthropology and media anthropology. Such connections have developed in the production of indigenous media anthropology and activist anthropology, which invite new forms of collaboration between anthropologists, local people, and activists. Much of this work follows in some way the agenda suggested by Hart Cohen and Juan Salazar, who argue that "intrinsically, digital anthropology must revise traditional power relations between research and its objects of study and look at increasing forms of empowerment offered by new digital media, in terms of access, participation and communication" (2005, 7).

Above I have highlighted how the interactivity and nonlinearity of digital media, and especially hypermedia, have been credited with potential for new forms of anthropological practice and communication. This is no less the case for the pronouncements made for applied uses. As Salazar proposes, "Interactive and non-linear narratives may . . . have the potential to disrupt anthropological authorship even further [than visual anthropological uses of graphics, sound, and time-based media have], but they are increasingly vital—not only for presentation and dissemination of information, but also for collaborative practice and applied action research" (2005, 65). As this work now develops in practice, variation is evident, although in some work the point of intervention is principally that of the ruptures in stereotyping that may be achieved when users engage with the text, rather than in the collaborative methods that are used to produce it.

In the past anthropologists have set up websites that welcome comments and contributions from the people they are doing research about or with. A good recent example is Jay Ruby's ethnographic study of Oak Park, Illinois.[19] New digital technologies provide possibilities for what Wesch calls "radically collaborative open-ended ethnography" by allowing more people to upload, share, modify, and attach tags to materials online. This new online context is being referred to as Web 2.0, a term that Wesch says "suggests that we do not fully understand the current webscape, only that it is different from what it just now ceased to be" (2007).

Clearly the collaborative possibilities that the Internet offers to visual anthropologists are yet to be explored. Even those, like Wesch, who have the technological expertise are deterred by the ethical issues that it invokes. However, others have taken up the potential for collaboration in processes by which knowledge is produced, either during fieldwork (see above) or during the editing of a film or multimedia project, where electronic media may be used in more controlled ways. Salazar writes about his own collaborative digital videomaking project, developed with the Mapuche videomaker Jeannette Paillan. Over three years the two worked together to produce the documentary video *From Land to Screen* (2004), using digital tools and maintaining communication between Salazar's base in Australia and Paillan in Chile through the electronic exchange of compressed video files. The final production included video files from some of Paillan's previous work, which were used as "a kind of 'visual quote.'" This made the postproduction process "a question of "negotiation" and a "form of collaborative authorship" (2005, 71–72). The work thus commented critically on the "hegemonic construction" of representations of similar topics by mainstream and other nonindigenous media.

Others also have strong hopes that digital technologies will provide visual anthropologists with ways to create critical interventions that go beyond those possible with documentary video. In his earlier work, Biella indicated that interactive and nonlinear hypermedia had potential to counter racism (e.g., Biella 1994). In a more recent essay he elaborates this argument: "Ethnographic films that depict the intimate confidences between anthropologists and informants, and show intimacies among informants, offer viewers the vicarious experience and discovery of close personal revelations and vulnerabilities by people in other cultural worlds. . . . They can promote a sense of *virtual intimacy*" through which "a strong component of cross-cultural racism is overcome" (2008). Because it brings to viewers a form of intimacy that does not require immediate reciprocation, "Visual Anthropology can present countermeasures to the blunted sensitivities of militaristic, racist and sexist ideology." Thus, "film intimacy is a safe first step into a world of increased awareness and compassion." Biella warns, however, that filmic representations alone are not enough. "Although images of intimacy have the power to transform negative emotions, they can also be used to reinforce stereotypes" (2008), since (recalling the reservations expressed by Wesch [2007] and myself) the "abuse of intimacy" is also possible.

As I have argued elsewhere (Pink 2006), a limitation of anthropological film is that it lacks the cultural contextualization and theoretical explicitness that are sometimes necessary to promote cross-cultural understanding. Biella takes a similar tack, suggesting that "new computer-based media," by using appropriately designed combinations of "scholarship, media interactivity and film shooting styles," can play an important role in the promotion of intimacy across cultures, and thus counter racism, militarism, and hypermasculinity. "The link between theory and visual media is particularly important for the goals of an anthropology of intimacy," he writes, suggesting that "if ethnographers wished to attack the problems of stereotypic readings, they could place footage on screen, expose and dissect the implicit default meanings, and subject them to counter-interpretations." This is the approach that Biella has taken in the production of his forthcoming work *Maasai Interactive*. Notably he publishes his projects on CD and DVD; the work is interactive and invites its users to forge their own pathways through it (Biella 2007). However, as a collaborative practice it is distinguished from the open-ended processes offered by Web 2.0 in that Biella maintains a degree of authorial control and designs his texts according to an agenda that seeks to challenge and shift the ways their users think about others.

Final Thoughts: Has Visual Anthropology Gone Digital?

Insofar as most visual anthropologists are by now using digital media to produce, store, edit, and disseminate their work, it would be fair to say that we are living in an age of a digital visual anthropology. However, if we shift this definition of digital visual anthropology to one that entails the establishment of new and innovative practices that stand to change the way the subdiscipline works both within academia and as a public anthropology, then the extent to which visual anthropology has "gone digital" is much narrower. At the beginning of this article I noted that I would be writing mainly about the work of a few "pioneers," those who are using digital media to push at the existing boundaries of visual anthropology to produce works that are collaborative, that traverse the frontiers of anthropology, that challenge existing practice, and that introduce novel combinations of multiple media. In this sense, digital visual anthropology is still in its infancy. Many visual anthropologists are now using digital video cameras and editing. However, they are not (although they have the technology to do so in their hands) producing interactive multimedia projects like Peter Biella and Jay Ruby, nor are they posting their video texts on YouTube or Mojiti like Michael Wesch. More are sharing their materials with those whom their work concerns or represents (e.g., Durington 2007; Martinez Perez 2007), as I did myself as I developed my current research on British Slow Cities. Some, like the ERA and DART projects, are using digital visual materials in teaching and learning or are designing software for visual methods. Although the number of practitioners of this type of digital visual anthropology is steadily increasing, as yet it is the domain of a narrow group.

For some, the funding sources available for hypermedia development present a serious limitation. For instance, Glowczewski complains, that "even though the DVD medium has taken over the video market, there are few interactive documentaries available on DVD. Only big production companies and TV channels can afford to pay the costs of such digital productions, including the copyright payments for distribution. This financial limitation is damaging to the future of visual anthropology and ethnographic films because DVD is the perfect format for documentation and analysis" (2005, 32). While such funding might be hard to obtain, there are other models for anthropological hypermedia production that are available to visual anthropologists. We do not need such big productions to create visual anthropology texts that are collaborative, that seek to make interventions in the public sphere, that students can learn with, and that at the same time contribute to academic debate. But we do need technical skills, an understanding of the potentials and powers of the medium (cf. Wesch 2007), and an appreciation of how visual and written text might work together in an interactive multimedia environment. While pedagogical projects such as ERA and DART have been developed with funding support, and *Yanomamö Interactive* was finally redeveloped by technical developers employed by its publisher, research-based anthropological hypermedia text have evolved along less costly routes. They require that visual anthropologists have access to digital equipment, software, and skills, but once these are acquired, in principle they should be no more costly to produce than are written texts. Here it is important to keep in mind the role of visual anthropologists themselves in driving the development of new digital visual anthropology practice. Salazar has suggested that "new digital media arguably have the potential to reinstate anthropology as a critical 'text' in the picturing of experiential knowledge and cultural phenomena in the context of emerging digital cultures and convergence" (Salazar 2005, 65). I would rephrase this to suggest that it is the practitioners who have the potential.

Finally, a digital visual anthropology needs to be theoretically and methodologically engaged in order to be meaningful to and influential in the mainstream debates in anthropology. A strand in the theorizing of visual anthropology, related to the phenomenological approach outlined above, focuses, in various incarnations, on the intimacy (Biella 1994, 2008) and corporeality (MacDougall 2006) of filmic representations, its potential for synesthetic and empathetic forms of communication.

Elsewhere, I have argued that for such filmic representations to achieve their potential to communicate in this way in any academic, public, or pedagogic context, they also need to be contextualized so that they are correctly situated in relation to culturally specific knowledge and academic meanings that are not represented in the film (Pink 2006).

Hypermedia can support this; the potential to combine media in hypermedia projects is also what gives it its social intervention, pedagogic, and academic advantages over separate written anthropology and anthropological documentaries (and viral videos). It allows us to combine the intimacy and corporeality through which ethnographic film invokes empathetic understandings, with, on the one hand, rigorous theorizing, and, on the other, detailed contextualizing knowledge. While I do not believe it will or should replace film/videomaking or writing, hypermedia has an important role to play in the future of visual anthropology.

Notes

1. http://youtube.com/watch?v=6gmP4nk0EOE (accessed February 9, 2007). At the time Wesch was assistant professor of cultural anthropology at Kansas State University.
2. http://www.media-anthropology.net (accessed March 12, 2007).
3. Visual Anthropology Review 23, no. 2 (2007).
4. Michael Wesch, interview with John Battelle, published on Battelle's Blog, http://battellemedia.com/archives/003386.php (accessed February 25, 2007).
5. In *The Future of Visual Anthropology* (Pink 2006) I suggest that applied visual anthropology be seen as the fourth component of visual anthropology (see esp. chap. 5) and that visual anthropology has a role to play in a public anthropology (see chap. 7).
6. For example in the work of Mike Fischer in the UK and Brian Schwimmer in the US. See http://www.umanitoba.ca/anthropology/kintitle.html (accessed March 12, 2007.)
7. http://www.alanmacfarlane.com/TEXTS/computerland.pdf (accessed February 9, 2007).
8. Funded by the Economic and Social Research Council, UK.
9. http://www.rsl.ox.ac.uk/isca/marcus.banks.01.html (accessed February 22, 2007).
10. http://www.usc.edu/dept/elab/welcome/codifications.html (accessed February 22, 2007).
11. Funded by Unilever Research.
12. Funded by the Nuffield Foundation.

13. For details on DART, see the documents at https://dart.columbia.edu/ project/projectdocuments/Project_Plan_1.doc (accessed February 22, 2007). The descriptions of ERA in this paragraph are quoted from http://era .anthropology.ac.uk; those of DART, from http://www.lse.ac.uk/collections/ anthropology/dart.htm.

14. "What's Going On?" http://clt011.lse.ac.uk:8383/steve/wgo/wgoLevel1 .html (accessed March 5, 2007).

15. http://www.aaanet.org/press/an/0405aa-news.htm. Lathrop names Charles Stafford (LSE) and Nicholas Dirks (Columbia) as principal investigators and Gustav Pebbles and Rashmi Sadana (LSE) and Luke Freeman and Jerome Lewis (Columbia) as the research fellows, but does not attribute this quotation to a particular individual.

16. See http://anthromethods.net/amwiki/AnthroTools/AnthroTools.html. For details on Image Interviewer, discussed below, see http://anthromethods .net/amwiki/AnthroTools/g1/g1/36.html?branch=1&language=1 (accessed March 2, 2007).

17. For details, see http://anthromethods.net/amwiki/AnthroTools/g1/g1/39. html?branch=1&language=1. Quote is from http://sourceforge.net/projects/ videogrok (both accessed March 2, 2007).

18. http://mediatedcultures.net/ksudigg/?page_id=61.

19. http://astro.temple.edu/~ruby/opp/ (accessed March 12, 2007).

NINE

Native Intelligence: A Short History of Debates on Indigenous Media and Ethnographic Film

FAYE GINSBURG

In the three final decades of the twentieth century, and into the twenty-first, as indigenous people began to gain control over film and video, technologies of representation that had long objectified them, a series of debates emerged that challenged this project. Some scholars questioned whether the radical alterity of indigenous cultural life might translate to the screen, some could scarcely tolerate the idea of natives using cameras and thought the very idea of indigenous media was an oxymoron, and some took more celebratory approaches, imagining that this work had displaced that which ethnographic film had previously engaged in. Now, as indigenous people are showing feature films at Cannes and starting their own national television networks—such as the Aboriginal People's Television Network (APTN), founded in Canada in 1999, and Maori TV, established in 2004—the debates have moved on. Is the separatism implied by the term "indigenous media" still appropriate in cases of deep collaboration, such as *The Journals of Knud Rasmussen*, which the Inuit filmmakers of Igloolik Isuma co-produced in collaboration with a Danish team, relying for their story and visuals on Rasmussen's ethnographic journals? On the other hand, will initiatives such as APTN, Maori TV, and the more recent Australian Aboriginal television station—National Indigenous Television—create sequestered media worlds that will become the televisual equivalent to "reservations"? This essay addresses this history of debates and the current issues that are shaping contemporary work.

The Anxieties and Possibilities of the Parallax Effect

In May 2007 a newspaper article in the *Australian* announced an indigenous protest in the real world concerning the virtual appropriation of a major Aboriginal sacred site into the trendy online world of Second Life 3-D (created in 2003). The protestors' concern was directed against Telstra, Australia's largest telecommunications corporation and creator of The Pond, a virtual island and popular destination representing things Australian on Second Life. The Anangu people, indigenous owners of Uluru in South Australia (well-known to tourists and others by its English name, Ayers Rock), were concerned about the possible desecration, albeit virtual, of the online representation of the site, a dramatic geological formation and part of their sacred ancestral heritage. The virtual Uluru, like its physical counterpart, was protected by barriers to discourage people from walking or flying over the site. Nonetheless, "representatives of the traditional owners . . . warned that even with the restrictions, it may be possible to view sacred sites around [the virtual] Uluru."

In the physical world, non-Aboriginal visitors have, since 1987, faced strict prohibitions against photography or filming without consent of the indigenous landowners. Telstra's spokesperson confirmed that the company had not sought the permission of Uluru's landowners to use images of the site for commercial purposes (Canning 2007). The case heated up in October 2008 when the telecommunications corporation posted billboards advertising its Big Pond Internet service in front of the virtual Uluru, as well as serving grog—alcohol—at the Billabong Bar, an adjacent pub. If the rules of the real world applied in Second Life, the bar would be right in the middle of the Mutitjulu community—a dry area. Telstra removed the billboards after protests. Meanwhile, many indigenous Australians living in remote areas wondered whether they might be served by the much publicized rollout of broadband services, a form of digital stratification that is too rarely discussed (figure 9.1).

This story seems profoundly contemporary in its concern with the virtual and the difficulties of containing cultural and intellectual property in a digital viral medium. Yet, it is emblematic of many of the epistemologically challenging issues that have been raised in the field of visual anthropology over the last three decades—if not longer—concerning the status and implications of indigenous media.[1] In this short history of debates in the field, the Second Life story reminds us that they are not only academic but also, of course, have consequences in the lives of

9.1. Cartoon by Peter Nicholson commenting on the digital age in indigenous Australia. From the *Australian* (newspaper); http://www.nicholsoncartoons.com.au.

indigenous people themselves, many of whom are avid producers and consumers of visual media of all kinds. Through these activities, they have become increasingly aware of how dominant cultural protocols regarding media—valorizing free and open access—are at times very different from those in their own cultures, where certain forms of mediation are restricted in their circulation.

This kind of conundrum shapes some of the central and enduring concerns in the field of indigenous media. These include:

- questions of cultural difference that frame not only media representation and indigenous aesthetics but also the very notion of what can or cannot be rendered visually accessible to those in or outside particular communities, a set of concerns that might fall under the rubric "image ethics" (Gross et al. 2003; Leuthold 1998);
- problems with control over the increasingly promiscuous circulation of images, with sacred objects, sites, and activities that should only be witnessed by initiated traditional owners offering an extreme case, the repatriation of archives another;
- ways in which both radical alterity—profound cultural, cosmological, political, aesthetic difference from Western norms—and rights to represent indigenous realities are negotiated through contemporary media worlds, both on and off screen; and
- the uptake of media practices as an extension of cultural and political activism to establish the presence of indigenous lives within their own communities, in nation-states, and on the world stage.

These questions—which hover around concerns regarding who has the right to represent indigenous lives and landscapes in both old and new media forms—are themselves not new. Indeed, they linger in the background of what is considered the foundational text in this field, Sol Worth and John Adair's classic study *Through Navajo Eyes*, first published in 1973. That book inaugurated a paradigm shift in the field of visual anthropology, albeit one that took some time to be more fully articulated. While Worth and Adair's book focused on whether novice Navajo filmmakers would make films that embodied the radical alterity of other cultural perspectives when brought to a new medium—that is, would their films "be Navajo" in some fundamental way—it also, perhaps unwittingly, opened the eyes of many Anglophone readers who at the time had not yet imagined (with the exception of those familiar with the work of French anthropologist/filmmaker Jean Rouch) that the camera might be put in the hands of those who had historically been objects of the anthropological gaze. The unexpected elegance of this idea—that this technology might allow many to encounter the native's point of view without the mediation of either the ethnographer or anthropological language—was exciting to some but apparently threatening to others, who continued to try to police the legitimacy of indigenous media throughout the 1990s, arguing that the technology of the camera was fundamentally Western.[2]

The logical if unintended consequence of Worth and Adair's interest in literally seeing other worldviews was to open people's minds as to who might have the right to represent other cultural worlds through a variety of media—including film, photography, and video. No longer could one assume that it was the exclusive domain of the anthropologist (or filmmaker) to make documentary or other photographic/moving-image representations of indigenous people. The fact that cameras were circulating among many of the world's subaltern subjects did not necessarily undermine the legitimacy of ethnographic film, but rather drew the genre into a salutary dialogue with another, emerging field of representations, creating what I have characterized elsewhere as a cultural "parallax effect." The idea of the parallax effect, as I have described it, was

originally invented to describe the phenomenon that occurs when a change in the position of the observer creates the illusion that an object has been displaced or moved. . . . In optics, the small parallax created by the slightly different angles of vision of each eye is recognized as that which enables us to judge distances accurately and see in three dimensions. Drawing on a similar principle, one might understand indigenous media as arising from a historically new positioning of the observed behind the camera so that the object—the cinematic representation of culture—appears to look different than it does from the observational perspective of ethnographic film. Yet, by juxtaposing these different but related kinds of cinematic perspectives on culture, one can create a kind of parallax effect; if harnessed analytically, these "slightly different angles of vision" can offer a fuller comprehension of the complexity—the three dimensionality, so to speak—of the social phenomenon we call culture and those media representations that self-consciously engage with it. It is my argument that resituating ethnographic film in relation to related practices such as indigenous media can help expand the field's possibilities and revive its contemporary interest and purpose beyond a narrowly defined field. The parallax created by the different perspectives in these media practices is one that is particularly important now as anthropology struggles to position itself in relation to contemporary critiques. (Ginsburg 1994b, 158)

Now, more than a decade after I wrote that essay, it is clear that both fields—indigenous media and ethnographic film—have continued to develop, in the context of the dizzying proliferation of media forms and images that distinguishes the contemporary era. From the vantage point of the early twenty-first century, it is hard to imagine that just over a decade ago, some scholars were assuming that the uptake of media in indigenous communities would be the death knell of "authentic cultural practices," despite considerable evidence to the contrary. The broader question this raised—what I called the Faustian contract in 1991—as to whether indigenous (or indeed, minority or dominated subjects anywhere) can assimilate dominant media to their own cultural and political concerns or are inevitably compromised by its presence, haunted much of the research and debate on the topic of the cross-cultural spread of media.

If anything, the opposite has turned out to be the case. Indigenous media work has shown itself to be a particularly robust form of contemporary cultural objectification. From small-scale video and local radio to archival websites to national television stations and feature films, indigenous media-makers have found opportunities for cultural creativity of all sorts. These projects often support the maintenance or even revival of ritual practices and local languages, while building forms of cultural labor that repair fraying intergenerational relationships and bring much-needed sources of productive activity, and at times income, into communities that suffer from high rates of poverty and unemployment. The work has developed across a range of technologies and community or institutional bases, most notably:

- small-format local productions, originally produced in analog video in the 1980s, and now increasingly on digital video;

- local and regional television created over the last two decades, facilitated initially by the launch of communication satellites over remote areas, as with CAAMA in Central Australia and Inuit Broadcasting in Canada, and now utilizing digital possibilities, as inaugurated in 2009 with Isuma TV in Nunavut, Canada, by Igloolik Isuma;[3]
- indigenously run national television stations, beginning with
  - Aboriginal People's Television Network (APTN) in Canada (1999),
  - Maori TV in New Zealand/Aoteoroa (2003) (and a second channel for Maori speakers in 2007),
  - Taiwan Indigenous Television (2005), and
  - National Indigenous Television (NITV) in Australia (2007);
- fiction filmmaking, including the production of approximately forty indigenously directed feature films, which have circulated not only through a lively, worldwide circuit of indigenous film festivals but also at mainstream venues, such as Cannes, the Toronto International Film Festival, and the Sundance Film Festival (where they have garnered both financial backing and cultural capital in the form of major prizes);
- digital media, with cross platforms and epistemologies, raising important questions about representation and the materiality of different media (from the virtual world issues of the opening example to concerns about the increasing stratification of media practices that are dependent on literacy-based media forms) and exploiting the possibilities of the digital to circulate indigenous media to remote communities around the world (as Isuma TV and its 2009 retooling, the Nunavut Independent TV Network, have done);[4] and
- indigenous archives based on the repatriation of ethnographic and other films and photographs made in earlier, often colonial/settler eras. These archives have become an increasingly important and exciting social practice and are enhanced by mindful use of digital technologies, often created through deeply collaborative creative partnerships with technically skilled nonindigenous fellow travelers. Together they have imagined and invented new ways to build in cultural protocols and support for nonalphabetic language use, as in the groundbreaking work of the Ara Irititja project in Australia.[5] For other important work in this area, see Anderson 2009; Bryson 2002; Christen 2005; Christie 2005; Ginsburg 2008; Lydon 2005; Salazar 2004, 2007; Srinivasan et al 2009.

While I cannot cover all of these areas in depth in the space of this chapter, I will attempt to give a broad sense as to how these technologies have differentially shaped the development of indigenous media under different media regimes.

FAYE GINSBURG

Indigenous Media: Mediating Culture and the Activist Imaginary

Since the 1980s Indigenous media has attracted ongoing and sometimes intense scholarly attention.[6] Central to much of this work is a recognition that the uptake of new media technologies by indigenous producers was often motivated—at least initially—by a desire to "talk back" to structures of power that have erased or distorted indigenous interests and realities. Many of the works and projects that have been produced might best be understood as forms of "cultural activism," a term I have used to underscore the intertwined sense of both political agency and cultural intervention that people bring to these efforts, part of a spectrum of practices of self-conscious mediation, and mobilization of culture more generally, that took on particular shape and velocity beginning in the late twentieth century (Ginsburg 1993, 1997; Mahon 2000). In the mid-1990s George Marcus coined another, related term, "the activist imaginary," to describe how subaltern groups turn to film, video, and other media not only to "pursue traditional goals of broad-based social change through a politics of identity and representation" but also out of a utopian desire for "emancipatory projects . . . raising fresh issues about citizenship and the shape of public spheres within the frame and terms of traditional discourse on polity and civil society" (1996, 6). Even as indigenous media practices have evolved in their sophistication and reach in many parts of the world, these central motivations continue to drive much of the work, from remote communities to urban centers, a point that is underscored in the writing about this work.

In two key locales—Canada and Australia—indigenous media first developed in response to the entry of mass media into the lives of First Nations people, primarily through the state's imposition of satellite-based commercial television over remote regions where more traditional populations lived, beginning in Canada in the late 1970s (Roth 2005) and in Australia in the 1980s. Remote communities vigorously opposed the "dumping" of mainstream media into their lives without the opportunity to shape their own media to meet local concerns. At the same time, the increasing availability of inexpensive, user-friendly, small-format analog video presented an opportunity for these groups to produce their own work, which some indigenous activists imagined, metaphorically, as a shield of local manufacture that might fend off the invasion of signals from the dominant culture.

This happened with the early foundational case made famous by activist researcher Eric Michaels, a student of Jay Ruby, who built on and transformed Ruby's ideas when he was hired to study the impact of media on indigenous people living in the Central Desert of Australia. In the 1980s he worked with Warlpiri people to help them develop their own analog video practices and low-power television—what he called *The Aboriginal Invention of Television in Central Australia* (1986)—created as an alternative to the onslaught of commercial television via the satellite. Michaels's work was foundational for the emergence of indigenous media as a topic in visual anthropology. He showed how local indigenous media might be particularly well suited for anthropological inquiry; small in scale and sustaining an alternative to the mass media industries that dominate late capitalist societies, these practices occupy a clear position of difference from dominant cultural assumptions about media aesthetics and practices. Thus they provided a kind of natural laboratory for understanding the possibilities of radically different media practices that are "off the grid" of most media scholarship (which is largely Eurocentric) or for research addressing indigenous lives (in which media practices are too easily regarded as either epiphenomenal or insufficiently traditional). As Michaels pointed out in the 1980s:

[Aboriginal] art or video objects become difficult to isolate for analysis because the producer's intention is the opposite. Warlpiri artists demonstrate their own invisibility in order to assert the work's authority and continuity with tradition. They do not draw attention to themselves or to their creativity. (1984, 34)

Building on this insight, I have pointed to the significance of "embedded aesthetics" in indigenous media being produced in traditional Aboriginal communities, the producers of which maintain a system of evaluation that refuses a separation of textual production and circulation from broader arenas of social relations. Rather, the quality of a work is assessed according to its capacity to embody, sustain, and even revive or create certain social relations. Indigenous media, then, can be seen as a new and complex object operating in a number of domains as an extension of collective self-production (Ginsburg 1994b, 368). As another instance of this complex sense of aesthetics, Jennifer Deger's book on her work with Yolngu media-making in northern Australia focuses on what one might call an indigenous (Yolngu) theory of "media effects," in which traditional concepts of the impact of revelation/witnessing/showing can be constitutive of identity, a kind of active viewing that empowers and catalyzes ancestral power, rendered evident even if it is not actually visible (Deger 2006). In other parts of the world, for example among the

Aymara and Quechua filmmakers who make up the Bolivian indigenous media collective CEFREC, there is a refusal of authorship in the production of films and a "noncapitalist" economy that shapes the circuits of exhibition and exchange that are fundamental to the Andean indigenous media world (Himpele 2007).

Debates about such work contribute to and reflect the changing and sometimes contested status of "culture" both in local worlds and in a globalizing world where culture is increasingly commodified, as well as in social/anthropological theory and, importantly, in the writings of indigenous filmmakers and intellectuals (Barclay 1990; Langton 1993; Masayesva 1995; Mita 1995; Muenala 1995; Raheja, forthcoming; Singer 2001). "Culture" is a category that is increasingly objectified and mediated as it becomes a source of claims for political and human rights both within the nation-states encompassing indigenous people and on the world stage. As Terry Turner has shown in regard to the work of Kayapo media-makers, cultural claims "can be converted into political assets, both internally as bases of group solidarity and mobilization, and externally as claims on the support of other social groups, governments and public opinion all over the globe" (1993, 424).

The Politics of Research

Indigenous media projects have often been a site for activist participation on the part of anthropologists and communications scholars (like Michaels and many others since then), as they and indigenous intellectuals alike have been quick to see the political promise and cultural possibilities of indigenously controlled media-making. Such collaborations include work such as Harald Prins's advocacy media productions with Micmac, Apache, and other groups (2002), my own work with Aboriginal Australians (Ginsburg 1991, 2002), Terry Turner and Vincent Carelli's successful projects helping to launch Amazonian media (Aufderheide 1995; Carelli 1988; Turner 2002), and a host of others (see Wilson and Stewart 2008). These collaborative research projects—what Jean Rouch called *anthropologie partagée* (shared anthropology)—have helped to produce and promote as well as analyze the making of film and video as part of indigenous projects of cultural revival, whether through recording traditional rituals or through the use of video, film, and media events as a persuasive tool for claims to political sovereignty. These scholars and others have actively supported indigenous media production, while recognizing the dilemmas that such work can present. Prins, for example, who has helped to catalyze indigenous filmmaking for Native American claims to land and cultural rights, nonetheless points out "the paradox of primitivism," in which traditional imagery of indigenous people in documentaries about native rights, while effective (perhaps even essential) as a form of political agency, may also distort the cultural processes that indigenous peoples are committed to preserving (2002).

Often doing fieldwork among and sympathizing with dominated groups, anthropologists feel a responsibility to support projects by non-Western or postcolonial groups that are resisting the impositions of Western or global capitalist media. While the media we study may be "off the map" of dominant media cartographies, they are no less crucial to the transformations of the twenty-first century. Those studying indigenous media seek to grasp the ways media are integrated into communities that are parts of nations and states, as well as transnational networks and circuits produced in the worlds of late capitalism and postcolonial cultural politics. Our relations with those we study are changing as our cultural worlds grow closer in ways that push the boundaries of anthropology; it is difficult to exoticize others or to maintain fictions of bounded or untouched communities of difference when one includes media in one's purview, if only because it forces a recognition that "natives" are deeply engaged in establishing their own multiple representational strategies and objectifications on their own terms, through forms marked as resolutely modern, yet which are indigenized in multiple ways. Local uses and meanings of media and of comparative political economies of media production and consumption (including real constraints posed by the unreliability of electricity and the vicissitudes of poverty) suggest the persistence of difference and the importance of locality, while highlighting the forms of inequality that continue to structure our world.

While anthropologists and media scholars debate the impact that media technologies might have on the communities with which they work and whence they come, indigenous media-makers are busy using and rethinking the technologies for their own purposes. Activists are documenting traditional activities with elders and working with them to repatriate archival material; creating works to teach young people literacy in their own languages, using many forms, including the radically underappreciated but deeply significant radio; engaging with dominant circuits of mass media to project political struggles through mainstream as well as alternative arenas; communicating among dispersed kin and communities on a range of issues; using video as legal documents in negotiations with states; presenting videos on state television to assert their presence televisually within national imaginaries; and creating award-winning feature films. Whatever the contradictions, when new technologies are embraced as powerful forms of collective self-production, they enable indigenous cultural activists to assert their presence in the polities that encompass them, and to more easily enter into much larger movements for social transformation for the recognition and redress of human and cultural rights, processes in which media play an increasingly important role (Castells 1996).

Perhaps the most articulate theorization of indigenous media has come from the work of the late Maori filmmaker and intellectual Barry Barclay, who coined the term "Fourth Cinema" in his book *Our Own Image*, published in 1990. In that publication, and in almost all of his writing until his death in 2008, he argues for indigenous filmmaking as a *hui* (the term for a Maori gathering or meeting), drawing on the power of community on and off the screen. As film scholar Stuart Murray explains in his book *Images of Dignity*:

> In keeping with his developing ideas about Fourth Cinema, Barclay saw all of his features as comprising multiple elements—from the pre-production consultation with the communities to be filmed, to the actual detail of the shooting, and on to the questions of distribution, reception and film use. (2008, 6)

Barclay's emphasis on *korero*, or protocols, and on ensuring that the end product was appropriately returned to those who had given it, has established a notion of total filmmaking, an inclusive process of discussion and advice (2008, 69).

As Barclay and others suggest, indigenous media worldwide represent a countercurrent to neoliberal trends that seek to deracinate and commodify culture. Often working against the grain of a late-capitalist economy, indigenous producers seek to circulate their work based on terms other than profit. Instead, productions are understood as based on embedded notions of reciprocity, cultural rights, and the need for communities to maintain guardianship over work so that circulation and archives are managed according to local protocols.

The Case of Indigenous Television

Given the prominence of experiments in television in the broader debates concerning indigenous media in visual anthropology, I want to explore the issues raised by this medium in some depth. Television—from low power operations to terrestrial national channels to satellite—has been used for almost four decades by indigenous communities around the world. This usage began with the launch of communications satellites over the Canadian Arctic in the 1970s, which motivated Inuit communities to create their own productions, with the Inuit Broadcasting Corporation being established in 1982 (Meadows and Molnar 2001; Roth 2005). Indigenous television experiments offer a power alternative to the notion of television as a "vast wasteland," the term coined and made famous in 1961 by Newton Minow, in his first speech as chairman of the US Federal Communications Commission. Rather, they show how the medium can be reimagined to promote and develop the cultural resurgence of minoritized communities, providing a provocative case study around which the global impact of television can be reexamined and understood.

Over the last three decades, television has spread from centers to peripheries and from earth to sky, as media technology has expanded from terrestrial TV to the more flexible range of satellite and small-format video and, increasingly, digital convergence with the Internet (Jenkins 2007). The result has been what some call "Planet TV" (Parks and Kumar 2002). The localized possibilities in this form of globalization are especially apparent in the uptake of such media forms in First Peoples' communities throughout the world, creating "something new in the air" (Roth 2005), modes of communication that could be seen as having much longer histories—from "songlines to satellites" (Meadows and Molnar 2001) or "from birchbark talk to digital dreamspeaking" (Buddle-Crowe 1991), to use the poetics of some key studies. The capacity of such media to communicate the concerns of indigenous people to many audiences has created, some argue, a discursive space for an emergent indigenous public sphere (Hartley and McKee 2000); this view is countered, however, by the most pessimistic, who suggest that these projects inevitably entail a corrupt relationship that involves "getting into bed with the state" (Batty 2003).

Concerns about compromise haunt much of the early research and debate on indigenous media, echoing the suspicions of indigenous communities as they struggled to imagine how they might turn the imposition of technologies such as television—described early on by Inuit leader Rosemary Kuptana as a potential neutron bomb—to their advantage. Generally, this has involved recognition of the cultural possibilities of indigenously controlled media-making as a way of rendering the nations that encompass indigenous communities more aware of their concerns, while also strengthening internal intergenerational and intercommunity knowledge. When indigenous producers can control or even redesign the circumstances of production and circulation, indigenous activists have embraced television and other media as allowing them some degree of agency and enhanced cultural expression, albeit within hegemonic forms of representation, and often under less than ideal conditions (Ginsburg 1991).

To some extent, indigenous concerns about compromise were lessened by the fact that many of the communication technologies they wanted to use initially were regarded as experimental and marginal. Indeed, the very idea of indigenous television was regarded as somewhat of an oxymoron, which often made it possible for early projects to develop under the radar of state scrutiny, unfolding at their own pace, in line with indigenously based ideas of appropriate production and circulation practices, as well as aesthetics (Leuthold 1998). As indigenous television has come to play more of a role in the global mediasphere, however, concern has resurfaced that it will be increasingly compromised by the homogenizing demands of "broadcast standards" (Stefanoff 2009).

Local indigenous television projects first emerged, as I have noted, in Canada in the 1970s and Australia in the 1980s; these were followed, in the 1990s, by other varieties of indigenous television in the United States, Brazil, Bolivia, and Mexico. The vehicles for these ventures include localized, low-power television, as with Radio y Video Tamix in Mexico or PAW TV in Yuendumu, Australia (*television sin reglas*—television without rules—as one scholar of Mexican indigenous media puts it; Wortham 2002, 265); regional remote networks, such as the Central Australian Aboriginal Media Association (Stefanoff 2009); units affiliated with national television, such as the Indigenous Production Units inaugurated in 1988 as part of Australia's ABC and SBS stations; and national stations underwritten by the government, as with the Aboriginal People's Television Network in Canada (Hafsteinsson 2007; Roth 2005), Maori TV in Aotearoa/New Zealand (Ginsburg and Strickland 2004), Taiwan Indigenous Television in Taiwan, and National Indigenous Television in Australia.

Following on the heels of broader movements for indigenous rights, activists in a number of locales pushed government bodies to allocate resources for their communities to produce and circulate representations of themselves, their histories, and their worldviews. Of particular concern was the capacity to create programming for all age groups and in local languages, to combat the overwhelming effects of exposure to the dominant culture and its language elsewhere on television. This debate was active in the 1970s and resurfaced in 2005 regarding language policy on Canada's APTN and New Zealand's Maori TV. Eventually, the indigenous appropriation of television was recognized as an important technology in the development of indigenous citizenship for those living in both remote and urban areas, and for their recognition by the surrounding settler societies as well. Significantly, these developments have also served as incubators of indigenous talent, as indigenous producers, directors, actors, and editors have enjoyed opportunities that never before existed; increasingly, indigenous work from different parts of the world circulates internationally, forming a regular part of programming for these television stations.

Scholars and researchers have been attracted to indigenous television since the mid-1980s, seeking in it the empirical evidence for a kind of embedded cultural critique, an aesthetic and political alternative to mass media that is beholden to governmental or late-capitalist interests. This sense of possibility was first articulated in the work of Eric Michaels (mentioned earlier), which showed the complex epistemologies surrounding image production in traditional Aboriginal life—including the significance of kin groups and cosmologies in the off-screen production of work as a source of authentication as to the truth value of the final product, and the extension of traditional linguistic taboos on using the names of those who had died to prohibitions on circulating images of the dead.

As indigenous media productions have developed under these regimes, the work has increasingly circulated beyond the televisual moment of broadcast to other native communities, through the circulation of tapes, films, DVDs, and Internet portals, as well as to non-Aboriginal audiences, via regional, national, and even international television. Such extensions of the life of this work help overcome the risk of indigenous media's being restricted to particular channels or programming slots—what one scholar has termed "media reservations" (Roth 2005). More broadly, the telling and circulation of indigenous stories and histories through media forms that can circulate beyond the local has been an important force for constituting claims for land and cultural rights and for developing alliances with other communities.

Getting indigenous histories into mainstream media—as indigenous units affiliated with national broadcasters have done—has been a critical goal everywhere, as Aboriginal citizens feel their contributions to national narratives have largely been erased or ignored. The broadcast in Australia in late 2008 of the seven-part, indigenously directed series *First Australians* was widely regarded as a major breakthrough, offering a compelling counternarrative of the nation's history, from the precontact period to the present, from an indigenous point of view. The prominent indigenous filmmaker Rachel Perkins (Arrente/Kalkadoon) directed four of the episodes, while Beck Cole (Warramungu/Luritja) directed three. In addition to its paradigm-changing effect on the Australian public sphere, the series demonstrated the productivity of colonial archival film and photography when it is appropriated, resignified, and repurposed by indigenous media-makers as visible evidence of their experiences. The series received lengthy and laudatory coverage in the mainstream press; it was, said one writer in *The Age*, "one of the most significant documentary series in the history of Australian television. For the first time, the story of Aboriginal Australia has been condensed into a coherent narrative that begins with the mythological birth of humanity on this continent."[7] The series was accompanied by a book, *First Australians: A Visual History* (2009), edited by Rachel Perkins and Marcia Langton, which elaborated on the historical and visual archival sources that were used in the films.

Six months later, *American Experience*, a production of the Public Broadcasting Service in the United States, televised its five-part series *We Shall Remain*, which focused on key moments in Native American history. Four of the five episodes were directed by established indigenous directors, including three by Chris Eyre (Cheyenne/Arapaho) and one by Dustinn Craig (Apache), and each was guided by a team of scholars. The project, as the series' website proclaimed, created "a provocative multi-media project that establishes Native history as an essential part of American history."[8]

The most recent and perhaps most innovative experiment in indigenous television has been the launch of the Nunavut Independent TV Network (NITV) on Isuma TV on May 29, 2009. NITV is the latest venture of the long-standing and always groundbreaking remote collective Igloolik Isuma, perhaps the best known of the world's indigenous media groups, thanks in large part to the global success of its film *Atanarjuat, the Fast Runner* (2000), the first Inuit feature film, created through their distinctive community-based production process. Isuma's most recent film, *Before Tomorrow* (2008, Arnait women's collective), is likewise gathering prizes on its festival run. The group developed its video style in the 1980s and formed officially in 1990, turning televisual technologies into vehicles for cultural expression of Inuit lives and histories. Headed by director Zacharias Kunuk, Isuma engages Igloolik community members, while Brooklyn-born filmmaker and Isuma partner Norman Cohn leads a support team in Montreal. Frustrated by the difficulty of showing its work to other Inuit communities, the group, in 2008, launched Isuma TV, a free Internet video portal for global indigenous media, making its productions available to both local audiences and worldwide viewers. NITV on Isuma TV is a digital distribution project, bringing a high-speed version of Isuma TV into remote Nunavut communities where the bandwidth is often inadequate even to view YouTube. NITV allows films to be uploaded from anywhere, rebroadcast through local cable or low-power channels, or downloaded to digital projectors. The bigger story here concerns the unanticipated possibilities presented to indigenous cultural activists at moments of media innovation. As Cohn explains:

We saw the historical technological "moment of opportunity" for the Internet, the way we saw the analog video moment in 1970 and the *Atanarjuat* digital/film moment in 1998: the brief window in the technology of communication where marginalized users with a serious political and cultural objective could bypass centuries of entrenched powerlessness with a serious new idea at a much higher level of visibility than usual in our top-down power-driven global politics. In 2007, internet capacity allowed us to end-run the film industry entirely and launch a video website that could take aspects of YouTube to a much higher level of thematic seriousness, and see what happens. So this is a serious experiment in the history of alternate media experiments since the early 70s, as Isuma has been from the start, helping viewers see indigenous reality from its own point of view.[9]

First Nations/First Features

Feature film offers a different kind of practice, creating new opportunities for the recognition of the complex realities of a range of indigenous experiences, with stories emerging from the multiple legacies of settler colonialism that have shaped Aboriginal lives, including those that have been less clearly marked in public discourse until now. Many of the films made by indigenous people since the late 1980s offer alternative and complex accountings of histories and subjectivities, providing a site for a counter public articulation of a broader range of indigenous experience than the depleted repertoire of long-standing cinematic stereotypes. What role do these films—and especially feature films—play in reconceptualizing national imaginaries, destabilizing unified national narratives? Fundamentally, this work can be understood as part of broader efforts to "decolonize the screen." As the respected Maori filmmaker and writer Merata Mita put it:

Swimming against the tide becomes an exhilarating experience. It makes you strong. For 90 minutes or so, we have the capability of indigenizing the screen in any part of the world our films are shown. This represents power and is one reason that we make films that are uniquely and distinctly Maori. (1995, quoted in Dowell 2006a, 377)

Such work also demonstrates that a textual analysis of what we see on-screen is not sufficient if it does not also take into account the cultural and political labor of indigenous activists whose interventions have made support for this possible, revealing how contemporary states and their indigenous citizens negotiate diversity. This is a problematic central to current discussions of cultural citizenship, a topic that has gained considerable currency over the last decade in anthropology and in other fields: in other words, citizenship is not just a legal status, defined by a set of rights and responsibilities, but also an identity, an expression of one's membership in a political community that must be accommodated and recognized within liberal democracies.

Indigenous filmmakers who have wanted to develop their own capacities—their voices and visions—as well as the social and financial capital needed to enter into feature filmmaking, have faced a far more complex and costly field of cultural production than the infrastructure needed by those who have been working in small-scale video. To understand works such as indigenously directed feature films, it is as important to attend to the off-screen circumstances that shape cultural production as it is to understand the on-screen narratives, including (1) the cultural and institutional conditions that helped bring at least some of this work into being and (2) the crucial role played by indigenous cultural activists and their fellow travelers to get support for the programs and resources necessary to create the kind of films that can expand, if not transform, a national cinema.

The histories of initiatives to develop indigenous feature film first launched in a systematic way with two groundbreaking films that debuted in 1987 at the Cannes Film Festival: *Ngati*, by Maori director Barry Barclay, and *Pathfinder*, by Sami director Nils Gaup. In May 2009 *Samson and Delilah*, a feature film by indigenous Australian director Warwick Thornton, won the Camera d'Or, the prize for the best first feature at the Cannes. On getting the prize, Thornton spoke of the significance of filmmaking in his life:

I grew up on the streets of Alice Springs, getting into trouble with the police. I needed direction and somehow I found cinema, or cinema found that direction for me. It saved my life. The original story came out of anger at the neglect of our children, not only by the government and wider society, but even by parents. So it came from a dark place. I had to think about it for a year in order to present something that wasn't angry, where people could just go on a journey with these children. I've got so many more stories to tell, what I believe are beautiful stories, that are fires inside me that I desperately need to show the world.[10]

These success stories are instructive as experiments in testing the limits of multicultural arts policies, as works that transcend the bounded world suggested by restrictive funding categories, demonstrating their value on the world stage as well as in local indigenous worlds. Increasingly, these films have been circulating internationally and are thus implicated in the nation's broader trade relations and the political economies in which "culture" is increasingly caught up. For example, in his book discussing the Bolivian indigenous film collective CEFREC, Jeff Himpele argues that the circulation of indigenous videomakers and their work is made possible in part by a wider international political shift in which "indigeneity" has become a valuable political image, as well as through transcontinental technologies, networks, and resources (2007). The travels of indigenous films and filmmakers to the United States, Europe, and elsewhere are not only a form of cultural expansion and strength; an ever-expanding circuit of indigenous film festivals allows them to form significant alliances with native media-makers across the world.

Rethinking the Digital Age

Let me end by returning to the domain indexed in my opening example: "the digital age." How might we understand what this feels and looks like in indigenous communities in remote regions of the world where access to telephone landlines can still be difficult? As Kyra Landzelius asks in her 2006 collection, *Native on the Net*: "Can the info-superhighway be a fast track to greater empowerment for the historically disenfranchised? Or do they risk becoming 'roadkill': casualties of hyper-media and the drive to electronically map everything?" (2006, 1). Recent developments give some insight into what it might actually mean for indigenous subjects and how digital technologies might indeed be indigenized, from the design of hardware and software to the questions raised in the first example regarding protocols in new media environments.[11] As Prins (2001) has argued regarding the place of indigenous people in "cyberia":

Although indigenous peoples are proportionally underrepresented in cyberspace—for obvious reasons such as economic poverty, technological inexperience, linguistic isolation, political repression, and/or cultural resistance—the Internet has vastly extended traditional networks of information and communication. . . . Together with the rest of us, they have pioneered across the new cultural frontier and are now surfing daily through Cyberia.

While indigenous use of digital technologies is uneven at best, Prins points optimistically to the circumstances in which the cross-platformed use of digital technologies is being taken up in indigenous communities on their own terms, furthering the development of political networks and the capacity to extend their traditional cultural worlds into new domains.

Indigenous digital media have raised important questions about the politics and circulation of knowledge at a number of levels; within communities this may be about who has had access to and understanding of media technologies, and who has the rights to know, tell, and circulate certain stories and images. Within nation-states, media are linked to larger battles over cultural citizenship, racism, sovereignty, and land rights, as well as struggles over funding, airspace and satellites, networks of broadcasting and distribution, access to archives, and digital broadband services that may or may not be available to indigenous communities. Norman Cohn, who has been working with the Nunavut-based media collective Igloolik Isuma for over two decades, articulates the extremities of this kind of hardware stratification, while at the same time inventing new ways to put digital technologies to use in the radically different circumstances:

At present, Inuit and other Indigenous people are on the brink of being left out of the most important new communication technology since the printing press. Almost everything in the 21st century will be conducted at least partly by internet. Being left off, even for another decade or two, is like a linguistic, cultural and economic death sentence. Isuma's commitment to create Isuma TV even in the face of these disadvantages is our recognition of how access to the internet cannot be "negotiable" for Indigenous communities struggling to survive. This is particularly the case since the new 2.0 multimedia internet actually offers a practical tool especially suitable for oral cultures in remote regions. Unlike the literary medium of print, or the 1.0 print-based internet which is all about reading, in which oral cultures traditionally have been disadvantaged by participating in their second languages, the 2.0 audiovisual internet advantages people using sophisticated aural and visual skill-sets in their own first languages. (2009)

Efforts such as Igloolik Isuma's NITV (discussed earlier) are evidence of how indigenous media projects formed over the last decades are now positioned at the juncture of a number of historical developments: these include the circuits opened by new media technologies, ranging from satellites to compressed video and cyberspace, as well as the ongoing legacies of indigenous activism worldwide, most recently by a generation comfortable with media and concerned with making their own representations as a mode of cultural creativity and social action. They also represent the complex and differing ways that encompassing settler states have responded to these developments—the opportunities of media and the pressures of activism—and have entered into new relationships with the indigenous nations that they encompass.[12]

Conclusion

I conclude on a note of cautious optimism. The evidence of the growth and creativity of indigenous media over the last two decades, whatever problems may have accompanied it, is nothing short of remarkable, whether working out of grounded communities or broader regional or national bases. While indigenous media activism alone certainly cannot unseat the power asymmetries that underwrite the profound inequalities that continue to shape the activists' worlds, the issues and images that their media interventions raise about their cultural futures are on a continuum with the broader issues of self-determination, cultural rights, and political sovereignty and may help bring some attention to these profoundly interconnected concerns.

While activism and policy concerns initially shaped much of indigenous media, it is important to acknowledge the current range of genres being produced: drama, current affairs, political analysis, humor, cooking shows, variety shows, music videos, and sports. Additionally, the media technologies being deployed range from low-format video to satellite, cable to Web 2.0, radio to feature film and television. As indigenous media has grown more robust over the last two decades—in part through an increasing convergence of media forms that makes it hard to know where to draw the boundary demarcating television from film from web-based work—a remarkably diverse array of works suggest that this synthesis of media technology with new forms of collective self-production has much to offer indigenous communities as they redefine themselves and future generations in the twenty-first century.

Notes

Many thanks to Jay Ruby and Marcus Banks for their interest in this topic and their patience as editors. This essay is based on ongoing research that began in 1988 in Australia and has continued since then in many locations. The work has been funded over the years by fellowships and grants from New York

University and the Guggenheim and Macarthur Foundations. I am indebted to a number of people for ongoing conversations that have informed this paper, including Jane Anderson, Philip Batty, Sally Berger, Vincent Carelli, Norman Cohn, Jennifer Deger, Francoise Dussart, Samia Gaudie, Sara Hourez, Darlene Johnson, Frances Jupurrula Kelly, Merata Mita, Rachel Naninaaq Edwardson, Alanis Obamsawim, Frances Peters, Rachel Perkins, Jolene Rickard, Sally Riley, Juan Salazar, Wal Saunders, Beverly Singer, Ramesh Srinivasan, Loretta Todd, David Vadiveloo, Pegi Vail, Elizabeth Weatherford, Amalia Cordova, and Michelle Raheja, as well as current and former graduate students Lucas Bessire, Ernesto de Carvalho, Kristin Dowell, Danny Fisher, Aaron Glass, Lisa Stefanoff, April Strickland, Sabra Thorner, and Erica Wortham. As always, I am grateful to Fred Myers for his thoughtful comments and enthusiastic support.

1. While "indigenous" can index a social formation "native" to a particular area (e.g., I Love Lucy is "indigenous" to America), I use it here in the strict sense of the term, as interchangeable with the neologism "First Peoples" to indicate the original inhabitants of areas later colonized by settler states (Australia, the United States, New Zealand, Canada, most of Latin America). These people, an estimated 5 percent of the world's population, are struggling to sustain their own identities and claims to culture and land, surviving as internal colonies within encompassing nation-states. The impact of the last two or more decades of indigenous activism throughout the world, and especially in the Americas, and the catalytic effect of the formation of groups such as the UN Working Group on Indigenous Populations, formed in 1977, and the UN decade of Indigenous People (1994–2004)—part of the globalization of social life that has caught the attention of so many scholars and built significant networks for many of the players—has had a significant impact on the uptake and development of media of all sorts in indigenous communities and on the development of Fourth World theory beginning in the mid-1970s. See also Linda Tuhiwai Smith's important book *Decolonising Methodologies* (1999).

2. Some anthropologists have expressed alarm at these developments (Faris 1992); they see indigenous media practices as destructive of cultural difference and the study of such work as "ersatz anthropology" (Weiner 1997), an argument that echoes the concerns over the destructive effects of mass culture first articulated by intellectuals of the Frankfurt school. However, absolutely no evidence to support this position has ever been put forward. For this debate in the context of indigenous media see the spring 1997 issue of *Current Anthropology* (Weiner et al.) and the spring 1998 issue of *Lingua Franca* (Palatella).

3. http://www.isuma.tv.

4. See my article "Beyond Broadcast: Launching NITV on Isuma TV," In Media Res, May 4, 2009, http://mediacommons.futureofthebook.org/imr/2009/05/01/beyond-broadcast-launching-nitv-and-isuma-tv (accessed May 29, 2009).

5. As its website explains, Ara Irititja means "stories from a long time ago" in the language of Anangu (Pitjantjatjara and Yankunytjatjara people) of Central Australia. The aim of Ara Irititja is to bring home materials of cultural and historical significance, including photographs, films, sound recordings, and documents. Ara Irititja has designed a purpose-built computer archive that digitally stores repatriated materials and other contemporary items. Anangu are passionate about protecting their archival past, accessing it today, and securing it for the future. http://www.irititja.com (accessed May 29, 2009).

6. E.g., Asch 1991; Aufderheide 1995; Berger 1995; Carelli 1988; Dowell 2006b; Fleming 1991; Ginsburg 1991; Leuthold 1998; Meadows and Molnar 2001; Philipsen and Markussen 1995; Prins 1989; Roth 2005; Salazar 2004; Turner 1991a, 1991b, 1992a, 1995; Vail 1997; Weatherford 1990; Wortham 2000).

7. Sacha Molitorisz, "The Story of Black Australia," *The Age*, October 9, 2008, http://www.theage.com.au/articles/2008/10/08/1223145363254.html (accessed May 2, 2009). The commentary on the series' website, http://www.sbs.com.au/firstaustralians/, is uniformly positive, with many people posting comments as to how little they knew of Australia's black history.

8. For more on this series see http://www.pbs.org/wgbh/amex/weshallremain/the_films/index (accessed May 14, 2009).

9. http://mediacommons.futureofthebook.org/imr/2009/05/01/beyond-broadcast-launching-nitv-and-isuma-tv (accessed May 23, 2009).

10. Stephanie Bunbury, "Australian love story wins Cannes prize," *The Age* (Melbourne), May 25, 2009, http://www.theage.com.au/news/entertainment/film/2009/05/25/1243103459083.html (accessed June 3, 2009).

11. See Christie 2005; Christen 2005; Dyson et al. 2007; Ginsburg 2008; Latukefu 2006; Rickard 1999; Salazar 2004, 2007; Wilson and Stewart 2008.

12. http://mediacommons.futureofthebook.org/imr/2009/05/01/beyond-broadcast-launching-nitv-and-isuma-tv.

TEN

Productive Dissonance and Sensuous Image-Making: Visual Anthropology and Experimental Film

KATHRYN RAMEY

In contrast to recent works in cultural studies and film theory (e.g., Russell 1999) that conceive ethnographic and experimental film in the widest possible sense, encompassing a vast array of film, video, and performance practice, this chapter will establish links between the project of sociocultural anthropology as practiced in the last fifty years and works of film, video, and performance by experimental or avant-garde filmmakers. Central to this research is an analysis of how and why luminaries within the world of avant-garde film such as Chick Strand and Maya Deren moved between these two seemingly discreet and incompatible worlds. What use is anthropology to an experimental filmmaker? What use are the community and ideas of experimental film to someone concerned with anthropological research? Formal experimentation in these film and video works will be tied to an analysis of their intended function, both as works of art or aesthetic utterances and as "visual communications with anthropological intent" (Ruby 2000b). In answer to calls for new modes of ethnographic filmmaking this essay will analyze how and if experimental techniques can be incorporated into and made to reinvigorate contemporary anthropological film.

This chapter is an investigation into the interconnections between two very distinct types of moving-image production: experimental film and films made with anthropological intent. While the history of visual anthropology should be familiar to readers of this volume, the film avant-garde, if known at all, will very likely be understood as typified by a few well-known works and not as a community with its own rituals, organizations, and social networks. Many volumes exist on the subject, some canonizing particular persons, groups, or periods (e.g., Arthur 2005; Renan 1967; Sitney 2002), others seeking to redress perceived faults or absences in the former (e.g., Mellancamp 1990; Rabinowitz 1991) and in those that attempt to chart a history along national or geographic lines (e.g., Brenez and Lebrat 2001; James 2005). In the past I have argued that these histories and counterhistories of the film avant-garde cannot be seen as separate from the field of cultural production (Bourdieu 1993) in which the filmmakers operate (Ramey 2006). Rather, like the art critics in Howard Becker's *Artworlds* (1982), historians and theorists of the film avant-garde are enmeshed in the social network in which these things called "experimental films" and "experimental filmmakers" are produced and upon which they bestow symbolic capital in the form of reviews or writings, receiving in return acclaim that helps them maintain their own position in the field. If the reader wishes to gain a deeper understanding of the historic and contemporary community of experimental film these histories would be a good place to start, but despite various proclamations about the death of the film avant-garde (Camper 1986–1987; Sanborn 1988; Turvey 2002), a vibrant community continues to exist and in the age of listservs (Deren 2007) and alternative distribution (Bachar and Kwiatkowski 2008; Chodorov 2008; McCormick 2008) is easier to access than ever.[1]

In her 1999 tome *Experimental Ethnography*, Catherine Russell purports to connect experimental and ethnographic film through textual and comparative analysis, showing how some experimental filmmakers work is ethnographic and how some films by anthropologists are experimental or can be viewed through an avant-garde lens. While Russell's comparative exercise is interesting it stretches the term "ethnographic" to the point where it includes any sort of image-making that can be seen to be *about* culture. In turn, its expansive view of the experimental and anthropological film communities eclipses important historical and social contiguities that give the groups form and have helped to shape the offerings of their members. By omission Russell also denies the real, lived histories of interconnection between anthropologists and experimental filmmakers and the similarities between their twisted histories.

Although an exhaustive history of either experimental or anthropological film is beyond the scope of this essay, links between these two modes of production can be mapped through individuals in various capacities as makers, scholars, and audience members, as well as through overlaps in viewing contexts and funding resources. In addition, commonalities in distribution and reception practices and problems and community organization are explored to see how similar contexts for these small-scale, academically oriented filmmakers create varied responses. A question central to this research is: is it useful for makers of ethnographic films to use the image-making strategies of avant-garde cinema?[2] The final segment of this chapter examines a variety of "experimental" tactics used by anthropologists and experimental filmmakers engaged in creating productive dissonance and sensuous exploration of the visual world.

Paths That Sometimes Crossed: Visual Anthropology and Experimental Film

The term "avant-garde" was first used in relation to artistic production by Henri de Saint-Simon, a nineteenth-century French utopian socialist who imagined that the arts would be at the vanguard of social change because of their availability to the people as a communicative force (Nochlin 1989). Avant-garde cinema is both historically and currently the production of films by predominantly Western European and North American filmmakers whose intentions are to critique, subvert, and provide an alternative to dominant, mainstream media production. Except for the best-known, "crossover" or critically acclaimed filmmakers, most of this work has always been made, distributed, and viewed within a noncommercial network comprised almost solely of audience-producers operating on the fringes of the mainstream film industry, the art world, and, as of the 1950s, the academy.

Avant-garde and experimental film work does not adhere to any standard in terms of length, style, or even format. There are experimental films that are less than a minute long and one, the *Magellan Cycle* by Hollis Frampton, that was to have run thirty-six hours.[3] Avant-garde films can be abstract, narrative, poetic, or even documentary in nature. As with ethnographic films made from the 1950s to the 1980s, the majority of experimental films are produced on 16-millimeter stock, although there are 35-millimeter, Super-8, and regular 8-millimeter films as well. In the late 1960s, with the advent of the Sony Portapak video camera and recorder, certain filmmakers moved into video as a means of production. As digital video production and postproduction technology has increased in quality and decreased in cost, some filmmakers have moved into digital video as a production or postproduction medium.

Similar to visual anthropology, what truly unites avant-garde film-makers is a common history, community gatherings at festivals and screenings, and an artisanal practice that is, with few exceptions, both marginalized and self-marginalizing from the mainstream film and television industries. Like ethnographic filmmakers, experimental filmmakers fund their films through teaching positions in universities, artist or humanities grants, and personal wealth or work. To understand the film avant-garde, it must not be looked at as a genre with specific formal characteristics but rather as a social practice with a variety of practitioners engaged in a network of production, distribution, and exhibition that constitutes a community of practice.

In the earliest days, what helped to solidify core audiences and communities of experimental filmmakers and fans and to connect them across geographical distances were the alternative screening venues and the networks and communication between them. With obscenity laws barring all but the tamest experimental films from public screening, distribution and exhibition of experimental film in the United States was constrained within members-only venues for much of the 1940s and 1950s. Two of the most central venues were the Art in Cinema series at the San Francisco Museum of Art, founded by Frank Stauffacher and Richard Foster, and Cinema 16 in New York, founded by Austrian émigré Amos Vogel, who brought his experience of ciné clubs from his native Vienna. At the height of its popularity, Cinema 16 claimed more than five thousand members; it also distributed films that Vogel deemed of great artistic merit and soon became the leading distributor of avant-garde films in America (MacDonald 2002).

Throughout the late 1940s and 1950s, Art in Cinema and Cinema 16 showed a variety of experimental, international, and nonfiction films that could not be shown in commercial cinemas. Art in Cinema was an unpaid labor of love for its programmers, who were also filmmakers. Because it depended on the largesse of its sponsoring institution, the San Francisco Museum of Art, Stauffacher felt he had to keep the films in the realm of art and not delve too deeply into political work or even other types of nonfiction, such as documentary. In a letter to Vogel, he writes:

In my effort to keep the films of Art in Cinema on a liberal aesthetic par with the rest of the modern art that is hung on the walls here, and on a par with the presentations of the San Francisco Symphony Orchestra which holds forth next door at the Opera House, the keynote has been strictly just what it says: Art in cinematic form; the cinema as art. If I get too ideological or partisan you can bet the audience will no longer remain the liberal and highly discriminating one it is. I've got to keep these films in line with the Museum's attitude towards all other manifestations of art. (Vogel 1997, 139)

In contrast, Vogel, who was responsible to no one but his members and needed only to stay financially solvent, would regularly program very political work as well as documentary and experimental films. This intermingling of the "independents" in the 1950s encouraged a sense of common purpose among noncommercial filmmakers of all stripes. Thus in the formative decades of the film avant-garde, there was much cross-pollination and exchange between what we would now call documentary and ethnographic filmmakers and those whose work is labeled art film or avant-garde. Both groups claim Russian filmmaker Denis Kaufman, otherwise known as Dziga Vertov, as a significant ancestor. Both groups claim eminent filmmaker and anthropologist Jean Rouch as a progenitor. Paul Fejos, an anthropologist and director of the Wenner-Gren Foundation, who began his career directing films in Europe and spent some time in Hollywood, is also claimed by some as an early experimental filmmaker (Horak 1995; James 2005; Renan 1967). Robert Gardner, the Harvard-trained anthropologist and highly contentious ethnographic filmmaker, spent some time in the 1950s, between his bachelor's and graduate degrees, living in Seattle, where he cofounded Orbit Films, Ltd. with eminent experimental filmmaker and pedagogue Sidney Peterson.[4] Orbit Films was a company dedicated to the production of documentary nonfiction. With Orbit, Gardner produced two films on the Kwakiutl tribe, *Bluden Harbour* (1951a) and *Dances of the Kwakiutl* (1951), as well as a self-described experimental film on Seattle painter Mark Tobey (Gardner 2007b).[5] Although Peterson is known predominantly as an experimental filmmaker, throughout his career he moved between documentary, educational, and experimental film, even working for a time in Hollywood for Walt Disney (Peterson 1980). Gardner continued to admire experimental filmmakers and interviewed a number of them on *Screening Room*, a television program he hosted from 1972 to 1981 in Boston, including Stan Brakhage (1973 and 1980), Michael Snow (1975), and Jonas Mekas (1975) (http://www.studio7arts.org).

Perhaps the most infamous anthropologist-turned-experimental filmmaker from this early period is Harry Smith, who is primarily known for his contribution to the preservation of American folk music (he received a Grammy for lifetime achievement in 1991). Smith grew up in the Pacific Northwest and developed an interest in Native American language and rituals at an early age. His mother was a schoolteacher on a Lummi

10.1 Harry Smith recording Native Americans. Promotional material for the film *The Old Weird America: Harry Smith's Anthology of American Folk Music,* produced by the Harry Smith Archives, New York.

reservation, and while in high school Smith attended performances and recorded the music there (Igliori 1996) (figure 10.1).

Smith spent two years studying anthropology at the University of Washington in Seattle in the 1940s (Singh 1999) and two years in Berkeley working with anthropologist and folklorist Paul Rabin (Igliori 1996).[6] The move to California was predicated on a trip to San Francisco in mid-1940, when Smith experienced marijuana for the first time while listening to folk and jazz music and talking with bohemian intellectuals. After moving to San Francisco, he gradually became involved in Stauffacher's Art in Cinema series and began making paintings and films that were visual representations of the music he admired. These films were abstract animation drawn directly on the celluloid and were set to tunes by Dizzy Gillespie, Thelonious Monk, and others. According to Smith's friend and fellow abstract animator Jordan Belson, Smith was influenced by the surrealists and Dadaists (Igliori 1996; Singh 1999) and claimed at times that his paintings and films were efforts at achieving synesthesia, transcribing the colors and forms that he saw when listening to music. Smith had many interests—Kabbalah, Tibetan Buddhism, tarot, psychedelic drugs—and was an avid collector of, among other things, Ukrainian Easter eggs, paper airplanes, and string figures.

Smith was constantly recording himself and other people, including Allen Ginsberg, Rabbi Nuftali Zvi Margolies Abulafia, and the Kiowa, and was an avid recorder and collector of music of all kinds. Moe Asch initially distributed many of these recordings at Folkways Records. Smith received two Guggenheim fellowships that contributed significantly to his ability to produce films, but he was terrible at preserving his own work and is reported to have destroyed many of his paintings and films. Without the efforts of Jonas Mekas at Anthology Film Archives, his personal secretary Rani Singh, and his friend Paola Igliori, it is doubtful that any of his film work would have survived.[7] In recent years an online archive of Smith's work has been created, funded in part by a trust from his late friend Allen Ginsburg and featuring an online store that showcases the diversity of his influence in art, music, and film (Singh 2008). In 2006 Rani Singh, Smith's longtime friend and secretary and the director of his archive, produced a film documenting his anthology of folk music *The Old Weird America*.

Every discipline has those central characters who helped to give shape to the community as it emerged. In visual anthropology Margaret Mead is seen as an early champion. Maya Deren holds that role for experimental film. Born Eleanora Derenkowsky in 1917 in Kiev, Deren moved to the United States with her family when she was seven. She was educated in Switzerland and went to college at Syracuse University and New York University. She earned a master's degree in English from Smith College and after various jobs began work as the personal secretary to anthropology-trained dancer, choreographer, and educator Katherine Dunham. During her time with Dunham, Deren was exposed to urban, contemporary, African, and Caribbean dance and developed her interest in ritual dance and possession. Deren went with Dunham to Los Angeles, where she became acquainted with artists and filmmakers, among them her soon-to-be husband, Czech-born filmmaker Alexander Hackensmied, who changed his last name to Hammid when he became a US citizen. At that time, Derenkowsky changed her first name to "Maya," meaning "illusion" in Sanskrit, and shortened her last name to Deren (James 2005, 170). Together, Deren and Hammid made *Meshes in the Afternoon* (1943), deemed by many to be the best-known avant-garde film of all time and a pivotal moment in the history of the film avant-garde in the United States. Although in terms of thematic and stylistic characteristics the film has much in common with mainstream cinema from the period (see James 2005), it is remarkable for a visual and narrative style that positions the filmmaker as a central and subjective character. More importantly, through the distribution, exhibition, and reception of this and subsequent films, Deren was able to build a career for herself and others based on an art world model, outside of film industry production. After *Meshes*, Deren and Hammid moved to New York, where their apartment became the community center for this emerging alternative film practice (figure 10.2).[8]

In addition to her community-building, Deren was the first experimental filmmaker to write extensively about the unique ability of film to represent temporal and spatial qualities within a shot and to "suture" time and space through editing, creating temporal and spatial dimensions that exceed our experience in the real world (Deren 1946a/2005; see also Deren 1946b/2005). She was also the first person to use the medium as a means to explore body motion, dance, and social ritual, not as documentation but by using her embodied knowledge as a dancer to shoot and edit material (Deren 1945/2005). Because of Deren's performance experience and her critical thinking, the exploration of filmic space through movement is a central feature in all of her experimental film work. Although many film historians and theorists have attempted to read her work through a Freudian lens, Deren insisted that it was in fact responding to mythology and employed a symbolic reading.

Although Deren's interest in non-Western performance and ritual dates from her time with Dunham, it was her relationship with Gregory Bateson that introduced her to anthropological theory as well as early efforts in ethnographic cinema (Deren 1953/1983). Through her relationship with Bateson, she was able to see much of his and Mead's Balinese footage and to engage him in anthropological discussion. In the introduction to her monograph *Divine Horsemen*, Deren states:

It was the non-sectarian quality of his anthropological intelligence—his readiness to engage every sensibility and every possible point of view in the effort to illuminate the structure of society—that, in my eyes once more reaffirmed anthropology as the study of man, restoring to both words their major meaning. (Deren 1953/1983, 12)

From Bateson she took what separated culture from culture, finding the "major human pattern" in Voudon practice. However, it was from Joseph Campbell that she drew her inspiration to relate these things to what she claimed are metaphysical mythological structures. This exposure,

10.2 Maya Deren shooting with a Bolex camera. Promotional material for *In the Mirror of Maya Deren* (2002). Courtesy of Zeitgeist films.

coupled with the interest in dance and possession sparked during her time working with Dunham, inspired her to apply for a Guggenheim fellowship for a film project focusing on dance in Haiti. Once there, she took more than twenty thousand feet of 16-millimeter film, along with audio and stills. Deren credits her openness as an artist, along with her understanding of being the "artist/other" in an industrialized context, for the ease with which she developed a rapport with her Haitian dancer subjects. Her original plan for editing the project was discarded as she became more and more involved in Voudon ritual as a participant. Her experience led her to write the book *Divine Horseman: The Living Gods of Haiti* (1953), which explores Voudon religion in depth. For years, Deren's Haiti footage was stored at Anthology Film Archives in New York and occasionally screened in part or in its entirety.

Deren was not an anthropologist, though many have claimed that her work is anthropological. However, her notes about her experience as a dancer and an artist in another culture and the way she moved between roles, from observer to participant to initiate, resonates with the ethnographic method of participant observation. By moving from behind the camera, ceasing to use it as a capturing device, and becoming a participant in the sensuous experience of the dance and ritual, Deren gained tremendous anthropological insight into the purpose and practice of Voudon. She died, though, before she could complete the film, and it was subsequently edited by her ex-husband Tejiri Ito and his wife Cheryl, according to an outdated script that Deren herself had rejected. Thus, whatever insight she might have gained from her status as a participant observer that could have helped structure the film was lost. Nonetheless, there is much to be learned from Deren's cinematography and her writing about how to film dance and dancelike activities.

Deren had significant "embodied knowledge" as a dancer, singer, and Voudon participant that she brought to all of her filmmaking. In the biographical film *In the Mirror of Maya Deren* (2002), filmmaker Martina Kudláček uses recordings of Deren's many film lectures as a voice-over during selections from her films. Over a portion of *Meditation on Violence*, Deren describes how remarkable it is that the tai chi performed by Chao-Li Chi looks as balanced when played backward in film as it does when played forward. She notes that this is very atypical of dance or of other martial arts. While the film itself is not meant to be an anthropological investigation, Deren's experimentation with speed, film direction, and editing has yielded anthropological insight. This is even more true of her slow-motion photography in *Divine Horseman*, which allows the viewer to analyze the body motion of the participants for their symbolic meanings in the rituals.

Chick Strand is another filmmaker who has traversed the fields of anthropology and experimental film (figure 10.3). Although I was privileged to be in dialogue with her through most of the writing of this essay, Strand passed away July 11, 2009. Strand, a university-trained anthropologist, was an observer of and participant in the 1960s formation of what many term the "alternative" west coast American film avant-garde.

10.3 Chick Strand's official head shot, photographed by Neon Park. Courtesy of Canyon Cinema.

Strand received a bachelor's degree in anthropology from the University of California–Berkeley in the early 1960s. While she was finishing up that degree, she met experimental filmmaker Bruce Baillie, who helped expose her to the burgeoning west coast experimental film community. Strand said that from early childhood she was interested in art and music, but it was when she saw the films of experimental filmmakers Stan Brakhage and Bruce Conner that she realized that this was an art form she could do (Haug 1998). With Baillie, Strand began to host screenings of experimental film in the Bay Area, and the two eventually cofounded Canyon Cinema Cooperative—the second oldest cooperatively run distributor of experimental films in the United States. Baillie taught Strand how to use his spring-wound 16-millimeter film camera, and her first film, *Eric and the Monsters* (1964), premiered at a Canyon Cinema screening (Leimbacher 1998b).

After receiving her undergraduate degree, Strand spent a year in graduate school for anthropology but became disenchanted, saying that anthropologists, in their move toward greater acceptance within universities and as a science, had allowed the field to become stagnant:

There was no excitement and enthusiasm leading to new discoveries. . . . No longer were they mavericks, the crazy people who spent years in the field trying to sort out the wealth of information they encountered for the joy of it. . . . Their method became one of getting in and out of the field as rapidly as possible in order to come back, organize their material and publish it. (Strand 1978, 46)

Strand decided that she would prefer to use her creative energies making "personal experimental films" (Strand 1978), and so in the mid-1960s she moved to Los Angeles, began graduate school for film at UCLA, and became a part of the Ethnographic Film Program. Strand made three films at UCLA: *Anselmo* (1967a), *Waterfall* (1967b), and *Mosori Monika* (1970). The first two are each less than five minutes long and experiment with optical printing and collage (Leimbacher 1998b). The later film, *Mosori Monika*, was made as her thesis, produced by Colin Young (Furst 1971) and paid for by UCLA.[9]

Mosori Monika takes place in the Orinoco Delta in Venezuela. In the film, Strand contrasts the viewpoint of Carmilita, a Warao Indian, with a Spanish missionary nun, loosely following the narrative of Carmilita's life and her gradual assimilation of Western values. But this assimilation and the assertion by the nun that before the missionaries the Indians "lived like animals" is contradicted by Strand's visualizing contemporary indigenous practice and by Carmilita's own voice emphasizing Warao culture and practices. In her shooting and editing, Strand plays with the disjunctures between these portrayals, creating a film that "counter-manded the distanced objectivity of positivist ethnography of the time" (James 2005). Strand insisted that she approached shooting this film as an anthropologist (Haug 1998), and in 1971 it was positively reviewed by Peter Furst in *American Anthropologist*. But for some reason, neither this film nor any of Strand's later work is included in the canonical texts on visual anthropology (Crawford 1992; Heider 1976/2006; Loizos 1993), and her mention in Jay Ruby's *Picturing Culture* (2000b) is as a "film artist."

Film historian David James puzzles over Strand's exclusion from the central texts and venues of visual anthropology. He sees her work as an "exemplary solution to the social and semiotic contradictions generated in the interaction between self and other that troubled documentary filmmaking of the period" (James 2005). James cites the multivocality of Strand's films, working across various languages and translations, as being what Barbara Myerhoff called for when she proposed filmmakers seek a "third voice." According to Ruby, a "third voice" is a "blending of the voice of the investigator with that of the person portrayed in such a manner as to make it impossible to know who is author" (2000b). Strand experimented with this kind of collaboration and blending throughout her oeuvre. However, her work is generally not mentioned alongside other anthropological filmmakers, primarily because, although she espoused her role as an ethnographic filmmaker (Strand 1974, 1978), her work did not circulate within anthropological film circuits. In spite of all her anthropological training, she has remained most connected to the experimental film community in California and to Canyon Cinema, the film cooperative she helped form.

Marginalized and Self-Marginalizing: Similarities in Production, Distribution, and Reception of Visual Anthropology and Experimental Film

Beyond these anthropologist–experimental filmmaker hybrids, there are significant similarities between the organizational structures of the two communities of makers. Outside of the heyday of anthropological film-making, where there was some production for mass media (e.g., the British television series *Disappearing World*), and the heyday of experimental film (Andy Warhol films screening in some mainstream theaters), avant-garde and anthropological film are, for the most part, similar in production methods (single-author or small-crew productions), distribution (producer-distributed or specialized small distributors), exhibition types and venues (noncommercial and academic venues, festivals, and conferences), and audience types (producer-viewers, students, scholars, and interested lay persons). Both sorts of films also generate the majority of their meaning and value through extended discussion among the "communicative circle" that comprises the core audience for the work and its related production of conference papers, scholarly articles, books, listservs, and discussions. Perhaps it is because of the similarity in scope and scale of the projects that over the years experimental filmmakers and those whose interest is anthropological have found themselves sharing resources, venues, and sometimes ideas.

In the film avant-garde, programming films is considered an art form, akin to sophisticated museum or gallery display or disc jockeying. In these circumstances, ethnographic films are placed within the experimental film context and viewed for the visual construction of their arguments and the ways in which they imagine the viewer.[10] For example, during the late 1960s and early 1970s a type of filmmaking emerged within the avant-garde that was alternately labeled "materialist" or "structuralist." These films are organized according to rigorous principles developed by filmmakers who eschew all but the most fragmented or minimal narrative and whose work instead "insists on its shape" (Sitney 2002). Since the early 1980s programmers who saw similarities between these efforts and films such as Tim Asch's *Ax Fight* (1975) or Ray Bridwhistell's *Microcultural Incidents at 10 Zoos* (1969) have screened them in avant-garde film programs. In the early 1990s, during my tenure as a programmer at 911 Media Arts Center in Seattle, Washington, the work of John Marshall, Robert Gardner, Tim Asch, and Jean Rouch was screened alongside that of experimental filmmakers Hollis Frampton, Stan Brakhage, Chick Strand, Maya Deren, and others. To a certain degree, seeing the resonance between these works arose from their sharing screen space at the Flaherty Film Seminar beginning in the early 1970s and the ripple effect that collaboration had within the experimental film community (discussed below). It was also due to the emergence of feminist, postcolonial, and subaltern filmmakers, visual artists and theorists whose work began circulating within the experimental film community in the early 1980s. Offering simultaneously a critique of some of the rigidities of the experimental film community (its historic masculine whiteness) and of the problems with anthropology (Behar and Gordon 1995; Clifford and Marcus 1986), these artists raised awareness of ethnographic film and visual anthropology among experimental filmmakers.

On an anecdotal level, the processes and methods followed by experimental filmmakers reflect standard anthropological practices. Beyond the handful of historic connections between experimental filmmakers and anthropologists listed above, experimental filmmakers are expert gatherers. They peruse the dustbins and trim bins of visual culture and make use of things that fit the argument of their film. In *Land without Bread* (1933) (a.k.a. *Las Hurdes*), Luis Buñuel's surrealist sendup of ethnographic travelogue, he introduces the audience to the Hurdanos using a dispassionate voice, creating a caricature of the objective anthropologist putting the sufferings of a "lost people" on display. Although Buñuel makes it very clear that the whole thing is a farce, to this day students are taken in by the ruse. Similar to museum attendees who believed that Coco Fusco and Guillermo Gómez-Peña were actually representatives of a "lost tribe" in their performance *Couple in a Cage* (1993), the viewer's willingness to lend credibility to the ethnographic farce emphasizes that the codes for objectification and humiliation are more ingrained and normalized than one would like to think. This is part of the impetus for avant-garde and experimental filmmakers to continue to challenge viewers through reworking visual culture documents. One such filmmaker, Craig Baldwin, almost exclusively detours nonfiction films in works that function as cultural critique.

In the 1980s there were also a number of postcolonial filmmakers whose work circulated within the experimental film community but who were not self-identified as experimental or avant-garde filmmakers. Philippine filmmaker Kidlak Tahimik created auto-ethnography that incorporated nonfiction film and performance in a presentation that Frederic Jameson says "foregrounds the inauthenticity of the Western spectator" (Jameson 1992, 192). Similarly, in her two short films *Nice Coloured Girls* (1987) and *Night Cries: A Rural Tragedy* (1989), visual artist and filmmaker Tracey Moffat uses theatrical performance and experimental film and audio techniques to accentuate the dissonance between her Australian Aboriginal characters and their white counterparts. By revealing the "fakeness" of the sound-stage setting and the set pieces, Moffat encourages the viewer to think about the historical constructedness of the postcolonial reality of the protagonists in her films and the legacy of violence and cruelty that has led them to this place in her narratives.

Perhaps the most controversial filmmaker ever to negotiate the anthropological-experimental film terrain, Trinh Minh-ha rounds out the list of prominent postcolonial filmmakers. Her film *Reassemblage* (1982) launched her into both the experimental and anthropological film communities. With its jump cuts, nonsynchronous and untranslated location audio, and feminist film theory voice-over, the film challenged the male-dominated ethnocentrism of the experimental film community just at a time when it was beginning to critique itself. Trinh's work was also well received by the art community, as her work *Naked Spaces Living Is Round* (1985) toured with the 1987 biennial of the Whitney Museum of American Art. For the last twenty years, her influence within the experimental film community has also been felt as a pedagogue, as she has taught film and film theory, first at San Francisco State and then at University of California–Berkeley. Her books and articles have been widely used within both experimental film and documentary film courses.

Besides specific filmmakers, there are screening events and institutions that have helped to link the realms of experimental and anthropological film. Most readers of ethnographic film theory are familiar with Ruby's assertion that anthropologists look to experimental or avant-garde film and filmmakers. One of the reasons he seems so enamored with these filmmakers is that they are "content to produce works with no commercial potential designed for a very small audience" (Ruby 2000b, 244). Although one could take issue with his suggestion that all avant-garde filmmakers are "content" with what sociologist Todd Bayma argues is their "economic irrationality" (Bayma 1995), they do continue to make work that they know most people won't understand or appreciate. Ruby suggests that films made with anthropological intent should be selective in their target audience, not aspiring to mass consumption or even to "teaching" those uninitiated in anthropological theory. He also asserts that perhaps there is something to be gained from the ways in which some experimental filmmakers make films from or with theoretical concepts and employ potentially difficult visual and thematic structure despite the possibility that doing so may alienate an audience.

Ruby's familiarity with experimental film dates from his time spent in Los Angeles during the 1960s, but his association with individual experimental filmmakers comes from his experience as an attendee, board member, president, and programmer at the Flaherty Film Seminar during the 1970s and 1980s. The Flaherty seminar is a weeklong event dedicated to independent, mostly nonfiction films, sometimes with a very international scope, always very politically charged. Both ethnographic and experimental films and filmmakers have been shown alongside documentary, often causing debate and sometimes even clashing with the seminar's old guard. In 1963 experimental filmmakers Ken Jacobs, Jonas Mekas, and others stormed the Flaherty farm, taking over the barn for a midnight screening of their work. Jacobs was invited back in 1970, but he remembers little discussion after his screening: "The film is abstract, we were told; abstraction is entirely open offering nothing tangible to discuss" (Zimmerman and Barnouw 1995, 33). In 1993 a screening of Jacobs's ended with a screaming match. Verbal fisticuffs are not uncommon at the Flaherty; avant-garde film historian and repeated attendee Scott MacDonald argues that, while many seminar participants are very aware of the abuses of commercial cinema, they are unwilling to challenge their expectations as viewers and "use the cinema as a perceptual and/or ideological adventure." He goes on to say, "They blame the 'guilty' avant-garde filmmakers for their pretentiousness, their arrogance, their brutality, whatever; but in my view, this blame is often an obfuscation of attendees' own refusal either to grapple with the complex set of privileges and confirmations of the status quo that underlies their Flaherty experience, or even to have a sense of humor about themselves" (MacDonald 1995, 267).

This experience points out the underlying expectation of most experimental filmmakers. It is up to the audience to finish a film, and when they cannot or will not engage with it, it remains unfinished. This attitude is a substantial departure from the way a majority of filmmakers, including those who are anthropologists, approach an audience. With regard to anthropologists, there is an expectation that their films have something specific to communicate, and the relative success of this is a subject of intense concern (Martinez 1990, 1992).

The idea that the onus is on the audience to keep investigating and viewing a film until they understand it is best exemplified in a retort by experimental filmmaker Hollis Frampton to a perturbed audience member who, after watching one of his films, asked whether Frampton thought he had communicated with the audience:

If you mean, do I think I communicated to those in the audience who tramped indignantly out of my films, the answer is no, but I think there is a problem with your idea of communication. You seem to work on the assumption that you have this hole and I have this thing, and you want me to put my thing in your hole and that will be "communication." My idea of communication is very different. It involves my trying to say something I think is important and into which I have put all my thought and substantial labor. Necessarily, what I have to say will be difficult to apprehend, if it is original enough to be worth saying at all. That is my half of the communicative process. Yours must be to sensitize and educate yourself fully enough to be able to understand. It is only when two people—filmmaker and viewer in this case—can meet as equals that true communication can take place. (MacDonald 1978, 8)

In general, experimental films are produced for an audience that is willing to work to understand them. This audience is usually composed of other experimental filmmakers and scholars, students, and curators of experimental film. It is expected that the films—and increasingly, videos—will be difficult to understand, refer to obscure knowledge or to other films and filmmakers or to concepts from outside the "film text," and engage in visual and formal strategies that challenge the viewer. Film screenings are only one part of a "communicative circle" (Perin 1992) that includes scholarly articles and books, college and university classes, lectures by and about the films and filmmakers, and informal discussion. It is only by "traveling" this entire circle that one may grasp the film's meaning and significance.

As with Faye Ginsburg's assessment of the place of visual anthropology within mainstream anthropology college and university courses, experimental film is marginalized within a mainstream film education (Ginsburg 1998). Although a handful of the best-known experimental films are used in media history survey courses that all students of film and video must take, these films are only briefly contextualized, either within the body of work of the maker or within the period they come from. There simply isn't enough time within such a course to give broader or more in-depth coverage that might foster deeper research and interest by the student. Thus, unless they are already sensitized to modernist art or political movements, most students are turned off by their first viewings of experimental work, and some develop significant antipathy to it, despite the fact that its formal strategies have been consistently migrating into mainstream film practice for more than thirty years.

In other words, much like the situation with Martinez's students and ethnographic film, most experimental films, when consumed raw (not properly contextualized for the uninitiated), make viewers sick (turned off, prejudiced against them and those that they represent). The fact that this sickness is occasionally turned into transcendence (the sickened viewer later realizes that s/he has been challenged, likes it, and returns for more) is never investigated by Martinez. In research conducted with experimental filmmakers, many reported that an essential part of their conversion experience—the process by which they were made into an experimental filmmaker—involved initial anger or revulsion that was subsequently interrogated and revealed to be a fear of something that went against the conventions of cinema they were accustomed to. Once they recognized how this work challenged them and their assumptions about what film or video could do, they were seduced. As I was conducting my research with experimental filmmakers (Ramey 2006), I asked that they recount their first encounter with avant-garde cinema. The following response was not uncharacteristic:

273

I went to undergraduate school in Orlando, really determined that I was going to be the female equivalent to Steven Spielberg. And . . . then I was just about ready to graduate, it was my last year. And I was in the library, working on a project and a friend of mine came by and said that there was a strange little program of films that was going on at the student center, and I might be interested in going to see them. And I was really kind of rather annoyed, because I had this big project to do, but he convinced me to go over and take a look. So, I did and in the program there was a piece called *Chinese Fire Drill* [by experimental filmmaker Will Hindle]. And, after the program was over, we had this great debate. And my perspective was that a film like *Chinese Fire Drill* was a supreme waste of celluloid. And why would anybody waste their time making a piece like that? Why you know and where did this filmmaker get off you know making me sit through a half an hour of this torture. And I graduated and went on and really studied narrative and mainstream movies, and saw dozens and dozens of them, which were immediately forgettable. But I never forgot *Chinese Fire Drill*. And I could play back that whole sequence of that film in my head, after having seen it one time. And slowly over the course of the next two years I realized that that film was going to be with me the rest of my life.

Subsequent to this experience the filmmaker enrolled in graduate school to work with the filmmaker whose work she had been so alienated by a few years before and went on to become a well respected experimental filmmaker and pedagogue in her own right. As this filmmaker's experience attests, the initial alienation or confusion provoked by experimental film is, to a certain degree, a part of the process of reproducing experimental filmmakers.

While Martinez may not have come up with proscriptions for what to do when your students get sick, contextualizing difficult ethnographic films has been a concern among certain filmmakers. John Marshall and Tim Asch both developed study guides to go with their films, and David MacDougall writes about his process and projects. Although Jayasinjhi Jhala engaged in a reception study (1996) in which well-known (within the field) ethnographic films were shown to an "unintended audience" (non-anthropologists) in rural India, there has been no writing within visual anthropology in which the dissonance created by screening anthropological films to an uninitiated audience has been examined for its potentially transformative properties. Only MacDougall has questioned the visual anthropologist's "burden" to avoid potential misreadings, the arousal of "dangerous feelings," and the reinforcement of prejudice (MacDougall 1998). While he acknowledges that films made with anthropological intent cannot be expected to "compromise their approach to accommodate insensitive viewers," he does place the responsibility for contextualization—or, in Hollis Frampton's terms, for making the right-size film to fit into the audience's hole—on the filmmaker.

One of the major critiques Jay Ruby has waged against ethnographic filmmakers is that in shooting and editing their films they conform to storytelling strategies used in more mainstream documentary filmmaking. This has been particularly true of anthropologists making work for broadcast. As Jean Lydall writes of her experience in making *The Women Who Smile* (1990), although the impetus to make the film arose from her fieldwork experience, as well as the desire to countermand previous films about the Hamar, such as Robert Gardner's *Rivers of Sand* (1973), because she was making the film for BBC she had not only to have a director and crew who were not anthropologists but to ensure the film would have "popular appeal" (Lydall 1992, 145). What if, instead of making films and videos that worked to make more sense to a student, uninitiated, or general audience, anthropologists experimented with a visual language and formal strategies (methods of shooting, editing, and presentation) that emerged from the experience of their fieldwork and anthropological practice? Efforts to this end can be seen in David MacDougall's *Doon School Chronicles* (2000) and Jay Ruby's *Oak Park Stories* (2004–2006), but both are still to a large degree based around the ethnographic interview and observational photography.

This is where we find the major difference between experimental film and its makers and those who make images with anthropological intent. No matter how you slice it, in order for a film or video or hypermedia or any means currently employed or as yet undiscovered to transmit anthropological information visually and aurally, that information must be in dialogue with the academic *discipline* of anthropology. No matter that mainstream anthropology has a difficult time recognizing the validity of moving images as scholarship, and no matter that many mainstream anthropologists remain unsophisticated in either the use or analysis of images. Anthropology makes use of and is influenced by other disciplines and practices such as philosophy, geography, psychology, and so on, but there is a core of common texts and ideas and debate around these ideas with which something must be in dialogue to be considered *anthropological*. Experimental film does not have a core academic discipline but a *practice* of small-scale, artisanal film, and increasingly videomaking, that derives its meaning and purpose from its exhibition and reception among other filmmakers. What follows is an analysis of efforts from recent commingling between anthropologists and experimental filmmakers with the aim of exploring how experimental film *practice* can be in dialogue with the *discipline* of anthropology.

Dissonance and Sensuality: Experiments in Contemporary Ethnographic Film

The remainder of this chapter examines specific practices of experimental or artisanal moving-image makers and of some anthropologists working in alternative methods. In the case of the experimental filmmakers, most have no intention of contributing in any way to anthropological knowledge, but their experiments could be fruitful for anthropologists.[11] Conversely, the anthropologists cited in this piece frequently had no intention of making "experimental" film in the sense that avant-garde filmmakers do. Instead, they were working with the tools in front of them in a new way. That their work went on to have a life in the same venues and circuits as experimental film attests to the inclusiveness of experimental film networks. These particular works are discussed because they exemplify a filmmaking practice that emerges from a blend of art and literary experience and the anthropologists' experiences in the field.

With the exception of Harry Smith, most of the filmmaker-anthropologists discussed thus far worked with images taken in the "real world." In what would seem like a complete departure from standard ethnographic film practice, Robert Ascher, a UCLA-trained anthropologist and self-taught sculptor and filmmaker, drew on myths to inspire his hand-drawn anthropological animations. Within anthropology, Ascher is primarily known for his archaeological work in the 1960s and early 1970s (Ascher 1974; Ascher and Fairbanks 1971) and his work with his mathematician wife, Marcia Ascher, on decoding quipu—knotted cords and strands of cords used as recording devices by preconquest Andean and Incan people (Ascher and Ascher 1978, 1980). Despite the fact that his films have been reviewed within anthropological journals by noted anthropologists (Myers 1988; Pastner 1989; Stoller 1992a) and that he wrote about his own process (Ascher 1990, 1993), Ascher's animations have scarcely been viewed within anthropology and have received little attention from scholars of visual anthropology (Ruby 2000b). To a certain degree this can be attributed to the fact that Ascher was not an active participant in the "communicative circle" of visual anthropology. With the exception of a few articles he did not seem to take an active part in screening or promoting his work within the community of visual anthropology makers and scholars of the 1980s and early 1990s. Ascher's film *Cycle* (1986) showed at the Flaherty Film Seminar, curated by then Cornell Cinema director Richard Herskowitz. As for a more mainstream presence within anthropology, there does not seem to have been much serious consideration of his work for classroom purposes, with the exception of Fred Myers (1988) and Paul Stoller (1992a). Even within Myers's consideration of Ascher's films, there is an expectation that they would be more easily used in the classroom if they came with a written guide (1988, 245).

Ascher's films are explorations of myths, drawn frame by frame onto 35-millimeter celluloid and then rephotographed onto 16-millimeter with a soundtrack.[12] Hand drawing on film has been an accepted process within abstract animation since the 1930s, with the work of Len Lye and Oskar Fischinger. Harry Smith's first films in the 1940s and 1950s were also drawn directly on celluloid and, like Ascher's, were drawn in response to mythology and folklore. Canadian filmmaker Norman McLaren brought "direct animation" to a mass audience and even has a direct animation instructional film, *Pen Point Percussion*, produced by the National Film Board of Canada (McLaren 1952). Ascher was unaware of these technical predecessors when he decided to make films this way. In discussing his motivation for producing these films, Ascher begins discussing his last archaeological dig,[13] a slave cabin on Cumberland Island, Georgia (Ascher and Fairbanks 1971). The write-up of this research blends scientifically descriptive information from the dig with pictures and a (written) soundtrack culled from literature and oral histories of slaves and other eyewitnesses who lived through that period of history. Despite the constrictions of presenting this information in a paper format, the article attempts to engage the senses, urging the reader to read the soundtrack aloud and imagine the texture, smell, and sound of the artifacts.

With this project, Ascher felt that he had gone as far as he could in the traditional mode of presentation of anthropological knowledge, and thus lost interest in archaeology and the scholarly write-up as a means of contributing to anthropological discourse (Ramey 2006). Initially he attempted sculpture as a means of expressing anthropological knowledge. While he was considering working in film, he read an article on Steven Spielberg that described him using a thirty-thousand-dollar lens. Ascher knew he couldn't even afford that much for an entire film, let alone a lens, so he decided to work in the most minimal way possible. He began experimenting with drawing on clear film with pens and ink. When Ascher shared this with his colleague Don Fredericksen in the Department of Theatre Arts at Cornell University, Fredericksen turned him on to the work of Norman McLaren. Ascher contacted McLaren, who was then in his seventies, and from him learned many tricks that would aid him in his production.

In discussing motivations for his working practice, besides the financial considerations, Ascher invoked Sam Yazzi's famous question to Sol

Worth and John Adair: would the films be "good for the sheep"? Ascher argued that it was an anthropologist's responsibility to "do no harm" with filmmaking (Ascher 1990). He spent approximately two years in production for each of his four films, each of which has a running time of between three and six minutes. The animation style is representational, in that biomorphic images play out a narrative. The first film, *Cycle* (1986), explores a Wulamba (Australian Aboriginal) myth and has an untranslated narration of a linguist friend of Ascher's telling a Wulamba myth. Ascher's intention was *not* to illustrate the myth so that the audience obtain a clear understanding of it, but rather to create a dissonance so that audience members have an emotional or aesthetic response but simultaneously realize that they cannot understand this myth and what it means to the people. As Ascher said, "Myths from another culture are very, very complex and if you think you understand a myth from another culture, you're probably all wrong, from an anthropological perspective. You have to be deep in a culture to understand it" (Ramey 2006).

When he was critiqued for using a myth from a culture whose language he did not speak (Myers 1988), Ascher decided to draw on his own experience with the Jewish mystical tradition Kabbalah for his next film. The result, *Bar Yohai* (1988), was funded by the Wenner-Gren Foundation, courtesy of Paul Fejos's widow (Ramey 2006). For this film, Ascher, along with two hundred thousand other people, made a trip to Mount Miron, near Safed, Israel, to the tomb of Shimon Bar Yohai. Although it is contested, many people believe that Bar Yohai wrote the Zohar, a book of commentary on the Torah that is a central Kabbalist text. While in Israel, Ascher took 35-millimeter slides and recorded the audio that is used in the piece. He then spent two years reading the Zohar and other Kabbalist texts and making his drawings on film. All the images in *Bar Yohai* emerged from this process, which is representative of the seriousness of the research that Ascher engages in for each film. Figure 10.4 is a single frame from the film; in an e-mail, Ascher explains its imagery: "There are nine men observing the tree of life as it goes through the seasons. The tree has a pomegranate, an important figure in Kabbalah thought. In Jewish practice, ten men are needed for a group to pray. So you, the viewer, make up the tenth man."[14]

Ascher made two more films: *Blue: A Tlinglit Odyssey* (1991), based on a Tlinglit myth, and *The Golem* (1995). All of his films were very well received in the art and experimental film worlds, garnering awards and helping him get artists' grants. But outside of a few isolated screenings, these films did not play in the anthropological world. In recent years re-

10.4 Frame from Robert Ascher's *Bar Yohai* (1988). Courtesy of the filmmaker.

quests for his films from his main distributor, Canyon Cinema, slowed, and the cooperative asked him either to begin distributing his films in video so that they could sell them or to withdraw his films from their collection. Ascher, believing that video transfers of his work were wholly inadequate, took his films back and currently has no distributor.

The final two filmmakers under discussion, like Maya Deren, moved from different representational practices into anthropology. Alan Passes is a French anthropologist, novelist, playwright, and coscreenwriter with Stephen Quay on the Brothers Quay feature films *Institute Benjamenta or This Dream People Call Human Life* (1995) and *The Piano Tuner of Earthquakes* (2005).[15] Brothers Stephen and Timothy Quay gained interest among experimental filmmakers in the 1990s as stop-motion animators utilizing found materials and exhibiting a dark Victorian vision. Their feature films could be characterized as experimental narrative and in the United States are circulated in art house venues that operate between the mainstream multiplexes of commercial cinema and the art world– or community-based venues of experimental film communities.[16]

Passes writes fiction and had published two novels (Passes 1977, 1986) and a short story before earning a PhD from the University of St. Andrews, Scotland, in 1998. His fieldwork was done among the Pa'ikwené (Palikur) of northern Brazil and southern French Guiana, and his (unpublished) dissertation was written simultaneously with *Piano Tuner* (News 2006). Passes has published a handful of articles on the Pa'ikwené, including an analysis of the social productivity of traditional work processes (Passes 2000), an analysis of the political power of women's speech in everyday life (Passes 2004b), and an ethnohistorical analysis of the making of the Palikur nation (Passes 2004a). He has also published a "fictional" radio play that comes closest to giving insight into the ways in which he blends his literary and anthropological pursuits. This radio play relates the experience of a man with malaria in a small Amerindian village on the Oyapock River, which separates Brazil from French Guiana (Passes 2006). Woven throughout this piece are references, in music and voice-over, of a possibly autobiographical Yiddish and Jewish past in France and Great Britain during World War II. The style of the piece is clearly inspired by Central American magical realism.

The Passes-Quay scripts draw on this tradition of magic realism, or what Passes calls "fantastical film" (Anonymous 2006), and on Eastern European literature (authors such as Bruno Schulz and Franz Kafka). Passes met the Quay brothers in 1985, and they began collaborating by writing a longer version of one of their short films, *Gilgamesh* (Graham 2006). That piece was never made; instead they collaborated on a new scenario to be funded by Britain's Channel 4. The film, *Institute Benjamenta or This Dream People Call Human Life* (1995), is adapted from a book by Robert Walser, an early twentieth-century novelist who spent the last twenty-six years of his life in an asylum (Rose 2004). While the film's attention to detail and aesthetic sensibilities are similar to that in the Quays' earlier animation, Passes's contribution seems to be on the level of myth and symbolism.

In the film a man, Jakob, attends an institute for the reproduction of servants. The school is run by a brother and sister and seems to exist as a huge organic machine in which the students—all male—are simultaneously producers and produced by the headmaster and mistress. The black-and-white cinematography and the mise-en-scène is replete with erotic symbolism, predominantly hooves and stag antlers, from turn-of-the-century Europe. The narrative centers on Jakob's sexual awakening of the schoolmistress. The film teems with repressed Victorian desire as the students, "caught in the grips of the rules and indulg[ing] in monotonous repetition" (Quay, Quay, and Passes 1995), engage in intricate simultaneous performances as they learn to reproduce the movements and voice of servile submission. The story draws on tropes from European folklore, including Sleeping Beauty, and at one point Jakob asks, "Am I living in a fairy tale?"

10.5 Automata from Stephen and Timothy Quay's *Piano Tuner of Earthquakes* (2005). Courtesy of Zeitgeist Films.

Eventually Jakob, the would-be servant, and Liza, the headmistress, kiss and the woman dies, but not before Kraus, the model student, takes Jakob into the inner sanctum. There Jakob says, "I have finally been inside the inner chambers and I have to say that they don't exist. Instead of a mystery there is only a goldfish and Kraus has told me how to clean out its bowl, change its water and feed it" (Quay, Quay, and Passes 1995). After the headmistress's death, the institute closes and, in an inversion of the normative rules of fairy tales, the headmaster, Herr Benjamenta (who also desires Jakob), and a dazed Jakob "escape" into the snow. But this is a false resolution, as the finale of the film features Jakob alone in the "inner chambers," feeding the goldfish. The film can be read as an allegory for the process of social reproduction or enculturation in contemporary society, where we search for meaning in "this dream people call human life, only to find servile labor.

Piano Tuner of Earthquakes (2005), which Passes also cowrote with the Quays, begins with an on-screen text, "these things never happen but always are," cluing the viewer that what they are about to see is as authentic as dreams and operates not in "real" calendrical time but in mythic time. Like the previous Passes-Quay film, *Piano Tuner* explores mythological themes within an arcane human universe, employing elements of tragedy in a man's failed attempt to save a beautiful and cursed woman. Human beings and automata, made in the Quay brothers characteristic animated style, interact and influence each other (figure 10.5).

In discussing the way the script evolved, Passes has said, "It's true we were playing around with classical mythological elements not always in a straight line" (Graham 2006). Similarly, although neither film is meant to be anthropological, Passes and the Quays explore issues of interest to anthropologists, playing with them in an intense and curious way. While these films are exhibited on the fringe of the mainstream, at art house cinemas and major film festivals, they are nothing like other "independent" films, to the point of alienating audiences and viewers (Bradshaw 2006). In a way, the films engage with tropes from a whole variety of genres, both literary and dramatic, and spin them into multilayered webs that invites repeated and engaged viewing.[17]

Another film that engages theatricality in a wholly different way is Jenna Grant's *Sakamapeap* (meaning "action" or "activity" in Khmer) (2005). In 2005 this film was awarded the Jean Rouch Prize by the Society for Visual Anthropology. Grant is currently a doctoral candidate in anthropology at the University of Iowa, focusing on science studies and visual and medical anthropology. She shot the footage for *Sakamapeap* in 2003–2004 during her initial fieldwork in Cambodia and edited it in a postproduction class in the Department of Cinema and Comparative Literature.[18] Like Ascher, Grant felt compelled to "do no harm" with her filmmaking, to avoid exploiting and exoticizing her Cambodian neighbors Siang, Ro, Chenda, and Lorn, who, along with her, are the main "actors" of the film. But Grant was interested in them and what they did every day, and she also wanted to know what they thought of her. So she elected to engage in a participatory film activity, wherein each "actor" was given an opportunity to direct the others and the filmmaker herself. One participant, Siang, also acts as videographer for Grant's "performance."

The twenty-seven-minute film follows the five principals as they act out an activity they have chosen for themselves as well as one chosen by each of the other participants. It was inspired by Sam Shephard's play *Action*; short stories by Latin American feminist writers such as Clarice Lispector and Elena Poniatowska; critiques of documentary photography; and works of feminist art, video, and performance such as Martha Rosler's *Semiotics of the Kitchen* (1975). She stated an interest in doing something "collaborative" as her motivation for its design (Grant, personal communication, 2007a).[19] Although Grant was the instigator of this film activity and retained authorial control over the editing, she did return with the film to Cambodia to receive feedback. The work embraces Rouch's notion of a "shared anthropology," in which both the anthropologist and those she interacts with are "modified" by the ethnographic process and create knowledge together (Rouch 1975). Grant asserts that *Sakamapeap* also works to separate voice from agency by having one social actor embody an action at the request of another, and that following Keane (1991), this "delegation of voice" is characteristic of Anakalangese social rituals that

10.6 Filmmaker Jenna Grant, studying. Courtesy of the filmmaker.

are uncertain or involve risk or failure (Grant, personal communication, 2007b).

The film is lush and beautiful and pleasurable to watch. It is also amusing, as Grant engages in activities chosen for her—picking up leaves, cooking, cleaning, and dancing—that are not "hers" and that she performs awkwardly. For her chosen activity, Grant decided to be filmed as she sees herself, a student practicing the alphabet. Through these performances of other and self, the film achieves a rich, humorous multivocality. It does not reveal insights beyond the frame into the political, economic, or social conditions of its participants, but that does not seem to be its intention.[20] Instead it is specific, not presenting "whole bodies, whole people, whole lives" (Heider 1976/2006) but instead revealing the participants as people who, for a time, have the opportunity to hang out and make a film together. The film gives the viewer a sense of what it might have been like to live in that house in Serey Sophoan District in Cambodia in the summer of 2004 with a curious American and her video camera. In this sense, Grant is engaging in "sensuous scholarship" (Stoller 1997) that is grounded in her own body and the bodies of her friends as they live, work, and act together (figure 10.6).

Conclusion

This chapter draws parallels and shows the interconnections between two moving-image practices that are at the same time marginal and self-marginalizing, separate from both the mainstream of theatrical and broadcast production and distribution and the academic disciplines that help to support them and provide an audience for their work. Alliances and crossovers between individual social actors and groups in these communities have been uncovered. In response to a call by Jay Ruby and others to move away from the documentary film mode, the efforts of several filmmakers who move between experimental film and anthropology have been explored. Some of these works have moved within the "communicative circle" that is visual anthropology, and some have not. Although Chick Strand's and Robert Ascher's work didn't really find a home within the world of anthropology at the time, a reevaluation of their efforts as anthropologists is overdue. In the meanwhile, if Jenna Grant is any indication, the lessons that experimental films and filmmakers have to teach will continue to trickle into the minds and films of anthropologists. As for experimental filmmakers, they've been watching, interacting with, and making use of the products of visual anthropologists for some time. Examples abound of their making use of anthropological texts, films, and methods, such as Su Friedrich's use of kinship charts in *Sink or Swim* (1990) or Rebecca Baron's reexamination of the Great Britain's Mass Observation movement in *How Little We Know Our Neighbors* (2005). Experimental filmmaker Sharon Lockhart worked directly with anthropologists to develop her *Teatro Amazonas* (1999), and Jennifer Hardacker mined the history of ethnographic film to produce her visually stunning *Night Gardener* (2008). While these films, like those of the Quay brothers, are not *anthropological*, they may be looked at for the ways in which non-anthropologists utilize anthropological theory and incorporate it into their own moving image practice.

Notes

1. Experimental films are also available through more "traditional" cooperatives for experimental film: the filmmakers' cooperative in New York City (http://www.film-makerscoop.com), Canyon Cinema in San Francisco (http://www.canyoncinema.com), Light Cone in Paris (http://www

.lightcone.org), and the Canadian Filmmakers Distribution Center (http://www.cfmdc.org), among others.

2. Throughout this text I will use the terms "avant-garde" and "experimental" interchangeably to refer to work by film- and videomakers who may refer to their work using these terms or as, for instance, abstract, personal, underground, alternative, or independent. While I acknowledge that for many within the community these terms have specific connotations—and in fact, wars of words have been fought over their use—my intention is to convey a community of practice (Wenger 1998) that shares similar artisanal production methods, exhibition spaces, and social and distribution networks.

3. Frampton intended the *Magellan Cycle* to be a film for every day of the year. It remained unfinished when he died, although with its thirty films and over eight hours of material it is a sizable accomplishment.

4. In the late 1940s Peterson founded a workshop at the California School of Fine Arts (now the San Francisco Art Institute) and was very active in the San Francisco and New York experimental film communities, screening his films at Art in Cinema and Cinema 16 and frequently coming to the aid of Amos Vogel in locating other west coast filmmakers and their films (see Vogel 1997). For a detailed, if rambling, description of his life and work, see his memoir, *The Dark of the Screen* (Anthology Film Archives, 1980).

5. For more on Gardner's work at Orbit see Jacknis (2000) and Stan Brakhage's *Sidney Peterson: A Lecture by Stan Brakhage* (1983).

6. It is unclear whether Smith was Rabin's gardener, assistant, or both. Smith had a habit of making up stories about his life, including the claim that he was the illegitimate child of Aleister Crowley and the son of Czarina Anastasia. Biographical information included in this essay has been corroborated through various interviews with associates who were working with him at the time, as well as primary sources.

7. Mekas and Anthology Film Archives spearheaded a restoration of Smith's film *Mahagonny* and along with Singh have been responsible for keeping his film work in circulation.

8. In addition to published texts by and about Deren, I was able to examine the Maya Deren collection in the Howard Gotlieb Archival Research Center at Boston University. Much of my knowledge about her day-to-day life comes from this research.

9. In a 1998 interview with Irina Leimbacher, Strand describes the production of *Mosori Monika*:

> *Strand*: So there was that kind of thing going on, where people were really interested in an art form but had not had the experience of looking at a lot of experimental work because we weren't shown that at UCLA.
> *Leimbacher*: And that's where you made *Mosori Monika*?

> *Strand*: Yes. They sent me to Venezuela to the Orinoco River. They had got a grant to do this program and they had excellent equipment. I went in 1969, and there had been several other years that they went with a real portable camera and a recorder. They bought a few éclairs, a few nagras and lights, and everything you would need on a field trip. And they sent people to Africa and Ireland, and they finally decided that they were going to send women to the jungles of Venezuela. So they sent me and another woman. We were paid as research assistants, everything was paid for including the film, and I own it. And the only thing they have is the right to a print. (Leimbacher 1998a, 144)

10. Constructing screening programs from various types of nonfiction and experimental work was not new, although it had fallen out of fashion in the late 1960s and 1970s. In the United States, Amos Vogel, one of the earliest cinéastes, programmed documentary, experimental, and narrative work together.

11. I would like to distance this writing from the idea of "experimental ethnography" put forward by film and cultural studies theorists in the late 1990s, particularly in the work of Catherine Russell in *Experimental Ethnography* (1999). While I very much respect the work of the experimental filmmakers she writes about and think that their work can inform anthropologists, to make claims that their work is anthropological in the same way as ethnographies produced by anthropologists are dilutes the meaning of the word "ethnographic."

12. Ascher's films used to be distributed in New York by filmmaker, historian, and cinemaphile Cecile Starr, and were available from Cornell University Audio-Visual Center and from Canyon Cinema. According to Ascher, Starr has grown too old to continue her distribution business, Cornell shut its distribution services down, and Canyon ceased to distribute his films due to his refusal to transfer the work to video. Currently the films are only available directly from Ascher.

13. Unless otherwise noted, information regarding Robert Ascher was obtained during an interview and screening of his work at Cornell Cinema in Ithaca, NY. I would like to thank Dr. Ascher for taking the time to meet with me, as well as the director of Cornell Cinema Mary Fessendon, the projectionist Paul, and my friend and fellow experimental filmmaker Jason Livingston, a former student of Ascher's and present faculty member at Ithaca College, for helping to set up this meeting. It was truly a delight for me to be able to see this work on celluloid.

14. Robert Ascher, e-mail to the author, May 15, 2008.

15. For Alan Passes's current curriculum vitae, which includes novels, stage plays, poetry, radio plays, television programs, translation work, and anthropology, check his listing on the *Piano Tuner of Earthquakes* website, http://www.thepianotunerofearthquakes.com/bio_alanpasses.html.

16. Although the Quays where born in the United States, they have spent

most of their adult lives in Great Britain and much of their early animation was produced by the BBC. While an extensive analysis of the differences between the acceptance and funding of experimental film work in various European countries, Canada, and the US has yet to be conducted, anecdotally there seems to be a link between the more generous public funding of art/film/video and documentary work in Great Britain and Canada and its broader public appeal and acceptance. Thus what is considered edgier and more experimental in the US (the Quay brothers) may be seen as more mainstream, if no less experimental or "artsy," in Europe.

17. In 2008 I gave a talk at the Society for Cinema and Media Studies conference in which I discussed the ritual and symbolic aspects of the Quays' films. Afterward a colleague approached me and said that until then he had found the films' narratives circular and confusing, but through my examination he had begun to see their narrative logic.

18. Grant completed the editing of the film in a postproduction course with Sasha Waters. Waters works in both documentary and experimental film modes and graduated with an MFA from the Department of Film and Media Arts at Temple University. While a student there, she took a number of courses with Jay Ruby and was exposed to most of the literature in visual anthropology up through the late 1990s. Thus she was able to direct Grant to writings on and by Jean Rouch, which had a large impact on the editing of *Sakamapeap* (Grant, personal communication, 2007a).

19. Grant also cites ten years of living in the Bay Area, watching experimental films and seeing artwork and performance, as an impetus for wanting to do something visual during her fieldwork. During her undergraduate degree at the University of California–Berkeley, studying psychology, she attended film screenings and courses with her filmmaker friend, including classes taught by Trinh T. Minh-ha and Craig Baldwin, and had experienced experimental film and critiques of documentary style in their classrooms.

20. Grant is aware of this as she writes, "Before I shot it I had worked through how it would be possible for me to film in Cambodia. I know that sounds silly, but I do remember thinking about how what I made would be exploitative (for many reasons, e.g., of my neighbors' limited will or capacity to refuse, by the fact that the images would be beautiful and exoticize/culturalize poverty, by the inevitability of the 'subject' not being the audience, etc.) to an uncomfortable extent. My film doesn't escape this, in fact, I do think that both the humor and lushness of image and sound obscure struggles. And it has been pointed out to me that the focus on 'everyday' tells us nothing about their larger life situations, e.g., in political economic terms" (Grant, personal communication, 2007b).

ELEVEN

Anthropology and the Problem of Audience Reception

STEPHEN PUTNAM HUGHES

As anthropologists have become increasingly engaged with the study of media, the issues of "audience" and "reception" have emerged as central concerns. In this review article I pose two related questions: How have anthropologists come to focus on media audiences and reception? And what does an anthropological approach contribute to these issues? I argue that in focusing on media audiences and reception, anthropologists have been part of a larger critical interrogation of these issues within media and cultural studies over the last several decades. In response to perceived inadequacies of textual formalism, top-down theories of media domination, and lifeless statistical surveys for studying how audiences engage with media, those in media and cultural studies have taken an "ethnographic turn." By the 1990s when anthropologists began to take media more seriously as an object of study, they found an obvious convergence with media and cultural studies on the use of ethnographic approaches for studying the issues of media reception and audiences. Over the last decade there has been a significant interdisciplinary exchange around the problems of media reception, which has pushed anthropological research in new directions. But anthropologists have also made important contributions to this larger debate with their greater attentiveness to the social and cultural specificity of audience reception within contexts of everyday life, which has helped to challenge the Eurocentricism of media and cultural studies.

The term "audience" is not part of the classical analytic lexicon of anthropology. Yet in a keynote address to the Royal Anthropological Institute's Ethnographic Film Festival in

11.1   Detail from an educational wall poster entitled "Indian Families." Publisher unknown.
Purchased by the author in Chennai, India, 1997.

1990 David MacDougall claimed that visual anthropologists were "finally
beginning to take more seriously how audiences interact with films to
produce meanings" (1992a, 90). The importance of audiences to visual anthropology seems so fundamental and obvious, it hardly seems necessary
to have to elaborate. One cannot even begin to speak about visual media
without at least assuming some relationship with an audience. Indeed,
what is the purpose of visual anthropology and visual representation more
generally if they are not meant for someone? Yet, MacDougall's claim was
in part a tacit recognition that the question of "audience," either as theoretical issue or methodological problem, had not featured prominently
as part of the history of visual anthropology, especially when compared
to film, media, and cultural studies. Within the disciplinary space of anthropology, early promoters of visual anthropology as a definitive subfield placed explicit emphasis upon wrenching the discipline away from
its addiction to words (Mead 1975) and on establishing the legitimacy
of visual representation as a mode of anthropological inquiry and knowledge about others (Heider 1976/2006; Hockings 1975/2003). The stress

has been on how anthropologists use the visual as an analytical tool and not on the ways that people meaningfully engage with visual media. Moreover, insofar as much of the literature on visual anthropology has been predominantly concerned with ethnographic film and filmmakers, the perspectives of production have been privileged over those of reception.

MacDougall's claim also more positively announced that visual anthropology had in 1990 started to address more seriously the issues of audience. What exactly was this shift in emphasis to which he was referring? Since MacDougall is one of the most eminent of all ethnographic filmmakers and was addressing a roomful of ethnographic and documentary film enthusiasts, it is reasonable to assume that he was in part speaking about a growing recognition of the importance of considering how audiences make sense of ethnographic films. MacDougall was most certainly referring to his own considerable efforts to address filmmaking as a three-way encounter between filmmaker, subject, and audience (1975, 1978). And he was also very likely referring to a number of other attempts to highlight the issues of ethnographic film spectatorship, which had already suggested that more was to come (Ginsburg 2005; Martinez 1990). But in retrospect we can see that these early efforts, however significant, did not in themselves constitute the major reorientation, the retheorizing of ethnographic film in terms of its audiences, that MacDougall seemed to be suggesting.

Beyond an exclusive and narrow focus on ethnographic film spectatorship, MacDougall was also undoubtedly referring to another shift in visual anthropology. As he has argued elsewhere, visual anthropology was at the time caught up in a much broader intellectual shift as part of what W. J. T. Mitchell (1994) has called the "pictorial turn," away from the linguistic and textual privileging of structuralism, semiotics, poststructuralism, and deconstruction (MacDougall 1997; 1998, 61). As the visual in visual anthropology took on greater importance and was seen to be implicated in a much broader range of media practices, film viewing seemed to take on added importance alongside other viewing practices as part of the larger dynamics of visual culture. In the 1970s and 1980s anthropology had also gone through its own crisis of questioning the limits of ethnographic representation, which helped to alter and expand the project of visual anthropology (Banks and Morphy 1997). We can now recognize this shift as what in the 1970s Sol Worth described as a process whereby the naming of "visual anthropology" logically led to the possibility of another "anthropology of visual communication" (1981, 185). Once it was no longer a simple matter of *us* (that is, anthropologists addressing other anthropologists) with cameras looking at *them* as passive objects of study (Ginsburg 1994b), and once anthropologists realized that they did not own an ethnographic monopoly on the production and interpretation of visual representation, it began to be possible to think more broadly about how people everywhere relate to visual media as part of their everyday lives. Moreover, with visual anthropologists beginning to question the politics of visual representation, the issues of how visual media matter to those with whom they study helped focus attention on audiences as a significant concern. These shifts helped anthropologists to articulate a new and crucial distinction in visual anthropology between "using a medium and studying how a medium is used" (Worth 1981, 190; also discussed in Ruby 1976 and MacDougall 1997).

By the time MacDougall spoke about taking audiences more seriously, what Worth and Ruby had earlier envisaged as an anthropology of visual communication was finally beginning to coalesce as an anthropology of media (Spitulnik 1993; Ginsburg 1994b, 1997b). Even if MacDougall did not have such a project in mind, anthropologists were then responding to an important interdisciplinary and critical interrogation of audiences among film, media, and cultural studies. Outside of visual anthropology circles but within this cluster of emergent disciplines, the issues of spectatorship, audience, and reception had already been among the most important, if not the most important, areas of research, theorization, and debate over the 1970s and 1980s. So there is a sense that at the time MacDougall was heralding the turn toward audiences in visual anthropology, it had already been largely overtaken and carried along in the wake of the 1980s boom in audience studies.

It may seem that I am putting too much effort into discussing the implications of what was for MacDougall probably only a casual comment, one that was, even in the context of the original address, slightly off his main topic about how film styles relate to cultural styles. I have started here because I consider this early 1990s conjuncture as a crucial pivot around which the issues of ethnographic film spectatorship within visual anthropology have become part of a more general anthropological concern with media audiences. In this chapter I will use this moment as a kind of turning point in plotting the history of how audiences have been implicated within the history of visual anthropology, ethnographic film, and anthropology of media. I will also consider how the treatment of spectatorship and audiences in the emergent disciplines of film, media, and cultural studies has run parallel to and been interwoven with the history of visual anthropology.

An Unruly History of Audience Studies

Our commonsense understanding of the term "audience" seems disarmingly straightforward. In common English usage, an audience refers collectively to all those who watch, listen, read, or otherwise experience media or a live performance. It is a social category that encompasses a very broad and complex range of possibilities for how individuals engage with different media, involving diverse activities and enmeshed with specific cultural contexts. Audiences are located in many forms, ranging from a physical face-to-face gathering at a specific time and place to an abstract and dispersed collectivity linked in neither time nor space. We can define an audience in terms of various different and overlapping coordinates—place, social categories, media technologies, media content, or specific times (McQuail 1997, 2). This commonsense rendering has proven to be sufficiently broad, ambiguous, malleable, and portable to become an indispensable part of how practitioners, regulators, entrepreneurs, users, and critics understand what media do.

To the extent that anthropologists have become interested in asking questions about the categories of audience and its various cognates, they have for the most part borrowed from other disciplines and debates that have long taken place outside the confines of anthropology. At this point there is a complicated and contested history of theories and debates as to why audiences matter to the study of visual media, which stretches back to at least the early decades of the twentieth century. There have been so many divergent historical responses to the problem of theorizing and studying audiences that there is a good deal of confusion and uncertainty surrounding what is by now a famously problematic term. To make matters worse there are a number of alternative terms—spectators, filmgoers, TV viewers, consumers—that are often treated as interchangeable with "audience" and used without much awareness of where they have come from, how they might be different, and what assumptions they rely upon. Moreover, it has become common to elide the term audience altogether by referring to a set of general and abstract processes such as spectatorship, reception, and consumption in ways that no longer directly refer to people.

Since the late 1980s the prevailing sense within audience studies has been one of crisis. At precisely the moment when various disciplines, most notably film, media, and cultural studies, were converging on the study of the audience, a general consensus was emerging about the impossibility of a comprehensive theory of audiences. In the first instance,

the problem of the audience seemed to defy all empirical or methodological solutions that promised a direct and immediate access to the complexity and diversity of an audience as a whole. As a matter of research,
audiences provided no stable entity or single object of study already out
there waiting to be discovered. The unstructured group that we refer to
as a media audience is continuously being constituted, dissolved, and
reconstituted with each media experience. As such, audiences are always
partial, indeterminant, unfinished and incomplete (Ang 1996, 67). Many
also argued that, given this radical uncertainty about audiences, the term
was more appropriately considered a fiction that is institutionally and
discursively produced for the purpose of the media industry. In any sociological, historical, or analytical sense, media audiences were increasingly
considered to be only an abstraction generated by the researcher. In a reframing similar to what the crisis of representation had provoked among
anthropologists, the problem for media and cultural studies shifted from
trying to grasp the reality of audiences to asking political and epistemological questions about what constitutes the authority to make claims
about the audience.

Perhaps the best indication of this confusion and ambiguity is the rise
of a new academic genre of writing devoted to providing a comprehensive overview and scholarly review of the literature on the topic of audiences (e.g., Abercrombie and Longhurst 1998; Alasuutari 1999; Ang 1996;
Katz et al. 2005; Mayne 1993; McQuail 1997; Moores 1993; Morley 1992;
Ross and Nightingale, 2003; Ruddock 2001). There are so many review
articles and books devoted to audience studies that we need a comprehensive review of the reviews in order to make sense of this overcrowded
field. I will leave this task to others, though I have serious doubts as to
whether the untidy history of audience studies will ever fit neatly into
a seamless progressive and comprehensive narrative overview. Accord-
ingly, my strategy here is more limited. I pose two related questions: How
have anthropologists come to focus on media audiences and reception?
And what does an anthropological approach contribute to these issues?

An Implicit History of Ethnographic Film Spectatorship

Even if they have not always been used self-consciously to set the agenda,
issues of audience have been implicitly central throughout the history of
visual anthropology. Submerged within a more obvious historical genealogy of visual anthropology, which would include obligatory mentions
of such luminaries as Alfred Haddon, Edward Curtis, Robert Flaherty,

and Margaret Mead and Gregory Bateson, one could excavate implicit modes of address to presumed audiences. Each of these early efforts to mobilize new means and techniques of visual representation also entailed assumptions as to whom they were meant for and how these audiences would understand and use visual materials. Along these lines, we can credit Alison Griffiths's (2002) excellent history of anthropology and visual culture at the turn of the twentieth century as an exemplary start to opening up the topic of how visual anthropology has historically related to its wider audiences. Her work has shown how the early history of the visual in anthropology was mutually implicated in and co-constituent with a larger Euro-American visual culture. She has characterized ethnographic films from the early history of cinema "as modes of enunciation that move freely between commercial genres such as the home movie, scientific demonstration film, observational ethnographic film and travelogue" (2002, 318). This early moment in history of visual anthropology thus overlapped with a remarkably extensive range of visual practices and multiple modes of address.

Likewise, we could investigate how subsequent developments in ethnographic film have mobilized their own modes of spectatorship. During the 1950s and 1960s, when filmmakers such as Jean Rouch, John Marshall, Robert Gardner, Asen Balikci, and Timothy Asch self-consciously experimented with modes of filmmaking, which we have eventually come to understand as defining an ethnographic film genre, they were also in their own ways, at least implicitly, addressing the issue of audience through their films. Every historical shift and every conscious choice about using a documentary film style—expository, poetic, observational, participatory, or reflexive—reconfigured the relation between film, film subject, and audience. In particular each mode of documentary makes a different set of demands upon and assumptions about how audiences relate to the films (Nichols 1991, 32–75). In this sense, audiences and their imagined modes of viewing are already part of the filmmaking process. Following Bakhtin we could say that film is formed through a kind of dialogic anticipation of response and inflected with the expectation of an answer from an audience, even if these viewers are not copresent and are largely unknown and unseen by the filmmaker. In this way audiences are already implicitly inscribed in film as it is being made.

Throughout much of the twentieth century ethnographic filmmakers were generally more concerned with recording reality than with whom would watch their films or how a general public might engage with them. Certainly at a time when film was primarily conceived as a form of visual documentation within a salvage paradigm of anthropology, there was less concern as to who might use them, or how, outside of academia. Film, understood as a kind of visual note taking, was useful as a research tool for recording data, for making an illustrated anthropology, and as a preserved document of a way of life for future scholars. This mode of filmic address was narrowly focused upon a small community of experts and anthropological specialists, who would be expected to view films as a transparent medium. The films of Alfred Haddon, Franz Boas (Jacknis 1987), or Margaret Mead (Jacknis 1988) were not widely circulated. They went unseen outside a small circle of anthropologists and specialists and were not accessible to a general public. This mode of ethnographic film tended to elide explicit concern with its potential audiences, even as it implicitly addressed them as an unmediated transcription of reality.

Though this early mode of ethnographic film has not entirely disappeared, an important shift in how and to whom ethnographic filmmakers address their work took place in the 1950s and 1960s. Part of what allowed ethnographic film to emerge as a self-consciously distinct documentary genre is that it was retooled for use in the teaching of anthropology and its practitioners began to consider explicitly how student audiences might engage with films. In fact, we can understand much of the effort to establish ethnographic film as a viable genre during the 1960s and 1970s as directly related to institutionalizing and promoting its newfound educational mode of address.[1] The Film Study Center at Harvard's Peabody Museum, established in 1958, helped launch the eminent filmmaking careers of John Marshall, Robert Gardner, Asen Balikci, and Timothy Asch, all within an institutional framework that assumed forms of educational spectatorship. This institutional center then went on the establish the Program in Ethnographic Film in 1966, for the explicit purpose of training, production, and teaching; its major contribution, according to Ruby (2002b), was the publication of Karl Heider's *Films for Anthropological Teaching* (Heider and Hermer 1995). Since its first publication, this periodically updated text in the form of a filmography has provided a standard reference and normative guide for how educators might use ethnographic films within the contexts of teaching. Along with a host of supporting study guides produced as supplements for ethnographic films, this publication has helped mediate films for their presumed student audiences by shaping their expectations and promoting a privileged interpretive framework (also see Ramey, this volume).

Another important early example of this educational mode of address is the film work done in the early 1960s by Asen Balikci as part of an educational project for US schools that resulted in the extensive Netsilik Eskimo film series (1966). Originally these films were part of a school curriculum called *Man, A Course of Study*, which was aimed at nine- and ten-year-old children and sent out to at least three thousand schools across the United States (Hockings 1975/2003). This project was eventually and controversially terminated in 1973 as a result of conservative political pressure, based not upon the quality or style of filmmaking but upon the presumed ill effects that the films were having on the cultural values of their young audiences. This incident forced Balikci to confront explicitly the issue of how ethnographic film related to its audiences in ways that would necessarily alter his understanding of filmmaking practice (Balikci 1988; and see Durington and Ruby, this volume).

To this list we can also add the films of John Marshall who, after *The Hunters* (1957), explicitly refined his filming techniques with an eye to the productions' use in teaching anthropology. Marshall started experimenting in Nyae Nyae during the late 1950s with a simple chronological style of filming, based on action sequences conceived around discrete social events. He claimed that these *cinéma vérité* or direct-cinema action sequences, which he later went on to edit together with Timothy Asch, comprised the most basic observable forms of human behavior and as such were "the most effective films for use in the classroom" (Marshall 1993, 20). Thus, even such innovations in film style as *cinéma vérité* and direct cinema were overdetermined by this educational mode of address. Marshall continued along these lines in his partnership with Asch, establishing, in 1967, the Center for Documentary Anthropology, which became Documentary Educational Resources, with an expanded educational remit, in 1971. These efforts yielded important and lasting institutional support for the production and distribution of ethnographic film as part of an educative agenda for student audiences.

More, perhaps, than any other of these first-generation ethnographic filmmakers, Asch was dedicated to using and promoting film as an instrument of education. From numerous biographical accounts we know that he was heavily influenced by the work he did for the Harvard educational psychologist Jerome Bruner as part of the project *Man, A Course of Study,* mentioned above (Ruby 2000b; Lutkehaus 2004). He also worked for several years in the late 1960s to develop a media-based curriculum for the public school system in Massachusetts. In his own filmmaking, Asch adopted a sequential style of single-concept films, originally developed from his collaborative efforts with Marshall, as a pedagogical strategy. This greatly informed his early classic films *The Ax Fight* and *The Feast*

(Ruby 2000a). Though Asch experimented with new filmmaking styles throughout his career, he was always explicit about his educational address (Ginsburg 2004). In 1988 he claimed that "all seventy some odd films that I've made have been made out of a teaching experience" (quoted in Martinez 1995, 55). He was so committed to this approach that he incorporated input from his student audiences in the editing of his films. He would try a film out on some students and then discuss it with them. If he had not been able to get his ideas across in a way that they could understand, he would go back, make changes, and then screen it to another group of students until he was satisfied (Martinez 1995).

The educational mode of address, which inflected so much of the ethnographic filmmaking of the 1960s and 1970s, produced a "way of seeing" (Berger 1972) framed within historically specific discourses, institutions, and practices. These films were ways of seeing cultural difference that addressed their spectators as impressionable and receptive to the anthropological messages of cultural relativism, presented as part of a pedagogic encounter between teachers and students within the institutional contexts of classroom screenings and reception. In this sense ethnographic films "assume that we will learn something experientially from images, and in some sense make them our own" (MacDougall 1998, 144). But within the reception context of the classroom, where attentive viewing and an ability to connect films to other reading materials, class discussions, and analytic frameworks set by the teacher are rewarded with higher marks, students are a kind of captive audience.

The educational mode of address helped the first generation of ethnographic film consolidate its status as a definitive genre with reference to student audiences and the teaching of anthropology. Yet, although this legacy is still very much with us today, the encounter between ethnographic films and their audiences took a significant turn starting in the 1970s, when television also emerged as an important mode of address. Ethnographic films within the classroom settings have in some senses been teaching to the converted, that is, to a small, select group of students who had for whatever reasons chosen to study anthropology. In contrast, anthropological television programming greatly expanded this reach to include audiences far beyond specialist anthropological circles and without any background in or indeed even understanding of anthropology. The emergence of television as an outlet for ethnographic films not only created a new mode of public address but also helped pose urgent questions about how mass audiences might make sense of them (Loizos 1980). More than any other previous ethnographic film format, made-for-television anthropologically themed programming led to an explicit and extensive focus on the question of audience (Ginsburg 1992, 97).

This has especially been the case in the UK, where Grenada Television's series *Disappearing World*, which ran from the early 1970s through the late 1980s, set the precedent for such documentaries (Henley 1985). Over fifty films were produced during this period by a well-financed team of filmmakers, TV producers, film editors, and anthropologists (Singer and Woodhead 1988). In Britain these were originally broadcast during primetime (at a time when there were still only three, and later four, channels) to an audience of millions. Many of the programs were subsequently rebroadcast around the world.[2] In keeping with the agenda of salvage anthropology the main objectives of the series were to focus on the forces that were annihilating tribal peoples around the world and to record their endangered ways of life before it was too late (Singer 1992). The films let the people speak for themselves as much as possible and tried to present other cultures in ways that would allow for basic human empathy and respect.

While these ethnographic films attempted to create trajectories of understanding that shared a great deal with the educational emphasis so characteristic of the early phase of ethnographic film, television brought anthropology into the orbit of a major commercial entertainment industry (Turton 1992; Woodhead 1992; Turner 1992b). At every point the producers were aware that they needed a style that would be accessible to the widest possible British television audiences (Loizos 1993). Asen Balikci has quoted the chairman of Grenada Television, Sir Denis Forman, as saying that in television "the viewer is king" (1989, 5). Thus, the overriding question informing the entire production process was what would best hold the TV audience's attention (Wright 1992). This encouraged renewed emphasis upon entertainment values, with compelling narrative forms, strong characters, and exotic ritual being brought to the fore at the expense of the more mundane activities of everyday life. But more than a matter of film content, anthropology on television brought a new, historically specific set of institutions and discursive practices into a context of reception that was markedly different from the educational mode of address. Once ethnographic film audiences were no longer confined to classrooms but comprised millions around the world, the problem of the audience crossed over into new uncharted terrain—one that, as it happens, was already being worked over by film, media, and cultural studies.

Film Studies' Spectatorship versus Cultural Studies' TV Audiences

During the 1960s and 1970s, at precisely the time that anthropologists began to think more seriously about ethnographic film and visual representation as legitimate disciplinary concerns, film, media, and cultural studies were taking shape as important academic disciplines. It is perhaps not coincidental that Margaret Mead (1975) was, during this same period, famously scolding anthropology for its myopic adherence to words and calling upon the discipline to develop visual representation as a mode of anthropological knowledge. Over the course of the twentieth century, first film and then television had emerged as the dominant forms of visual mass media. And within different institutional and intellectual histories, there developed a variety of divergent approaches to the study and theorizing of people's relation to the new media. The collective success of these approaches played a large part in informing how anthropologists began to engage with the problem of audience reception in the 1990s.

Given the spectacular and worldwide success of motion pictures over the last century, film studies arrived on the scene rather late. At about the same time as visual anthropology was becoming a distinct subfield of anthropology, film studies also began to emerge as an autonomous discipline with degree-granting programs, mostly in European and North American universities. Film studies had struggled to establish itself as an offshoot of literature departments, which were, if anything, even more of a discipline of words than was anthropology. Within this initial humanities framework, film studies first articulated a distinct brand of scholarship on the basis of theories of film aesthetics, authorship, genre, and textuality, with a primary focus upon European art film and the Hollywood commercial mainstream. Drawing upon a potent mix of semiotics, structural Marxism, psychoanalysis, and feminism, it created a new theoretical language for analyzing the implicit codes and hidden meanings of filmic texts. This newfound theoretical sophistication defined around the specificity of the cinematic medium also posed important new questions of spectatorship.

From about the mid-1970s "spectatorship" began to emerge as a central problem for film studies and was predominantly theorized within a general framework of semiotics. In this context, spectatorship was used as a theoretical concept to consider how film viewers are constituted and positioned by the *textual* aspects of films. Starting with the centrality of film texts, conceived as signifying practices, semiotic approaches theorized film spectatorship as an empty space determined systematically by signi-fication. Like, Levi-Strauss's myth, Barthes's codes, and Althusser's ideol-ogy, film positioned and fixed the subjectivity of its spectators through its narrative conventions and practices of realism. Theories of spectatorship, constituted in explicit opposition to the notion of audience (considered as those who actually attend the cinema), thus directly challenged the empirical premises of the then-dominant social science approach to the study of mass communications. The social reality of the audience was no longer an issue since film spectators were always caught up in textual strategies that position them and produce their subjectivity, sewn into the text as it were. This new paradigm is now most commonly associ-ated with what is known as "screen theory," in reference to the British film journal *Screen*, which was principally responsible for publishing this work.

One of the prime exemplars of this approach was Laura Mulvey's essay "Visual Pleasure and Narrative Cinema" (1975), which used a feminist-inspired psychoanalytic approach to theorize how mainstream Holly-wood films construct their images for male spectatorial satisfaction. Mul-vey argued that the visual pleasure of Hollywood cinema was based on the assumption of the male gaze directed at an objectified female, which replicated the structure of unequal power relations between men and women. This patriarchal regime of representation privileged the active male act of looking as the sole agent of desire, with women, displayed as the sexual objects of his pleasure, demoted to passive "to-be-looked-at-ness." Mulvey herself has long since moved on from this position, yet the article has been canonized as a foundational text of screen theory (Loshitzky 2003), which has overall placed the emphasis on the power of film texts in constituting spectators through a series of subject positions of identification.[3]

The success of film theory in promoting the issue of spectatorship in the 1970s was countered by the rise of cultural studies as an important model for the study of media audiences in the 1980s. From its beginnings in the 1960s at the Birmingham Centre for Contemporary Cultural Stud-ies, this new approach maintained much closer links to sociology in the UK; it went on to set a new agenda for audience studies, using television as its main example. Cultural studies has achieved rapid intellectual and institutional growth, especially since the 1980s, losing its "British" iden-tity tag as it transformed into a global academic phenomenon (Turner 1993; Stratton and Ang 1996; Chen 1998). Its success can in part be attrib-uted to a refusal to operate within traditional disciplinary boundaries or be limited by any one object of study or fixed theoretical paradigm. Stuart

Hall, who more than anyone else served as the key figure for this expansive phase of cultural studies, has most famously called it a provisional rendezvous whose only coherence is a shared commitment to examining cultural practices in relation to power (1996). For the purposes of this chapter, however, the emergence of cultural studies was an important transformative intervention in the field of audience studies.

For those at the Birmingham Centre, media emerged as a main concern in the 1960s and 1970s. As an initial orientation they set themselves the major task of reviewing, evaluating, and synthesizing all the major approaches to the study of media. As a summation and synthesis of the history of mass communication theory, Stuart Hall's (1981) "encoding/decoding model" was a decisive intervention. Hall brought semiotics and Marxism together in order to rework the earlier sender/receiver model of mass communication, which had assumed a fundamental relationship between an active sender and a passive receiver, bound as key points at the beginning and end of a linear process of direct influence whereby a message is transmitted. This minimal, stimulus-response model was posited almost as a mechanical circuit, a frictionless machine. The meaning of media messages was considered to be inherent. Hall, in contrast, argued that meaning was not contained within a message but was determined in relation to larger linguistic and cultural parameters. He conceptualized mass communications as a complex set of relations articulated in linked but distinctive, semi-autonomous moments of production, circulation, distribution, consumption, and reproduction. The meaning of a communicative event was not ultimately fixed or determined by any one of these moments and allowed for a potential plurality and contestation of meanings. By questioning the teleological determinism of media communication, Hall's model freed up reception to be seen as something more than a passive response completely determined by the encoded message, even though the sender still set the limits within which decoding took place.

The encoding/decoding model was initially put forward within the Media Studies Group at the Birmingham Centre "as a kind of diagnostic model and tool kit for their work in progress" (Scannell 2007, 211). The first two scholars to take up the challenge of testing the model were two students, Charlotte Brunsdon and David Morley, who proposed to study the processes of encoding and decoding from production to reception of the British television program *Nationwide*. Because of practical research constraints, the project was never completed as planned. Instead Morley focused on the decoding side of the equation, and his work was eventually published as *Nationwide Audience* (1980). Morley demonstrated that an individual's location within class, gender, ethnic, and national relations conditions the modes of media access and exposure as well as mediating their encounter with media texts. The success of this work helped to emphasize the decoding side of the model at the expense of encoding. Many media scholars latched on to the ostensible shift from passive receivers to active audiences with reformist zeal.[4] While Hall's original formulation of the encoding/decoding model sought a careful and complex balance, in subsequent use it was reduced to "a mandate for the study of how audiences decoded the messages of television" (Gurevitch and Scannell 2003, 243).[5] Nonetheless, Hall's article proved to be a critical intervention in the unraveling of the semiotic model of media communications.

The Ethnographic Turn in Audience Studies

Cultural studies helped to move the question of the audience back to the forefront of media studies and to spark a boom in media audience studies. Hall's article had helped to establish a renewed emphasis on reception and the active engagement of the receiver as part of the critical understanding entailed in the decoding process, but it did not explicitly spell out how to study audiences. When faced with the problem of figuring out how people engage with media, those in cultural studies increasingly turned to anthropological methods, in what amounted to a selective reinvention of ethnography. Since the 1980s there has been such a steady stream of good critical reflection on this ethnographic turn in media cultural studies (e.g., Radway 1988; Morley 1992; Moores 1993; Ang 1996; Abu-Lughod 1997; Murphy and Kraidy 2003) that I not need cover comprehensively it here. However, it is important for my argument to explain how this development in audience studies relates to the way anthropologists embraced these issues in the 1990s.

Coming from a background in literary studies, Janice Radway's *Reading the Romance* (1984) was one of the first explicit efforts to develop an ethnographic approach to the study of media audiences in the United States. In posing the research question of how to explain the increased popularity of the romance novel, Radway took the then radical step of "taking the real readers seriously"—not merely as subjectivities constructed by the text or abstract "ideal readers" defined by the mechanisms of textual address. She argued that cultural studies must instead shift its analytic focus from the text, taken in isolation, to the complex social event of reading, whereby a woman actively makes the book meaningful in the context of her ordinary life. Methodologically, Radway started with a group of forty-two women—a symbolic community of readers—then used their newsletter, her own questionnaires, discussions, interviews, and observation to grapple with the unruly, heterogeneous practices and accounts of flesh-and-blood readers. In this way, she rediscovered a Malinowskian truism that there is a distinction between what readers do with texts and what they say about them. This instability between theory and practice provided the analytic angle for Radway to explain the popularity of romance reading as a kind of psychological mechanism for coping with a range of everyday problems. Radway's functionalist rendition of reading practices had it own limitations (Ang 1996, 98–108), but her intervention significantly opened up audience ethnography as an important methodological alternative for cultural and media studies.

Among those in cultural and media studies, David Morley and Roger Silverstone were some of the most prominent early figures in theorizing the importance of ethnographic methods and applying them to the study of TV audience research. The new "ethnographic turn" in media studies was heralded as a way of critically addressing the perceived inadequacies of the textual formalism of film studies, top-down theories of media domination, and lifeless quantitative surveys for studying audiences (Morley 1992, 173–97). Much of what had passed for audience studies throughout the twentieth century had consisted of commercially sponsored market research, which used positivistic methods of counting box office returns, questionnaires, sample surveys, and statistical analyses. The study of audiences had largely been conceived as an empirical project of counting or categorizing people guided by an optimistic, positivist faith that enough data could eventually be collected to reveal their sociological reality. In this context, ethnography offered an important qualitative alternative.

But beyond providing a means of critique, the promotion of ethnography in audience studies was informed by a growing anthropological realization that the encounter between media and audiences needed to be studied within the contexts and routines of everyday life, which render them meaningful (Morley and Silverstone 1990). Ethnographic methods seemed to offer the possibility of more detailed research into how television was made part of the experiences and patterns of the daily life of audiences (Silverstone 1990). Drawing upon the work of Michel de Certeau (1984), Silverstone (1989) emphasized how TV was worked into the citations and recitations of everyday narratives, such as rumor, gossip, stories, jokes, fragments of recollection, and proverbs, all of which help to define individual and collective identities. The study of TV audiences should be much more than a matter of focusing on the act of watching TV; it should also attend to the more anthropological question of how audiences put media to work in social interaction and in the management of daily life through such activities as working, talking, dressing, or shopping. In developing "the practice of everyday life" as an analytic framework, media reception constituted a kind of active cultural production conceived as "ways of operating" or "doing things" (de Certeau 1984, xii, 30–31). Or, in the words of Ien Ang, "What ethnographic work entails is a form of "methodological situationalism," underscoring the thoroughly situated, always context-bound ways in which people encounter, use, interpret, enjoy, think, and talk about television and other media in everyday life (1996, 70).

The rise of ethnographic approaches to audience studies also came with its own historical narrative. Morley (1989, 1992; Morley and Chen 1996) has perhaps done more than anyone else (though many others have followed him) to promote this new audience research as part of a teleological progress from passive to active audiences, from text to context, from screen theory to cultural studies, from film spectators to television audiences, from top-down structuralism to bottom-up resistance, and from quantitative to qualitative methods. Working through this general set of recurring dichotomies, ethnographic audience research privileged a reading of media where there was no inherent meaning in fixed texts. Rather, meaning was created in the encounter with audiences and shaped by discursive formations and practices. Audiences were considered to be active and selective but not necessarily in control. This story of theoretical and methodical alternatives became something of a ritual invocation, which has launched many an audience study ever since the 1980s.[6] But in the context of this chapter, it is important in that this narrative provided the general discursive framework within which anthropologists began to start thinking seriously about the problems of audience research.

Anthropology Takes on Audience Studies

Returning now to where I began, we can in retrospect agree with David MacDougall's claim that visual anthropology was in 1990 finally ready to move in the direction of audience studies. The early 1990s represents a kind of turning point for anthropologists' willingness to embrace the problem of the audience. Prior to the 1980s visual anthropologists had for the most part only implicitly dealt with hypothetical audiences as a mode of address and not as a concrete research problem. Audiences were assumed, produced by models of semiotic communication, or simply left unknown and unexamined. However, the 1980s boom in audience studies helped prepare the way for anthropologists to start a significant interdisciplinary exchange around the problems of media audiences.[7] Audience ethnography was one of the main issues that helped bring media studies and anthropology into a useful dialogue. For our purposes here we can distinguish two main areas where anthropologists in the 1990s converged around the study of audiences. The first focused on the more specific issues of ethnographic film spectatorship and the second on much broader questions about media audiences in general.[8]

Ethnographic film spectatorship was opened up as research topic almost single-handedly by the work of Wilton Martinez (1990, 1992, 1995, 1996). Starting in the late 1980s Martinez's research investigated how undergraduate students at the University of Southern California responded to ethnographic film; he went on to publish a series of important articles that are still widely acknowledged as the most extensive study and sustained theoretical work on the audiences of ethnographic films (Ruby 2000b, 190–91; Banks 1996a, 121; Wogan 2006, 14). Following Martinez's example, a number of other scholars have extended the discussion of ethnographic films in educational settings (Pack 1998, 2002; Offler 1999; Wogan 2006; Bird and Godwin 2006).[9] However, this kind of research work represents only a small field and has not been widely taken up or developed within the field of visual anthropology into a more general concern with ethnographic film's student or TV audiences (Dornfeld 1992). If it seemed to MacDougall in 1990 that questions of audience presented a new horizon for the study of ethnographic film, now, twenty years later, it seems that this challenge has yet to be adequately addressed. Undoubtedly this is in part because much of this work was too narrowly conceived, focusing on the presumed didactic purpose of ethnographic film and limited to classroom settings (Banks 1996a, 122). To understand how student audiences make sense of ethnographic films, however, would involve much broader research practices, which would necessarily explore a wider range of media practices and settings well beyond those of the classroom. An ethnographic approach to ethnographic film audiences calls for a contextual approach more akin to Sherry Ortner's (1998) study of the public youth culture of "Generation X" in the media-saturated United States of the 1990s.

Alongside and complementary to this work on ethnographic film audiences, a self-identified anthropology of media began to take shape in the early 1990s. Anthropologists taking on media-related research have been far more prolific in exploring the problem of audiences than in addressing the topic of ethnographic film spectatorship. But before I discuss this, let me first explain what I mean by anthropology of media. The term "media anthropology" was originally proposed in the early 1970s as a kind of applied anthropology and referred to the use of mass media for the purposes of promoting awareness of anthropology to the general public (Eiselein 1976; Eislein and Topper 1975; Chalfen 1978). The logic was that if anthropologists were to remain relevant and reflect upon contemporary cultural conditions, the discipline would have to start taking the media more seriously as one of the most important, far-reaching, and powerful cultural phenomena. Further, if one was committed to the value of anthropology, then its message should be delivered to the widest possible audience. This implied that anthropologists needed to work with journalists, acquire basic media skills, and develop appropriate media materials and outlets for that material (Allen 1994). A good example of this trajectory is the work of Terence Turner, who originally got involved with ethnographic film for TV as part of his politics of indigenous support among the Kayapo (1992b).

Media anthropology thus conceived, as a kind of public relations branch of the discipline, was, despite its strategic focus, an important step toward contemplating the problem of media audiences in general. However, it did not really gather much momentum apart from specific political engagements, and it should be distinguished from subsequent developments, which I am referring to as "anthropology of media." I do not want to get involved in hairsplitting,[10] but I do want to emphasize the fundamental shift from a concern with how anthropologists use media to asking questions regarding why media matter to those whom anthropologists study.

There is no discrete point or single founding event that definitively marks this transition. Rather it was more of a gathering collective sense that anthropologists had been slow to address the importance of media within their research contexts. It was, perhaps, not so much a matter of anthropologists deciding to go out and make media their main object of study as a recognition that anthropologists were increasingly having to work around everyone else's busy television watching or filmgoing schedules. This emergent realization was finally articulated coherently in 1993, when Debra Spitulnik, who was then still a graduate student, wrote her influential review of anthropology and mass media. At the time she did not believe that there was yet an anthropology of media, but insofar as she had named it and claimed a broad intellectual territory, she helped open out a space for media anthropology to emerge. Just a year later Faye Ginsburg (1994c) and Victor Caldarola (1994) guest-edited a special issue of *Visual Anthropology Review* (based on an earlier conference panel), in which they announced with conviction and academic authority that the anthropology of media was a new anthropological subfield. These early efforts (along with Ginsburg 1994a) provided the first widely acknowledged programmatic statements and offered a common referent around which other anthropologists of media rallied.[11]

In many respects the emergence of an anthropology of media in the early 1990s was closely related to important shifts within visual anthropology. Many of the key contributions during this period were published in the journal *Visual Anthropology Review* by scholars with a background in and common interest with visual anthropology (Taylor 1994). Moreover, several influential edited volumes in the 1990s reflected this greater openness to the wider study of media among visual anthropologists (Crawford and Turton 1992; Banks and Morphy 1997). For my argument here, the most significant of these new collective efforts to link visual anthropology to a wider anthropology of media was the 1993 Nordic Anthropological Film Association conference, held in Reykjavik, Iceland, and the resulting edited volume (Crawford and Hafsteinsson 1996). This represented the first coordinated effort by visual anthropologists to explore the issue of audiences as a kind of interdisciplinary exchange. This helped position visual anthropology within what was emerging as a more general anthropology of media. This mutual implication was forcefully articulated in Ginsburg's diagnostic survey of visual anthropology and its possible futures, where she compellingly argued for maintaining a link between the production and study of ethnographic film and the research on the social practice of media (1997).

Sara Dickey's (1993) ethnographic monograph on cinema and the urban poor in south India was, in many respects, indicative of how anthropologists were beginning to take on audiences as an object of study. Her research method and narrative form were both recognizably anthropological, but much of her analysis of audiences replayed the moves of 1980s film and cultural studies. She employed the classic anthropological rhetoric of ethnographic authority based on a strong first-person narrative about having lived in close proximity over an extended period in a foreign setting with those among whom she was conducting research. Much of her descriptive prose presented a written phenomenology of being there—on the streets, going to a film, and conducting interviews—which conveyed a great deal of information about where she lived, her neighbors, and her extended research experience. This rhetorical framing of research methodology stands in stark contrast to the use by those in cultural studies of ethnography more as a theoretical intervention than as a way of doing long-term fieldwork. Dickey's research practices and her representation of them may have differed significantly from the cultural

STEPHEN PUTNAM HUGHES

studies version of ethnography, but her resulting analysis bore strong similarities. Albeit in a very different research setting, she confirmed Morley's TV audience studies when she claimed that Tamil filmgoers tend to interpret movies with reference to their daily lives and specific personal relationships—familial, gender, class, and caste. Dickey also joined in with the widespread move to valorize the agency of her audiences, arguing that they were not passive victims of a dominant ideology but were actively engaged with the cinema through processes of accommodation and resistance. The urban poor, whom she identified as the main filmgoing audience, watched films as one of their few leisure activities, through which they sought "escape" and "relief" from the problems of daily life.

In this way, Dickey explained the continuing popularity of Tamil films by way of their ability to soothe audience anxieties, create an emotional release, and present a desirable, utopian world of romance and luxury. This argument came very close to Radway's functionalist, causal explanation of the behavior of romance readers in the United States. Put simply, the urban poor of south India escape into utopian fantasy as a means of fulfilling deep psychological needs, which are not otherwise addressed in their difficult living conditions (figure 11.2).

While Dickey was largely sympathetic and stressed her common ground with cultural studies approaches to audience ethnography, most subsequent anthropologists of media were more critical. It became increasingly obvious that anthropologists were not simply following the lead of media and cultural studies but were developing their own distinctive approaches to the study of media audiences. The first and most cited difference involved anthropologists' practice of ethnographic audience research. In media and cultural studies there had been numerous programmatic manifestos about the importance of ethnographic approaches for the study of media audiences, but, while strong on theory, these were conspicuously lacking in "thick" description (Abu-Lughod 1997, 111). Ethnography, that is, was deployed more as a rhetorical trope than as a rigorous method of field research. With a few exceptions (Gillespie 1995), those in media studies approached audience ethnography more as a day job, relying on discussion groups, questionnaires, and interviews (Murphy and Kraidy 2003, 3). They tended not to do the kind of long-term ethnographic research that involved immersion in the everyday lives of media audiences.[12] In contrast, anthropologists have approached audience ethnography much as they might anything else, through the open-ended, labor-intensive, long-term engagement of participant observation (e.g., Caldarola 1990; Hahn 1994; Armbrust 1998; Mankekar 1999; Miller

308

11.2   Crowd waiting to purchase cinema tickets at Crown Talkies, Chennai, India, June 1997.
   Photo: Stephen Hughes.

and Slater 2000; Kulick and Wilson 2002; Bird 2003; Abu-Lughod 2004; Pack 2007; Larkin 2008).

   Ethnographic method is, of course, not the panacea for all the problems of audience research. And the distinctive anthropological take on audience is not merely a matter of how one does research, but lies also in how the object of research is constructed. This points to another key difference in approach from media and cultural studies: anthropologists have not been so interested in uniquely differentiating audiences as an object of study. That is, for anthropologists, how people engage with media as audiences has tended to be considered as always already just another social and cultural practice that needs to be understood in its own specificity and context. This amounts to what Spitulnik (2002, 338) has called a critical rethink on the notions of audience and reception from an anthropological perspective. In arguing that anthropology "de-essentialize[s] the audience" as an object of study and broadens the frame of reception beyond the point of individual point of media contact, Spitulnik helps shift questions of method and analytic focus toward the study of media-related practices as a starting point for an anthropology of media (Hobart 2006, 502–4). The emphasis on media-related practices forces a shift away from a priori and deterministic models of how media and audiences relate. To study media-related practices one cannot in principle or in advance know how some media technology, power, text, political economy, communication circuit, or cultural industry determines what people do with media (when I say "do," I construe this broadly to include production, distribution, and consumption as well as commentary, appropriation, indifference, or avoidance). The emphasis on media-related practices, like Foucault's notion of discursive practice, is a methodological and analytical tool to break up a totalizing notion of media audiences toward what Elizabeth Bird has called "real people in a media world" (2003, 188).

The notion of audiences that emerges from anthropological media scholarship since 1990 is not a unified, homogeneous object; rather, it is a category, not dissimilar to our old favorites "society" and "culture"—that is, contested, disparate, multiple, and constantly being redefined in a kind of territorial struggle over its representation and meaning. Recent anthropological work on media audiences is just as likely to be an exploration of practices of media production and distribution (Wilk 1993; Dornfeld 1998; Mankekar 1999; Himpele 2002, 2007; Mazzarella 2003; Abu-Lughod 2004; and Hughes 2005). Ethnographic approaches to the study of the specific institutions, discourses, and practices of media production and distribution have increasingly emphasized the multiple ways audiences are imagined and appropriated. In this regard Ien Ang's (1991) now-classic study, *Desperately Seeking the Audience*, is the key reference for approaching the ethnographic study of audience as a discursive construct, which in her case entailed laying out how television industries in Europe imagine their audiences through viewer ratings. Within anthropology, Tejaswini Ganti's (2002) work on production practices within the Bombay film industry is a good example of how audiences have been found in less than obvious places. In examining the processes that went into making production decisions when remaking foreign films for the Indian market, Ganti uncovered the centrality of a working discourse on Indian audiences. Producers anticipated their audiences in the course of production and made their films according to their understanding of those audiences, drawing imaginatively on their own experience as part of an audience, as well as on interactive online discussion forums, which were used like focus groups to try out story ideas.

Media audiences cannot be taken as a given but are historically contingent and constitutive activities. Thus, when I say that audience studies should be conceived as the study of media-related practices, the point is to investigate how *people actually argue, construct, and contest the media worlds in which they live and why they do or do not matter*. Methodologically, the task starts with an empirical problem about the historical contingency of media practices, that is, how some people at some time and at some place relate to media. But at the same time, we must deal with an analytical problem of how to evaluate the claims and presuppositions that people make about media audiences. We do not need a new theory of media audiences as such, so much as an approach that will help us address practical research problems of how to address why media matter to those with whom we study.

Notes

I would like to thank the editors not only for their patience but also for their constructive and insightful input on several drafts of this chapter. And as always my gratitude also goes out to Sarah Hodges for her careful reading and comments.

1. Rouch stands out as an exception in that he effectively bypassed the educational mode of address in his own filmmaking practice. He claimed to be uninterested in addressing general audiences with his films, preferring to privilege his film subjects as his primary audience. "In other words, for me, my prime audience is the other person, the one I am filming" (Rouch 1975, 99).
2. In the United States, for example, public television reedited many of the *Disappearing World* documentaries and telecast them as part of its series *Odyssey*.
3. See Judith Mayne's (1993) comprehensive overview of the film studies scholarship on spectatorship.
4. James Curran (1990) has argued that much of this work started out with

overexaggerated claims of theoretical innovation. He claimed that new audience studies reinvented earlier mass communication models.

5.   It is important to note that Hall himself gave up working on the encoding/decoding model and largely abandoned the communication model as being inadequate for understanding media by the late 1970s. Almost all references to the semiotics of communication dropped out of his writings as his work on the media/audience relationship shifted focus to the problems of ideology, hegemony, and power (1977, 1982, 1996).

6.   While the ethnographic turn in audience studies has been most closely associated with cultural studies, there have to a lesser extent been similar moves by those with film studies backgrounds. See, e.g., Kuhn 2002; Srinivas 2002, 2005.

7.   Though I will not cover it here, it is important to point out that there has been considerable debate as to the compatibility of anthropology and cultural studies. In contrast to the story I am telling about the anthropology of media, some anthropologists have reacted negatively to cultural studies as a kind of disciplinary border raid, an attempt to poach the concept of culture without performing the necessary anthropological rite of passage—the extended ethnographic experience (Nugent and Shore 1997; Wade 1996).

8.   It is important to note that audience and reception studies, whether from media studies, anthropology, or other disciplines, have overwhelmingly privileged film and television as their primary concerns. I have followed this narrow trend in this chapter, but it is worth considering why there have been comparatively so few attempts to study how people make sense of other visual media, such as photography or painting.

9.   For a useful and critical overview of this literature see Ruby (2000b, 181–93).

10.   Mihai Coman (2005) has recently devoted considerable attention to trying to sort out how "media anthropology" might differ from "anthropology of media" and has come up with an altogether more complicated rendering of these terms than I present here in this chapter. I think he is reading both too much and not enough into these terminological choices and has only managed to muddy the waters of an already murky problem. (Also see Rothenbuhler and Coman 2005.)

11.   There can be no doubt at present that anthropology of media has emerged as one of the most important new subfields in the discipline. With the publication in a short period of three large and wide-ranging readers (Ginsburg, Abu-Lughod, and Larkin 2002; Askew and Wilk 2002; Rothenbuhler and Coman 2005), the field has quickly consolidated its position since the early 1990s. The more recent success of the European Association of Social Anthropology, Media Anthropology Network (http://www.media-anthropology.net), is another clear indication that media is an important and growing concern among anthropologists.

12.   Abu-Lughod (1997, 110) cites Ang's admission (1996, 182n1) that media researchers' notion of ethnography barely resembles the anthropological ideal.

Ethical and Epistemic Reflections on/of Anthropological Vision

MICHAEL HERZFELD

Confessions of a Convert

It is something of an irony that I find myself asked to provide an afterword to this set of essays. I write as both a novice and a new convert—a former skeptic, who saw the use of film and other media as contaminating the purity of academic discourse in social and cultural anthropology. Some of the reasons behind my change of perspective—a revealing metaphor in itself—will emerge in the course of this concluding essay. I want to emphasize at the outset, however, that I write not as an authoritative observer but, rather, as a somewhat hesitant ethnographer of his own newly transformed epistemic space. This more modest horizon will allow readers to look beyond what I have to say and to seek their own inspirations in the genuinely exciting possibilities and realities unveiled in the pages of this book.

I think my original hesitations were all of a piece with my initial diffidence about anthropology itself—about the necessity of being inquisitive. To be sure, now that Bestor (2004, 41–42) has given us the methodological green light to perform "inquisitive observation," a wonderful illumination of what must be the vast majority of our interventions, it has become easier to conceptualize a space for such operations, but I also think that a Eurocentric and (in a Weberian sense) Protestant understanding of privacy does not stand up well to the peering and prying of most of our informants—a feature on which anthropologists from Evans-Pritchard (1940, 14–15) to Chagnon (1983, 15) have commented and complained (without always seeing it as corollary to their own ocular invasions of intimate space).

Informants are also in some sense anthropologists; if they had no such individual proclivity beforehand, they often respond to professionals' presence by reframing their understanding of their own culture in ways designed to compensate for the visitors' incomprehension. This becomes very clear when we place a camera or other recording device in their hands, but it also should long have been clear from the abundant space given to the theme of gossip in so many ethnographies.[1] The evil eye is itself an ocular instrument of visualism, both criticized and defended in anthropology (Fabian 1983; cf. Grasseni 2007b, 2–3), as much a tool of power as any panopticon.[2] Thus, visual anthropology does not so much reinvent the wheel as rediscover commonplace social dynamics, as Bourdieu (e.g., 1977, 36) would have said, *post festum*—in time to realize that our task is above all to systematize what our informants have known for a long time, but to do it as theory that will serve our comparative goals.[3]

If I have some hesitation about the term "visual anthropology" itself, this is for two reasons. First, creating ever-unfolding new "subfields" risks the kind of conceptual fragmentation that is already the administrative bane of anthropology's institutional life. The second reason, paradoxically, is that in some degree all anthropology is always both verbal and visual; we may wish, with many others (e.g., Classen 1993; Howes 1991; Jenkins 1994; Seremetakis 1993) that it could also become olfactory, auditory, and so on, and it does achieve these avatars at specific moments, but the fact remains that for the moment our main channels of communication and perception are verbal and visual, and our recording equipment cannot encompass much more than that. I shall have something to say below about the relation between the verbal and the visual, but for the moment my point is simply to reinforce the sense that good sociocultural anthropology has "always-already" been both self-consciously verbal and visual, and in a balance between these two dimensions that varied with shifting topical predilections as well as with technological developments—a point elegantly adumbrated in the editors' introductory remarks and confirmed by many of the essays gathered here.

Let me therefore set my terminological scruples aside. We can use "visual anthropology" as a shorthand for a group of activities defined more by a Wittgensteinian family resemblance than by classificatory fiat. Much hot air has been generated by the latter; in Italy, for example, there seems to be some uncertainty about how (if at all) to define the difference between *antropologia visuale* and *antropologia visiva*, but it is far from clear that either term represents a clearly bounded episteme. Indeed, the work of Italian scholars such as Paolo Chiozzi (1983), Francesco Faeta (2003), and Felice Tiragallo (2001) shows rather clearly that the visual dimensions of anthropology are important precisely because they cannot be separated in any but the most austerely abstract sense from all those other social and cultural aspects to which they give access and form—any more than anthropology constitutes an ivory tower separated from the "real" world.

An anthropologist who started out decidedly on the verbal end of things, I nonetheless found myself attracted to the visual in, appropriately, an unfolding sequence of snapshot moments. First, photography offered a means of engaging informants; it was a resident's curiosity about my wife's photographing his old house that led me directly to my interest in historic conservation (Herzfeld 1991, 2009). Then I began to film dyadic interactions between artisans and their apprentices, convinced that I could use this material to elicit commentary on the nature of these relationships (see below). When I began to work in Italy, I continued to some extent with this emphasis on artisans, but both there and in Thailand I also recorded endless meetings—community meetings, condominium meetings, political protests, and activist committees—and the resulting footage allowed me to reconstruct details of gesture and movement in ways that proved ethnographically rich and informative. Indeed, I felt subsequently that it also did wonders for my writing. Meanwhile I began work on a film about my Rome work and thus, for the first time, confronted the esthetics of filming and editing as something at least conceptually independent of the data-collecting dimension of visual work.[4]

In short, I write now with the advantage of hindsight. That word recasts in a visual frame both this postscript and the personal trajectory that informs it. It is thus not only revelatory of the serendipitous visualization through which anthropologists typically, and productively, discover their goals and move toward them. It also suggests the clarity that a visual approach induces, much as a video recording allows for better *hearing* through *seeing*—anyone who has first tried to decipher an audio recording of a meeting and then done the same with a video will know what relief the latter brings.[5] Such, wonderfully, was the sense of a productive time warp that I experienced a year after videotaping Thai community meetings at which I initially understood little of what I heard and saw (and not only for reasons of language, although these were paramount). Aside from all other considerations, this experience offers a real challenge to the temporal complacency of the "ethnographic present" while also putting in question the sense of rational sequence that a narrative in strictly past-historic (aorist) time inevitably generates. Much of what we understand in the field does not occur as a result of a linear sequence of deductive logic, and the sudden bursts of knowledge that a rich video archive can trigger throw a harsh light on the falsity of such self-serving historical purism.

Intimacies of Field and Frame

One theme that emerges from the essays in this volume concerns the greater intimacy that visual methods permit. This takes us right to the heart of ethnographic practice because, as I have argued elsewhere (Herzfeld 2005, 47), it is the social intimacy of the ethnographic encounter that allows access to the dirty laundry and popular secrets that I have called the "cultural intimacy" of the nation-state and other formal cultural organizations. This is nonetheless not an easy transition, and attention to visual methods allows us to consider some of the methodological and ethical problems it raises.

The first question concerns the relation between presence and intimacy. Is it necessary to "be there" in order to achieve intimacy? The seeming intimacies of e-mail and other electronic communications suggest otherwise, although one may wonder whether the willingness of some chat-room correspondents to reveal all bespeaks genuine intimacy or simply the deadening of sensibility that excessive and ill-considered media exposure can generate (see Das and Kleinman 2001)—a conditioning that has also led to the pornographic voyeurism with which media often treat some of the most disgusting forms of violence. On the other hand, the possibility of building a close cinematic relationship on the basis of a preexisting friendship, which is what I have attempted to do in my own film work (and in my writing), allows for a more nuanced form of access, albeit not one lacking in risks of other kinds.

What are these risks? In advocating for intimate filming based on existing social relations, and suggesting that this may be more useful than aesthetically pleasing but socially distant representations of various societies, I am encouraged by Waterson's recognition of the "sense of intimacy" achieved in a film that was nevertheless a team effort. One does nevertheless wonder how much more might have been possible had the anthropologist (Fiedermutz-Laun) done her own filming, editing, and directing, to say nothing of the reciprocal effect of such an engagement on her own and others' writing; Ruby points out that there are still rather few examples of writing that is drawn directly from film work.[6] This is unfortunate, especially because the act of converting the visual into the written is one important channel through which we can achieve a degree of conceptual pixellation—a disguising of personal identities from which we can thereby decouple the ethnographically interesting aspects of intimate encounters.

Aesthetic and technical issues are also not unrelated to the intimacy of the ethnographic encounter. The question of how far and when one should sacrifice technical virtuosity and the advantages of sophisticated equipment for the purpose of more intimate access shows that visual media have not yet been as fully domesticated in the discipline as writing, where style and a poetic sensibility are generally acknowledged as essential to the successful reporting of fieldwork and where the goal is to bring readers into the intimate spaces of everyday life without slipping into intellectually pointless voyeurism.

In my own case, this might be judged a case of making a virtue out of necessity. I was used to shooting with a small handycam and saw no reason to change what I was doing, especially as my informants were mostly—as we will see—rather comfortable with this kind of equipment. Of course, ethnographic intimacy and technical excellence are not necessarily mutually exclusive qualities, nor should they be; but the weight of public and professional cinematographic judgment, as opposed to that of ethnographers, may create a rift that is all to the advantage of the latter—a good cinematographer may not realize how important anthropologically some poorly shot detail might be. For example, I am currently working on a film about a Bangkok community that is facing eviction; the footage of the residents' preparation of nets to block access via the canal at the back of their space, shot in near darkness, is visually poor—but that very weakness is expressive of the physical and social constraints under which I was necessarily working, as well as of the intimate friendship with community leaders that allowed me to film at all.

In fact I would go further, arguing that there is a good case for encouraging the development of a "small camera" genre that emphasizes the ethnographic over the technical, to the extent that the choice has to be made. This is not to deny the attendant problems (such as pronounced camera-shake) or to claim that anthropologists would gain nothing from mastering professional-level filming—or, for that matter, photographic, drawing, and other representational skills—however imperfect the results may appear to narrowly (narrowed?) expert eyes. But the use of the light equipment of the amateur, especially in societies that already have a great deal of access to such technology, does not usually render the anthropologist an intrusive presence. To the contrary, introducing familiar equipment reduces the sometimes awkward distance between the two parts of our traditional methodology of "participant observation."[7] Many of us have found ourselves filming alongside locals intent on recording important community or family moments for posterity.

There is, for that matter, a useful ethnographic account to be made of the strains among technical expertise, aesthetics, and ethnographic depth. But how to infiltrate an impartial ethnographer into a festival selection committee or architecture school committee? What Ruby tells us about the Florentine Festival dei Popoli may be disturbingly predictive of what might happen elsewhere unless anthropologists assert their own particular interest in the intimate and ethnographic.[8] But they are often insufficiently, or at least unevenly, assertive where their challenges to established canons and power structures are concerned. A very serviceable definition of power is the capacity to keep anthropologists out; and, in the world of cinematography, the privileging of technical expertise risks exoticizing and marginalizing even the best of the indigenous filming of which, in this volume, Ginsburg writes so engagingly.

As Ruby and Durington note here, amplifying a point also made in the introductory essay, much of what claims the title of "ethnographic film" is actually an exercise in precisely the kind of exoticism that anthropologists have learned to repudiate (see also Ruby 2000b). To be sure, there are indigenous exoticisms that have some interest in their own right; some may be the result of well-meaning but perhaps ultimately misplaced anthropological and museological tutelage, as Paolo Chiozzi has indicated (1983, 80–81). Conversely, aesthetic pleasure does not automatically mean exoticism, although the two are often linked. Perhaps it would be more useful here to emphasize that the ethnographic encounter can itself be a work of art, an exercise in social poetics—the skill in managing social relations in which the ethnographer, always more of a learner than the informant, begins, however clumsily, to master that skilled elaboration of everyday habits that garners real appreciation in the host society. A truly reflexive ethnographic film may not focus narcissistically on the ethnographer but should at least register some of the informants' assessments—verbal, gestural, kinesic—of the ethnographer's role and actions. In my own film work, for example, I like to include locals' ironic descriptions of, or reactions to, my role: indigenous ethnography and analysis of the visiting ethnographer's actions.

Such interactions take place in a lived, and often built, environment. Waterson's essay is thus especially valuable for the pertinent observation that much anthropology concerns aspects of society and culture that are structured by architectonic principles. What architecture is to society as a whole, moreover, clothing is to the individual body. The corollary—echoing Dudley's timely call—is that clothing, like architecture, visually activates principles of exclusion and intimacy by visually and tactilely linking individuals to the social order. Such fundamentally spatial and embodied principles often remain relatively underreported in the moment of writing, although, for example, Fernandez's (1966) observation of the ways in which dance forms and church architecture reproduce each other in a South African society long ago pointed the way to their significance, while Gray's (2006) much more recent work on the Chhetri of Nepal offers a rich exploration of the reciprocal linkages among body, habitation, and cosmos. Despite such exemplary studies, one can only endorse Waterson's complaints about the general lack of cross-fertilization between architectural history and social anthropology, and about the corresponding Hobson's choice between poor or nonexistent illustrations and ethnographic superficiality.

Waterson, a Southeast Asia specialist, appropriately and effectively dwells on ethnographic examples from her own area of expertise. Her argument would nevertheless have found considerable reinforcement in work done on social aspects of architecture in the Greek context by at least two architect-anthropologist pairs of collaborators (Hirschon 1989, 121–32; Hirschon and Thakurdesai 1970; Pavlides and Hesser 1986). Hirschon's attention to the way dowry provisions mediate the effects of the pressures of urban life on architectural form anticipates by many years the discussion of urban adjustments to the Balinese *dadia* to which Waterson gives such appropriate prominence. As someone who has come more recently to Waterson's general geographic area from a background largely dominated by Greek research, I hope that our reciprocal engagement through this book will lead both of us to think in terms, not only of comparisons of these processes, but also of the overlapping historical backgrounds that perhaps gave rise to their comparability.[9]

While the reasons here may be very different, the absence of such European ethnographic material reproduces a common habit among anthropologists of excluding Europeanist work from general theoretical discussions. One wonders, in fact, whether this circumstance has been reinforced by Westerners' relatively much greater power to exclude visual invasion of their intimate spaces, rendering the ethnography of Europe less excitingly intimate than that of other areas.

There is another, and perhaps more important, dimension to the specific dearth of allusions to modern Greece, a dearth that is all the more surprising in view of its much vaunted light qualities and of the major achievements of Greek filmmakers and photographers. Greece's attributed importance to the canon of European civilization has generated a powerful and strongly architectonic sense of dichotomy between a classically inflected exterior (classicizing façades and Ionic columns having a particular durability) and an "indigenous," "traditional," or simply "simple" interior redolent of Slavic, Turkish, or otherwise "oriental" pasts (Herzfeld 1987, 117–19). But this spatial binarism is the result of official interventions, which anthropology would do well to avoid except as an object of critical analysis in its own right—a point that resonates nicely with Farnell's astute critique of dualism in modern anthropological thought. Edwards's very useful discussion of the Danforth-Tsiaras volume on funerary practices, especially her observation that reviewers focused on the text rather than the photographs, suggests that perhaps the *only* way Greece could enter the ethnographic canon was as a site of representation, not of analysis—a perspective that takes us right back to colonial and Cartesian perceptions and perpetuates the crypto-colonial limbo to which Greece has been consigned, as much by scholarship as by politics, until at least the late 1970s.

Embodiments and Ethics

Edwards's discussion subtly and usefully suggests, in fact, how easily Cartesian dualism can permeate a wide range of discourses—in this case, creating an opposition between text and image that in turn suggests a profoundly colonial privileging of verbal analytics over the (supposedly passive) objects of anthropological inquiry—those objects that anthropology "makes," in Johannes Fabian's (1983) telling phrase.

These assumptions are sneakily liable to recur even in the most critically anti-Cartesian discourse, and their consequences are both epistemological and ethical. Farnell, for example, describes Linnaeus's classification of the human races in terms of their bodily features. It would have been rewarding to see her also take on his analysis of clothing (see Hodgen 1964, 425–26) as part of her overall critique of mind-body dualism—to which, ironically, the omission of such a discussion risks letting careless readers revert.

Such further explorations, in the context of this volume, would especially have provided an interesting genealogy for the habits of thought that both Dudley and Farnell criticize. Indeed, if Linnaeus's schema could be detached from its evolutionist assumptions, it might actually nourish a critique of mind-body dualism; it does have the virtue of recognizing clothing as more than simply a way of covering the body. Thinking of the architectonics of dance, as Fernandez has done, is a promising start; so is attention to the spatiality of language use and choices of clothing. In each case, the neat evolutionary assumption of unilineal development, with pure intellect at its pinnacle, is undone. The corollary of mind-body dualism, moreover, is biological determinism; the apparent seamlessness of principle with which Linnaeus tackled biological morphology and human dress in the same breath exemplifies, *avant la lettre*, the social Darwinism with which anthropology has had to contend for most of its history, often permeating the discipline's intellectual *habitus* despite its best efforts at resistance. We may, as Edwards notes, discuss the problems of a scientific gaze that dominates its colonized subjects; but I suspect that we are rarely as genuinely free of such hierarchizing propensities as we would like to believe. One useful grounding that enables us to push back against their allure is knowledge of the historical antecedents, which is why I would like to see further analysis of the entire Linnaean schema and of humanity's place in it.

Arnd Schneider's brief discussion in these pages of a historical instance—not necessarily one of intentional exoticism—of anthropologists' posing in indigenous clothing suggests, at the very least, the fundamentally disruptive and category-busting aspect of our discipline (whatever the actual intentions behind the particular moment he describes). That aspect persists even at anthropology's most exoticizing moments, an ironic conjuncture that critics of its colonial past usually fail to appreciate; even those anthropologists who served in the colonial bureaucracies were rarely submissive servants of empire throughout their careers. Linnaeus, on the other hand, was arguably far more representative of entrenched Eurocentrism; he would surely have been horrified at the very idea of Westerners' dressing in indigenous clothing, an abuse of his beloved taxonomy and its hierarchization of the world's peoples in terms of the degree of self-control symbolized, as he thought, by their respective forms of dress.

The engagement of the body in schemata of such antiquity also raises the question of how anthropological knowledge and attitudes are transmitted. How do anthropologists come to work against the grain of such deeply embedded conceptual traditions? One thing is certain: much is left inexplicit, a suggestive fact in itself. Scholars learn by experience as much as through verbal instruction; Rabinow's (1977) celebrated critique of his own training shows that we, like apprentice artisans, are expected by our masters to learn experientially or to drop out of the profession. Apprenticeship directs, as Grasseni points out, our personal phenomenologies, and one of the skills we learn—as indeed do craft apprentices in many cultures—is to be sneaky in pursuit of new understandings of old practices. This is a particularly good reason to appreciate Grasseni's invocation of apprenticeship, which also resonates with Ramey's emphasis on "communities of practice" (see also Lave and Wenger 1991). Apprenticeship is a dynamic social process that often engages socially disreputable habits—stealing with the eyes, the hazing of new recruits, insubordination against a master artisan—that are not only important keys to local forms of cultural intimacy but also put social planks on the visual scaffolding of the spaces in which everyday activities take place.

The best way to find out what that means for our professional practices is to do something that forces it into the foreground of our consciousness. When I first found myself behind a video camera, the shift in my understanding of human relations—even if I was only dimly aware of it at first—was tectonic. (This is another reason for not ceding the physical and technical labor to professional filmmakers. We need the exercise—in both senses of the word.) I was not simply imitating, reproducing, some form of suppositious reality. I was learning new modes of perception, in ways that were only possible because I had elected to plunge into a risky new venture. In fact, I think my informants and some professional observers realized the political implications of my extended eye before I did; at a time when it was becoming clear that my active engagement in their struggle against the eviction of a small Bangkok community (Pom Mahakan) was affording some protection, a weekly newspaper portrayed me photographically shooting straight at the reader, with the nearby Temple of the Golden Mount drawn in as a place-setting background.[10]

But it is not only a perspectival shift that occurs at such a moment in the anthropologist's personal experience, although that is important. There is also a necessary expansion of the anthropologist's ethical horizon. Sarah Pink's discussion of the need for ethical responsibility in the use of digital media shows how far this expansion can go; the possibilities today seem infinite, and perhaps also infinitely daunting. The seeds for this concern have long been with us (and today will make more sense to the general public as a result of the furor over the infamous Danish cartoon depictions of the Prophet Mohammed).[11] Able for several generations to wield the fig leaf of anonymity as a protection of our informants, we did not even grapple with the potential violation of their intellectual property rights that such a move entailed (or discuss whether we were imposing our own anxieties on them!). But once ethnographers move from verbal description to filming and videotaping, the tact of the written word is whisked away and anthropologists' ethical vulnerability is brusquely exposed. They must get permission from informants to use both images and talk if the films are to have any kind of public existence.

Although it was not a major issue for most of my informants in Rome, for example, the shift from a projected book (Herzfeld 2009) to a film portraying some of the same people and incorporating some of the same utterances threatened to blow the cover of a few individuals who appeared in both works. As I edited the film, I became quite self-conscious about the need for a degree of self-censorship, a concern that was not as acutely present during the writing of the book. In the end, I determined that the couple who had led a dramatic, highly public, but ultimately unsuccessful fight against the eviction of themselves and their neighbors were not unhappy to be named in the book, thus allowing me to resolve the major ethical tension created by the divergent aims of two generically different but potentially synergistic works. But the situation did provoke considerable reflection on my part regarding the increased risks of identification—and concomitant exposure to criticism, ridicule, and misrepresentation—that the making of the film entailed.

Such reflections are not independent of the degree of agency we recognize in the involvement of our informants in our various projects. For example, Pink's observation that visual anthropologists become involved in the practice of place-making is highly germane. In making *Monti Moments*, one of my goals was to persuade some of those who appear in the film to take me through the walkways of their own memories. But which of us was creating the sense of place—the informant who invoked past memories to give a sense of how landmarks had shifted or gained and lost significance, or the ethnographer whose angle of vision determined the viewer's understanding of how the various parts of the place came together? I did try to make what I heard from my informants determine the emphases and choices I made; but ultimately these remain the product of my own moderately skilled vision,[12] itself in turn partially the product of their—more or less successful—cultural tutelage. So the visual encompassment of place that results is the product of a dialectical engagement, no less than is the verbal description.

One of the advantages of the visual over the verbal is the relative difficulty of retreating to abstraction; the traces that led to a particular representation may be easier to discern because the visual medium, while also selectively treated, seems to offer many more chinks through which a critical viewer can discern evidence of the ethnographer's motivations and choices. This is a short-term version of something that art historians (e.g., Gombrich 1961) have long known well: that the visual etymologies of design features, while as liable to functional refashioning as any words, can be reconstructed in a fairly precise archaeology of motifs. Something of the kind can also be seen with gesture, as De Iorio (1832/2000) noted nearly two centuries ago. While visual elements may not be directly translatable into words or their meanings subject to the reconstructions we encounter in historical linguistics of the *longue durée*, in the manner of Benveniste (1973), the apparent concreteness of the visual traces allows anthropologists to reconstruct those elements of the built environment that give consistency to the *habitus* (Bourdieu 1977) of those who dwell therein.

The spatial organization of social relations also has consequences for the distribution of social knowledge, particularly with regard to the classic distinction between insiders and outsiders that is the continuing preoccupation of anthropologists around the world (e.g., Gefou-Madianou 1993a, 1993b; Paritta 2002). Within a given physical space, with all its implications of belonging and *habitus*, it is relatively easy to discern the signs of discomfort or acceptance of the admission of strangers to cultural secrets—to the spaces, indeed, of cultural intimacy. The "parallax effect" that Ginsburg describes here as arising from the disjuncture between an outsider's and a local filmmaker's respective visualizations may also emerge in the tension between two informants' orientations toward the anthropologist and—this is perhaps the key—toward the anthropologist's camera.

For example, one of my Roman informants, an irreverent taxi driver with a talent for irony and a rich knowledge of the city's history, insisted that "what the professor wants to know is the events of the 'black chronicle' [*cronaca nera*]"—that is, scandals. (I leave it to the reader to evaluate this assessment!) But his interlocutor, a newsagent who had earlier in the film expatiated on the virtues of a pope who is in fact deeply unpopular in this left-leaning and powerfully anticlerical part of Rome, claimed not to know some of the stories the taxi driver recounted, and became notably ill at ease when the latter began to relate tales of the arrival of drugs in the district. In the film, he looks away with visible unease, shrugs his shoulders, and explicitly says he knows nothing about some of the other's more scandalous tales. Perhaps some of his discomfiture arose from a genuine lack of knowledge about, or interest in, such disreputable matters. But it was clear that the real stakes here concerned the cultural intimacy of the local community and of Rome. The knowledge that they were being filmed—while, I would argue, less threatening than being tape-recorded, because the camcorder is a family instrument where the sound recorder may still have implications of espionage and police investigation, especially for older informants—brought to the fore concerns about collective reputation and attendant consequences for their livelihoods.

That awkwardness also underscores the ethical dilemma of the filmmaker whose images show real faces. As Pink observes, while visual media may confer a sense of intimacy, they also raise concerns about abuse. How far is it fair to display such discomfiture, or to allow one informant to tell tales that manifestly breach another's sense of propriety? Pixellation is no answer; the one who is hanging out the dirty laundry would be outraged. In this particular case, both informants seemed, and seem, quite satisfied with the outcome; after all, one might suspect that the more sensitive individual was satisfied simply with the recording of his (largely gestural) refusal to endorse the other's scandalous revelations.

But this was a situation involving high jinks and good humor, with a considerable amount of mutual teasing and also some ironic framing of the anthropologist. When a film portrays real violence or humiliation, is what we see truly a product of intimacy? I would argue instead that it emerges from a *failure* of intimacy—a failure in which the amiable collusion that challenges norms of propriety collapses without being replaced by anything remotely acceptable to the principals. Because visual representation entails a much greater risk of personal identification—aside from pixellation, again, and the use of line drawings and cartoons[13]—it intensifies the ethical dilemmas and thereby makes them more accessible to critical dissection. But this conceptual advantage also means that, in individual cases, the use of media may already have gone too far.

One issue that the essays in this volume—notably those of Ginsburg and Waterson—nicely bring into focus is the relation between such ethical concerns and spatiality. Indeed, Waterson's concluding remarks about recognizing the significance of squatters' (and, more generally, urban proletarians') understanding about architectonic resources strikes me—as does Ginsburg's exaltation of indigenous media—as joining in a more general call for incorporating the perspectives of the repressed. It has been surprisingly difficult to get even anthropologists to acknowledge the theoretical resources of which their informants dispose; planners have been even more reluctant to admit, let alone deploy, these indigenous sources of wisdom and knowledge, while, at the same time, the persistent romanticization of "local knowledge" and "local history" has sometimes occluded power struggles that were taking place below the visible horizon of official discourse.

It has only recently been recognized that spatiality and rights are intimately interlinked, and the institutional framing of that recognition is still in its infancy.[14] Yet debates about the forms and uses of housing, often using models, are more easily captured in film than through note-taking; the processes whereby residents familiarize themselves with the components of new architectural forms and move the resulting small-scale models around on ground plans of their communities are, as I have discovered in my own work in Bangkok, a rich source of insight into the micropolitics of entitlement and symbolic transformation. Should the residents adopt a "traditional" form of row houses? Should they put professional needs first, with a weather eye cocked toward the gargantuan shiftings of the national and international economies? What advantages accrue to those who can make a plausible case for the more, or the less, visible sites within the community? Even the most assiduous note-taker cannot hope to record enough of these dynamics; a video record, by contrast, allows multiple viewings, perhaps in some cases with the help of others who were present, including key local actors. In such a process, issues of entitlement become relativized, with some claims nonetheless emerging as genuinely collective and as representing a far better adaptation—as Waterson's comments suggest—to the immediate needs of the community than any abstract planning document can offer.

Abstraction and Agency

Abstraction, indeed, is a key problem of theoretical practice, at once political and epistemological; and it is a problem that the visual emphasis of these essays brings into critical focus. It would be hard, in light of everything else I have said here, to disagree with Farnell's historically grounded and carefully analytic account of the shift to an "agentic" view of human movement—a shift that these new ethical concerns demand. That view is a crucial source of resistance to the crass positivism ("number-crunching" and "quick and dirty" analyses) that characterize so many official interventions. It is by reversing the closure of such arid approaches that a visually based anthropology can furnish tools for the struggle, creating a parallax effect that reveals the bureaucratic imagination as itself a form of agency that just happens to be exceptionally skilled at covering the traces of its own passage and of its own interventions, rendering as rules and principles what historically were in fact contingent, ad hoc "solutions" designed, in some cases, more for the ease of the bureaucrats than to serve the citizens' interests. What the editors of this volume say about visual media, rightly refusing to situate it in a convenient but meaning-less choice between "art" and "science," has also long been true of the best ethnographic writing; the scientistic pretensions of Malinowski's functionalist theorizing, for example, cannot disguise the sheer beauty of his prose.

The problem that Farnell addresses is a remarkably persistent one, and it is much harder to eradicate in our own discourse than to recognize in that of officials and even those of their clients who are adept in what Bourdieu (1977, 40) calls "officializing strategies." It is, for one thing, em-bedded in the category of human movement itself—ironically yet again, in her own work, replaying a persistence Farnell has perceptively identi-fied in, for example, the work of Thomas Csordas and Michael Jackson: "Csordas's work thus remains rooted in the spirit of the Cartesian tradi-tion, although that is certainly not his intent."

What Farnell does *not* mention is the trap posed by an overeager con-cern to avoid verbocentrism at all costs—a trap that could very easily produce a dangerous misreading of her own argument. Language-derived (as opposed to verbocentric) models, such as Jakobson's (1960) poetic function, are often easily adapted to the social uses of the body and its surroundings and can thereby be rescued from both the functionalism and the verbocentrism to which some guardians of an older perspective on his work have wished to anchor it (see Herzfeld 2005, 21–24, 189–90). I would not wish to alter the balance of Farnell's superb exposition, and perhaps what I am calling for is too much of a complication; but a social poetics, employing what Jakobson recognized as the effect of cultural forms not easily reduced to verbal equivalents, would permit a degree of resistance to the cantonization already implied in phrases like "the anthropology of the body." Farnell's argument is too important to end up confined to a self-proclaimed subspecialty; she would, I am sure, be among the first to acknowledge that what she is describing is not an "an-thropology of the body" but, as with "visual anthropology," anthropol-ogy *tout court*. Indeed, her call for wider use of a nuanced Labanotation parallels my call for wider anthropological adoption of some basic record-ing skills, and all these techniques should allow us to track the relation between small-scale cultural "de-formations" and cultural change in the relatively *longue durée*. I would argue further that it is only the intimacy of the truly ethnographic that permits such correlations—a far cry from the automatism of Lomax's choreometrics project, to name but the most obvious example (and here I certainly take my lead from Farnell).

Obviously I do not advocate a return to language as the basis for the analysis of all systems of meaning. Indeed, I thoroughly endorse and applaud Farnell's elegantly argued rejection of the harsh conceptual opposition that separates the verbal from other forms of meaning-making. My visual questionnaire was explicitly designed to resist the reduction of gesture to a set of lexeme-equivalents, a problem to which early work on "kinesics" (Birdwhistell 1970) was notoriously liable. Linguistic reductionism, to which the usual channels of academic discourse renders us highly susceptible, occludes understanding of precisely those often vague and ephemeral phenomena—the subtleties of quotidian micropolitics (see Bailey 1969, 1971)—that enrich, precisely in Jakobson's sense of the poetic function, the communicative capacities of human beings everywhere.

I would argue, rather, that the boot is on the other foot—that, far from reducing all semiotic expression to language, we should instead rescue models hitherto primarily regarded as "linguistic" from that tyrannical obsession (of what Farnell forcefully dubs "the dominant disembodied-language ideology within linguistics and linguistic anthropology") and see whether they work equally well, or perhaps better, for other modes of meaning-making.

Indeed, there is some evidence in the models that linguists have devised that these models should never have been viewed as primarily linguistic in their implications; spatiality seems to provide a more fundamental motivation for these models than does language. Diglossia (Ferguson 1959), for example, is a concept of clearly architectonic inspiration, in which speakers use a formal and archaizing language to shield interior intimacies from the often hostile and repressive inspection of outsiders, especially, in the Greek context, when the latter belonged to the censorious powers whose cultural bullying has warped national politics for most of the country's modern history. Inasmuch as modern Greece is a *locus classicus* for the study of diglossia (see e.g., Kazazis 1982; Mackridge 1985), it is thus noteworthy that local architecture has long displayed archaizing historical referents in its external decoration while often showing a predilection for Byzantine, vernacular, or even Ottoman elements of design and spatial organization on the inside.

While I would no longer argue in favor of such semiocentric terms as "disemia," except in very specific descriptive contexts, a more flexible sense of what is at stake is captured in the notion of "cultural intimacy" (Herzfeld 2005; see also Coe 2005; Festa 2007; Light 2008; Shryock 2004). Such formulations separate binarism—an in/out dichotomy would seem inevitable when we consider issues of spatiality, for example—from the specific heritage of Cartesianism, freeing the study of embodiment from a specific *kind* of binarism that has served scientism, colonialism, statism, and nationalism all too well.

To ignore the presence of binary oppositions in the experiential world is to commit an error of major proportions, since these are the product of both the engagement with physical space and the deployment of that space by the agents of massive state and colonial power—think of prisons, for example. What is important is to chronicle how people experience these binarisms and what they actually *do* with them—and, of course, as Grasseni argues in this volume in respect of visual techniques more generally, to track the prehistory of their modern uses in order to understand the genesis of their current capacity for repression and worse. If visualism is an instrument of power, so that anthropologists who frame everything in tabular terms risk complicity in projects of colonial and state domination, vision itself can also, like etymology in the writings of Giambattista Vico, be subversive and critical.[15]

This reconsideration of binarisms as *instruments* rather than as authoritative *representations* is also implicit in the shift that Farnell, largely following Edwin Ardener's inspired example (1989), notes from behavior to action. Anthropologists were actually rather slow to follow Ardener's lead, for a variety of reasons ranging from his untimely death and a consequent loss of immediacy in the reception of his ideas (audiences *are* important, after all [see Hughes, this volume], even in this negative sense) to the institutional tenacity of behaviorist and functionalist perspectives. But the various possibilities begin to coalesce in the present volume, with its grounding in the history of (anthropological) ideas. For example, Grasseni's careful (and ethnographically grounded) arguments for the idea that vision is a skilled activity, that it is the result of inculcation (see also Bourdieu 1977, 77), resonates fruitfully with Farnell's insistence on the dynamism of human action. Meanwhile, the growing sophistication *and* accessibility (a rare combination in human history!) of recording technology suggests that increasingly it will become easier to capture the sense and content of that dynamism.

Practical Considerations: Enabling a Clearer Vision

Digitization, as Pink points out, has made it possible to devise various kinds of interactive methods. These, too, are a source of the parallax effect. The simplest of these is playing back footage to one's informants while also, perhaps, recording their reactions. In an important early example, Jane K. Cowan (1990, 92) describes her attempts to get villagers to respond to the scenes of their dance moves, mostly in the hope of eliciting some of the associations that people made among gender, morality, and bodily movement in general. Cowan's work was inevitably constrained by the unwieldy equipment of the time, a difficulty that Pink also mentions.

I was more fortunate, or at least had the advantage of the subsequent development of small-scale electronics. Using a friendly family camcorder, I developed a "visual questionnaire" in order to get at informal interpretations of the dyadic interpretations between Cretan artisans and their apprentices.[16] That experience suggested to me that, rather than understanding "visual anthropology" as something apart from its social and cultural cousins, we would do better to insist that visual and other sensory recording be considered an integral part of ethnographic data collection.

Recalling that a distinguished anthropologist of an earlier generation than my own once expressed surprise that one might want to use a sound recording device, I cannot help suspecting that the increasing convenience and maneuverability of the equipment has played a major role in redirecting our preferences. It would be a pity if, at the very moment when many of us have become so much more amenable to both the technology and the rethinking of epistemological priorities that it enables, "visual anthropology" were to fall prey to the anthropological passion for classification and compartmentalization. Surely the point is that all good anthropology has always been about recording—even if it is that of notes and memory. The new technology does not replace the basic human equipment; to the contrary, it amplifies it.

Similarly, as I hope has become clear in this concluding essay, one of the great gifts of the visual emphasis in modern anthropology is the resistance it offers, like fieldwork more generally, to such backsliding—to the loss of perspective that complacency and taxonomic routinization inevitably bring. If visual technology is simply allowed to become a means of accumulating data, it will not open new paths of any great significance. But if it is deliberately, indeed agentively, employed to provoke and to discommode, it will break down some of the most pernicious barriers that bedevil the role of anthropology in the world today. Vision has practical consequences; it is our ethical predilections that will determine, at least to some extent, whether these will benefit the people with whom we work or reproduce the rigid antinomies through which privilege maintains the structural status quo.

Among those barriers, perhaps the most dangerous is that which separates our academic preoccupations from the world in which they are embedded. I would like to end these reflections with a comment on this mental apartheid, which I consider a symptom of a larger malaise. It also seems particularly appropriate to emphasize this connection in the context of a discussion of the visual, since cinematography and photography are perhaps the two major arenas in which the discipline continues to meet some popular recognition, and where, as several of the authors in this volume have suggested, it could do a great deal more in that direction.

Anthropology, after all, is one of the relatively few academic disciplines in which the link with social experience is never entirely severed. The anti-intellectual (and supremely Cartesian) separation of the "real" world of activism from the "ivory tower" of epistemology has never sounded entirely convincing to anthropologists, although sometimes their arcane choices of terminology have seemed to cut them off at home from the very categories of people they have gloried in knowing "in the field." Without yielding to the fallacy of misplaced concreteness, a visually sensitized anthropology can remind its interlocutors among the general public of its engagement with the realities that people face in their daily lives. True, a visual approach can encourage sensationalism and exoticism; but, by the same token, it can also induce shifts of perspective—not unlike my own gradual epiphany from behind the video camera as I have described it here—that induce the respect born of true engagement.

The tension between sensationalism and sensitivity perhaps explains why the histories outlined in these pages do not constitute an evolutionist paean to the great achievements of our discipline in the present age. The contributors have instead opted to point out risks and temptations, and to show how some promising paths were long left untraveled—or were hesitantly traveled only part-way, only to be abandoned until new research interests and improved technologies made them again both conceivable and practicable. Such a resolutely nonlinear reading of the past offers a productive basis for genuine reflection on the goals of the discipline as a whole because it exposes these lost opportunities and brings them back into play, rather than dismissing them as relicts of a simpler age now left far behind.

In particular, if the growing renewal of anthropological interest in the visual prompts a reassessment of our involvement in the lived world, it may also, in parallel (and especially by helping to recognize the embodied and artisanal nature of intellectual labor), generate greater recognition of the theoretical capacities of our informants; of the usefulness and desirability of local forms of knowledge in the reconstitution of urban (and other inhabited) space; and of the ethical risks and political possibilities that remain attendant on each and every one of our scholarly interventions in the lives of others. We might, to borrow a phrase from

Farnell's (1995a) sign language study, truly come to "see what they are saying"—and the public might also see what *we* are saying, and engage with it. Thanks to the developments described in this book, the achievement of such goals lies within our grasp.

Notes

I am very grateful to Marcus Banks and Jay Ruby for their warm invitation to write this piece, as well as for their critical response to an earlier version of it. Writing it has been an education in itself.

1. Among many distinguished examples, Bailey 1971 is especially relevant to this discussion.
2. This insight originates in a research proposal recently authored by Melissa Alejandra Nelson (University of Virginia) and is reproduced here by her kind permission.
3. This becomes an especially acute difficulty, as well as an advantage in terms of insight, when the ethnographer is working, in some sense, "at home"; see, e.g., Akin 2002, 2–3.
4. *Monti Moments: Men's Memories in the Heart of Rome*, filmed, edited, and produced by Michael Herzfeld, 2007. An En Masse Films Associated Production; distributed by Berkeley Media LLC.
5. Because my own hearing is somewhat restricted, I may have appreciated the advantages of the visual more deeply and more immediately than some others. This in fact reinforces my main point here; our bodies are the basic instruments of our data-collecting techniques. Thus, as long as sight continues to play a central role, even in respect of our ability to engage the other senses, anthropology will remain inherently visual at some level. It is perhaps worth recalling that the Sanskrit root of "wit," "wisdom," and "*Wissenschaft*" is a term that means "knowing through seeing" (cf. Thai *witthaya*, "academic discipline, science").
6. Recently, in a lengthy passage describing the interaction in a condominium meeting in Rome (Herzfeld 2009, 199–211), I draw heavily on the video footage I was allowed by the participants to make.
7. See also the remarks by Banks and Ruby on Schneider's paper; they discuss the move from filming to participation, but these days, as Ginsburg also shows, filming sometimes *is* participation—and the learning process is clearly multidimensional.
8. For a brief account of that festival reflecting the initial optimism with which it began, see Chiozzi 1993, 190.
9. In an early attempt to understand why I seemed to be ineluctably drawn to such a comparison, I attempted to demonstrate that Greece and Thailand shared features of "crypto-colonialism" (Herzfeld 2002). These certainly

include references to an architectural vocabulary that is directly linked to the spatial distinction between places for collective self-display and those where social life generates and maintains the very stuff of cultural intimacy.

10. "Anaanikhom amphrang 'taat tawantok,'"*Sawatdii Krungthaep*, August 6–12, 2004, p. 1.

11. The cartoons were published in the newspaper *Jyllands-Posten*, September 30, 2005. The resulting bibliography is vast; the complex emotions stirred by this event should certainly put an end to any doubts about the power of images to affect international events.

12. Here I again invoke Grasseni's apt phrase; see also Dudley's discussion of Felice Tiragallo's work in this volume.

13. See, for examples, the drawings that Michele Lamprakos made for me from video stills (Herzfeld 2004, 130).

14. The recent launching in Bangkok of the Centre for Architecture and Human Rights by a Canadian planner and architect, Graeme Bristol, has not received the attention or support it deserves, although his hard work may be starting to redress that situation. Some NGOs, notably the international Center on Housing Rights and Evictions, use film—notably under the direction of Fionn Skiotis—as a key form of documentation.

15. Vico's use of etymology is a wonderful example of what I have tried to demonstrate earlier in this essay with regard to the importance of "liberating" apparently linguistic models from the tyranny of verbocentrism. See especially Struever 1983.

16. See Fernandez and Herzfeld 1998, 91–101; Herzfeld 2004, 92–94.

Bibliography

Abercrombie, N., and B. Longhurst. 1998. *Audiences*. London: Sage.

Abu-Lughod, Lila. 1990. The romance of resistance: Tracing transformations of power through Bedouin women. *American Anthropologist* 1 (1): 41–55.

———. 1997. The interpretation of culture(s) after television. *Representations* 59:109–33.

———. 2004. *Dramas of nationhood: The politics of television in Egypt*. Chicago: University of Chicago Press.

Adam, Leonhard. 1949. *Primitive art*. Harmondsworth: Penguin. (Orig. pub. 1940.)

Adamowicz, Elza. 1993. Ethnology, ethnographic film and surrealism. *Anthropology Today* 9 (1): 21.

Adams, M. J. 1973. Structural aspects of a village art. *American Anthropologist* 75:265–79.

Ades, Dawn, and Simon Baker, eds. 2006. *Undercover surrealism: Georges Bataille and DOCUMENTS*. London: Hayward Gallery; Cambridge, MA: MIT Press.

Adrian, B. 2003. *Framing the bride: Globalizing beauty and romance in Taiwan's bridal industry*. Berkeley: University of California Press.

Ahmed, M. 2002. *Living fabric: Weaving among the nomads of Ladakh Himalaya*. Bangkok: Orchid Press.

Aird, Michael. 1993. *Portraits of our elders*. Brisbane: Queensland Museum.

———. 2003. Growing up with Aborigines. In *Photography's other histories*, ed. C. Pinney and N. Peterson. Durham, NC: Duke University Press.

Akin Rabibhadana, M. R. 2002. Kaphawb thisadii kap ngan sanaam sawng krajok duu tua eng. In *Khon nai: Prasobkaan phaakh sanaam khawng manusayawitthayaa thai*, ed. Paritta

Chalermpow Koanantakool, 1–21. Bangkok: Sirindhorn Anthropology Center.

Alasuutari, Pertti. 1999. *Rethinking the media audience: The new agenda*. Beverly Hills: Sage.

Allen, J., and Elizabeth Grosz, eds. 1987. Feminism and the body. Special issue. *Australian Feminist Studies* 5.

Allen, Susan. 1994. What is media anthropology? A personal view and a suggested structure. In *Media anthropology: Informing global citizens*, ed. Susan Allen. Westport, CT: Bergin and Garvey.

Allerton, C. 2007. The secret life of sarongs: Manggarai textiles as super-skins. *Journal of Material Culture* 12 (1): 22–46.

Alloula, Malek. 1986. *The colonial harem*. Trans. B. Harlo. Minneapolis: University of Minnesota Press.

Ambrose, Stanley H. 2001. Paleolithic technology and human evolution. *Science* 291:1748–53.

Amerlinck, Mari-Jose, ed. 1995. *Hacía una antropología arquitectónica*. Guadelajara: Universidad de Guadelajara.

———, ed. 2001. *Architectural anthropology*. Westport, CT: Bergin and Garvey.

Amerlinck, Mari-Jose, and Juan Fernando Bontempo. 1994. *El entorno construido y la antropologia: Introducción a su estudio interdisciplinar*. Mexico, DF: CIESAS.

Anderson, C. 2004. *Legible bodies: Race, criminality and colonialism in South Asia*. Oxford: Berg.

Anderson, Jane. 2009. *Law, knowledge, culture: The production of indigenous knowledge in intellectual property law*. London: Edward Elgar Press.

Ang, Ien. 1991. *Desperately seeking the audience*. London: Routledge.

———. 1996. Ethnography and radical contextualism in audience studies. In *Living room wars: Rethinking media audiences for a postmodern world*, 66–81. London: Routledge.

Anonymous. 2006. Ethnography and experimental film. *Anthropology Today* 22 (4): 27–28.

Anzieu, D. 1989. *The skin ego*. Trans. C. Turner. New Haven, CT: Yale University Press.

Appadurai, Arjun. 1986. *The social life of things: Commodities in cultural perspective*. Cambridge: Cambridge University Press.

———. 1996. *Modernity at large: Cultural dimensions of globalization*. Minneapolis: University of Minnesota Press.

Archer, W. G., and Robert Melville. 1949. Primitive influences on modern art. In *40,000 years of modern art: A comparison of primitive and modern*. Exh. cat., with a preface by Herbert Read. London: Institute of Contemporary Arts.

Ardener, Edwin. 1970. "Behavior": A social anthropological criticism. *Journal of the Anthropological Society of Oxford* 4 (3): 153–55.

———. 1989. *The voice of prophecy and other essays*. Ed. Malcolm Chapman. Oxford: Blackwell.

Ardizzone, H. 2006. Such fine families: Photography and race in the work of Caroline Bond Day. *Visual Studies* 21 (2): 106–32.

Armbrust, Walter. 1998. When the lights go down in Cairo: Cinema as secular ritual. *Visual Anthropology* 10 (2–4): 413–42.

Armstrong, David F., William F. Stokoe, and Sherman E. Wilcox. 1995. *Gesture and the nature of language*. New York: Cambridge University Press.

Aronson, Jerrold L. 1984. *A realist philosophy of science*. New York: St Martin's.

Arthur, L. 2006. The Aloha shirt and ethnicity in Hawai'i. *Textile* 4 (1): 8–35.

Arthur, Paul. 2005. *A line of sight: American avant-garde film since 1965*. Minneapolis: University of Minnesota Press.

Asad, Talal, ed. 1973. *Anthropology and the colonial encounter*. London: Ithaca Press.

Asch, Timothy.1972. Making ethnographic film for teaching and research. *Program in Ethnographic Film Newsletter* (American Anthropological Association) 3 (2): 6—10.

———. 1991. The story we now want to hear is not ours to tell—relinquishing control over representation: Toward sharing visual communication skills with the Yanomamo. *Visual Anthropology Review* 7 (2): 102–6.

———. 1993. Bias in ethnographic reporting and using the Yanomamo films in teaching. In *Yanomamo film study guide*, ed. Tim Asch and Gary Seaman. Los Angeles: Ethnographics Press.

Ascher, Marcia, and Robert Ascher. 1978. *Code of the quipu: Databook*. Ann Arbor: University of Michigan Press.

———. 1980. *Code of the quipu: A study in media, mathematics, and culture*. Ann Arbor: University of Michigan Press.

Ascher, Robert. 1961. Experimental archaeology. *American Anthropologist* 63:793–816.

———. 1974. Tin can archaeology. *Historical Archaeology* 8:7–16.

———. 1990. Approach, theory and technique in making *Bar Yohai*. *Visual Anthropology* 3:111–19.

———. 1993. Myth and film. In *Anthropological film and video in the 1990s*, ed. J. R. Rollwagen. Brockport, NY: Institute Press.

Ascher, Robert, and Douglas Fairbanks. 1971. Excavation of a slave cabin: Georgia U. S.A. *Historical Archaeology* 5:3–17.

Askew, Kelly, and Richard Wilk, eds. 2002. *The anthropology of media: A reader*. London: Blackwell.

Asquith, Lindsay, and Marcel Vellinga, eds. 2006. *Vernacular architecture in the twenty-first century: Theory, education and practice*. London: Taylor and Francis.

Aufderheide, Patricia. 1995. The Video in the Villages Project: Videomaking with and by Brazilian Indians. *Visual Anthropology Review* 11 (2): 83–93.

Bachar, Joel, and Patrick Kwiatkowski. 2008. Microcinema International. http://www.microcinema.com (accessed 18 August 2008).

Bachelard, Gaston. 1969. *The poetics of space*. Boston, MA: Beacon Press.

Bailey, F. G. 1969. *Stratagems and spoils: A social anthropology of politics.* Oxford: Basil Blackwell.

———. 1971. *Gifts and poison: The politics of reputation.* Oxford: Basil Blackwell.

Bal, Meike. 1996. A postcard from the edge. In *Double exposure: The subject of cultural analyses.* New York: Routledge.

Balikci, Asen. 1966. Ethnographic filming and the Netsilik Eskimos. *ESI Quarterly Reports,* Spring–Summer, 19–33.

———. 1988. Anthropologist and ethnographic filmmaking: A personal view. In *Anthropological filmmaking: Anthropological perspectives on the production of film and video for general public audiences,* ed. J. Rollwagen. New York: Harwood Academic Publishers.

———. 1989. Anthropology, film and the Arctic peoples: The first Forman Lecture. *Anthropology Today* 5 (2): 4–10.

Balikci, Asen, and Quentin Brown. 1966. Ethnographic filming and the Netsilik Eskimos. *ESI Reports,* pp. 19–33.

Banerjee, M., and D. Miller. 2003. *The sari.* Oxford: Berg.

Banks, Marcus. 1994. Interactive multimedia and anthropology: A skeptical view. Formerly available at http://www.rsl.ox.ac.uk/isca/marcus.banks .01.html.

———. 1996a. Constructing the audience through ethnography. In *The construction of the viewer: Media ethnography and the anthropology of audiences,* ed. P. Crawford and S. B. Hafsteinsson, 118–34. Proceedings from NAFA 3. Hojberg: Intervention Press.

———. 1996b. *Ethnicity: Anthropological constructions.* London: Routledge.

———. 1997. Representing the bodies of the Jains. In *Rethinking Visual Anthropology,* ed. Marcus Banks and Howard Morphy, 216–39. New Haven, CT: Yale University Press.

———. 2001. *Visual methods in social research.* London: Sage.

———. 2008. The burden of symbols: Film and representation in India. In *The cinema of Robert Gardner,* ed. Ilisa Barbash and Lucien Taylor. Oxford: Berg.

Banks, Marcus, and Howard Morphy. 1997. *Rethinking visual anthropology.* New Haven, CT: Yale University Press.

Banta, Melissa, and Curtis Hinsley. 1986. *From site to sight: Anthropology, photography and the power of images.* Cambridge, MA: Peabody Museum Press.

Barbash, Ilisa, and Lucien Taylor. 2008. *The cinema of Robert Gardner.* Oxford: Berg.

Barclay, Barry. 1990. *Our own image.* Auckland: Longman Paul.

Barish, Jonas. 1981. *The antitheatrical prejudice.* Berkeley: University of California Press.

Barnes, R. 1989. *The ikat textiles of Lamalera: A study of an Eastern Indonesian weaving tradition.* Leiden: E. J. Brill.

———. 1992. Women as headhunters: The making and meaning of textiles in a southeast Asian context. In *Dress and gender: Making and meaning in cultural contexts,* ed. R. Barnes and J. B. Eicher, 29–43. Oxford: Berg.

———. 1995. Textile design in southern Lembata: Tradition and change. In *Anthropology, Art and Aesthetics*, ed. J. Coote and A. Shelton, 160–80. Oxford: Clarendon Press.

———. 1997. *Textiles and the Indian Ocean trade*. 2 vols. Oxford: Ashmolean Museum.

Barnes, R., and J. B. Eicher, eds. 1992. *Dress and gender: Making and meaning in cultural contexts*. Oxford: Berg.

Barthes, R. 1972. *Mythologies*. London: Jonathan Cape.

———. 1977. *Image music text*. Trans. R. Howard. London: Fontana.

———. 1984. *Camera lucida*. Trans. R. Howard. London: Fontana.

———. 2006. *The Language of Fashion*. Oxford: Berg.

Basso, Keith. 1996. *Wisdom sits in places: Landscape and language among the western Apache*. Albuquerque: University of New Mexico Press.

Bastide, Roger. 1973. *Applied anthropology*. London: Croom Helm.

Bateson, Gregory, and Margaret Mead. 1942. *Balinese character: A photographic analysis*. New York: New York Academy of Sciences.

Batty, Philip. 2003. Governing cultural difference: The incorporation of the Aboriginal subject into the mechanisms of government with reference to the development of Aboriginal radio and television in central Australia. PhD thesis, School of Communication, Information and New Media, University of South Australia.

Batty, Philip, L. Allen, and J. Morton, eds. 2005. *The photographs of Baldwin Spencer*. Melbourne: Miegunyah Press/Museum Victoria.

Baumann, Hermann. 1927. Der Schwarze karikiret den Weifsen. *Die Woche* 29 (5): 722–24.

Baxandall, Michael. 1988. *Painting and experience in fifteenth century Italy: A primer in the social history of pictorial style*. Oxford: Oxford University Press. (Orig. pub. 1972.)

Bayma, Todd. 1995. Art world culture and institutional choices: The case of experimental film. *Sociological Quarterly* 36 (1): 79–95.

Bechhoefer, William, and Carl Bovill. 1994. Fractal analysis of traditional housing in Amasya, Turkey. In *Changing Methodologies in the Field of Traditional-Environment Research*, 1–21. Traditional Dwellings and Settlements Working Paper Series, vol. 61. Berkeley: University of California Center for Environmental Design Research.

Becker, Howard. 1981. *Exploring society photographically*. Evanston, IL: Block Gallery, Northwestern University.

———. 1982. *Art worlds*. Berkeley: University of California Press.

Behar, Ruth, and Deborah Gordon, eds. 1995. *Women writing culture*. Berkeley: University of California Press.

Behrend, Heike. 2000. Feeling global: The Likoni Ferry photographers in Mombassa. *African Arts* 33 (3): 70–77

Behrend, Heike, and J.-F. Werner, eds. 2001. Photographies and modernities in Africa. *Visual Anthropology* 14 (3).

Behrman, C. 1995. The fairest of them all: Gender, ethnicity and a beauty pageant in the Kingdom of Swaziland. In *Dress and Ethnicity*, ed. J. B. Eicher, 195–206. Oxford: Berg.

Bell, Joshua A. 2004. Looking to see: Reflecting on visual repatriation in the Purari Delta, Papua New Guinea. In *Museums and Source Communities*, ed. L. Peers and A. Brown. London: Routledge.

Belting, Hans. 2005. Image, medium, body: A new approach to iconology. *Critical Inquiry* 31:302–19.

Benedict, Ruth. 1934. *Patterns of Culture*. Boston: Houghton Mifflin.

Benjamin, David, David Stea, and David Saile, eds. 1995. *The home: Words, interpretations, meanings, and environments*. Aldershot: Avebury.

Benveniste, Emile. 1973. *Indo-European language and society*. Coral Gables, FL: University of Miami Press.

Berger, John. 1972. *Ways of seeing*. London: Penguin Books.

Berger, Sally. 1995. Move over Nanook. *Wide Angle* 17 (1–4): 177–92. Special issue on the Flaherty.

Berlin, B., and P. Kay. 1969. *Basic color terms: Their universality and evolution*. Berkeley: University of California Press.

Berthelot, J. M. 1986. Sociological discourse and the body. *Theory, Culture and Society* 3:155–64.

Besnier, N. 2002. Transgenderism, locality, and the Miss Galaxy beauty pageant in Tonga. *American Ethnologist* 29 (3): 534–66.

Best, David. 1974. *Expression in movement and the arts*. London: Lepus.

———. 1978. *Philosophy and human movement*. London: Allen & Unwin.

Bestor, Theodore C. 2004. Tsukiji: The fish market at the center of the world. Berkeley: University of California Press.

Bhaskar, Roy. 1975. *A realist theory of science*. Atlantic Highlands: Humanities Press.

Biella, P. 1993. Beyond ethnographic film: Hypermedia and scholarship. In *Anthropological Film and Video in the 1990s*, ed. J. Rollwagen, 131–76. Brockport, NY: The Institute.

———. 1994. Codifications of ethnography: Linear and nonlinear. Formerly available at http://www.usc.edu/dept/elab/welcome/codifications.html.

———. 1997. Mama Kone's possession: Scene from an interactive ethnography. *Visual Anthropology Review* 12 (2): 59–95.

———. 2004. *The ax fight* on CD-ROM. *Timothy Asch and ethnographic film*. Ed. E. D. Lewis. London: Routledge.

———. 2007. Coherent labyrinths. *Visual Anthropology Review* 23 (2). http://online.sfsu.edu/~biella/perry/coherent.html.

———. 2008. Visual anthropology in a time of war. In *Viewpoints: Visual anthropologists at work*, ed. Mary Strong and Laena Wilder. Austin: University of Texas Press.

Binney, Judith, and Elizabeth Chaplin. 1991. Taking the photographs home: The recovery of a Maori history. *Visual Anthropology* 4 (4): 341–442.

Bird, S. Elizabeth. 2003. *The audience in everyday life: Living in a media world.* London: Routledge.

Bird, S. Elizabeth, and Jonathan P. Godwin. 2006. Film in the undergraduate anthropology classroom: Applying audience response research in pedagogical practice. *Anthropology and Education Quarterly* 37 (3): 285–99.

———. 1970. *Kinesics in context: Essays on body motion communication.* Philadelphia: University of Pennsylvania Press.

Birdwhistell, Ray L. 1970. *Kinesics in context: Essays on body motion communication.* Philadelphia: University of Pennylvania Press.

Blanchard, Pascal, et al. 1995. *L'autre et nous: "Scènes et types."* Paris: ACHAS.

Blanton, Richard. 1994. *Houses and households: A comparative study.* New York: Plenum Press.

Bleichmar, D. 2007. Training the naturalist's eye in the eighteenth century: Perfect global visions and local blind spots. In *Skilled Visions*, ed. C. Grasseni, 166–90. Oxford: Berghahn.

Blier, Susan Preston. 1987. *The anatomy of architecture: Ontology and metaphor in Batammaliba architectural expression.* Cambridge: Cambridge University Press.

Bloch, Ernst. 1986. *The principle of hope.* Oxford: Basil Blackwell. (Orig. pub. 1959.)

Bloch, Maurice. 1971. *Placing the dead: Tombs, ancestral villages, and kinship organization in Madagascar.* London: Seminar Press.

———. 1995. The resurrection of the house amongst the Zafimaniry of Madagascar. In *About the house: Lévi-Strauss and beyond*, ed. Janet Carsten and Stephen Hugh-Jones, 69–83. Cambridge: Cambridge University Press.

Blumenbach, Johann Friedrich. 1776. *De generis humani varietate humane.* MD thesis, Jena, Germany.

Boas, Franz. 1888. On certain songs and dances of the Kwakiutl of British Columbia. *Journal of American Folklore* 1:49–64.

———. 1890. *Sign language: Second general report on the Indians of British Columbia.* In *Report for the 60th meeting of the Advanced Sciences*, 638–41. London: John Murray.

———. 1897. The social organization and secret societies of the Kwakiutl Indians. *Report of the U.S National Museum for 1895*, 311–738.

———. 1911. Editor's introduction. *The Handbook of American Indian Languages Bulletin* 40 (1): 1–83. Washington, DC: Bureau of American Ethnology, Smithsonian Institution.

———. 1927. *Primitive art.* New York: Dover.

———. 1944. Dance and music in the life of the Northwest Coast Indians of North America (Kwakiutl). In *The function of dance in human society*, ed. Franziska Boas, 7–18. New York: Dance Horizons.

Boas, Franziska M., ed. 1944. *The function of dance in human society.* New York: Dance Horizons.

Boggs, Ralph Steele. 1945. *Bibliografía completa, clasificada y comentada, de los artículos de Mexican Folkways (MF), con índice.* Mexico City: Instituto Panamericano de Geografía e Historia.

Bordo, Susan. 1993. *Unbearable weight: Feminism, Western culture and the body*. Berkeley: University of California Press.

Born, Georgina. 2005. On musical mediation: Ontology, technology and creativity. *Twentieth Century Music* 2 (1): 7– 36.

Born, G. 1997. Computer software as a medium: Textuality, orality and sociality in an Artificial Intelligence research culture. In *Rethinking visual anthropology*, ed. M. Banks and H. Morphy, 139–69. New Haven, CT: Yale University Press.

Boulay, Roger. 1990. *La maison Kanak*. Marseille: Editions Parenthèses/Agence pour la Développement de la Culture Kanak/Editions de l'Orstom.

Bouman, Jan C. 1954. Bibliography on filmography related to the social sciences. *Unesco Reports and Papers on Mass Communication*, no. 9, Paris.

Bouquet, Mary, ed. 2001. *Academic anthropology and the museum: Back to the future*. New York: Berghahn Books.

Bourdier, Jean-Paul, and Nezar Alsayyad, eds. 1989. *Dwellings, settlements and tradition: Cross-cultural perspectives*. New York: Lanham.

Bourdier, Jean-Paul, and Trinh Minh-ha. 1996. *Drawn from African dwellings*. Bloomington: Indiana University Press.

Bourdieu, Pierre. 1972. *Ésquisse d'une théorie de la pratique, précédé de trois études de ethnologie kabyle*. Paris: Librairie Droz.

———. 1973. The Berber house. In *Rules and meanings*, ed. Mary Douglas. Harmondsworth: Penguin.

———. 1977. *Outline of a theory of practice*. Trans. Richard Nice. Cambridge: Cambridge University Press.

———. 1993. *Field of cultural production*. New York: Columbia University Press.

Bourdieu, Pierre, and L. D. Wacquant. 1992. *An invitation to reflexive sociology*. Chicago: University of Chicago Press.

Bourriaud, Nicolas. 1999/2002. *Relational aesthetics*. Paris: Les Presses du Réel.

Brading, David A. 1988. Manuel Gamio and official indigenismo in Mexico. *Bulletin of Latin American Research* 7:75–89.

Bradshaw, Peter. 2006. The piano tuner of earthquakes. *Guardian* (London), 17 February, Features section, 9.

Brakhage, Stan. 1983. Sidney Peterson: A lecture by Stan Brakhage, Art Institute of Chicago, 1973. *Film Culture*, 70–71

Braun, Barbara. 1993. *Pre-Columbian art and the post-Columbian world: Ancient American sources of modern art*. New York: Abrams.

Braun, Peter. 1997. *Die doppelte Dokumentation: Fotografie und Literatur im Werk von Leonore Mau und Hubert Fichte*. Stuttgart: M & P Verlag für Wissenschaft und Forschung.

Bredekamp, Horst. 2003. A neglected tradition? Art history as Bildwissenschaft. *Critical Inquiry* 29 (3): 418–28.

Brenez, Nicole, and Christian Lebrat, eds. 2001. *Jeune, dure et pure! Une histoire du cinéma d'avant-garde et expérimental en France*. Milan: Mazzotta.

Brenner, Anita. 1929/1967. *Idols behind altars*. New York: Biblio and Tannen.

Brenner, S. 1996. Restructuring self and society: Javanese Muslim women and "the veil." *American Ethnologist* 23 (4): 673–97.

Breward, C., B. Conekin, and C. Cox. 2002. *The Englishness of English Dress.* Oxford: Berg.

Bridgwood, A. 1995. Dancing the jar: Girls' dress at Turkish Cypriot weddings. In *Dress and Ethnicity*, ed. J. B. Eicher, 29–51. Oxford: Berg.

Brink, Joram Ten. 2007. *Building bridges: The cinema of Jean Rouch.* London: Wallflower Press.

British Association for the Advancement of Science. 1912. *Notes and Queries on Anthropology*, 4th ed. London: BAAS.

Brown, Alison and Laura Peers. 2006. *Pictures bring us messages.* Toronto: University of Toronto Press.

Brown, Michael F. 2003. *Who owns native culture?* Cambridge, MA: Harvard University Press.

Brown, Peter. 1988. *The body and society: Men, women and sexual renunciation in early Christianity.* New York: Columbia University Press.

Brugger, Ingried, ed. 2001. *Emil Nolde und die Südsee.* Munich: Hirmer.

Bruno, G. 2003. Havana: Memoirs of material culture. *Journal of Visual Culture* 2 (3): 303–24.

Brydon, A., and S. Niessen, eds. 1998. *Consuming fashion: Adorning the transnational body.* Oxford: Berg.

Bryson, Ian. 2002. *Bringing to light: A history of ethnographic filmmaking at the Australian Institute of Aboriginal and Torres Strait Islander Studies.* Canberra: Aboriginal Studies Press.

Buck, A. 1958. *Handbook for museum curators*, pt. D, sect. 3. London: Museums Association.

Buckley, Liam. 2000–2001. Self and accessory in Gambian studio photography. *Visual Anthropology Review* 16 (2): 71–91.

———. 2006. Studio photography and the aesthetics of citizenship in the Gambia, West Africa. In *Sensible objects: Colonialism, museums and material culture*, ed. E. Edwards, C. Gosden, and R. Phillips. Oxford: Berg.

Buddle-Crowe, Kathleen. 2001. From birchbark talk to digital dreamspeaking: A partial history of aboriginal media activism in Canada. PhD thesis, Department of Anthropology, University of Ontario.

Bunzl, Matti. 1996. Franz Boas and the Humboldtian tradition. In *Volksgeist and Nationalcharakter to an anthropological concept of culture: Volksgeist as method and ethic. Essays on Boasian ethnography and the German anthropological tradition*, ed. George W. Stocking. Madison: University of Wisconsin Press.

Burgin, Victor, ed. 1986. *Thinking photography.* Basingstoke: Macmillan.

Burroughs, Catherine, and Jeffrey D. Ehrenreich, eds. 1993. *Reading the social body.* Iowa City: University of Iowa Press.

Burton, John W. 2001. *Culture and the human body: An anthropological perspective.* Prospect Heights: Waveland Press.

Butler, Judith. 1993. *Bodies that matter.* New York: Routledge.

Bynum, Cathryn W. 1991. *Fragmentation and redemption: Essays on gender and the human body in medieval religion*. New York: Zone Books.

Cairns, Stephen, ed. 2004. *Drifting: Architecture and migrancy*. London: Routledge.

Caldarola, Victor. 1990. *Reception as cultural experience: Visual mass media and reception practices in outer Indonesia*. PhD dissertation, University of Pennsylvania.

———. 1994. Embracing the media simulacrum. *Visual Anthropology Review* 10 (1): 66–69.

———. 1998. Imaging process as ethnographic inquiry. *Visual Anthropology* 1 (4): 433–51.

Calefato, P. 2004. *The clothed body*. Oxford: Berg.

Calisi, Romano. 1960. Sulla utilizzazione del film nella ricerca etnografica. *Rivista di Etnografia* 14:248–49.

Calzadilla, Fernando, and George Marcus. 2006. Artists in the field: Between art and anthropology. In *Contemporary art and anthropology*, ed. Arnd Schneider and Christopher Wright. Oxford: Berg.

Camper, Fred. 1986–1987. The end of avant-garde film. *Millennium Film Journal*, Fall/Winter (16/17/18).

Canning, Simon. 2007. Uluru row rocks Telstra. http://australianit.news.com .au/story/0,24897,21786053-15306,00.html (accessed 22 October 2007).

Caplan, Pat. 1988. Engendering knowledge: The politics of ethnography. *Anthropology Today* 4:8–12, 5:14–17.

———. 2005. In search of the exotic: A discussion of the BBC2 series *Tribe*. *Anthropology Today* 21 (2): 3–7.

Carelli, Vincent. 1988. Video in the Villages. *Commission on Visual Anthropology Bulletin*, May, 10–15.

Carey, B. S., and H. N. Tuck. 1896. *The Chin Hills: A history of the people, our dealings with them, their customs and manners, and a gazeteer of their country*. Rangoon: Superintendent Government Printing.

Carpitella, D. 1981a. Pratica e teoria nel film etnografico italiano prime osservazioni. *Ricerca Folklorica* 2/3:5–22.

———. 1981b. Cinesica 1 Napoli : Il linguaggio del corpo e le tradizioni popolari codici cinesici e ricerca cinematografica; Sceneggiatura. *Ricerca Folklorica* 2/3:61–70.

Carsten, Janet, and Stephen Hugh-Jones, eds. 1995. *About the house: Lévi-Strauss and beyond*. Cambridge: Cambridge University Press.

Casey, E. 1996. How to get from space to place in a fairly short stretch of time: Phenomenological prolegomena. In *Senses of place,* ed. S. Feld and K. Basso. Santa Fe: School of American Research Advanced Seminar Series.

Cassirer, Ernst. 1944/1953. *An essay on man: An introduction to a philosophy of human culture*. Garden City, NY: Doubleday.

Castells, M. 1996. *The rise of the network society*. London: Blackwell.

Centlives, Pierre. 1997. Julius Lips et la riposte du sauvage: L'homme blanc à travers le regard indigene. *Terrain* 28:73–86.

Ceram, C. W. 1965. *The archaeology of the cinemà*. New York: Harcourt, Brace and World.

Cerny, C. 1992. Quilted apparel and gender identity: An American case study. In *Dress and gender: Making and meaning in cultural contexts,* ed. R. Barnes and J. B. Eicher, 106–20. Oxford: Berg.

Ceruti, M. 1986. *Il vincolo e la possibilità*. Milan: Feltrinelli.

Chaat, Smith. 1992. Every picture tells a story. In *Partial recall,* ed. L. Lippard. New York: New Press.

Chagnon, Napoleon A. 1983. *Yanomamö: The fierce people*. 3rd edition. New York: Holt, Rinehart and Winston.

Chaiklin, S., and J. Lave, eds. 1993. *Understanding practice: Perspectives on activity and context*. Cambridge: Cambridge University Press.

Chalfen, Richard. 1978. Which way media anthropology? *Journal of Communication* 28 (3): 208–14.

Chalfen, R., and M. Rich. 2007. Combining the applied, the visual and the medical: Patients teaching physicians with visual narratives. In *Visual Interventions,* ed. S. Pink. Oxford: Berghahn.

Chandra, Mohini. 2000. Pacific album: Vernacular photography in the Fiji Indian diaspora. *History of Photography* 2000 (3): 236–42.

Chapman, M. 1995. "Freezing the frame": Dress and ethnicity in Brittany and Gaelic Scotland. In *Dress and Ethnicity,* ed. J. B. Eicher, 7–28. Oxford: Berg.

Chen Voon Fee, ed. 1998. *Encyclopedia of Malaysia,* vol. 5, *Architecture*. Singapore: Archipelago Press.

Cheung, Sidney C., ed. 2005. Wedding photography in South East Asia. Special issue. *Visual Anthropology* 19 (1).

———. 2006. Visualising marriage in Hong Kong. *Visual Anthropology* 19 (1): 21–37.

Child, Brenda. 1998. *Boarding school seasons*. Lincoln: University of Nebraska Press.

Chiozzi, Paolo. 1993. *Manuale di antropologia visuale*. Milan: Unicopli.

Chodorov, Pip. 2008. Re-voir. http://www.re-voir.com (accessed 18 August 2008).

Christen, Kim. 2005. Gone digital: Aboriginal remix in the cultural commons. *International Journal of Cultural Property* 12:315–44.

Christie, Michael. 2005. Words, ontologies and Aboriginal databases. *Media International Australia* 116 (August). Special issue: Digital Anthropology.

Cieraad, Irene. 1999. *At home: An anthropology of domestic space*. New York: Syracuse University Press.

Cinatti, Ruy. 1987. *Arquitectura Timorense*. Lisbon: Instituto de Investigação Ciientifica Tropical, Museu de Etnologia.

Clapp, J. A. 2005. "Are you talking to *me*?" New York and the cinema of urban alienation. *Visual Anthropology* 18:1–18.

Classen, Constance, ed. 1993. *Worlds of sense: Exploring the senses in history and across cultures*. London: Routledge

———. 2005. *The book of touch*. Oxford: Berg Publishers.

Clifford, James. 1988. *The predicament of culture*. Cambridge, MA: Harvard University Press.

Clifford, James, and George E. Marcus, eds. 1986. *Writing culture: The poetics and politics of ethnography*. Berkeley: University of California Press.

Cline, Ann. 1997. *A hut of one's own: Life outside the circle of architecture*. Cambridge, MA: MIT Press.

Coe, Cati. 2005. *Dilemmas of culture in African schools: Youth, nationalism, and the transformation of knowledge*. Chicago: University of Chicago Press.

Cohn, B. S. 1989. Cloth, clothes, and colonialism: India in the nineteenth century. In *Cloth and human experience*, ed. A. B. Weiner and J. Schneider, 303–54. Washington, DC: Smithsonian Books.

Cohn, Norman. 2009. Hi-speed, low-speed communities. Commentary on "Beyond broadcast: Launching NITV on Isuma TV" by Faye Ginsburg. *In Media Res*, May 3. http://mediacommons.futureofthebook.org/imr/2009/05/03/beyond-broadcast-launching-nitv-iuma-tv (accessed 7 February 2011).

Cohen, C. B., R. Wilk, and B. Stoeltje, eds. 1996. *Beauty queens on the global stage: Gender, contests and power*. London: Routledge.

Cohen, H., and J. F. Salazaar. 2005. Introduction: Prospects of a digital anthropology. *Media International Australia* 116:5–9. Special issue: Digital Anthropology.

Colchester, C., ed. 2003. *Clothing the Pacific*. Oxford: Berg.

———. 2005. Relative imagery: Responses to the revival of archaic chiefly dress in Fiji. In *Clothing as Material Culture*, ed. S. Küchler and D. Miller, 139–58. Oxford: Berg.

Cole, M. 1997. *Culture and cognitive science*. San Diego: Laboratory of Comparative Human Cognition. http://lchc.ucsd.edu/People/Localz/MCole/santabar.html.

Cole, M., Y. Engeström, and O. Vasquez, eds. 1997. *Mind, culture, and activity: Seminal papers from the Laboratory of Comparative Human Cognition*. Cambridge: Cambridge University Press.

Collier, J. 1973. *Alaskan Eskimo education*. New York: Holt, Rinehart, Winston.

Collier, John, Jr. 1967. *Visual anthropology: Photography as a research method*. New York: Holt, Rinehart and Winston.

Collier, Malcolm. 2001. A personal and professional appreciation of Edward T. Hall. Unpublished paper prepared for the Origins of Visual Anthropology Conference, Göttingen, Germany, 21–25 June.

Colloredo-Mansfeld, Rudi. 1999. *The native leisure class: Consumption and cultural creativity in the Andes*. Chicago: University of Chicago Press.

Colquhoun, A. R. 1885. *Amongst the Shans*. London: Field Tuer.

Coman, Mihai. 2005. *Media anthropology: An overview*. European Association of Social Anthropology, Media Anthropology Network, working paper, 17–24 May. http://www.media-anthropology.net/coman_maoverview.pdf (accessed 1 September 2006).

Comaroff, J. L., and J. Comaroff. 1992. *Ethnography and the historical imagination*. Boulder, CO: Westview Press.

———. 1997. Fashioning the colonial subject. In *Of revelation and revolution*, vol. 2, *The dialectics of modernity on a South African frontier*, ed. J. L. Comaroff and J. Comaroff, 218–73. Chicago: University of Chicago Press.

Conklin, Harold 1955. Hanunóo color categories. *Southwestern Journal of Anthropology* 11:339–44.

———. 1980. *Ethnographic atlas of Ifugao: A study of environment, culture and society in Northern Luzon*. New Haven, CT: Yale University Press.

Constable, N. 2006. Nostalgia, memory, and modernity: Bridal portraits in contemporary Beijing. *Visual Anthropology* 19 (1): 39–55.

Conway, S. 2000. Dress and cultural identity: Court costumes and textiles of 19th century Lan Na. PhD thesis, University of Brighton.

Cooper, Meriam C. 1925. *Grass*. New York: G. P. Putnam's Sons.

Corbey, Raymond. 1988. The colonial nude. *Critique of Anthropology* 8 (3): 75–92.

Courtney-Clarke, Margaret. 1990. *African canvas: The art of West African women*. New York: Rizzoli.

Cowan, Jane K. 1990. *Dance and the body politic in northern Greece*. Princeton, NJ: Princeton University Press.

Crawford, Peter. 2006. "Big men" and the representation of local communities on film: Some practical and theoretical implications based on the Reef Islands ethnographic film project. In *Reflecting visual ethnography: Using the camera in anthropological research*, ed. Peter Crawford and Metje Postma. Leiden: CNWS Publications; Intervention Press Hjobjerg.

Crawford, P., and S. B. Hafsteinsson, eds. 1996. *The construction of the viewer: Media ethnography and the anthropology of audiences*. Hojbjerg, Denmark: Intervention Press.

Crawford, Peter, and David Turton, eds. 1992. *Film as ethnography*. Manchester: Manchester University Press.

Crick, Malcolm. 1976. *Explorations in language and meaning:Towards a semantic anthropology*. London: Malaby.

Crouch, Dora, and June Johnson. 2001. *Traditions in architecture: Africa, America, Asia and Oceania*. New York: Oxford University Press.

Csordas, Thomas J. 1989. Embodiment as a paradigm for anthropology. *Ethos* 18 (1): 5–47.

———. 1994. Introduction: The body as representation and being-in-the-world. In *Embodiment and experience: The existential ground of culture and self*, 1–24. Cambridge: Cambridge University Press.

———. 1999. The body's career in anthropology. In *Anthropological theory today*, ed. Henrietta Moore, 172–205. Cambridge: Polity Press.

Cunningham, Clark. 1964. Order in the Atoni house. *Bijdragen tot de Taal, Land en Volkenkunde* 120:34–68.

Curran, James. 1990. The new revisionism in mass communications research: A reappraisal. *European Journal of Communication* 5:130–64.

Danforth, Loring, with Alexander Tsiaras. 1982. *The death rituals of rural Greece.* Princeton, NJ: Princeton University Press.

Darish, P. 1989. Dressing for the next life: Raffia textile production and use among the Kubo of Zaire. In *Cloth and human experience,* ed. A. B. Weiner and J. Schneider, 117–40. Washington, DC: Smithsonian Books.

Darwin, Charles. 1872. *The expression of emotion in man and animals.* London: Murray.

Das, Veena, and Arthur Kleinman. 2001. Introduction. In *Remaking a world: Violence, social suffering, and memory,* ed. Veena Das, Arthur Kleinman, Margaret Lock, Mamphela Ramphele, and Pamela Reynolds, 1–30. Berkeley: University of California Press.

Daston, Lorraine, and Peter Galison. 1992. The image of objectivity. *Representations* 40:81–128.

Davis, Martha. 2001. Film projectors as microscopes: Ray L. Birdwhistell and microanalysis of interaction, 1955–1975. Unpublished paper prepared for the Origins of Visual Anthropology Conference, Göttingen, Germany, June 21–25.

Davison, Julian, and Goh Geok Yian, eds. 1998. *Encyclopedia of Indonesian heritage.* Vol. 6, *Architecture.* Singapore: Archipelago Press.

Davison, Julian, and Bruce Granquist. 1999. *Balinese architecture.* Singapore: Periplus.

De Brigard, Emilie. 1995. The history of ethnographic film. In *Principles of visual anthropology,* ed. Paul Hockings. 2nd ed. Berlin: Mouton de Gruyter. (Orig. pub. 1975.)

de Certeau, Michel. 1984. *The practice of everyday life.* Berkeley: University of California Press.

De France, Claudine. 1982. *Cinéma et anthropologie.* Paris: Editions de la Maison des Sciences de l'Homme.

De Heusch, Luc. 1962. The cinema and the social science: A survey of ethnographic and sociological films. *Unesco Reports and Papers in the Social Sciences,* no. 16.

———. 2007. Jean Rouch and the birth of visual anthropology: A brief history of the Comité international du film ethnographique. *Visual Anthropology* 20 (5): 365–86.

De Iorio, Andrea. 1832/2000. *Gesture in Naples and gesture in classical antiquity.* Trans. Adam Kendon. [La mimica degli antichi investigata nel gestire napoletano (Naples: Fibreno).] Bloomington: Indiana University Press.

de Kloet, J. 2005. Authenticating geographies and temporalities: Representations of Chinese rock in China. *Visual Anthropology* 18:229–55.

De Lorenzo, Catherine. 2000. Appropriating anthropology? Document and rhetoric. *Journal of Material Culture* 5 (1): 91–113.

de Wita, B. 1994. *French bourgeois culture*. Cambridge: Editions de la Maison des Sciences de l'Homme/Cambridge University Press.

Deger, Jennifer. 2006. *Shimmering screens: Making media in an Aboriginal community*. Visible Evidence, no. 19. Minneapolis: University of Minnesota Press.

Dell, E., ed. 2000. *Burma frontier photographs, 1918–1935*. London: Merrell.

Dell, E., and S. Dudley, eds. 2003. *Textiles from Burma*. London: Philip Wilson.

Delpar, Helen. 1992. *The enormous vogue of things Mexican: Cultural relations between the United States and Mexico, 1920–1935*. Tuscaloosa: University of Alabama Press.

Demello, M. 1993. The convict body: Tattooing among male American prisoners. *Anthropology Today* 9:10–13.

Deren, Maya. 1953/1983. *Divine horsemen: The living gods of Haiti*. New York: Documentext/McPherson and Company.

———. 1953. *Divine horsemen*. London: Thames & Hudson.

———. 1945/2005. Choreography for the camera. In *Essential Deren: Collected writings on film by Maya Deren*, ed. B. R. McPherson, 220–24. Kingston, NY: Documentext.

———. 1946a/2005. Cinema as an art form. In *Essential Deren: Collected writings on film by Maya Deren*, ed. B. R. McPherson, 19–34. Kingston, NY: Documentext.

———. 1946b/2005. Creating movies with a new dimension: Time. In *Essential Deren: Collected writings on film by Maya Deren*, ed. B. R. McPherson, 131–38. Kingston, NY: Documentext.

———. 2007. Frameworks listserv archive. http://www.hi-beam.net/fw/index .html (accessed 6 June 2007).

Deren, Maya, and Gregory Bateson. 1980. An exchange of letters between Maya Deren and Gregory Bateson. *October*, no. 14, 16–20.

Devereaux, Leslie, and Roger Hillman, eds. 1995. *Fields of vision: Essays in film studies, visual anthropology and photography*. Berkeley: University of California Press.

Dias, Nelia. 1994. Photograpier et mesurer: Les portraits anthropologiques. *Romantisme* 84:37–49.

———. 1997. Images et savoir anthropologique au XIXe siècle. *Gradhiva* 22:87–97.

Dickey, Sara. 1993. *Cinema and the urban poor in South India*. Cambridge: Cambridge University Press.

———. 1996. Consuming utopia: Film watching in Tamil Nadu. In *Consuming modernity: Public culture in contemporary India*, ed. Carol Breckenridge, 131–56. Oxford: Oxford University Press.

———. 1997. Anthropology and its contributions to studies in mass media. *International Social Science Journal* 153:413–27.

Dicks, B., B. Mason, A. Coffey, and P. Atkinson. 2005. *Qualitative research and hypermedia: Ethnography for the digital age*. London: Sage.

Diran, R. K. 1997. *The vanishing tribes of Burma*. London: Weidenfeld Nicolson.

Dodds, John W. 1973. *The several lives of Paul Fejos*. New York: Wenner-Gren Foundation.

Domenig, Gaudenz. 1980. *Tektonik in Primitiven Dachbau* [Tectonics (principles of harmonious structure) of primitive roof construction]. Zürich: ETH.

Dornfeld, Barry. 1992. Representation and authority in ethnographic film/video: Reception. *Ethnomusicology* 36 (1): 95–98.

———. 1998. *Producing public television, producing public culture*. Princeton, NJ: Princeton University Press.

Dorward, D. C. 1976. Precolonial Tiv trade and cloth currency. *International Journal of African Historical Studies* 9: 576–91.

Douglas, M. 1967. Raffia cloth distribution in the Lele economy. In *Tribal and peasant economies: Readings in economic anthropology*, ed. G. Dalton. New York: American Museum of Natural History Press.

Douglas, Mary. 1972. Symbolic orders in the use of domestic space. In *Man, settlement and urbanism*, ed. P. Ucko et al., 513–21. Cambridge, MA: Schenckman.

Dow, Peter. 1991. *Schoolhouse politics: Lessons from the Sputnik era*. Cambridge, MA: Harvard University Press.

Dowell, Kristin. 2006a. Honoring stories: Aboriginal media, art, and activism in Vancouver. PhD thesis, Department of Anthropology, New York University.

———. 2006b. Indigenous media gone global: Strengthening indigenous identity on- and offscreen at the First Nations/First Features Film Showcase. *American Anthropologist* 108 (2): 376–84.

Dubin, Margaret. 1999. Native American image making and the spurious canon of the 'of-and-the-by' (review article). *Visual Anthropology Review* 15 (1): 70–74.

Dudding, J. 2003. Photographs of Maori as cultural artefacts and their positioning within the museum. *Journal of Museum Ethnography* 15:8–18.

Dudley, S. 1998. Aspects of research with Karenni refugees in Thailand. *Bulletin of the International Committee on Urgent Anthropological and Ethnological Research (UNESCO)* 39:165–84.

———. 1999. "Traditional" culture and refugee welfare in north-west Thailand. *Forced Migration Review* 6:5–8.

———. 2000. Displacement and identity: Karenni refugees in Thailand. DPhil thesis, University of Oxford.

———. 2002. Diversity, identity and modernity in exile: "Traditional" Karenni clothing. In *Burma: Art and archaeology*, ed. A. Green and R. Blurton, 143–51. London: British Museum Press.

———. 2003a. Whose textiles and whose meanings? In *Textiles from Burma*, ed. E. Dell and S. Dudley, 37–47. London: Philip Wilson.

———. 2003b. Appendix: Museum collections of textiles from Burma. In *Textiles from Burma*, ed. E. Dell and S. Dudley, 179–80. London: Philip Wilson.

Duggan, G. 2004. Woven traditions, collectors and tourists: A field report from Savu, Eastern Indonesia. In *Performing Objects: Museums, material Culture and performance in Southeast Asia*, ed. F. Kerlogue, 103–18. London: Horniman Museum.

Duly, Colin. 1978. *The houses of mankind*. London: Thames & Hudson.

Durington, Matthew. 2004. John Marshall's Kalahari family. *American Anthropologist* 106 (3): 589–94.

———. 2007. *The Hunters redux*: Applied participatory visual strategies among the Botswana !Xo. In *Visual Interventions*, ed. S. Pink. Oxford: Berghahn.

Dyson, L. E., M. A. N. Hendriks, and S. Grant, eds. 2007. *Information technology and indigenous people*. Hershey, PA: Idea Group.

Eckman, Paul, W. Friesen, and T. Taussig. 1969. VID-R and SCAN: Tools and methods for the automated analysis of visual records. In *Content Analysis*, ed. George Gerbner. New York: Wiley & Sons.

Edwards, Eiluned. 2005. Contemporary production and transmission of resist-dyed and block-printed textiles in Kachchh District, Gujarat. *Textile* 3 (2): 166–201.

Edwards, Elizabeth. 1988. Representation and reality: Science and the visual image. In *Australia in Oxford*, ed. H. Morphy and E. Edwards. Oxford: Pitt Rivers Museum.

———. 1990. Photographic types: The pursuit of method. *Visual Anthropology* 3 (2–3): 235–58.

———. 1992. Science visualized: E. H. Man in the Andaman Islands. In *Anthropology and photography, 1860–1920*, ed. E. Edwards, 108–21. New Haven, CT: Yale University Press; London: Royal Anthropological Institute.

———. 1997. Beyond the boundary. In *Rethinking visual anthropology*, ed. Marcus Banks and Howard Morphy. New Haven, CT: Yale University Press.

———. 1998. Performing science. In *Cambridge and the Torres Strait*, ed. A. Herle and S. Rouse, 106–35. Cambridge: Cambridge University Press.

———. 1999. Torres Strait islanders. *Anthropology Today* 15 (1): 17–19.

———. 2001. *Raw histories: Photographs, anthropology and museums*. Oxford: Berg.

———. 2004. Talking visual histories. In *Museums and source communities*, ed. A. Brown and L. Peers, 83–99. London: Routledge.

———. 2006. Photographs and the sound of history. *Visual Anthropology Review* 21 (1/2): 27–46.

Edwards, Elizabeth, ed. 1992. *Anthropology and photography, 1860–1920*. New Haven, CT: Yale University Press; London: Royal Anthropological Institute.

Edwards, Elizabeth, Chris Gosden, and Ruth Phillips, eds. 2006. *Sensible objects: Colonialism, museums and material culture*. Oxford: Berg.

Edwards, Jay. 1980. The evolution of vernacular architecture in the Western Carribean. In *Cultural traditions and Carribean identity: The question of patrimony*, ed. S. Jeffrey and K. Wilkerson, 291–342. Gainsville: Center for Latin American Studies, University of Florida.

———. 1988. *Louisiana's remarkable French vernacular architecture, 1700–1900*. Baton Rouge: Geoscience Publications, Louisiana State University Press.

————. 2001. Architectural creolization: The importance of colonial architecture. In *Architectural anthropology*, ed. Mari-Jose Amerlinck, 83–120. Westport, CT: Bergin and Garvey.

Edwards, Jay, and Nicholas Kariouk. 2004. *A Creole lexicon: Architecture, landscape, people*. Baton Rouge: Louisiana State University Press.

Edwards, Steve. 2006. *Photography: A very short introduction*. Oxford: Oxford University Press.

Efron, David. 1942. *Gesture and environment*. New York: Kings Crown.

Eicher, J. B., ed. 1995a. *Dress and ethnicity*. Oxford: Berg.

————. 1995b. Introduction: Dress as expression of ethnic identity. In *Dress and Ethnicity*, ed. J. B. Eicher, 1–5. Oxford: Berg.

————. 1997. Social change and dress among the Kalabari of Nigeria. In *Changing rural social systems: Adaptation and survival*, ed. N. E. Johnson and C. Wang. East Lansing: Michigan State University Press.

————. 2000. The anthropology of dress. *Dress* 27: 59–70.

Eicher, J. B., and M. E. Roach-Higgins. 1992. Definition and classification of dress: Implications for analysis of gender roles. In *Dress and gender: Making and meaning*, ed. R. Barnes and J. B. Eicher. Oxford: Berg.

Einstein, Carl. 1915. *Negerplastik*. Leipzig: Verlag der Weissen Bücher.

————. 1915/2004. Negro sculpture. Trans. Charles W. Haxthausen and ebastian Zeidler; introduced by Sebastian Zeidler. *October*, no. 107, 122–38.

————. 1921. *Afrikanische Plastik*. Berlin: Ernst Wasmuth.

————. 1926/1931. *Die Kunst des 20 Jahrhunderts*. Propyläen Weltgeschichte der Kunst, vol. 16. Berlin: Propyläen-Verlag.

Eiselein, E. B. 1976. Applied anthropology in broadcasting. *Human Organization* 35 (2): 165–72.

Eiselein, E. B., and Martin Topper. 1975. Media anthropology: A theoretical framework. *Human Organization* 35 (2): 113–23.

Eisenstein, E. 1979. *The printing press as an agent of change: Communications and cultural transformations in early modern Europe*. Cambridge: Cambridge University Press.

El Guindi, Fadwa. 1999. *Veil: Modesty, privacy and resistance*. Oxford: Berg.

————. 2004. *Visual anthropology*. New York: Altamira Press.

Elleh, Nnamdi. 1997. *African architecture: Evolution and transformation*. New York: McGraw-Hill.

Emmons, G. T. 1907. The Chilkat blanket. *Memoirs of the American Museum of Natural History* 3 (4): 329–409.

Engelbrecht, Beate, ed. 2007. *Memories of the origins of ethnographic film*. New York: Peter Lang.

Engeström, Y., and D. Middleton, eds. 1998. *Cognition and communication at work*. Cambridge: Cambridge University Press.

Enriquez, C. M. 1923. *A Burmese Arcady: An account of a long and intimate sojourn amongst the mountain dwellers of the Burmese hinterland and of their engaging characteristics and customs*. London: Seeley Service Co.

Entwistle, J. 2000. *The fashioned body*. Cambridge: Polity Press.

Entwistle, J., and E. Wilson. 2001. *Body dressing*. Oxford: Berg.

Eric, K. 2006. Realising wedding imaginations in south China. *Visual Anthropology* 19 (1): 57–71.

Evans-Pritchard, E. 1937. *Witchcraft, oracles and magic amongst the Azande*. Oxford: Clarendon Press.

———. 1940. *The Nuer: A description of the mode of livelihood and political institutions of a Nilotic people*. Oxford: Clarendon.

Fabian, Johannes. 1983. *Time and the other: How anthropology makes its object*. New York: Columbia University Press.

Faeta, Francesco. 2003. *Strategie dell'occhio: Saggi di antropologia visiva*. Milan: Franco Angeli.

Fagg, William. 1949. Primitive and modern art in London. *Man* 49:9.

———. 1960. *The Epstein collection of tribal and exotic sculpture*. London: Arts Council.

Fardon, Richard. 2006. *Lela in Bali: History through ceremony in Cameroon*. Oxford: Berghahn.

Faris, James C. 1972. *Nuba personal art*. London: Duckworth.

———. 1992. Anthropological transparency: Film, representation and politics. In *Film as ethnography*, ed. P. Crawford and D. Turton, 171–82. Manchester: University of Manchester Press.

———. 1996. *The Navajo and photography: A critical history of the representation of an American people*. Albuquerque: University of New Mexico Press.

Farnell, Brenda M. 1994. Ethno-graphics and the moving body. *Man* 29 (4): 929–74.

———. 1995a. *"Do you see what I mean?" Plains Indian sign talk and the embodiment of action*. Austin: University of Texas Press.

———. 1995b. Introduction. In *Human action signs in cultural context: The visible and the invisible in movement and dance*, ed. B. Farnell, 1–28. Metuchen, NJ: Scarecrow Press.

———. 1996a. Metaphors we move by. *Visual Anthropology* 8 (2–4): 311–35.

———. 1996b. Paradigms lost? (a reply to Prost). *Visual Anthropology* 8:359–63.

———. 1996c. Gesture and movement. In *Encyclopedia of cultural anthropology*, 536–41. Human relations area files, Yale University, American Reference Publishing.

———. 1996d. Movement writing systems. In *The world's writing systems*, ed. P. Daniels and W. Bright, 855–79. Oxford: Oxford University Press.

———. 1999. Moving bodies, acting selves. *Annual Review of Anthropology* 28:341–73.

———. 2000. Getting out of the *habitus*: An alternative model of dynamically embodied social action. *Journal of the Royal Anthropological Institute* 6:397–417.

———. 2001. Rethinking verbal and non-verbal in discursive performance. *Textus* 14:417–36.

————. 2003. Birdwhistell, Hall, Lomax and the origins of visual anthropology. *Visual Anthropology* 16:43–55.

Farnell, Brenda, and Charles Varela. 2008. The second somatic revolution. *Journal for the Theory of Social Behavior* 38 (3): 215–40.

Featherstone, Mike, Mike Hepworth, and Bryan S. Turner, eds. 1991. *The body: Social process and cultural theory*. London: Sage.

Feely-Harnik, G. 1989. Cloth and the creation of ancestors in Madagascar. In *Cloth and human experience*, ed. A. B. Weiner and J. Schneider, 73–116. Washington, DC: Smithsonian Books.

Fehar M, R. Naddaff, and N. Tazi, eds. 1989. *Fragments for a history of the human body*. 3 vols. New York: Zone.

Feld, Steven, ed. and trans. 2003. *Ciné-ethnography: Jean Rouch*. Minneapolis: University of Minnesota Press.

Feld, Steven, and K. Basso. 1996. *Senses of place*. School of American Research Advanced Seminar Series. Santa Fe: School of American Research Press.

Feld, Steven, and Carroll Williams. 1975. Towards a researchable film language. *Studies in the Anthropology of Visual Communication* 2 (1): 25–32.

Feldman A. 1994. On cultural anesthesia: From Desert Storm to Rodney King. In *The senses still: Perception and memory as material culture in modernity*, ed. N. Seremetakis, 87–107. Chicago: University of Chicago Press.

Feldman, S., and K. Morarji. 2007. Highway courtesans. *Visual Anthropology* 20 (2): 251–54.

Ferguson. Charles A. 1959. Diglossia. *Word* 15: 325–40.

Fernandez, James. 1966. Principles of opposition and vitality in Fang aesthetics. *Journal of Aesthetics and Art Criticism* 25:53–64.

Fernandez, James W., and Michael Herzfeld. 1998. In search of meaningful methods. In *Handbook of methods in cultural anthropology*, ed. H. Russell Bernard, 89–219. Walnut Creek: Altamira.

Fernandez, N. P. 1998. Review of *Unraveling the stories: Quilts as a reflection of our lives* by Luanne Bole-Becker and Bob Becker. *Journal of American History* 85 (3): 1200–1201.

Festa, Paul. 1966. Principles of opposition and vitality in Fang aesthetics. *Journal of Aesthetics and Art Criticism* 25: 53–64.

————. 2007. Mahjong agonistics and the political public in Taiwan: Fate, mimesis, and the martial imaginary. *Anthropological Quarterly* 80: 93–125.

Fienup-Riordan, A. 1998. Yup'ik elders in museums: Fieldwork turned on its head. *Arctic Anthropology* 35 (2): 49–58.

Fine, B., and E. Leopold. 1993. *The world of consumption*. London: Routledge.

Firth, Raymond. 1965. *We, the Tikopia*. Boston: Beacon Press. (Orig. pub. London: George, Allen & Unwin, 1936.)

Fischer, M. 1994. *Applications in computing for social anthropologists*. ASA Research Methods Series. London: Routledge.

Fischer, Michael D. and David Zeitlyn. 2003. Visual anthropology in the digital mirror: Computer-assisted visual anthropology. http://lucy.ukc.ac.uk/dz/layers_nggwun.html (accessed 2 March 2007).

Fleckner, Uwe. 2006. *Carl Einstein und sein Jahrhundert.* Berlin: Akademie Verlag.

Fleming, Kathlee. 1991. Zacharias Kunuk: Videomaker and Inuit historian. *Inuit Art Quarterly*, Summer, 24–28.

Fleming, P. R., and J. Luskey. 1986. *The North American Indians in early photographs.* New York: Dorset Press.

Forrest, J., and D. Blincoe. 1995. *Natural history of the traditional quilt.* Austin: University of Texas Press.

Fox, J. J. 1977. *Harvest of the palm: Ecological change in Eastern Indonesia.* Cambridge, MA: Harvard University Press.

Fox, James. 1993. *Inside Austronesian houses: Perspectives on domestic designs for living.* Canberra: Department of Anthropology, Research School of Pacific and Asian Studies.

Foucault, Michel. 1973. *The birth of the clinic.* London: Tavistock.

———. 1977. *Discipline and punish: The birth of the prison.* Trans. Alan Sheridan. New York: Pantheon.

———. 1978. *An introduction: The history of sexuality.* Trans. R Hurley. New York: Random House.

Fourmile, Henrietta. 1990. Possession is nine tenths of the law—and don't Aboriginal people know it. *COMA* 23:57–67.

Frank, Arthur. 1990. Bringing bodies back in: A decade review. *Theory Culture and Society* 7:131–62.

———. 1991. For a sociology of the body: An analytical review. In *The Body: Social Process and Cultural Theory*, ed. Mike Featherstone, Mike Hepworth, and Bryan S. Turner, 36–102. London: Sage.

Fraser, Douglas. 1968. *Village planning in the primitive world.* New York: Brasilier.

Freedberg, David. 2004. Pathos at Oraibi: What Warburg did not see. [Trans. of Pathos a Oraibi: Ciò che Warburg non vide. In *Lo Sguardo di Giano, Aby Warburg fra tempo e memoria*, ed. Claudia Cieri Via and Pietro Montani, 569–611 (Turin: Nino Aragno).] http://columbia.edu/cu/arthistory/pdf/freed_pathose_at_orabi.pdf (accessed July 11, 2007).

———. 2005. Warburg's mask. In *Anthropologies of art*, ed. Mariët Westermann. Williamstown: Clark Art Institute; New Haven, CT: Yale University Press.

———. 2006. On the circulation of ethnographic knowledge. http://www.materialworldblog.com (accessed June 19, 2007).

Frembgen, J. W. 2004. Tying and untying the trouser-cord: Dimensions of normativity, morality, and emotion in Pakistani body behaviour. *Asian Pacific Journal of Anthropology* 5 (1): 49–70.

Freud, Sigmund. 1919. *Totem and taboo.* London: Routledge.

Freund, Peter E. S. 1988. Bringing society into the body: Understanding socialized human nature. *Theory and Society* 17:839–64.

Fuchs, Peter, ed. 1988. Special issue on ethnographic film in Germany. *Visual Anthropology* 1 (3).

Furst, Peter. 1971. Review: Mosori Monika. *American Anthropologist* 73 (6): 1476–77.

Gaines, J. 1990. Introduction: Fabricating the female body. In *Fabrications and the female body*, ed. J. Gaines and C. Herzog, 1–27. London: Routledge.

Gaines, J., and C. Herzog, eds. 1990. *Fabrications: Costume and the human body.* New York: Routledge & Kegan Paul.

Galison, P., and C. Jones, eds. 1998. *Producing art, picturing science.* London: Routledge.

Ganti, Tejaswini. 2002. And yet my heart is still Indian: The Bombay film industry and the (H)Indianization of Hollywood. In *Media worlds: Anthropology on new terrain*, ed. F. Ginsburg, L. Abu-Lughod, and B. Larkin. Berkeley: University of California Press.

Gardner, Robert. 1968. *Gardens of war.* New York: Random House.

———. 1970. Program in ethnographic film: A review of its history. *Program in Ethnographic Film Newsletter* 1 (1): 3–5.

———. 2007a. *The impulse to preserve: Reflections of a filmmaker.* Cambridge, MA: Harvard University Press.

———. 2007b. Robert Gardner. http://robertgardner.net/gardner_final.swf (accessed 6 June 2007).

Gardner, Robert, and Akos Ostor. 2002. *Making Forest of Bliss: Intention, circumstance, and chance in nonfiction film: a conversation between Robert Gardner and Akos Ostor.* Cambridge, MA: Harvard Film Archive.

Garfinkel, H., M. Lynch, and E. Livingston. 1981. The work of a discovering science construed with materials from the optically discovered pulsar. *Philosophy of the Social Sciences* 2:131–58.

Geary, Christraud. 1988. *Images from Bamum: German colonial photography at the court of King Njoya.* Washington, DC: Smithsonian Institution Press.

Geddes, William. 1971. Review of *Gardens of war. American Anthropologist* 73 (2): 346–47.

Gefou-Madianou, Dimitra. 1993a. Mirroring ourselves through Western texts: The limitations of an indigenous anthropology. In *The politics of ethnographic reading and writing: Confrontation of Western and indigenous views*, ed. Henk Driessen, 160–81. Saarbrucken: Breitenbach.

———. 1993b. Anthropoloyiki iki: Yia mia kritiki tis "ithayenous anthropoloyias." *Dhiavazo* 323:44–51.

Geismar, Haidy. 2010. Photographs and foundations: Visualizing the past on Atchin and Vao. In *Moving images: John Layard, fieldwork and photography in Malakula since 1914*, ed. H. Geismar and A. Herle. Bathurst: Crawford House Publishing; Honolulu: University of Hawaii Press.

Gell, Alfred. 1993. *Wrapping in images: Tattooing in Polynesia.* Oxford: Clarendon Press.

———. 1998. *Art and agency: An anthropological theory.* Oxford: Clarendon Press.

Gibbs, Phillip. 1987. *Building a Malay house*. Singapore: Oxford University Press.

Gibson, James J. 1966. *The senses considered as perceptual systems*. Boston: Houghton Mifflin.

———. 1979. *The ecological approach to visual perception*. Boston: Houghton Mifflin.

Gibson, Katherine R., and Tim Ingold, eds. 1993. *Tools, language and cognition in human evolution*. Cambridge: Cambridge University Press.

Gillespie, Marie. 1995. *Television, ethnicity and cultural change*. London: Routledge.

Gillow, J., and B. Sentence. 1999. *A visual guide to traditional techniques*. London: Thames & Hudson.

Gilman, S. 1987. *Disease and representation: Images of illness from madness to AIDS*. Ithaca, NY: Cornell University Press.

Gilmore, D. 1994. The beauty of the beast: Male body image in anthropological perspective, In *The good body: Asceticism in contemporary culture*, ed. M. Winkler and L. Cole, 191–214. New Haven, CT: Yale University Press.

Ginsburg, Faye. 1991. Indigenous media: Faustian contract or global village? *Cultural Anthropology* 6 (1): 92–112.

———. 1992. Television and the mediation of culture: Issues in British ethnographic film. *Visual Anthropology Review* 8 (1): 97–102.

———. 1993. Aboriginal media and the Australian imaginary. *Public Culture* 5 (3): 557–78.

———. 1994a. Culture/media: A (mild) polemic. *Anthropology Today* 10 (2): 5–15.

———. 1994b. Embedded aesthetics: Creating a discursive space for indigenous media. *Cultural Anthropology* 9 (2): 365–82.

———. 1994c. Some thoughts on culture/media. *Visual Anthropology Review* 10 (1): 136–41.

———. 1997. "From little things, big things grow": Indigenous media and cultural activism. In *Between resistance and revolution: Cultural politics and social protest*, ed. R. Fox and O. Starn, 118–44. London: Routledge.

———. 1999a. Institutionalizing the unruly: Charting a future for visual anthropology. *Ethnos* 63 (2): 173–201.

———. 1999b. Shooting back: From ethnographic film to the ethnography of media. In *A companion to film theory*, ed. Toby Miller and Robert Stam, 295–322. London: Blackwell.

———. 2002. Mediating culture: Indigenous media, ethnographic film, and the production of identity. In *The anthropology of media: A reader*, ed. Kelly Askew and Richard Wilk. London: Blackwell.

———. 2004. Producing culture: Shifting representations of social theory in the films of Tim Asch. In *Timothy Asch and ethnographic film*, ed. E. D. Lewis. London: Routledge.

———. 2005. Media anthropology: An introduction. In *Media anthropology*, ed. Eric W. Rothenbuhler and Mihai Coman. Thousand Oaks, CA: Sage.

―――. 2008. Rethinking the digital age. In *Global indigenous media: Cultures, practices and politics*, ed. Pamela Wilson and Michelle Stewart, 287–306. Durham, NC: Duke University Press.

Ginsburg, Faye, L. Abu-Lughod, and B. Larkin, eds. 2002. *Media worlds: Anthropology on new terrain*. Berkeley: University of California Press.

―――. 2002. Introduction. In *Media worlds: Anthropology on new terrain*, 1–38. Berkeley: University of California Press.

Ginsburg, Faye, and April Strickland. 2005. The latest in reality TV? Maori Television stakes a claim on the world stage. *FlowTV* 2 (9), 22 July. http://flowtv .org/2005/07/maori-television-global-television-first-peoples-television (accessed 7 February 2011).

Gittinger, M. 1979. *Splendid symbols: Textiles and tradition in Indonesia*. Washington, DC: Textile Museum.

Glass, Aaron. 2006. On the circulation of ethnographic knowledge. http://www .materialworldblog.com (accessed 27 March 2007).

Glassie, Henry. 1975. *Folk housing in middle Virginia: A structural analysis of historic artifacts*. Knoxville: University of Tennessee Press.

―――. 1982. *Passing the time in Ballymenone: Culture and history of an Ulster community*. Philadelphia: University of Pennsylvania Press.

―――. 1993. *Turkish traditional art today*. Bloomington: Indiana University Press.

―――. 1997. *Art and life in Bangladesh*. Bloomington: Indiana University Press.

―――. 1999. *Material culture*. Bloomington: Indiana University Press.

―――. 2000. *Vernacular architecture*. Philadelphia: Material Culture; Bloomington: Indiana University Press.

Glenn Penny, H. 2003. Bastian's museum: On the limits of empiricism and the transformation of German ethnology. In *Worldly provincialism: German anthropology in the age of empire*, ed. H. Glenn Penny and Matti Bunzl. Ann Arbor: University of Michigan Press.

Glowczewski, B. 2005. Lines and criss-crossings: Hyperlinks in Australian indigenous narratives, anthropology. *Media International Australia* 116:24–35. Special issue: Digital Anthropology.

Goffman, Erving. 1963. *Behavior in public places: Notes on the social organization of gathering*. New York: Free Press.

―――. 1969. *The presentation of self in everyday life*. Harmondsworth: Penguin.

Goldwater, Robert. 1986. *Primitivism in modern art*. Cambridge, MA: Harvard University Press. (Orig. pub. 1938.)

Gombrich, Ernst H. 1961. *Art and illusion: A study in the psychology of pictorial representation*. 2nd ed. Princeton, NJ: Princeton University Press.

Goodwin, C. 1994. Professional vision. *American Anthropologist* 96 (3): 606–33.

―――. 1996. Practices of color classification. *Ninchi Kagaku (Cognitive Studies: Bulletin of the Japanese Cognitive Science Society)* 3 (2): 62–82.

———. 1997. The blackness of black: Color categories as situated practice. In *Discourse, tools and reasoning: Essays on situated cognition*, ed. L. B. Resnick, R. Säljö, C. Pontecorvo, and B. Burge, 111–40. Berlin: Springer.

———. 2000. Practices of seeing. Visual analysis: An ethnomethodological approach. In *Handbook of visual analysis*, ed. T. van Leeuwen and C. Jewitt, 157–82. London: Sage.

Goodwin, C., and M. H. Goodwin. 1998. Formulating planes: Seeing as a situated activity. In *Cognition and communication at work*, ed. D. Middleton and Y. Engeström. Cambridge: Cambridge University Press.

Goodwin, C., and N. Ueno, eds. 2000. Vision and inscription in practice. Special issue. *Mind, Culture and Activity* 7 (1–2).

Gordon, Robert. 1997. *Picturing bushman: The Denver African Expedition of 1925*. Athens: Ohio University Press.

Gould, Stephen J. 1981/1996. *The mismeasure of man*. New York: Norton.

———. 1994. The geometer of race. *Discover* 15 (November): 65–69.

Gow, Peter. 1995. Land, people and paper in western Amazonia. In *The anthropology of landscape: Perspectives on place and space*, ed. Eric Hirsch and Michael O'Hanlon, 43–62. Oxford: Clarendon Press.

Graburn, Nelson. 1976. *Ethnic and tourist arts: Cultural expressions from the fourth world*. Berkeley: University of California Press.

———. 1982. The dynamics of change in tourist arts. *Cultural Survival Quarterly* 6:7–12.

Grady, J. 1991. The visual essay and sociology. *Visual Sociology* 6 (2): 23–38.

Graham, Daniel. 2006. An interview with the Quay brothers and Alan Passes. *The piano tuner of earthquakes* (DVD). New York: Zeitgeist Films.

Grasseni, Cristina. 2004a. Skilled vision: An apprenticeship in breeding aesthetics. *Social Anthropology* 12 (1): 1–15.

———. 2004b. Skilled landscapes: Mapping practices of locality. *Environment and Planning D: Society and Space* 22:699–717.

———. 2005a. Designer cows: The practice of cattle breeding between skill and standardization. *Society and Animals* 13 (1): 33–50.

———. 2005b. Disciplining vision in animal biotechnology. *Anthropology in Action* 12 (2): 44–55.

———. 2007a. Communities of practice and forms of life: Towards a rehabilitation of anthropological vision? In *Ways of knowing*, ed. Mark Harris. Oxford: Berghahn.

———. 2007b. Introduction. In *Skilled visions: Between apprenticeship and standards*, ed. Cristina Grasseni, 1–19. Oxford: Berghahn.

———, ed. 2007c. *Skilled visions: Between apprenticeship and standards*. Oxford: Berghahn.

Gray, John. 2006. *Domestic mandala architecture of lifeworlds in Nepal*. Aldershot: Ashgate.

Green, David. 1984. Classified subjects. Photography and anthropology: The technology of power, *Ten-8* (14): 30–37.

———. 1985. Veins of resemblance. *Oxford Art Journal* 7 (2): 3–16.

Green, J. H. 1934. The tribes of upper Burma north of 24° latitude and their classification. PhD dissertation, University of Cambridge.

Griaule, M. 1938. *Masques dogons*. Paris: Trav. Mém. Inst. Ethnol. XXXIII.

———. 1965. *Conversations with Ogotemmêli*. Oxford: Oxford University Press, for International African Institute.

Griffiths, Alison. 2002. *Wondrous difference: Cinema, anthropology and the turn of the century visual culture*. New York: Columbia University Press.

———. 2004. The largest picture ever executed by man: Panoramas and the emergence of large-screen and 360-degree technologies. In *Screen culture: History and textuality*, ed. John Fullerton. London: John Libbey.

Grimshaw, Anna. 1997. The eye in the door. In *Rethinking visual anthropology*, ed. Marcus Banks and Howard Morphy. New Haven, CT: Yale University Press.

———. 2001a. *The ethnographer's eye: Ways of seeing in modern anthropology*. Cambridge: Cambridge University Press.

———. 2001b. The anthropological television of Melissa Llewlyn-Davies. In *The ethnographer's eye: Ways of seeing in modern anthropology*, 149–71. Cambridge: Cambridge University Press.

———. 2002 Eyeing the field: New horizons for visual anthropology. *Journal of Media Practice* 3 (1): 7–15.

Grimshaw, Anna, and Amanda Ravetz, eds. 2005. *Visualizing anthropology*. Bristol: Intellect Books.

Groning, K. 1998. *Body decoration: A world survey of body art*. New York: Vendome Press.

Gross, Larry, John Katz, and Jay Ruby, eds. 1988. *Image ethics: The moral rights of subjects in photography*. New York: Oxford University Press.

———. 2003. *Image ethics in the digital age*. Minneapolis: University of Minnesota Press.

Grosz, Elizabeth. 1991. Feminism and the body. *Hypatia* 6 (3): 1–3.

———. 1994. *Volatile bodies: Towards a corporeal feminism*. Bloomington: Indiana University Press.

———. 1995. *Space, time and perversion: Essays on the politics of bodies*. New York: Routledge.

Guidoni, Enrico. 1978. *Primitive architecture*. New York: Abrams.

Gumbrecht, H. U. 1998. Perception versus sciences: Moving pictures and their resistance to interpretation. In *Inscribing science: Scientific texts and the materiality of communication*, ed. T. Lenoir, 351–64. Stanford, CA: Stanford University Press.

Habermas, Jürgen. 1971. *Knowledge and human interests*. Trans. Jeremy J. Shapiro. Boston: Beacon Press.

Hacking, I. 1983. *Representing and intervening*. Cambridge: Cambridge University Press.

Haddon, Alfred Cort. 1895. *Evolution in art: As illustrated by the life-histories of designs*. London: Walter Scott.

Hafsteinsson, Sigurjon. 2007. Unmasking deep democracy: Aboriginal people's television network and culture production. PhD diss., Temple University, Department of Anthropology.

Hahn, Elizabeth. 1994. The Tongon tradition of going to the movies. *Visual Anthropology Review* 10 (1): 103–11.

Hall, Edward T. 1959. *The silent language*. Garden City, NY : Doubleday/Anchor.

———. 1966. *The hidden dimension*. New York: Doubleday.

———. 1968. Proxemics. *Current Anthropology* 9 (2–3): 83–108.

Hall, Stuart. 1977. Culture, the media and the "ideological effect." In *Mass communication and society*, ed. J. Curran et al. London: Open University.

———. 1981. Encoding and decoding in the TV discourse. In *Culture, media, language*, ed. S. Hall et al. London: Hutchinson.

———. 1982. The rediscovery of "ideology": Return of the repressed in media studies. In *Culture, society and the media*, ed. Michael Gurevitch et al., 56–90. London: Methuen.

———. 1996. Cultural studies and its theoretical legacies. In *Stuart Hall: Critical dialogues in cultural studies*, ed. D. Morley and K. Chen, 262–75. London: Routledge.

Hallowell, A. Irving. 1955. Cultural factors in spatial orientation. In *Culture and experience*, 184–202. Philadelphia: University of Pennsylvania Press.

Halperin, I. 1999. *Shut up and smile. Supermodels: The dark side*. Los Angeles: Ogo Books.

Halvaksz, Jamon. 2008. Photographing spirits: Biangai photography, ancestors and the environment in Morobe Province, Papua New Guinea. *Visual Anthropology* 21 (4): 310–26.

Hamilton, J. A., and J. W. Hamilton. 1989. Dress as a reflection and sustainer of social reality: A cross-cultural perspective. *Clothing and Textiles Research Journal* 7 (2): 16–22.

Hanna, Judith Lynn. 1979. *To dance is human: A theory of non-verbal communication*. Austin: University of Texas Press.

Hansen, H. H. 1960. *Some costumes of highland Burma at the Ethnographical Museum of Gothenburg*. Göteborg: Etnografiska Museet.

Hansen, K. T. 2000a. *Salaula: The world of secondhand clothing in Zambia*. Chicago: University of Chicago Press.

———. 2000b. Other people's clothes? The international second-hand clothing trade and dress practices in Zambia. *Fashion Theory* 4 (3): 245–74.

———. 2003. Fashioning: Zambian moments. *Journal of Material Culture* 11 (8): 301–9.

———. 2004. The world in dress: Anthropological perspectives on clothing, fashion, and culture. *Annual Review of Anthropology* 33:369–92.

Harlan, Teresa. 1995. Creating a visual history: A question of ownership. In *Strong hearts: Native American visions and voices*, 20–32. New York: Aperture.

———. 1998. Indigenous photographies: A space for indigenous realities. In *Native nations: Journeys in American photography*, ed. J. Allison, 233–45. London: Barbican Art Gallery.

Harper, Doug. 1987. The visual ethnographic narrative. *Visual Anthropology* 1 (1): 1–19.

———. 1994. A conversation with Tim Asch. *Visual Sociology* 9 (2): 97–101. Special issue: Cape Breton 1952: The photographic vision of Tim Asch, ed. D. Harper.

———. 2002. Talking about pictures: A case for photo-elicitation. *Visual Studies* 17 (1): 13–26.

Harré, Rom. 1971. The shift to an anthropomorphic model of man. *Journal of the Anthropological Society of Oxford* 2 (1): 33–37.

———. 1984. *Personal being*. Cambridge, MA: Harvard University Press.

———. 1986a. *Varieties of realism*. Oxford: Basil Blackwell.

———. 1986b. Persons and power. In *Philosophy in Britain today*, ed. G. Shankar. Albany: State University of New York Press.

———. 1991. *Physical being*. Oxford: Blackwell.

———. 1998. *The singular self: An introduction to the psychology of personhood*. Thousand Oaks, CA: Sage.

Harré, Rom, and Grant Gillett. 1994. *The discursive mind*. London: Sage.

Harré, Rom, and E. H. Maddon. 1975. *Causal powers*. Oxford: Blackwell.

Harré, Rom, and Peter F. Secord. 1972. *The explanation of social behavior*. Oxford: Blackwell.

Harris, Clare. 2004. The photograph reincarnate. In *Photographs objects histories: On the materiality of the image*, ed. E. Edwards and J. Hart, 132–47. London: Routledge.

Hartley, John. 2004. Television, nation, and indigenous media. *Television & New Media*, 5 February (1): 7–25.

Hartley, John, and Alan McKee. 2000. *The indigenous public sphere: The reporting and reception of Aboriginal issues in the Australian media*. Oxford: Oxford University Press.

Hartmann, W., J. Silvester, and P. Hayes, eds. 1998. *The colonising camera: Photographs and the making of history in Namibia*. Cape Town: University of Cape Town Press.

Harvey, J. 2007. Showing and hiding: Equivocation in the relations of body and dress. *Fashion Theory* 11 (1): 65–94.

Hastrup, Kirsten. 1992. Anthropological visions: Some notes on visual and textual authority. In *Film as ethnography*, ed. P. I. Crawford and D. Turton. Manchester: Manchester University Press.

Haug, Kate. 1988. An interview with Chick Stand. *Wide Angle* 20 (1–2): 106–37.

Haugan, Eingar. 1957/1969. The semantics of Icelandic orientation. In *Cognitive anthropology*, ed. S. A. Tylor, 330–42. New York: Holt, Reinhart and Winston.

Hauser-Schäublin, Brigitta. 1989. *Kulthäuser in Nordneuguinea* [Cult houses in northern New Guinea]. Berlin: Akademie-Verlag.

Hebdige, D. 1979. *Subculture: The meaning of style*. London: Methuen.

Heidegger, Martin. 1965. Building, dwelling, thinking. In *Poetry, language, thought*. New York: Harper and Row.

Heider, Karl G. 1976/2006. *Ethnographic film*. Austin: University of Texas Press.

———. 2007. Robert Gardner: The early years. In *Memories of the origins of ethnographic film*, ed. Beate Engelbrecht. New York: Peter Lang.

Heider, Karl. and Carol Hermer. 1995. *Films for anthropological teaching*. Washington, DC: American Anthropological Association.

Henare, Amiria. 2005a. *Museums, anthropology, and imperial exchange*. Cambridge: Cambridge University Press.

———. 2005b. *Nga Aho Tipuna* (Ancestral threads): Maori cloaks from New Zealand. In *Clothing as material culture*, ed. S. Küchler and D. Miller, 121–38. Oxford: Berg.

Henare, Amiria, Martin Holbraad, and Sari Wastell, eds. 2007. *Thinking through things: Theorising artifacts ethnographically*. London: Routledge.

Henley, Paul. 1985. British ethnographic film: Recent developments. *Anthropology Today* 1 (1): 5–17.

Herle, Anita. and Jude Philp. 1998. *Torres Strait islanders: An exhibition marking the centenary of the 1898 Cambridge Anthropological Exhibition*. Cambridge: Museum of Archaeology and Anthropology.

Herzfeld, Michael. 1987. *Anthropology through the looking-glass: Critical ethnography in the margins of Europe*. Cambridge: Cambridge University Press.

———. 1991. *A place in history: Social and monumental time in a Cretan town*. Princeton, NJ: Princeton University Press.

———. 2002. The absent presence: Discourses of crypto-colonialism. *South Atlantic Quarterly* 101: 899–926.

———. 2004. *The body impolitic: Artisans and artifice in the global hierarchy of value*. Chicago: University of Chicago Press.

———. 2005. *Cultural intimacy: Social poetics in the nation-state*. 2nd ed. New York: Routledge.

———. 2007. Envisioning skills: Insight, hindsight and second sight. In *Skilled visions*, ed. C. Grasseni, 207–18. Oxford: Berghahn.

———. 2009. *Evicted from eternity: The restructuring of modern Rome*. Chicago: University of Chicago Press.

Hethorn, J., and S. Kaiser. 1999. Youth style: Articulating cultural anxiety. *Visual Sociology*, 14: 109–25.

Hewes, Gordan. 1955. World distribution of certain postural habits. *American Ethnologist* 57 (2): 231–44.

Highlands, Delbert. 1990. What's indigenous? An essay on building. In *Vernacular architecture: Paradigms of environmental respon*, ed. Mete Turan, 31–62. Aldershot: Avebury.

Hill, Richard W., Sr. 1998. Developed identities: Seeing the stereotypes and beyond. In *Spirit capture*, ed. T. Johnson, 139–60. Washington, DC: Smithsonian Institution.

Himpele, Jeff. 1996. Film distribution as media: Mapping difference in the Bolivian cinemascape. *Visual Anthropology Review,* 12 (1): 47–66.

———. 2002. Arrival scenes: Complicity and media ethnography in the Bolivian public sphere. In *Media worlds: Anthropology on new terrain,* ed. F. Ginsburg, L. Abu-Lughod, and B. Larkin, 301–16. Berkeley: University of California Press.

———. 2007. *Circuits of culture: Media, politics and indigenous identity in the Andes.* Minneapolis: University of Minnesota Press.

Hinsley, Curtis M., Jr., and Bill Holm. 1976. A cannibal in the National Museum: The early career of Franz Boas in America, *American Anthropologist* 78:306–16.

Hirsch, Eric. 2004. "Techniques of vision": Photography, disco and renderings of present perception in highland Papua. *Journal of the Royal Anthropological Institute* 10 (1): 19–39.

Hirschon, Renée. 1989. *Heirs of the Greek catastrophe: The social life of Asia Minor refugees in Piraeus.* Oxford: Clarendon.

Hirschon, Renée, and Thakurdesai. 1970. Society, culture and spatial organization: An Athens community. *Ekistics* 178: 187–96.

Hitchcock, M., and L. Norris. 1995. *Bali, the imaginary museum: The photographs of Walter Spies and Beryl de Zoete.* Oxford: Oxford University Press.

Hobart, Mark. 2006. Just talk? Anthropological reflections on the object of media studies in Indonesia. *Asian Journal of Social Science* 34 (3): 492–519.

Hocart, Arthur Maurice. 1937. Cinematic anthropology. *Nature* 139, supplement, 13 March, 447–48.

Hockings, Paul, ed. 1975/2003. *Principles of visual anthropology.* The Hague: Mouton.

Hodgen, Margaret T. 1964. *Early anthropology in the sixteenth and seventeenth centuries.* Philadelphia: University of Pennsylvania Press.

Hollis, M., and S. Lukes, eds. 1982. *Rationality and relativism.* Oxford: Blackwell.

Holman, Nigel. 1996. Curating and controlling Zuni photographic images. *Curator* 39 (2): 108–22.

Hopkins, M. C. 2005. The cultural construction of self: Cloth, fashion, and agency in Africa. *Reviews in Anthropology* 34 (1): 79–101.

Horak, Jan-Christopher, ed. 1995. *Lovers of cinema.* Madison: University of Wisconsin Press.

Hoskins, J. 1989. Why do ladies sing the blues? Indigo dyeing, cloth production and gender symbolism in Kodi. In *Cloth and human experience,* ed. A. B. Weiner and J. Schneider, 141–73. Washington, DC: Smithsonian Institution Press.

Houtman, Gustaaf. 1988. Interview with Maurice Bloch. *Anthropology Today* 4 (1): 18–21.

Howard, A. 1988. Hypermedia and the future of ethnography. *Cultural Anthropology* 3 (3): 304–15.

Howes, David. 1991. *The varieties of sensory experience: A sourcebook in the anthropology of the senses.* Toronto: University of Toronto Press.

———. 2004. *Empire of the senses*. Oxford: Berg.

Hubbard, Jim, ed. 1994. *Shooting back from the reservation: A photographic view of life by Native American youth*. New York: New Press.

Hugh-Jones, Stephen. 1985. The Maloca: A world in a house. In *The hidden peoples of the Amazon*, ed. Elizabeth Carmichael, Stephen Hugh-Jones, Brian Moser, and Donald Tayler, 76–93. London: British Museum Publications.

Hughes, Stephen Putnam. 2005. House full: Film genre, exhibition and audiences in south India. *Indian Economic and Social History Review* 43 (1): 31–62.

Hughes-Freeland, Felicia. 2006. Tribes and tribulations: A response to Pat Caplan. *Anthropology Today* 22 (2): 22–23.

Hughes-Freeland, F., S. Pink, G. Bowman. and C. Grasseni. 2007. Editors' introduction. *Visual Anthropology* 20 (2): 91–101.

Humphrey, Caroline. 1974. Inside a Mongolian tent. *New Society,* 31 October, 273–75.

Hutchins, E. 1986. Mediation and automatization. *Quarterly Newsletter of the Laboratory of Comparative Human Cognition* 8 (2): 47–58.

———. 1993. Learning to navigate, understanding practice. In *Perspectives on activity and context*, ed. S. Chaiklin and J. Lave, 35–63. Cambridge: Cambridge University Press.

———. 1995. *Cognition in the wild*. Cambridge, MA: MIT Press.

Hutchins, E., and T. Klausen. 1998. Distributed cognition in an airline cockpit. In *Cognition and communication at work*, ed. Y. Engeström and D. Middleton, 15–34. Cambridge: Cambridge University Press.

Hutnyk, John. 1994. Comparative anthropology and Evans-Pritchard's African photography. *Critique of Anthropology* 10 (1): 81–102.

Hymes, Dell. 1971. Competence and performance in linguistic theory. In *Language acquisition models and methods*, ed. R Huxley and E. Ingram, 3–28. New York: Academic Press.

Igliori, Paola, ed. 1996. *American magus: Harry Smith, a modern alchemist*. New York: In and Out Press.

Im Thurn, E. 1896. Anthropological uses of the camera, *Journal of the Anthropological Institute* 22:184–203.

Ingold, Timothy. 1993a. Tool-use, sociality and intelligence. In *Tools, language and cognition in human evolution*, ed. K. R. Gibson and T. Ingold, 429–45. Cambridge: Cambridge University Press.

———. 1993b. Technology, language, intelligence: A reconsideration of basic concepts. In *Tools, language and cognition in human evolution*, ed. K. R. Gibson and T. Ingold, 449–72. Cambridge: Cambridge University Press.

———. 1993c. The art of translation in a continuous world. In *Beyond boundaries: Understanding, translation and anthropological discourse*, ed. G. Pálsson, 210–30. London: Berg.

———. 2000. *The perception of the environment: Essays in livelihood, dwelling and skill*. London: Routledge.

———. 2001. From the transmission of representations to the education of attention. In *Mind, evolution and cultural transmission*, ed. H. Whitehouse, 113–53. Cambridge: Cambridge University Press.

———. 2007. *Lines: A brief history*. London: Routledge.

Innes, R. A. 1957. *Costumes of Upper Burma and the Shan states in the collections of the Bankfield Museum, Halifax*. Halifax: Halifax Museums.

Isaac, Gwyniera. 2007. *Mediating knowledges: Origins of a museum for the Zuni people*. Tucson: University of Arizona Press.

Jablonko, Allison. 1968. Dance and daily activities among the Maring people of New Guinea. PhD dissertation, Department of Anthropology, Columbia University, New York.

———. 1991. Patterns of daily life in the dance of the Maring of New Guinea. *Visual Anthropology* 4:367–77.

———. 2001. An intersection of disciplines: The development of choreometrics in the 1960's. Unpublished paper prepared for the Origins of Visual Anthropology Conference, Göttingen, Germany, June 21–25.

———. 2008. Seeing ideas. In *Imparare a guardare*, ed. C. Grasseni. Milano: Franco Angeli.

Jacknis, Ira. 1984. Franz Boas and photography. *Studies in Visual Communication* 10 (1): 2–60.

———. 1987. The picturesque and the scientific: Franz Boas' plan for anthropological filmmaking. *Visual Anthropology* 1 (1): 59–64.

———. 1988. Margaret Mead and Gregory Bateson in Bali: Their use of photography and film. *Cultural Anthropology* 13 (2): 166–77.

———. 1992. In search of the image maker: James Mooney as ethnographic photographer. *Visual Anthropology* 3 (2): 179–212.

———. 1996. The ethnographic object and the object of ethnology in the early career of Franz Boas. In *Volksgeist as method and ethic: Essays on Boasian ethnography and the German anthropological tradition*, ed. George W. Stocking. Madison: University of Wisconsin Press.

———. 2000. Visualizing Kwakwaka'wakw tradition: The films of William Heick. *BC Studies*, no. 125–26, 99–146.

———. 2002. *The storage box of tradition: Kwakiutl art, anthropologists, and museums, 1881–1981*. Washington, DC: Smithsonian Institution Press.

Jackson, H. O. and G. S. O'Neal. 1994. Dress and appearance responses to perceptions of aging. *Clothing and Textiles Research Journal* 12 (4): 8–15.

Jackson, Michael. 1989. *Paths toward a clearing*. Bloomington: Indiana University Press.

Jackson, Renata. 2002. *The modernist poetics and experimental film practice of Maya Deren, 1917–1961*. Lewiston: Edwin Mellen Press.

Jahn, Jens, ed. 1983. *Colon: Das schwarze Bild vom weissen Mann*. Munich: Rogner & Bernhard.

Jagger, Angela, and Susan Bordo, eds. 1989. *Gender/body/ knowledge: Feminist reconstructions of being and knowing*. New Brunswick, NJ: Rutgers University Press.

Jakobson, Roman. 1960. Linguistics and poetics. In *Style in language*, ed. Thomas A. Sebeok, 350–77. Cambridge, MA: MIT Press.

James, David. 2005. *The most typical avant-garde: History and geography of minor cinemas in Los Angeles*. Berkeley: University of California Press.

James, W. 1981. *Pragmatism: A new name for some old ways of thinking*. Indianapolis: Hackett. (Orig. pub. 1907.)

Jameson, Fredric. 1992. *The geopolitical aesthetic: Cinema and space in the world system*. London: British Film Institute.

Jasanoff, S. 1998. The eye of everyman: Witnessing DNA in the Simpson trial. *Social Studies of Science* 28 (5/6): 713–40. Special issue: Contested identities: Science, law and forensic practice.

Jay, M. 1993. *Downcast eyes. The denigration of vision in twentieth-century French thought*. Berkeley: University of California Press.

Jenkins, Henry. 2007. *Convergence culture: Where old and new media collide*. New York: NYU Press.

Jenkins, Timothy. 1994. Fieldwork and the perception of everyday life. *Man*, n.s., 29:433–55.

Jhala, Jayasinjhi. 1996. The unintended audience. In *The construction of the viewer*, ed. P. I. Crawford and S. B. Halfsteinsson, 207–28. Højbjerg, Denmark: Intervention Press.

Jirousek, C. A. 1996. Dress as social policy: Change in women's dress in a southwestern Turkish village. *Dress* 23:47–62.

Johnson, D. C., and H. B. Foster, eds. 2007. *Dress sense: Emotional and sensory experiences of the body and clothes*. Oxford: Berg.

Johnson, Mark. 1987. *The body in the mind: The bodily basis of meaning, imagination and reasoning*. Chicago: University of Chicago Press.

Jonaitis, Aldona, ed. 1995. *A wealth of thought: Franz Boas on Native American art*. Seattle: University of Washington Press.

Jones, Caroline, ed. 2006. *Sensorium: Embodied experience, technology, and contemporary art*. Cambridge, MA: MIT Press.

Joshi, O. P. 1992. Continuity and change in Hindu women's dress. In *Dress and gender: Making and meaning in cultural contexts*, ed. R. Barnes and J. B. Eicher, 214–31. Oxford: Berg.

Josselin de Jong, P. E. De. 1977. *Structural anthropology in the Netherlands*. The Hague: Nijhoff.

Joyce, Conor. 2002. *Carl Einstein in Documents*. New York: Xlibris.

Joyce, R. A. 2005. Archaeology of the body. *Annual Review of Anthropology* 34:139–58.

Joyce, Rosemary, and Susan Gillespie. 2000. *Beyond kinship: Social and material reproduction in house societies*. Philadelphia: University of Pennsylvania Press.

Kaeppler, Adrienne. 1967. *The structure of Tongan dance*. PhD dissertation, University of Hawai'i.

———. 1978. The dance in anthropological perspective. *Annual Review of Anthropology* 7:31–39.

Kahlenberg, M. H. 1979. *Rites of passage: Textiles of the Indonesian archipelago*. San Diego: Mingei Museum of World Folk Art.

Kaiser, S. B. 1989. Clothing and the social organization of gender perception: A developmental approach. *Clothing and Textiles Research Journal* 7 (2): 46–56.

Kapfer, R., W. Petermann, and R. Thoms, eds. 1989. *Ritual von Leben und Tod: Robert Gardner und seine Filme*. Munich: Trickster Verlag.

Karp, Ivan, and Steven D. Levine, eds. 1991. *Exhibiting cultures: The poetics and politics of museum display*. Washington, DC: Smithsonian Institution Press.

Katz, Elihu, Yosefa Loshitsky, John Durham Peters, Tamar Liebes, and Avril Orloff, eds. 2003. Thoughts on Mulvey's "Visual pleasure in the age of cultural studies." *Polity* 35:248–59. (Special issue: Canonic texts in media research: Are there any? Should there be? How about these?)

Kawashima, Chuji. 1986. *Minka: Traditional houses of rural Japan*. Tokyo: Kodansha International.

Kazazis, Kostas. 1982. Partial linguistic autobiography of a schizoglossic linguist. *Glossologia* [Athens] 1:109–17.

Keali'inohomoku, Joann W. 1976. Caveat on causes and correlations. *CORD News* 6 (2): 20–24.

———. 1979. Dance and human history: A film by Alan Lomax (review essay). *Ethnomusicology* 25 (1): 169–76.

Keane, W. 2005. Signs are not the garb of meaning: On the social analysis of material things. In *Materiality*, ed. D. Miller. Durham, NC: Duke University Press.

Keane, Webb. 1991. Delegated voice: Ritual speech, risk, and the making of marriage alliances in Anakalang. *American Ethnologist* 18 (2): 311–30.

Keller, Janet, and Charles Keller. 1996. *Cognition and tool use: The blacksmith at work*. Cambridge: Cambridge University Press.

Kendall, L. 1985. Ritual silks and kowtow money: The bride as daughter-in-law in Korean wedding rituals. *Ethnology* 24: 253–69.

Kendall, L., Ross Miller, and B. Mathé. 1997. *Drawing shadows to stone*. Seattle: University of Washington Press.

Kendon, Adam. 1972. Some relationships between body motion and speech: An analysis of an example. In *Studies in dyadic communication*, ed. Aaron W. Siegman and Benjamin Pope, 177–210. Elmsford: Pergamon Press.

———. 1980. Gesticulation and speech: Two aspects of the process of utterance. In *The relationship of verbal and nonverbal communication*, ed. M. R. Key, 207–27. The Hague: Mouton.

———. 1982. The study of gesture: Some observations on its history. *Semiotic Inquiry* 2:45–62.

———. 1983. Gestures and speech: How they interact. In *Non-verbal communication*, ed. J. M. Wieman and R. P. Harrison, 2:13–46. Beverly Hills: Sage.

———. 1988 *Sign languages of Aboriginal Australia: Cultural semiotics and communicative perspectives*. Cambridge: Cambridge University Press.

———. 1997. Gesture. *Annual Review of Anthropology* 26:109–28.

———. 2004. *Gesture: Visible action as utterance*. Cambridge: Cambridge University Press.

Kent, K. 1983. *Pueblo Indian textiles: A living tradition*. Albuquerque: University of New Mexico Press.

Kent, Susan, ed. 1990. *Domestic architecture and the use of space: An interdisciplinary cross-cultural study*. Cambridge: Cambridge University Press.

Khan, N. 1992. Asian women's dress: From burquah to bloggs—changing clothes for changing times. In *Chic thrills: A fashion reader*, ed. J. Ash and E. Wilson, 61–74. London: Pandora Press.

Kirshenblatt-Gimblett, Barbara. 1998. *Destination culture: Tourism, museums, and heritage*. Berkeley: University of California Press.

Kis-Jovak, Jowa, Reimar Schefold, Hetty Nooy-Palm, and Ursula Schultz-Dornburg. 1988. *Banua Toraja: Changing patterns in architecture and symbolism among the Sa'danToraja, Sulawesi, Indonesia*. Amsterdam: Royal Tropical Institute.

Klima, Alan. 2002. *The funeral casino: Meditation, massacre and exchange with the dead in Thailand*. Princeton, NJ: Princeton University Press.

Knapp, Ronald. 1989. *China's vernacular architecture: House form and culture*. Honolulu: University of Hawai'i Press.

Knappet, Carl. 2005. *Thinking through material culture: An interdisciplinary perspective*. Philadelphia: University of Pensnsylvania Press.

———. 1999. *China's living houses: Folk beliefs, symbols and household ornamentation*. Honolulu: University of Hawai'i Press.

———. 2000a. *China's old dwellings*. Honolulu: University of Hawai'i Press.

———. 2000b. *China's walled cities*. Honolulu: University of Hawai'i Press.

———. 2003. *Asia's old dwellings: Tradition, resilience and change*. Honolulu: University of Hawai'i Press.

Knapp, Ronald, and Kai-Yin Lo. 2005. *House home family: Living and being Chinese*. Honolulu: University of Hawai'i Press.

Knappet, Carl. 2005. *Thinking through material culture: An interdisciplinary perspective*. Philadelphia: University of Pennsylvania Press.

Knight, Alan. 1990. Racism, revolution and the revolutionary state in Mexico, 1910–1940. In *The idea of race in Latin America, 1870–1940*, ed. Richard Graham. Austin: University of Texas Press.

Kopytoff, I. 1986. The cultural biography of things. In *The social life of things: Commodities in cultural perspective*, ed. Arun Appadurai, 64–91. Cambridge: Cambridge University Press.

Koselleck, Reinhart. 2004. *Futures past: On the semantics of historical time*. Trans. Keith Tribe. New York: Columbia University Press. (Orig. pub. 1979.)

Kostof, Spiro. 1985. *A history of architecture, settings and rituals*. New York: Oxford University Press.

Kramer, Fritz. 1993. *The red fez: Art and spirit possession in Africa*. London: Verso. (Orig. pub. 1986.)

Kratz, Corinne. 2002. *The ones that are wanted: Communication and the politics of representation in a photographic exhibition*. Berkeley: University of California Press.

Krauss, Rosalind. 1982. Photography's discursive spaces. *Art Journal* 42 (4): 311–19.

Kries, Mateo, and Alexander von Vegesack, eds. 2000. *Grow your own house: Simón Vélez and bamboo architecture*. Weil-am-Rhein: Vitra Design Museum.

Krinsky, Carol Herselle. 1996. *Contemporary Native American architecture: Cultural regeneration and creativity*. New York: Oxford University Press.

Krouse, M. B. 1999. Gift giving, identity, and transformation: The AIDS Memorial Quilt. *International Journal of Sexuality and Gender Studies* 4 (3): 241–56.

Krupat, Arnold. 1990. Irony in anthropology: The work of Franz Boas. In *Modernist anthropology: From fieldwork to text*, ed. Marc Manganaro. Princeton, NJ: Princeton University Press.

Kubler, George. 1991. *Esthetic recognition of ancient Amerindian art*. New Haven, CT: Yale University Press.

Küchler, S. 2003. The poncho and the quilt: Material Christianity in the Cook Islands. In *Clothing the Pacific*, ed. C. Colchester, 97–116. Oxford: Berg.

———. 2005. Why are there quilts in Polynesia? In *Clothing as material culture*, ed. S. Küchler and D. Miller, 175–92. Oxford: Berg.

Küchler, S., and D. Miller, eds. 2005. *Clothing as material culture*. Oxford: Berg.

Kuhn, Annette. 2002. *An everyday magic: Cinema and cultural memory*. London: I. B. Tauris.

Kulick, D., and M. Wilson. 2002. Rambo's wife saves the day: Subjugating the gaze and subverting the narrative in a Papua New Guinean swamp. In *The anthropology of media: A reader*, ed. Kelly Askew and Richard Wilk, 270–86. London: Blackwell.

Kuper, H. 1973. Costume and identity. *Comparative Studies in Society and History* 15 (3): 348–67.

Kymlicka, Will. 1995. *Multicultural citizenship: A liberal theory of minority rights*. Oxford: Clarendon Press.

La Barre, Weston. 1947. The cultural basis of emotions and gestures. *Journal of Personality* 16:49–68.

Lakoff, George. 1987. *Women, fire, and dangerous things*. Chicago: University of Chicago Press.

Lalvani, Suren. 1996. *Photography, vision and the production of modern bodies*. Albany: State University of New York Press.

Lancret, Nathalie. 1997. *La maison balinaise en secteur urbain: Etude ethno-architecturale*. Paris: Association Archipel.

Landzelius, Kyra, ed. 2006. *Going native on the net: Indigenous cyber-activism and virtual diasporas over the World Wide Web*. London: Routledge.

Langer, Suzanne. 1942. *Philosophy in a new key*. New York: New American Library.

Langton, Marcia. 1993. *Well, I heard it on the radio and I saw it on the television: An essay for the Australian Film Commission on the politics and aesthetics of filmmaking by and about Aboriginal people and things*. Sydney: Australian Film Commission.

Larkin, Brian. 1998–1999. Theaters of the profane: Cinema and colonial urbanism. *Visual Anthropology Review* 14 (2): 46–62.

————. 2008. *Signal and noise: Media, infrastructure and urban culture in Nigeria.* Durham, NC: Duke University Press.

Larson, Heidi. 1981. Photography that listens. *Visual Anthropology* 1:415–32.

————. 1993. Anthropology exposed: Photography and anthropology since *Balinese Character. Yearbook of Visual Anthropology* 1:13–27.

Lathrop, S. 2004. Bringing digital media into anthropology classrooms. *Anthropology News* (May), http://www.aaanet.org/press/an/0405aa-news.htm (accessed 5 September 2008).

Latour, B. 1986. Visualization and cognition: Thinking with eyes and hands. *Knowledge and Society: Studies in the Sociology of Culture Past and Present* 6:1–40.

————. 1990. *Drawing things together: Representation in scientific practice*, ed. M. Lynch and S. Woolga. Cambridge, MA: MIT Press.

————. 1991. *Nous n'avons jamais été modernes.* Paris: Editions La Découverte.

————. 1995. The "Pedofil" of Boa Vista: A photo-philosophical montage. *Common Knowledge* 4 (1): 144–87. (Also published, with revisions, as Circulating reference: Sampling the soil in the Amazon forest. In *Pandora's hope: Essays on the reality of science studies*, ed. B. Latour. Cambridge, MA: Harvard University Press, 1999.)

Latour, B., and S. Woolgar. 1979. *Laboratory life: The social construction of scientific facts.* London: Sage.

Latukefu, A. 2006. Remote indigenous communities in Australia: Questions of access, information, and self-determination. In *Going native on the net: Indigenous cyber-activism and virtual diasporas over the world wide web,* ed. K. Landzelius, 1–42. London: Routledge.

Lave, Jean M., and Etienne Wenger. 1991. *Situated learning: Legitimate peripheral participation.* Cambridge: Cambridge University Press.

Layton, Robert. 1991. *The anthropology of art.* Cambridge: Cambridge University Press.

————. 2003. Art and agency: A reassessment. *Journal of the Royal Anthropological Institute* 9 (3): 447–64.

Leimbacher, Irena. 1998a. An interview with Chick Strand. *Discourse* 20 (1–2): 140–51.

————. 1998b. An introduction to the films of Chick Strand. *Discourse* 20 (1–2): 127–39.

Lenoir, T., ed. 1998. *Inscribing science: Scientific texts and the materiality of communication.* Stanford, CA: Stanford University Press.

Lentz, C. 1995. Ethnic conflict and changing dress codes: A case study of an Indian migrant village in highland Ecuador. In *Dress and ethnicity*, ed. J. B. Eicher, 269–93. Oxford: Berg.

Leuthold, Steven. 1998. *Indigenous aesthetics.* Seattle: University of Washington Press.

Lévi-Strauss, Claude. 1963. Split representation in the art of Asia and America. In *Structural anthropology.* New York: Basic Books

————. 1969. Do dual organizations exist? In *Structural Anthropology*, 132–63. Harmondsworth: Penguin.

————. 1983. *The way of the masks*. Trans. S. Modelski. London: Cape. (Orig. French pub. 1979.)

————. 1987. *Anthropology and myth: Lectures, 1951–1982*. Trans. R. Willis. Oxford: Blackwell. (Orig. French pub. 1984.)

Levinson, David, and M. Ember, eds. 1996. *Encyclopedia of cultural anthropology*. New York: Henry Holt and Company.

Lewis, E. O. 2003. *Timothy Asch and ethnographic film*. London: Routledge.

Lewis, E., and P. Lewis. 1984. *Peoples of the golden triangle*. London: Thames & Hudson.

Lewis-Harris, J. A. 2004. Not without a cost: Contemporary PNG art in the 21st century. *Visual Anthropology* 17 (3–4): 273–92.

Light, Nathan. 2008. *Intimate heritage: Creating Uyghur muqam song in Xinjiang*. Berlin: Lit Verlag.

Linnaeus, Carl. 1758. *Systema naturae*. 10th rev. ed. The Netherlands.

Linton, R. 1933. *The Tanala, a hill tribe of Madagascar*. Chicago: Field Museum.

Lippard, Lucy R., ed. 1992. *Partial recall*. New York: New Press.

Lips, Julius. 1966. *The savage hits back*. New York: University Books. (Orig. pub.: London: Lovat Dickinson; New Haven, CT: Yale University Press, 1937.)

Lock, Margaret. 1993. Cultivating the body: Anthropology and epistemologies of bodily practice and knowledge. *Annual Review of Anthropology* 22:133–55.

Loizos, Peter. 1980. Granada television's *Disappearing World* series: An appraisal. *American Anthropologist* 82:573–94.

————. 1993. *Innovation in ethnographic film: From innocence to self-consciousness*. Chicago: University of Chicago Press.

————. 2006. Sudanese engagements: Three films by Arthur Howes (1950–2004). *Visual Anthropology* 19 (3): 353–63.

Lomawaima, Tsianina. 1994. *They called it prairie light*. Lincoln: University of Nebraska Press.

Lomax, Alan. 1968. *Folk song style and culture*. Washington, DC: American Association for the Advancement of Science.

————. 1971. Choreometrics and ethnographic filmmaking. *Filmmakers' Newsletter* 4 (4): 22–30.

Low, Setha, and Denise Lawrence-Zúñiga, eds. 2003. *The anthropology of space and place: Locating culture*. Oxford: Blackwell.

Lowe, J. W., and G. E. D. Lowe. 1982. Cultural pattern and process: A story of stylistic change in women's dress. *American Anthropologist* 84 (3): 521–44.

Lowis, C. C. 1906. *A note on the Palaungs of Hsipaw and Tawpeng: Ethnographical survey of India, Burma, no. 1*. Rangoon: Government Printing.

Lozada, E. 2006. Framing globalisations: Wedding pictures, funeral photography, and family snapshots in rural China. *Visual Anthropology* 19 (1): 87–103.

Lull, James. 1991. *Inside family viewing*. London: Routledge.

Lutkehaus, Nancy. 2004. Man, a course of study: Situating Tim Asch's pedagogy and ethnographic films. In *Timothy Asch and ethnographic film*, ed. E. D. Lewis. London: Routledge.

Lydall, Jean. 1992. Filming the women who smile. In *Ethnographic film aesthetics and narrative tradition*, ed. P. I. Crawford and J. K. Simonsen, 141–58. Arhaus, Denmark: Intervention Press.

Lydon, Jane. 2005. *Eye contact: Photographing indigenous Australians*. Durham, NC: Duke University Press.

Lynch, A., D. F. Detzner, and J. B. Eicher. 1995. Hmong American New Year rituals: Generational bonds through dress. *Clothing and Textiles Research Journal* 13 (2): 111–20.

———. 1996. Transmission and reconstruction of gender through dress: Hmong American New Year rituals. *Clothing and Textiles Research Journal* 14 (4): 257–66.

Lynch, M. 1985. *Art and artifact in laboratory science: A study of shop work and shop talk in research laboratory*. London: Routledge & Kegan Paul.

———. 1990. The externalized retina: Selection and mathematization in the visual documentation of objects in the life sciences. In *Representation in scientific practice*, ed. M. Lynch and S. Woolgar, 153–86. Cambridge, MA: MIT Press.

———. 2001. Ethnomethodology and the logic of practice. In *The practice turn in contemporary theory*, ed. T. Schatzki, K. Knorr Cetina, and E. von Savigny, 131–48. London: Routledge.

Lynch, M., and S. Woolgar, eds. 1990. *Representation in scientific practice*. Cambridge, MA: MIT Press.

Maas, Pierre, and Geert Mommersteeg. 1992. *Djenne: Chef-d'oeuvre architectural*. Bamako: Université de Technologie; Eindhoven: Institut des Sciences Humaines.

Macdonald, Charles. 1987. *De la hutte au palais: Sociétés "à maison" en Asie du sud-est Insulaire*. Paris: CNRS.

MacDonald, Gaynor. 2003. Photos in Wiradjuri biscuit tins: Negotiating relatedness and validating colonial histories. *Oceania* 73 (4): 225–42.

MacDonald, Scott. 1978. Hollis Frampton's *Hapax Legomena*. *After-Image* 5:8–13.

———. 1995. Avant-garde at the Flaherty. *Wide Angle* 17 (1–4): 257–68.

———. 1996. The challenge of television for anthropology. Talk delivered at Television and Anthropology and the Anthropology of Television, 5th International Festival of Ethnographic Film, University of Kent, 1996. http://www.unimainz.de/Organisationen/SORC/fileadmin/texte_lydall/Anthropology_20for_20TV.pdf (accessed 6 March 2007).

———. 2002. *Cinema 16: Documents toward a history of the Film Society*. Philadelphia: Temple University Press.

MacDougall, David. 1975. Beyond observational cinema. In *Principles of visual anthropology*, ed. Paul Hockings. Paris: Mouton.

———. 1978. Ethnographic film: Failure and promise. *Annual Review of Anthropology* 7:405–26.

———. 1992a. Complicities of style. In *Film as ethnography*, ed. Peter Ian Crawford and David Turton. Manchester: Manchester University Press.

———. 1992b. Photo hierarchicus: Signs and mirrors in Indian photography. *Visual Anthropology* 5 (2): 103–29.

———. 1997. The visual in anthropology. In *Rethinking visual anthropology*, ed. Marcus Banks and Howard Morphy, 276–95. New Haven, CT: Yale University Press.

———. 1998. *Transcultural cinema*. Princeton, NJ: Princeton University Press.

———. 2006. *The corporeal image: Film, ethnography, and the senses*. Princeton, NJ: Princeton University Press.

MacFarlane A. 2004. Forty years work with computers and visual media: A preliminary overview written in November 2004. http://www.alanmacfarlane .com/TEXTS/computerland.pdf (accessed 9 February 2007).

Mackridge, Peter. 1985. *The modern Greek language: A descriptive analysis of standard modern Greek*. Oxford: Clarendon Press.

MacMahon, A. R. 1876. *The Karens of the Golden Chersonese*. London: Harrison.

Maddigan, L. 2003. Kachin textiles. In *Textiles from Burma*, ed. E. Dell and S. Dudley, 69–75. London: Philip Wilson Publishers.

Mageo, J. 1994. Hair dos and don'ts: Hair symbolism and sexual history in Samoa. *MAN* 29:407–23.

Mahon, Maureen. 2000. The visible evidence of cultural producers. *Annual Review of Anthropology* 29:467–92.

Malinowski, Bronislaw. 1922. *Argonauts of the western Pacific*. London: Routledge & Kegan Paul.

———. 1929. Practical anthropology. *Africa* 2:22–38.

———. 1935. *Coral gardens and their magic*. London: Allen & Unwin.

Mallery, Garrick. 1880a. *Introduction to the study of sign language among the North American Indians as illustrating the gesture speech of mankind*. Washington, DC: Smithsonian Institution, Bureau of American Ethnology.

———. 1880b *A collection of gesture signs and signals of the North American Indians, with some comparisons*. Washington, DC: Government Printing office.

———. 1881. Sign language among North American Indians compared with that among other peoples and deafmutes. In *First annual report of the Bureau of American Ethnology for 1879–80*, 269–552. Washington, DC.

Man, E. H. 1883. On the aboriginal inhabitants of the Andaman Islands. *Journal of the Anthropological Institute* 12:69–175, 327–434.

Manicus, Peter T. 2006. *A realist philosophy of social science*. Cambridge: Cambridge University Press.

Mankekar, Purnima. 1999. *Screening culture, viewing politics: An ethnography of television, womanhood and nation in postcolonial India*. Durham, NC: Duke University Press.

———. 2002. National texts and gendered lives: An ethnography of television viewers in a north Indian city. In *The anthropology of media: A reader*, ed. Kelly Askew and Richard Wilk. London: Blackwell, 299–322. (Orig pub.: *American Ethnologist* 20, no. 3 [1993].)

Marazzi, A. 2002. *Antropologia della visione*. Roma: Carocci.

Marcus, A. 2006. *Nanook of the North* as primal drama. *Visual Anthropology* 9 (3–4): 201–22.

Marcus, George. 1996. Introduction. In *Connected: Engagements with media*, ed. G. Marcus, 1–18. Late Editions 3. Chicago: University of Chicago Press.

———. 1998. A report on two initiatives in experiments with ethnography a decade after the "writing culture" critique. *Anthropological Journal on European Cultures* 7 (1): 9–24.

Marcus, George, and Michael M. J. Fischer. 1986. *Anthropology as cultural critique: An experimental moment in the human sciences*. Chicago: University of Chicago Press.

Marcus, George E., and Fred Myers, eds. 1995. *The traffic in culture: Refiguring art and anthropology*. Berkeley: University of California Press.

Marshall, H. I. 1922/1997. *The Karen people of Burma: A study in anthropology and ethnology*. Bangkok: White Lotus.

Marshall, John. 1993. Filming and learning. In *The cinema of John Marshall*, ed. Jay Ruby. New York: Harwood Academic Publishers.

Marshall, Lorna. 1965. The !Kung bushmen of the Kalahari Desert. In *Peoples of Africa*, ed. J. Gibbs Jr., 241–78. New York: Holt, Rinehart and Winston.

Martin, Emily. 1988. *The woman in the body*. Boston: Beacon.

Martinez, D. 1995. Naked divers: A case of identity and dress in Japan. In *Dress and Ethnicity*, ed. J. B. Eicher, 79–94. Oxford: Berg.

Martinez Perez, A. 2007. The rhythm of our dreams: A proposal for an applied visual anthropology. In *Visual interventions*, ed. S. Pink. Oxford: Berghahn.

Martinez, W. 1990. Critical studies and visual anthropology: Aberrant versus anticipated readings of ethnographic film. *Commission for Visual Anthropology Review*, Spring, 34–47.

———. 1992. Who constructs anthropological knowledge? Toward a theory of ethnographic film spectatorship. In *Film as ethnography*, ed. Peter Crawford and David Turton, 131–61. Manchester: Manchester University Press.

———. 1995. The challenge of a pioneer: Tim Asch, otherness, and film reception. *Visual Anthropology Review* 11 (1): 53–82.

———. 1996. Deconstructing the "viewer": From ethnography of the visual to critique of the occult. In *The construction of the viewer: Media ethnography and the anthropology of audiences*, ed. P. Crawford and S. B. Hafsteinsson, 69–100. Proceedings from NAFA 3. Hojbjerg, Denmark: Intervention Press.

———. 2004. Tim Asch, otherness and film reception. In *Timothy Asch and ethnographic film*, ed. P. Crawford and S. Hafsteinsson. London: Routledge.

Masayesva, Victor, Jr. 1995. The emerging Native American aesthetics in film and video. *Felix: A Journal of Arts and Media* 2 (1): 156–61.

Mascia-Lees, F. E., and P. Sharpe, eds. 1992. *Tattoo, torture, mutilation, and adornment: The denaturalization of the body in culture and text.* Albany: SUNY Press.

Mason, F. 1868. On dwellings, work of art, c of the Karens. *Journal of the Asiatic Society of Bengal* 37 (3): 125–69.

Mau, Leonore. 1976. *Xango: Die afroamerikanischen Religionen I—Bahia, Haiti, Trinidad.* Texte Hubert Fichte. Frankfurt am Main: Fischer.

Mauss, Marcel. 1934. Les techniques du corps. *Journal de Psychologie* 32 (3–4). Reprinted in Mauss, *Sociologie et anthropologie* (Paris: PUF, 1950).

———. 1935/1979. Techniques of the body. In *Sociology and psychology: Essays*, 95–123. London: Routledge & Kegan Paul.

Maxwell, R. 1990. *Textiles of Southeast Asia: Tradition, trade, and transformation.* Melbourne: Oxford University Press.

Mayne, Judith. 1993. *Cinema and spectatorship.* London: Routledge.

Mazzarella, William. 2003. *Shoveling smoke: Advertising and globalization in contemporary India.* Durham, NC: Duke University Press.

McCormick, Matt. 2008. Peripheral Produce catalogue. http://www.peripheralproduce.com/catalog.php (accessed 18 August 2008).

McNeill, David, ed. 2000. *Language and gesture.* Language, Culture and Cognition series, ed. Stephen C. Levinson. Max Plank Institute for Psycho-linguistics, Nijmegan. Cambridge: Cambridge University Press.

Mcquail, Dennis. 1997. *Audience analysis.* Beverly Hills: Sage.

McVeigh, B. J. 2000. *Wearing ideology: State, schooling and self-presentation in Japan.* Oxford: Berg.

Mead, Margaret. 1928/1959. *Coming of age in Samoa.* New York: Mentor Books.

———. 1975. Visual anthropology in a discipline of words. In *Principles of visual anthropology*, ed. Paul Hockings, 3–10. The Hague: Mouton.

———. 1977. *Letters from the field, 1925–1975.* New York: Harper & Row.

Meadows, Michael, and Helen Molnar. 2001. *Songlines to satellites: Indigenous communications in Australia, the South Pacific, and Canada.* Leichardt: Pluto Press.

Mellancamp, Patricia. 1990. *Indiscretions: Avant-garde film, video and feminism.* Bloomington: Indiana University Press.

Merleau-Ponty, M. 1962. *The phenomenology of perception.* Trans. C. Smith. London: Routledge & Kegan Paul.

Messick, B. 1987. Subordinate discourse: Women, weaving and gender relations in North Africa. *American Ethnologist* 14:20–35.

Michaelis, Anthony R. 1955. *Research films in biology, anthropology, psychology, and medicine.* New York: Academic Press.

Michaels, Eric. 1986. *The Aboriginal invention of television in central Australia, 1982–1985.* Canberra: Australian Institute of Aboriginal Studies, Institute Report.

————. 1991. A primer of restrictions on picture-taking in traditional areas of Aboriginal Australia. *Visual Anthropology* 4 (3–4): 259–75.

————. 1994. *Bad Aboriginal art: Tradition, media and technological horizons*. Minneapolis: University of Minnesota Press.

Michaels, Eric, with Frances Jupurrurla Kelly. 1984. The social organization of an Aboriginal video workplace. *Australian Aboriginal Studies* 1:26–34.

Michelman, S. O. and J. B. Eicher. 1995. Dress and gender in Kalabari women's societies. *Clothing and Textiles Research Journal* 13 (2): 121–30.

Miller, D. 2005. Introduction. In *Clothing as material culture*, ed. S. Küchler and D. Miller, 1–19. Oxford: Berg.

Miller, Daniel, and Don Slater. 2000. *The Internet: An ethnographic approach*. Oxford: Berg.

Miller, D. P., and P. H. Reill, eds. 1996. *Visions of empire: Voyages, botany, and representations of nature*. Cambridge: Cambridge University Press.

Miller, K. A. 1997. Dress: Private and secret self-expression. *Clothing and Textiles Research Journal* 15 (4): 223–34.

Mills, J., and S. Sen, eds. 2004. *Confronting the body: The politics of physicality in colonial and post-colonial India*. London: Anthem Press.

Mita, Merata. 1995. Opening comments. *Felix: A Journal of Arts and Media* 2 (1): 152–53.

Mitchell, W. J. T. 1986. *Iconology: Image, text, ideology*. Chicago: University of Chicago Press.

————. 1994. *Picture theory*. Chicago: University of Chicago Press.

Moeller, Magdalena M., and Janina Dahlmanns, eds. 2002. *Emil Nolde in der Südsee*. Berlin: Brücke-Museum.

Moore, Henry. 1951. Tribal sculpture: A review of the exhibition at the Imperial Institute. *Man*, July, 96–97.

Moores, Shaun. 1993. *Interpreting audiences: The ethnography of media consumption*. London: Sage.

Morgan, Louis Henry. 1881/1965. *Houses and house life of the American aborigines*. Chicago: University of Chicago Press.

Morgan, William. 1988. *Prehistoric architecture in Micronesia*. Austin: University of Texas Press.

Morley, David. 1980. *The "nationwide" audience: Structure and decoding*. London: British Film Institute.

————. 1989. Changing paradigms in audience studies. In *Remote control*, ed. E. Seiter. London: Routledge.

————. 1992. Towards an ethnography of the television audience. In *Television, audiences and cultural studies*, 173–97. London: Routledge.

Morley, David, and K. Chen, eds. 1996. *Stuart Hall: Critical dialogues in cultural studies*. London: Routledge.

Morley, David, and Roger Silverstone. 1990. Domestic communication: Technologies and meanings. *Media Culture and Society* 12:31–55.

Morphy, Howard. 1994. The anthropology of art. In *Companion encyclopedia to anthropology*, ed. Tim Ingold, 648–85. London: Routledge.

———. 2005. Spencer and Gillen and the evolution of anthropological method. In *The photographs of Baldwin Spencer*, ed. Philip Batty, L. Allen, and J. Morton. Melbourne: Miegunyah Press/Museum Victoria.

———. 2007. *Becoming art: Exploring cross-cultural categories*. Oxford: Berg.

———. 2009. Art as a mode of action: Some problems with Gell's *Art and agency*. *Journal of Material Culture* 14 (5): 5–27.

Morphy, Howard, and Morgan Perkins. 2006. The anthropology of art: A reflection on its history and contemporary practice. In *The anthropology of art: A reader*, ed. Howard Morphy and Morgan Perkins. Oxford: Blackwell.

Morris, W. F. 1986. Maya time warps. *Archaeology* 39:52–59.

Morton, Chris. 2005. The anthropologist as photographer: Reading the monograph and reading the archive. *Visual Anthropology* 18 (18): 389–405.

Muenala, Alberto. 1995. Cinema as an instrument for indigenous people's identity. *Felix: A Journal of Arts and Media* 2 (1): 154–56.

Mulvey, Laura. 1975. Visual pleasure and narrative cinema. *Screen* 6 (3): 6–18.

Munn, Nancy D. 1973. *Walbiri iconography: Graphic representation and cultural symbolism in a central Australian society*. Ithaca, NY: Cornell University Press.

Murphy, Patrick, and Marwan Kraidy. 2003. Towards an ethnographic approach to global media studies. In *Global media studies: Ethnographic perspectives*, ed. Patrick Murphy and Marwan Kraidy. London: Routledge.

Murra, J. 1962. Cloth and its function in the Inca state. *American Anthropologist* 64:710–28.

Murray, Stuart. 2008. *Images of dignity: Barry Barclay and fourth cinema*. Wellington: Huia Publishers.

Mustafa, Hudita Nura. 2002. Portraits of modernity: Fashioning selves in Dakarois popular photography. In *Images and empires: Visuality and colonial and post-colonial Africa*, ed. P. Landau and D. Kaspin, 172–92. Berkeley: University of California Press.

Myers, Fred. 1988. Cycle by Robert Ascher. *American Anthropologist* 90 (1): 245–46.

Nabokov, Peter, and Robert Easton. 1989. *Native American architecture*. New York: Oxford University Press.

Neimann, Catrina. 1980. An introduction to the notebook of Maya Deren, 1947. *October*, no. 14, 3–15.

Netz, R. 1999. *The shaping of deduction in Greek mathematics: A study in cognitive history*. Cambridge: Cambridge University Press.

———. 2004. *Barbed wire: An ecology of modernity*. Middletown, CT: Wesleyan University Press.

Neumann, Klaus. 1991. Hubert Fichte as ethnographer. *Cultural Anthropology* 6 (3): 263–84.

Nichols, Bill. 1991. *Representing reality: Issues and concepts in documentary*. Bloomington: University of Indiana Press.

———. 1993. The ethnographer's tale. In *Blurred boundaries*, 63–91. Blooming-ton: Indiana University Press.

———. 2004. What really happened: A reassessment of the *Ax Fight*. In *Timothy Ash and ethnographic film*, ed. E. D. Lewis. London: Routledge.

Niessen, Sandra. 1991. "More to it than meets the eye": Photo-elicitation amongst the Batak of Sumatra. *Visual Anthropology* 4:415–30.

———. 1993. *Batak cloth and clothing: A dynamic Indonesian tradition*. Oxford: Oxford University Press.

Niessen, S. A., A. M. Leshkowich, and C. Jones, eds. 2003. *Re-orienting fashion: The globalization of Asian dress*. Oxford: Berg.

Nimis, E. 2006. The rise of Nigerian women in the visual media. *Visual Anthropol-ogy* 19 (5): 423–41.

Noble, Andrea. 2001. *Tina Modotti: Image, texture, photography*. Albuquerque: University of New Mexico Press.

Nochlin, Linda. 1989. *The politics of vision: Essays on nineteenth-century art and society*. New York: Harper & Row.

Nooy-Palm, Hetty. 2001. The ancestral house of the Sa'dan Toeaja, Sulawesi, Indonesia. In *Architectural anthropology*, ed. Mari-Jose Amerlinck, 145–69. Westport, CT: Bergin and Garvey.

Nordström, A. 1994. Photographies of art and science. *Visual Sociology* 9 (2): 97–101. Special issue: Cape Breton 1952: The photographic vision of Tim Asch, ed. D. Harper.

Norman, D. 1988. *The psychology of everyday things*. New York: Basic Books.

———. 1993. *Things that make us smart*. Cambridge, MA: Perseus Books.

Norris, L. 2004. Shedding skins: The materiality of divestment in India. *Journal of Material Culture* 9 (1): 59–71.

———. 2005. Cloth that lies: The secrets of recycling in India. In *Clothing as material culture*, ed. S. Küchler and D. Miller, 83–106. Oxford: Berg.

Nugent, Stephen. 1997. Introduction: Brother, can you share a paradigm? In *An-thropology and cultural studies*, ed. Stephen Nugent and Chris Shore. London: Pluto Press.

Nugent, Stephen, and Chris Shore, eds. 1997. *Anthropology and cultural studies*. London: Pluto Press.

Nussbaum, Martha. 1995. *Poetic justice: The literary imagination and public life*. Boston: Beacon Press.

O'Connor, K. 2005. The other half: The material culture of new fibres. In *Cloth-ing as material culture*, ed. S. Küchler and D. Miller, 41–60. Oxford: Berg.

Odo, D. 2000. Anthropological boundaries and photographic frontiers: J. H. Green's visual language of salvage. In *Burma frontier Photographs, 1918–1935*, ed. E. Dell, 41–49. London: Merrell.

O'Donnell, Joan Kathryn. 1980. Review of Odyssey series. *Rain* 41:7–9 + 1.

Offler, Naomi. 1999. Shock, judgement and the stereotype: Exploring the role of the emotional response in ethnographic film reception. *SIGHTS—Visual*

Anthropology Forum. http://cc.joensuu.fi/sights/naomi.htm (accessed 7 March 2007).

Okely, J. 1998. Picturing and placing Constable country. In *Siting culture*, ed. K. Fog Olwig and K. Hastrup. London: Routledge.

———. 2001. Visualism and landscape: Looking and seeing in Normandy. *Ethnos* 66:99–120.

Oles, James. 1993. *South of the border: Mexico in the American imagination, 1914–1947*. Washington, DC: Smithsonian Institution Press.

Oliver, Paul, ed. 1969. *Shelter and society*. London: Barrie and Rockliff.

———, ed. 1971. *Shelter in Africa*. London: Barrie and Jenkins.

———, ed. 1975. *Shelter, sign and symbol*. London: Barrie and Jenkins.

———. 1987. *Dwellings: The house across the World*. Austin: University of Texas Press.

———, ed. 1997. *Encyclopaedia of vernacular architecture of the world*. 3 vols. Cambridge: Cambridge University Press.

———. 2003. *Dwellings: The vernacular house worldwide*. Oxford: Phaidon.

———. 2006a. *Built to meet needs: Cultural issues in vernacular architecture*. Oxford: Elsevier Architectural Press.

———. 2006b. Afterword: Raising the roof. In *Vernacular architecture in the twenty-first century: Theory, education and practice*, ed. Lindsay Asquith and Marcel Vellinga, 262–68. London: Taylor and Francis.

O'Neale, L. M. 1945. *Textiles of highland Guatemala*. Washington, DC: Carnegie Institute.

Ong, A. 1990. State versus Islam: Malay families, women's bodies, and the body politic in Malaysia. *American Ethnologist* 17 (2): 258–76.

Onians, R. B. 1951. *The origins of European thought about the body, the mind, the soul, the world, time and fate*. Cambridge: Cambridge University Press.

Orozco, José Clemente. 1929. A correction. *Mexican Folkways* (5): 8–9.

Ortiz, A. 1969. *The Tewa world: Space, time, being and becoming in a Pueblo society*. Chicago: University of Chicago Press.

Ortner, Sherry. 1984. Theory in anthropology since the sixties. *Comparative Studies in Society and History* 26 (1): 126–66.

———. 1998. Generation X: Anthropology in a media saturated world. *Cultural Anthropology* 13 (3): 414–40.

Osborne, Robin, and Jeremy Tanner, eds. 2007. *Art's agency and art history*. Oxford: Blackwell.

Ossenbruggen, F. D. E. van. 1977. Java's Monca-pat: Origins of a primitive classification system. In *Structural anthropology in the Netherlands*, ed. P. E. de Josselin de Jong, 32–60. The Hague: Nijhoff. (Orig. pub. 1918.)

Pack, Sam. 1998. Beauty and the beast. Paper delivered at a panel at the American Anthropological Association meetings, 2 December.

———. 2002. Familiarizing the exotic in ethnographic film. In *Strategies in teaching anthropology*, 2nd ed., ed. Patricia Rice and David McCurdy, 162–66. Upper Saddle River, NJ: Prentice Hall.

————. 2003. Television's unintended audience. In *Television: Critical concepts in media and cultural studies*, ed. Toby Miller, 163–80. London: Routledge.

————. 2007. Watching Navajos watch themselves. *Wicazo Sa Review*, Fall, 111–27.

Page, Joanne. 1996. Images for understanding: Movement notations and visual recordings. *Visual Anthropology* 8 (2–4): 171–96.

Palatella, John. 1998. Pictures of us. *Lingua Franca* 8 (5): 50–57.

Palmer, A., and H. Clark, eds. 2004. *Old clothes, new looks: Second-hand fashion.* Oxford: Berg.

Paolozzi, Eduardo. 1985. *Lost magic kingdoms and six paper moons from Nahuatl.* London: British Museum Publications.

Paritta Chalermpow Koanantakool, ed. 2002. Kham nam: Prasopkaan manusay-awitthayaa thai baan koed. In *Khon nai: Prasobkaan phaakh sanaam khawng manusayawitthayaa thai*, ed. Paritta Chalermpow Koanantakool, ix–xx. Bangkok: Sirindhorn Anthropology Center.

Park, S., P. C. Warner, and T. K. Fitzgerald. 1993. The process of westernization: Adoption of Western-style dress by Korean women, 1945–1962. *Clothing and Textiles Research Journal* 11 (3): 39–47.

Park Redfield, Margaret. 1928. Nace un niño en Tepoztlán [A child is born in Tepoztlán]. *Mexican Folkways* 4:102–9.

Parks, Lisa, and Shanti Kumar, eds. 2002. *Planet TV: A global television reader.* New York: NYU Press.

Passes, Alan. 1977. *Big step.* London: Allison and Busby.

————. 1986. *Private diary of Rembrandt Harmenszoon van Rijn painter, 1661.* Scranton, PA: HarperCollins.

————. 2000. The value of working and speaking together: A facet of Pa'ikwené (Palikur) conviviality. In *The anthropology of love and anger: The aesthetics of conviviality in native Amazonia*, ed. J. Overing and A. Passes, 97–113. London: Routledge.

————. 2004a. The gathering of the clans: The making of the Palikur *Naoné*. *Ethnohistory* 51 (2): 257–91.

————. 2004b. The place of politics: Powerful speech and women speakers in everyday Pa'ikwené (Palikur) life. *Journal of the Royal Anthropological Institute*,10:1–18.

————. 2006. Chaos theory: A footnote. *Anthropology and Humanism* 31 (1): 75–82.

Pastner, Stephen. 1989. *Bar Yohai* by Robert Ascher. *American Anthropologist* 91 (2): 523.

Pasztory, Esther. 2005. *Thinking with things: Toward a new vision of art.* Austin: University of Texas Press.

Pauwels, L. 1993. Visual essay: Affinities and divergencies between the social scientific and the social documentary modes. *Visual Anthropology* 6:199–210.

Pavlides, Eleftherios, and Jana Hesser. 1986. Women's roles and house form and decoration in Evessos, Greece. In *Gender and power in rural Greece*, ed. Jill Dubisch, 68–96. Princeton, NJ: Princeton University Press.

Pels, Peter. 1996. Visions of anthropology. *Society for the Comparative Study of History and Society* 38 (2): 376–79.

Perani, J., and N. H. Wolff. 1999. *Cloth, dress and art patronage in Africa.* Oxford: Berg.

Perin, Constance. 1992. The communicative circle. In *Museums as communities, museums and communities,* ed. Ivan Karp, 182–220. Washington, DC: Smithsonian.

Perkins, Rachel, and Marcia Langton, eds. 2009. *The first Australians: An illustrated history.* Melbourne: Melbourne University Press

Peterson, Nicolas. 2003. Changing the photographic contract: Aborigines and image ethics. In *Photography's other histories,* ed. C. Pinney and N. Peterson, 119–45. Durham, NC: Duke University Press.

Peterson, Sidney. 1980. *The dark of the screen.* Vol. 4. New York: Anthology Film Archives/New York University Press.

Phillips, Ruth B., and Christopher B. Steiner, eds. 1999. *Unpacking culture: Art and commodity in colonial and postcolonial worlds.* Berkeley: University of California Press.

Philipsen, Hans Henrik, and Birgitte Markussen. 1995. *Advocacy and indigenous film-making.* Aarhaus, Denmark: Intervention Press.

Piault, Colette. 2007. Festivals, conferences, seminars and networks in visual anthropology in Europe. In *Memories of the origins of ethnographic film,* ed. Beate Engelbrecht. New York: Peter Lang.

Pickering, A., ed. 1992. *Science as practice and culture.* Chicago: University of Chicago Press.

Picton, J. 1995. *The art of African textiles: Technology, tradition and Lurex.* London: Lund Humphries.

Pierce, S., and A. Rao, eds. 2006. *Discipline and the other body: Correction, corporeality, colonialism.* Durham, NC: Duke University Press.

Pink, S. 2001. *Doing visual ethnography.* London: Sage.

———. 2003. Interdisciplinary agendas in visual research: Reinstating visual anthropology. *Visual Studies* 18 (2): 179–92.

———. 2004. *Home truths.* Oxford: Berg.

———. 2006 *The future of visual anthropology: Engaging the senses.* London: Routledge.

———. 2007a. *Doing visual ethnography.* London: Sage. (Orig. pub. 2001.)

———. 2007b. Walking with video. *Visual Studies.* 22 (3): 240–52.

———, ed. 2007c. *Visual interventions: Applied visual anthropology.* Oxford: Berghahn.

———. 2009. *Doing sensory ethnography.* London: Sage.

Pink, S., A. Afonso, and L. Kurti, eds. 2004. *Working images: Visual research and representation in ethnography.* London: Routledge.

Pink, S., and A. Martinez Perez. 2006. A fitting social model: Culturally locating telemadres.com. *Home Cultures* 3 (1): 63–86.

Pinney, Christopher. 1990. Classification and fantasy in the photographic construction of caste and tribe. *Visual Anthropology* 3 (2–4): 259–88.

———. 1992a. Parallel histories. In *Anthropology and photography, 1860–1920*, ed. E. Edwards, 74–95. New Haven, CT: Yale University Press; London: Royal Anthropological Institute.

———. 1992b. The lexical spaces of eye-spy. In *Film as ethnography*, ed. P. Crawford and D. Turton, 26–49. Manchester: Manchester University Press.

———. 1997. *Camera indica: The social life of Indian photographs*. London: Reaktion.

———. 2001. Piercing the skin of the idol. In *Beyond aesthetics*, ed. C. Pinney and N. Thomas, 157–79. Oxford: Berg.

———. 2004. *Photos of the gods*. London: Reaktion.

Pinney, Christopher, and Nick Peterson, eds. 2003. *Photography's other histories*. Durham, NC: Duke University Press.

Pinney, Christopher, and Nicholas Thomas, eds. 2001. *Beyond aesthetics: Art and the technologies of enchantment*. Oxford: Berg.

Plattner, Stuart. 1996. *High art down home: An economic ethnography of a local art market*. Chicago: University of Chicago Press.

Poch, Rudolf. 1907. Reisen in New-Guinea in den Jahren 1904–1906. *Zeitschrift fur Ethnologie* 39:382–400.

Poignant, Roslyn. 1990. *Observers of man*. London: Photographers' Gallery/RAI.

———. 1992a. Surveying the field of view. In *Anthropology and photography, 1860–1920*, ed. E. Edwards, 42–75. New Haven, CT: Yale University Press; London: Royal Anthropological Institute.

———. 1992b. Wurdayak/Baman (life history) photo collection: Report on the setting up of a life history photo collection at the Djomi Museum, Maningrida. *Australian Aboriginal Studies* 2:71–77.

———. 1994–1995. About friendship; about trade; about photographs. *Voices: Quarterly Journal of the National Library of Australia* 4 (45): 55–70.

———. 1996. *Encounter at Nagalrramba*. Canberra: National Library of Australia.

Polakoff, C. 1982. *African textiles and dyeing techniques*. London: Routledge.

Polanyi, M. 1958. *Personal knowledge: Towards a post-critical philosophy*. Chicago: University of Chicago Press.

Poole, Deborah. 1997. *Vision race and modernity: A visual economy of the Andean image world*. Princeton, NJ: Princeton University Press.

———. 2005. An excess of description: Ethnography, race and visual technologies. *Annual Reviews in Anthropology* 24:159–79.

Portman, M. V. 1896. Photography for anthropologists. *Journal of the Anthropological Institute* 15:75–87.

Powers, E. 2007. A lesson in viral video. *Inside Higher Ed*, 7 February. http://www.insidehighered.com/news/2007/02/07/web (accessed 9 February 2007).

Powers, Willow. 1996. Images across boundaries: History, use, and ethics of photographs of American Indians. *American Indian Culture and Research Journal* 20 (3): 20–33.

Press, I. 1969. Ambiguity and innovation: Implications for the genesis of the culture broker, *American Anthropologist* (71)205–17.

Price, Sally. 1989. *Primitive art in civilized places*. Chicago: University of Chicago Press

———. 2007. *Paris primitive: Jacques Chirac's museum on the Quai Branly*. Chicago: University Press.

Prins, Harold. 1989. American Indians and the ethnocinematic complex: From native participation to production control. In *Eyes across the water*, ed. R. Boonzajer Flaes, 80–90. Amsterdam: Het Spinhof.

———. 1997. The paradox of primitivism: Native rights and the problem of imagery in cultural survival films. *Visual Anthropology* 9 (3–4): 243–66.

———. 2001. Digital revolution: Indigenous peoples in Cyberia. In *Cultural anthropology*, 10th ed., ed. William A. Haviland, 306–8. Fort Worth, TX: Harcourt College Publishers.

———. 2002. Visual media and the primitivist perplex: Colonial fantasies, indigenous imagination, and advocacy in North America. In *Media worlds: Anthropology on new terrain*, ed. F. Ginsburg, L. Abu-Lughod, and B. Larkin, 58–74. Berkeley: University of California Press.

Prost, J. H. 1996. Body language in the context of culture (review essay). *Visual Anthropology* 8 (2–4): 337–43.

Prussin, Labelle. 1995. *African nomadic architecture: Space, place and gender*. Washington, DC: Smithsonian Institution Press; London: National Museum of African Art.

Putti, R. 2008. Gente in Mostra: Una riflessione tra spazi, corpi e sguardi. In *Imparare a Guardare*, ed. C. Grasseni. Milano: Franco Angeli.

Pützstück, Lothar. 1995. *"Symphonie in Moll": Julius Lips und die Kölner Völkerkunde*. Pfaffenweiler: Centaurus Verlagsgesellschaft.

Rabine, L. W. 2002. *The global circulation of African fashion*. Oxford: Berg.

Rabinow, Paul. 1977. *Reflections on fieldwork in Morocco*. Berkeley: University of California Press.

Rabinowitz, Laura. 1991. *Points of resistance: Women, power and politics in the New York avant-garde cinema, 1943–1971*. Urbana: University of Illinois Press.

Radcliff-Brown, A. R. 1913/1964. *The Andaman islanders*. Glencoe, IL: Free Press.

Radway, Janice. 1984. *Reading the romance*. London: Verso.

———. 1988. Reception study: Ethnography and the problems of dispersed audiences and nomadic subjects. *Cultural Studies* 2 (3): 359–76.

———. 1996. The hegemony of "specificity" and the impasse in audience research: Cultural studies and the problem of ethnography. In *The audience and its landscape*, ed. James Hay, Lawrence Grossberg, and Ellen Wartella, 235–46. Boulder: Westview Press.

Raheja, Michelle. Forthcoming. *Reservation reelism: Redfacing, visual sovereignty, and Native American film*. Lincoln: University of Nebraska Press.

Rajgopal, Arvind. 2000. Mediating modernity: Theorizing reception in a non-Western society. In *De-westernizing media studies*, ed. James Curran and Myung-Jin Park, 293–304. London: Routledge.

Ramey, Kathryn. 2006. Is the film avant-garde still avant-garde: Economics and culture of artisanal moving-image makers. PhD thesis, Anthropology Department, Temple University.

Rapoport, Amos. 1969. *House form and culture*. Englewood Cliffs, NJ: Prentice-Hall.

———. 1982. *The meaning of the built environment: A non-verbal communication approach*. Beverly Hills: Sage.

———. 2004. *Culture, architecture and design*. Chicago: Locke Science Publishing.

Rapport, Nigel. 1994. *The prose and the passion: Anthropology, literature and the writing of E. M. Forster*. Manchester: Manchester University Press.

Rasmussen, S. 1991. Veiled self, transparent meanings: Tuareg headdress as social expression. *Ethnology* 30:101–17.

Reed, Susan A. 1998. The poetics and politics of dance. *Annual Review of Anthropology* 27:503–32.

Regnault, Felix-Louis. 1900. La chronophotographie dans l'ethnographie. *Bulletin de la Societe D'Anthropologie de Paris* 11:421–22.

Reischer, Erica, and Kathryn S. Koo. 2004. The body beautiful: Symbolism and agency in the social world. *Annual Review of Anthropology* 33:297–317.

Renan, Sheldon. 1967. *The underground film: An introduction to its development in America*. New York: Dutton.

Renne, E. P. 1995. Becoming a Bunu bride: Bunu ethnic identity and traditional marriage dress. In *Dress and ethnicity*, ed. J. B. Eicher, 117–37. Oxford: Berg.

———. 2000. Cloth and conversion: Yoruba textiles and ecclesiastical dress. In *Undressing religion: Commitment and conversion from a cross-cultural perspective*, 9th ed., ed. L. B. Arthur, 7–24. Oxford: Berg.

Rhodes, Colin. 1994. *Primitivsm and modern art*. London: Thames & Hudson.

Richardson, Vicky. 2001. *New vernacular architecture*. London: Lawrence King.

Rickard, Jolene. 1995. Sovereignty: A line in the sand. In *Strong hearts: Native American visions and voices*, 51–54. New York: Aperture.

———. 1999. First Nation territory in cyber space declared: No treaties needed. In *CyberPowWow: An aboriginally determined territory in cyberspace*. http://www.cyberpowwow.net/nation2nation/jolenework.html.

Riefenstahl, Leni. 1974 *The last of the Nuba*. London: William Collins.

Roach-Higgins, M., and J. B. Eicher. 1992. Dress and identity. *Clothing and Textiles Research Journal* 10 (4): 1–8.

Roberts, John. 1998. *The art of interruption: Realism, photography and the everyday*. Manchester: Manchester University Press.

Rogoff, B. 1990. *Apprenticeship in thinking: Cognitive development in social contexts*. Cambridge, MA: Harvard University Press.

———. 2003. *The cultural nature of human development*. Oxford: Oxford University Press.

Rohde, Rick. 1998. How we see each other: Subjectivity, photography and ethnographic re/vision. In *Colonising camera*, ed. W. Hartmann et al., 198–204. Cape Town: Cape Town University Press.

Rohner, Ronald, ed. 1969. *The ethnography of Franz Boas: Letters and diaries of Franz Boas written on the north west coast from 1886 to 1931*. Chicago: University of Chicago Press.

Rollwagen, Jack R., ed. 1988. *Anthropological filmmaking: Anthropological perspectives on the production of film and video for general public audiences*. New York: Harwood Academic Publishers.

Rony, Fatimah Tobing. 1996. *The third eye: Race, cinema, and ethnographic spectacle*. Durham, NC: Duke University Press.

Ronzon, F. 2007. Icons and transvestites: Notes on irony, cognition and visual skill. In *Skilled visions*, ed. C. Grasseni, 67–88. Oxford: Berghahn.

Roodenberg, Linda, ed. 2002. *De Bril van Anceaux: Volkerkundige fotographie vanaf 1860*. Leiden: Rijksmuseum Museum voor Volkerkunde.

Rosaldo, Renato. 1986. From the door of his tent: The fieldworker and the inquisitor. In *Writing culture: The poetics and politics of ethnography*, ed. J. Clifford and G. E. Marcus, 75–97. Berkeley: University of California Press.

Rose, James. 2004. Stephen and Timothy Quay. In *Senses of cinema*, "Great directors." http://www.sensesofcinema.com/contents/directors/04/quay_brothers.html.

Ross, Karen, and Virginia Nightingale. 2003. *Media and audiences: New perspectives*. Maidenhead: Open University Press.

Roth, H. L. 1934. *Studies in primitive looms*. Reprinted (1977) from the original Bankfield Museum Notes, Halifax, England. Carlton: Ruth Bean.

Roth, Lorna. 2005. *Something new in the air: Indigenous television in Canada*. Montreal: McGill Queens University Press.

Rothenbuhler, Eric, and Mihai Coman. 2005. The promise of media anthropology. In *Media anthropology*, ed. Eric W. Rothenbuhler and Mihai Coman. London: Sage.

Rouch, Jean. 1975. The camera and the man. In *Principles of visual anthropology*, ed. Paul Hockings. New York: Mouton.

Royal Anthropological Institute. 1951. *Notes and queries on anthropology*. 6th ed. London: Routledge, Kegan & Paul.

Ruan, Xing. 2006. *Allegorical architecture: Living myth and architectonics in southern China*. Honolulu: University of Hawai'i Press.

Rubin, William, ed. 1984. *"Primitivism" in 20th century art*. New York: Museum of Modern Art.

Ruby, Jay. 1976. In a pic's eye: Interpretative strategies for deriving significance and meaning from photographs. *Afterimage*, March, 5–6.

———. 1980a Exposing yourself: Reflexivity, anthropology and film. *Semiotica* 3 (1–2): 153–79.

———. 1980b. Franz Boas and early camera study of behavior. *Kinesis Reports* 3 (1): 6–11.

———. 1981. A Re-examination of the early career of Robert J. Flaherty. *Quarterly Review of Film Studies* 5 (4): 431–57.

———. 1989a. Robert Gardner und der Anthropologische Film. In *Ritual von Leben und Tod: Robert Gardner und seine Filme*, ed. R. Kapfer, W. Petermann, and R. Thoms. Munich: Trickster Verlag.

———. 1989b. The emperor and his clothes: A comment. *SVA Newsletter* 5 (1): 9–11.

———. 1991. Speaking for, speaking about, speaking with, or speaking alongside: An anthropological and documentary dilemma. *Visual Anthropology Review* 7 (2): 50–67.

———. 1992. *The films of John Marshall*. New York: Gordon & Breech.

———. 1995a. Out of sync: The cinema of Tim Asch. *Visual Anthropology Review* 11 (1): 19–37.

———. 1995b. The moral burden of authorship in ethnographic film. *Visual Anthropology Review* 11 (2): 83–93.

———. 2000a. Out of sync: The cinema of Tim Asch. In *Picturing culture: Explorations of film and anthropology*, 115–35. Chicago: University of Chicago Press.

———. 2000b. *Picturing culture: Explorations of film and anthropology*. Chicago: University of Chicago Press.

———. 2002. The professionalization of visual anthropology in the United States: The 1960s and the 1970s. *Visual Anthropology Review* 17 (2): 5–12.

———. 2003a. The camera and man. In *Cine-ethno\graphy Jean Rouch* (Visible Evidence, vol. 13), ed. S. Feld. Minneapolis: University of Minnesota Press. (Orig. pub. 1973.)

———. 2003b. On the vicissitudes of the self: The possessed dancer, the magician, the sorcerer, the filmmaker, and the ethnographer. In *Cine-ethnography Jean Rouch* (Visible Evidence, vol. 13), ed. S. Feld, 87–101. Minneapolis: University of Minnesota Press.

Ruby, J., and R. Chalfen. 1974. The teaching of visual anthropology at Temple. *Society for the Anthropology of Visual Communication Newsletter* 5 (3): 5–7.

Ruddock, A. 2001. *Understanding audiences: Theory and method*. London: Sage.

Rudofsky, Bernard. 1964. *Architecture without architects*. London: Academy Editions.

———. 1977. *The prodigious builders*. London: Secker and Warburg.

Russell, Catherine. 1999. *Experimental ethnography: The work of film in the age of video*. Durham, NC: Duke University Press.

Ryan, James. 1997. *Picturing empire*. London: Reaktion.

Salazar, Juan Francisco. 2004. Imperfect media: The poetics of indigenous media in Chile. PhD thesis, University of Western Sydney.

———. 2005. Digitising knowledge: Anthropology and new practices of digi-textuality. *Media International Australia* 116:64–74. Special issue: Digital Anthropology.

———. 2007. Indigenous peoples and the cultural construction of information and communication technology (ICT) in Latin America. In *Information technology and indigenous people*, ed. Laurel Dyson, Max Hendricks, and Stephen Grant, 14–26. London: Information Science Publishing.

Samian, Etienne. 1995. Bronsilaw Malinowski et la photographie anthro-pologique. *L'Ethnographie* 91 (2): 107–30.

Sanborn, Keith. 1988. Modern, all too modern. *Cinematograph* 3:107–16.

Sanchez del Valle, Carmen, and Amr Abdel-Kawi. 1994. Al Muizz voyager: City portrait. In *Changing methodologies in the field of traditional-environment research*, 49–73. Traditional Dwellings and Settlements Working Paper Series, vol. 61. Berkeley: University of California Center for Environmental Design Research.

Sandiki, Ö., and G. Ger. 2005. Aesthetics, ethics and politics of the Turkish headscarf. In *Clothing as material culture*, ed. S. Küchler and D. Miller, 61–82. Oxford: Berg.

Sansi, Roger. 2005. Making do: Agency and objective change in the psychoge-netic portraits of Jaume Xifra. *Quaderns de l'Institut Català d'Antropologia* 21:91–106.

Sapir, Edward. 1949. Communication. In *Selected writings of Edward Sapir in lan-guage, culture and personality*, ed. D. Mandelbaum, 104–9. Berkeley: Univer-sity of California Press.

Sather, Clifford. 1993. Posts, hearths and thresholds: The Iban longhouse as a ritual structure. In *Inside Austronesian houses: Perspectives on domestic designs for living*, ed. J. Fox, 65–115. Canberra: Research School of Pacific Studies, ANU.

Scannell, Paddy. 2007. *Media and communication*. London: Sage.

Schefold, Reimar. 2009. The house as group: Traditional dwellings on Siberut, Mentawai. In *Indonesian houses*. Vol. 2, *Survey on the traditional house in west-ern Indonesia*, ed. Reimar Schefold, Gaudenz Domenig, Peter Nas, and Robert Wessing. Leiden: KITLV.

Schefold, Reimar, Gaudenz Domenig, and Peter Nas, eds. 2004. *Indonesian houses*. Vol. 1, *Tradition and transformation in vernacular architecture*. Leiden: KITLV.

Schefold, Reimar, Peter Nas, Gaudenz Domenig, and Robert Wessing, eds. 2009. *Indonesian houses*. Vol. 2, *Survey of vernacular architecture in western Indonesia*. Leiden: KITLV.

Scheper Hughes, Nancy, and Margaret Lock. 1987. The mindful body: A prole-gomenon to future work in medical anthropology. *Medical Anthropology Quarterly* 1:6–41.

Scherer, Joanna Cohan. 1988. The public faces of Sarah Winnemucca. *Cultural Anthropology* 3 (2): 178–204.

———. 1995. Ethnographic photography in anthropological research. In *Principles of visual anthropology*, 2nd ed., ed. Paul Hockings, 201–16. Berlin: Mouton de Gruyter.

———. 2006. *Benedicte Wrensted: A Danish photographer of Idaho Indians*. Norman: University of Oklahoma Press.

Schevill, M. B. 1985. *Evolution in textile design from the highlands of Guatemala*. Berkeley, CA: Lowie Museum of Anthropology.

Schildkrout, Enid. 2004. Inscribing the body. *Annual Review of Anthropology* 33:319–44.

Schindlbeck, M, ed. 1989. *Die Ethnographische Linse*. Berlin: SMPK.

Schneider, Arnd. 2003. On "appropriation": A critical reappraisal of the concept and its application in global art practices. *Social Anthropology* 11 (2): 215–29.

———. 2006. *Appropriation as practice: Art and identity in Argentina*. New York: Palgrave.

———. 2008. Three modes of experimentation with art and ethnography. *Journal of the Royal Anthropological Institute*, n.s., 14:171–93.

Schneider, Arnd, and C. Wright, eds. 2006. *Contemporary art and anthropology*. Oxford: Berg.

———. 2001. *Between art and anthropology*. Oxford: Berg.

Schneider, J. 1980. Trousseau as treasure: Some contributions of late nineteenth-century change in Sicily. In *Beyond the myths of culture: Essays in cultural materialism*, ed. E. B. Ross, 323–59. New York: Academic Press.

———. 1987. The anthropology of cloth. *Annual Review of Anthropology* 16: 409–48.

———. 1988. Rumplestiltskin's bargain: Folklore and the merchant capitalist intensification of linen manufacture in early modern Europe. In *Cloth and human experience*, ed. A. B. Weiner and J. Schneider, 177–214. Washington, DC: Smithsonian Books.

Schneider, J., and A. B. Weiner. 1986. Cloth and the organization of human experience. *Current Anthropology* 27 (2): 178–84.

Schoeller, Winfried F. 2005. *Hubert Fichte und Leonore Mau: Der Schriftsteller und die Fotografin*. Frankfurt: M. Fischer.

Schulte Nordholt, H. G. 1971. *The political system of the Atoni of Timor*. The Hague: Nijhoff.

Schwarz, R. A. 1979. Uncovering the secret vice: Towards an anthropology of clothing and adornment. In *The fabrics of culture*, ed. J. M. Cordwell and R. A. Schwarz, 23–46. The Hague: Mouton.

Scott, J. G. 1911. *Burma: A handbook of practical information*. London: Alexander Moring Ltd.

Seaman, G., and H. Williams. 1992. Hypermedia in ethnography. In *Film as ethnography*, ed. P. Crawford and D. Turton. Manchester: University of Manchester Press.

Sekula, Alan. 1989. The body and the archive. In *The contest of meaning*, ed. R. Bolton, 342–89. Cambridge, MA: MIT Press.

Seng, Y. J., and B. Wass. 1995. Traditional Palestinian wedding dress as a symbol of nationalism. In *Dress and ethnicity*, ed. J. B. Eicher, 227–54. Oxford: Berg.

Seremetakis, C. Nadia. 1993. Memory of the senses: Historical perception, commensal exchange and modernity. *Visual Anthropology Review* 9 (2): 2–18.

———. 1994. *The senses still: Perception and memory as material culture in modernity*. Chicago: University of Chicago Press.

Serres, Antoine-Étienne-Renaud-Augustin. 1845. Observations sur l'application de la photographie a l'étude des races humaine. *Comptes rundus hebdomadaires des séances de l'Académic des Sciences* 21 (3): 242–46 (séance du lundi 21 juillet, Paris).

Sharma, U. 1978. Women and their affines: The veil as a symbol of separation. *Man* 13: 218–33.

Sherwin, R. K., N. Feigenson, and C. Spiesel. 2007. What is visual knowledge, and what is it good for? Potential ethnographic lessons from the field of legal practice. *Visual Anthropology* 20 (2): 143–78.

Shilling, Chris. 1993. *The body and social theory.* London: Sage.

Shirazi, F. 2001. *The veil unveiled.* Gainesville: University Press of Florida.

Shotter, John. 1993. *Conversational realities.* London: Sage

Shryock, Andrew, ed. 2004. *Off stage/on display: Intimacy and ethnography in the age of public culture.* Stanford, CA: Stanford University Press.

Silver, H. R. 1979. Ethnoart. *Annual Review of Anthropology* 8:267–307.

Silverstone, Roger. 1985 *Framing science: The making of a BBC documentary.* London: British Film Institute.

———. 1989. Let us then return to the murmuring of everyday practices: A note on Michel de Certeau, television and everyday life. *Theory, Culture & Society* 6:77–94.

———. 1990. Television and everyday life: Towards an anthropology of the television audience. In *Public communication: The new imperatives,* ed. M. Ferguson, 173–89. London: Sage.

Simoni, Simonetta. 1996. The visual essay: Redefining data, presentation and scientific truth. *Visual Sociology* 11 (2): 75–82.

Singer, Andre. 1992. Anthropology in broadcasting. In *Film as ethnography,* ed. Peter Ian Crawford and David Turton, 264–73. Manchester: University of Manchester Press.

———. 2002. Beyond primetime: Anthropology and television at war. Forman Lecture, Manchester Conference Centre, 14 May.

Singer, Andre, and Leslie Woodhead. 1988. *Disappearing World: Television and anthropology.* London: Boxtree Limited and Granada Television.

Singer, Beverly. 2001. *Wiping the warpaint off the lens: Native American film and video.* Visible Evidence, vol. 10. Minneapolis: University of Minnesota Press.

Singh, Rani, ed. 1999. *Think of the self speaking: Harry Smith—selected interviews.* Seattle: Elbow/Cityful Press.

———, ed. 2008. Harry Smith archives. http://www.harrysmitharchives.com/index.html (accessed 18 August 2008).

Sitney, P. Adams. 2002. *Visionary film: The American avant-garde, 1943–2000.* 3rd ed. New York: Oxford University Press.

Skalnik, Peter. 1995. Bronislaw Kasper Malinowski and Stanislaw Ignacy Witkiewicz: Science versus art in the conceptualization of culture. In *Fieldwork and footnotes: Studies in the history of European anthropology,* ed. Han F. Vermeulen and Arturo Alverez Roldan. New York: Routledge.

Smallacombe, S. 1999. Indigenous peoples access rights to archival records. http://www.archivists.org.au/events/con99/smallacombe.html (accessed 20 February 2002).

Smith, Benjamin M. 2003. Images, selves and the visual record: Photography and ethnographic complexity in central Cape York Peninsula. *Social Analysis* 47 (3): 8–26.

Smith, Benjamin M., and Richard Vokes. 2008. Haunting images: The affective power of photography. *Visual Anthropology Review* 21 (4). Special issue.

Smith, Linda Tuhiwai. 1999. *Decolonizing methodologies: Research and indigenous peoples*. London: Zed Books.

Somsanouk Mixay et al. 2004. *Luang Prabang: An architectural journey*. Vientiane: Les Ateliers de la Péninsule.

Sontag, Susan. 1979. *On photography*. Harmondsworth: Penguin.

Sorenson, E. Richard. 1967. A research film program in the study of changing man: Research filmed materials as a foundation for continued study of non-recurring human events. *Current Anthropology* 8 (5): 443–69.

Spitulnik, Deborah. 1993. Anthropology and mass media. *Annual Review of Anthropology* 22:293–315.

———. 2002. Mobile machines and fluid audiences: Rethinking reception through Zambian radio culture. In *Media worlds: Anthropology on new terrain*, ed. F. Ginsburg, L. Abu-Lughod, and B. Larkin, 337–54. Berkeley: University of California Press.

Spyer, Patricia. 2001. Photography's framings and unframings: A review article. *Comparative Studies in Society and History* 43 (1): 181–92.

Srinivas, Lakshmi. 2002. The active audience: Spectatorship, social relations and the experience of cinema in India. *Media, Culture and Society* 24:155–73.

———. 2005. Imaging the audience. *South Asian Popular Culture* 3 (2): 101–16.

Srinivasan, Ramesh, Jim Enote, Katherine M. Becvar, and Robin Boast. 2009. Critical and reflective uses of new media technologies in tribal museums. *Museum Management and Curatorship* 24 (2): 169–89.

Stafford, B. M. 1996. *Good looking: Essays on the virtue of images*. Cambridge, MA: MIT Press.

Stalp, M. C. 2007. *Quilting: The fabric of everyday life*. Oxford: Berg.

Stanton, John. 2004. Snapshots on the dreaming: Photographs of past and present. In *Museums and source communities*, ed. L. Peers and A. Brown. London: Routledge.

Star, S. L., and J. Griesemer. 1989. Institutional ecology, translations, and boundary objects: Amateurs and professionals in Berkeley's Museum of Vertebrate Zoology, 1907–1939. *Social Studies of Science* 19:387–420.

Start, L. 1917. *Burmese textiles from the Shan and Kachin districts*. Halifax: Bankfield Museum.

Stefanoff, Lisa. 2009. Productions: Listening, revelation, and cultural intimacy at the Central Australian Aboriginal Media Association. PhD diss., New York University, Department of Anthropology.

Steiner, Christopher. 1985. Another image of Africa: Toward an ethnohistory of European cloth marketed in west Africa, 1873–1960. *Ethnohistory* 32 (2): 91–110.

———. 1994. *African art in transit*. Cambridge: Cambridge University Press.

Stocking, George W., Jr. 1983. *Observers observed: Essays on ethnographic fieldwork*. Madison: University of Wisconsin Press.

———, ed. 1996. *Volksgeist as method and ethic: Essays on Boasian ethnography and the German anthropological tradition*. Madison: University of Wisconsin Press.

Stoler, A., and K. Strassler. 2000. Casting for the colonial. *Comparative Studies in Sociology and History* 42 (1): 4–48.

Stoller, Paul. 1989. *The taste of ethnographic things: The senses in anthropology*. Philadelphia: University of Pennsylvania Press.

———. 1992a. *Blue: A Tinglit Odyssey* by Robert Ascher. *American Anthropologist* 94 (2): 521–22.

———. 1992b. *The cinematic griot: The ethnography of Jean Rouch*. Chicago: University of Chicago Press.

———. 1997. *Sensuous scholarship*. Philadelphia: University of Pennsylvania Press.

Strand, Chick. 1974. Woman as ethnographic filmmaker. *Journal of the University film Association* 26 (1–2): 16.

———. 1978. Notes on ethnographic film by a film artist. *Wide Angle* 2 (3): 44–51.

Strathern, A., and M. Strathern. 1971. *Self-decoration in Mount Hagen*. London: Gerald Duckworth and Co.

Stratton, Jon, and Ien Ang. 1996. On the impossibility of a global cultural studies: "British" cultural studies in an "international" frame. In *Stuart Hall: Critical dialogues in cultural studies*, ed. D. Morley and K. Chen, 361–91. London: Routledge.

Strecker, Ivo. 1988. Filming among the Hamar. *Visual Anthropology* 1 (4): 369–78.

Streeck, Jürgen. 1993. Gesture as communication I: Its coordination with gaze and speech. *Communications Monographs* 60:275–99.

———. 1994. Gesture as communication II: The audience as co-author. *Research on Language and Social Interaction* 27:239–67.

Struever, Nancy S. 1983. Fables of power. *Representations* 4 (Fall): 173–85.

Sturken, M., and L. Cartwright. 2001. *Practices of looking: An introduction to visual culture*. Oxford: Oxford University Press.

Suchman, L. 1987. *Plans and situated action: The problem of human-machine communication*. Cambridge: Cambridge University Press.

———. 1998. Constituting shared workspaces. In *Cognition and communication at work*, ed. Y. Engeström and D. Middleton, 35–60. Cambridge: Cambridge University Press.

Suchman, L., and R. H. Trigg. 1993. Artificial intelligence as craftwork. In *Understanding practice: Perspectives on activity and context*, ed. S. Chaiklin and J. Lave, 144–78. Cambridge: Cambridge University Press.

Suleiman, S., ed. 1986. *The female body in Western culture: Contemporary perspectives*. Cambridge, MA: Harvard University Press.

Sullivan, Gerry. 1992. *Margaret Mead, Gregory Bateson, and highland Bali: Fieldwork photographs of Bayang Gedé 1936–1939*. Chicago: University of Chicago Press.

Sumberg, B. 1995. Dress and ethnic differentiation in the Niger delta. In *Dress and ethnicity*, ed. J. B. Eicher, 165–81. Oxford: Berg.

Summers, L. 2001. *Bound to please: A history of the Victorian corset*. Oxford: Berg.

SVA (Society for Visual Anthropology). 2001. Guidelines for the evaluation of ethnographic visual media. http://www.societyforvisualanthropology .org/Resources/svaresolutiona.pdf (accessed September 2008).

Svašek, Maruška. 2007. *Anthropology, art and cultural production*. London: Pluto Press.

Tagg, John. 1988. *The burden of representation*. Basingstoke: Macmillan.

Tambiah, Stanley. 1973. Classification of animals in Thailand. In *Rules and meanings*, ed. Mary Douglas, 127–66. Harmondsworth: Penguin. (Orig. pub. 1969.)

Tarlo, E. 1996. *Clothing matters: Dress and identity in India*. Chicago: University of Chicago Press.

Taureg, Martin. 1983. The development of standards for scientific films in German ethography. *Studies in Visual Communication* 9 (1): 9–29.

Taussig, Michael. 1993. *Mimesis and alterity*. London: Routledge.

Tauzin, A. 2007. Women of Mauritania: Cathodic images and presentation of the self. *Visual Anthropology* 20 (2): 3–18.

Tayler, Donald. 1992. Very lovable human beings: The photography of Everard im Thurn. In *Anthropology and photography*, ed. E. Edwards, 187–92. New Haven, CT: Yale University Press.

Taylor, Charles. 1964. *The explanation of behaviour*. London: Routledge & Kegan Paul; New York: Humanities Press.

Taylor, L. 2002. *The study of dress history*. Manchester: Manchester University Press.

———. 2004. *Establishing dress history*. Manchester: Manchester University Press.

Taylor, Lucien, ed. 1994. *Visualizing theory: Selected essays from V.A.R. 1990–1994*. London: Routledge.

———. 1998 Visual anthropology is dead, long live visual anthropology. *American Anthropologist* 100 (2): 534–37.

Theye, T., ed. 1989. *Der geraubte Schatten: Photographie als ethnographisches Dokument*. Munich: Münchner Stadtmuseum.

Thomas, Elizabeth Marshall. 1989. *The harmless people*. Rev. ed. New York: Vintage.

Thomas, Nicholas. 1991. *Entangled objects: Exchange, material culture and colonialism in the Pacific*. Cambridge, MA: Harvard University Press.

———. 1997. Collectivity and nationality in the anthropology of art. In *Rethinking visual anthropology*, ed. Marcus Banks and Howard Morphy. New Haven, CT: Yale University Press.

———. 1999. *Possessions: Indigenous art/colonial culture*. London: Thames & Hudson.

Tiragallo, Felice. 2001. Sentivo le pernici cantare nel territorio di Armungia: Note su una documentazione audiovisiva dei mutamenti nel territorio del Gerrei. In *Il senso dei luoghi*, ed. Franco Lai, Carlo Maxia, Felice Tiragallo, and Laura Draetta. Cagliari: CUEC.

———. 2007. Embodiment of the gaze: Vision, planning and weaving between filmic ethnography and cultural technology. *Visual Anthropology* 20 (2): 201–19.

Trachtenberg, Alan. 2004. *Shades of Hiawatha: Staging Indians, making Americans, 1880–1930*. New York: Hill and Wang.

Trevor-Roper, H. 1983. The invention of tradition: The highland tradition of Scotland. In *The invention of tradition*, ed. E. Hobsbawm and T. Ranger, 15–43. Cambridge: Cambridge University Press.

Trinh T. Minh-ha. 1989. *Woman, native, other*. Bloomington: Indiana University Press.

Tsinhnahjinnie, Hulleah. 1998. When is a photograph worth a thousand words? In *Native nations: Journeys in American photography*, ed. J. Allison, 41–55. London: Barbican Art Gallery.

Tufte, Edward. 1983. *The visual display of quantitative information*. Cheshire, CT: Graphics Press.

Turan, Mete, ed. 1990. *Vernacular architecture: Paradigms of environmental response*. Aldershot: Avebury.

Turner, Bryan S. 1984. *The body and society*. Oxford: Basil Blackwell.

———. 1991. Recent developments in the theory of the body. In *The body: Social process and cultural theory*, ed. M. Featherstone, Mike Hepworth, and Bryan S. Turner, 1–35. London: Sage.

Turner, G. 1954. *Hair embroidery in Siberia and North America*. Oxford: Pitt Rivers Museum.

Turner, Terence. 1980. The social skin. In *Not work alone: A cross-cultural view of activities superfluous to survival*, ed. J. Cherfas and R. Lewin, 112–40. London: Temple Smith.

———. 1990. Visual media, cultural politics and anthropological practice: Some implications of recent uses of film and video among the Kayapo of Brazil. *Visual Anthropology Review* 6:8–13.

———. 1991a. The social dynamics of video media in an indigenous society: The cultural meaning and the personal politics of video-making in Kayapo communities. *Visual Anthropology Review* 7 (2): 68–76.

———. 1991b. Representing, resisting, rethinking: Historical transformations of Kayapo culture and anthropological consciousness. In *Colonial situations*, ed. G. Stocking, 285–313. Madison: University of Wisconsin Press.

———. 1992a. Defiant images: The Kayapo appropriation of video. *Anthropology Today* 8 (6): 5–16.

———. 1992b. The Kayapo on television: An anthropological viewing. *Visual Anthropology Review* 8 (1): 107–12.

———. 1993. Anthropology and multiculturalism: What is anthropology that multiculturalists should be mindful of it? *Cultural Anthropology* 8 (4): 411–29.

———. 1994. Bodies and anti-bodies: Flesh and fetish in contemporary social theory. In *Embodiment and experience: The existential ground of culture and self*, ed. Thomas J. Csordas, 27–47. Cambridge: Cambridge University Press.

———. 1995. Representation, collaboration, and mediation in contemporary ethnographic and indigenous media. *Visual Anthropology Review* 11 (2): 102–6.

———. 2002. Representation, politics, and cultural imagination in indigenous video: General points and Kayapo examples. In *Media worlds: Anthropology on new terrain*, ed. F. Ginsburg, L. Abu-Lughod and B. Larkin, 75–89. Berkeley: University of California Press.

Turton, David. 1992. Anthropology on television: What next? In *Film as ethnography*, ed. Peter Ian Crawford and David Turton, 283–99. Manchester: University of Manchester Press.

Turvey, Malcom, et al. 2002. Round table: Obsolescence and the American avant-garde film. *October*, no. 100 (Spring), 115–32.

Tyler, Stephen. 1987. On writing it up/off as speaking for. *Journal of Anthropological Research* 43 (4): 339–42.

Tylor, Edward B. 1865. *Researches into the early history of mankind and the development of civilization*. London: Murray.

Urciuoli, Bonnie. 1995. The indexical structure of visibility. In *Human action signs in cultural context: The visible and the invisible in movement and dance*, ed. B. Farnell, 189–215. Metuchen, NJ: Scarecrow Press.

Vail, Pegi. 1997. Producing America: The Native American Producer's Alliance. Master's thesis, New York University.

Varela, Charles R. 1994a. Harré and Merleau Ponty: Beyond the absent moving body in embodied social theory. *Journal for the Theory of Social Behavior* 24 (2): 167–85.

———. 1994b. Pocock, Williams, Gouldner: Initial reactions of three social scientists to the problem of objectivity. *Journal of the Anthropological Study of Human Movement* 8 (1): 43–64

———. 1995. Cartesianism revisited: The ghost in the moving machine or the lived body. In *Human action signs in cultural context: The visible and the invisible in movement and dance*, ed. B. Farnell, 216–93. Metuchen, NJ: Scarecrow Press.

———. 1996. The Prost review. *Visual Anthropology* 8 (24): 367–37.

———. 2006. Biological structure and agency: The problem of instinctivism. *Journal of the Theory of Social Behavior* (1): 95–123.

Varela, Charles R., and Rom Harré. 1996. Conflicting varieties of realism: Causal powers and the problems of social structure. *Journal for the Theory of Social Behavior* 26 (3): 313–25.

Vellinga, Marcel. 2004. *Constituting unity and difference: Vernacular architecture in a Minangkabau village*. Leiden: KITLV.

————. 2006. Engaging the future: Vernacular architecture studies in the twenty-first century. In *Vernacular architecture in the twenty-first century: Theory, education and practice*, ed. Lindsay Asquith and Marcel Vellinga, 81–94. London: Taylor and Francis.

Vellinga, Marcel, Paul Oliver, and Alexander Bridge. 2007. *Atlas of vernacular architecture of the world*. New York: Routledge.

Verdon, Michel. 2007. Franz Boas: Cultural history for the present or obsolete natural history. *Journal of the Royal Anthropological Institute*, n.s., 13: 433–51.

Vickery, A. 1998. *The gentleman's daughter: Women's lives in Georgian England*. New Haven, CT: Yale University Press.

Vizenor, G. 1998. Fugitive poses. In *Excavating voices: Listening to photographs*, ed. M. Katakis, 7–15. Philadelphia: University of Pennsylvania Museum of Archaeology and Anthropology.

Vogel, Amos. 1997. The documents: The Cinema 16 programs, and selected letters, program notes, and reviews from the Cinema 16 files. *Wide Angle* 19 (1): 103–92.

Vogel, Susan, ed. 1989. *Art/artifact: African art in anthropological collections*. New York: Center for African Art.

Vokes, Richard. 2008. On ancestral self-fashioning: Photography in the times of AIDS. *Visual Anthropology* 21 (4): 345–63.

Wade, Peter, ed. 1996. *Cultural studies will be the death of anthropology*. Group for Debates in Anthropological Theory (GDAT), no. 8.

Walker, G., and R. Vanderwal, eds. 1982. *The Aboriginal photographs of Baldwin Spencer*. Ringwood, Vic.: Viking O'Neil.

Wallis, Brian. 1995. Black bodies, white science: Louis Agassiz's slave daguerreotypes. *American Art* 9 (2): 335–61.

Warburg, Aby. 1938–1939. A lecture on serpent ritual. *Journal of the Warburg Institute* 2:277–97.

————. 1988. *Schlangenritual: Ein Reisebericht*. Berlin: Wagenbach.

Wariboko, N. 2002. Three against four: A cultural analysis of disappearance of women in Kalabari. *Journal of Asian and African Studies* 37 (2): 66–95.

Warner, C. Terence. 1990. Locating agency. *Annals of Theoretical Psychology* 6:133–45.

Warwick, A., and D. Cavallaro. 1998. *Fashioning the frame: Boundaries, dress and the body*. Oxford: Berg.

Wasserman, T., and J. Hill. 1981. *Bolivian Indian textiles: Traditional designs and costumes*. New York: Dover Press.

Waterbury, R. 1989. Embroidery for the tourists: A contemporary putting-out system in Oaxaca, Mexico. In *Cloth and human experience*, ed. A. B. Weiner and J. Schneider, 243–71. Washington, DC: Smithsonian Books.

Waterson, Roxana. 1986. The ideology and terminology of kinship among the Sa'dan Toraja. *Bijdragen tot de Taal, Land en Volkenkunde* 142 (1): 87–112.

———. 1988. The house and the world: The symbolism of Sa'dan Toraja house carvings. *RES (Peabody Museum, Harvard, Journal of Anthropology and Aesthetics)* 15:34–60.

———. 1989. Hornbill, naga and cock in Sa'dan Toraja woodcarving motifs. *Archipel* 38:53–73.

———. 1995a. Houses and hierarchies in island Southeast Asia. In *About the house: Lévi-Strauss and beyond*, ed. Janet Carsten and Stephen Hugh-Jones, 47–68. Cambridge: Cambridge University Press.

———. 1995b. Houses, graves, and the limits of kinship groupings among the Sa'dan Toraja. *Bijdragen tot de Taal, Land en Volkenkunde* 51 (2): 194–217.

———. 1997. The contested landscapes of myth and history in Tana Toraja. In *The poetic power of place: Comparative perspectives on Austronesian ideas of locality*, ed. James Fox, 63–90. Canberra: Department of Anthropology, Research School of Pacific and Asian Studies, Australian National University.

———. 2002. Vernacular architectures in the 21st century: The fragile power of heritage. *KILAS (Journal of the Dept. of Architecture, Universitas Indonesia)* 4 (2): 97–106.

———. 2003. The immortality of the house in Tana Toraja. In *The house in Southeast Asia: A changing social, economic and political domain*, ed. Stephen Sparkes and Signe Howell, 34–52. London: NIAS; Copenhagen: Curzon Press.

———. 2009. *The living house: An anthropology of architecture in Southeast Asia*. 4th ed. Kuala Lumpur: Oxford University Press; London: Thames & Hudson. (Orig. pub. 1990.)

Weatherford, Elizabeth. 1990. Native visions: The growth of indigenous media. *Aperture*, 58–61.

Weiner, A. 1976. *Women of value, men of renown: New perspectives in Trobriand exchange*. Austin: University of Texas Press.

———. 1985. Inalienable wealth. *American Ethnologist* 12:210–27.

Weiner, James. 1997. Televisualist anthropology: Representation, aesthetics, politics. *Current Anthropology* 38 (2): 197–236.

Weiss, Pegg. 1995. *Kandinsky and old Russia: The artist as ethnographer and shaman*. New Haven, CT: Yale University Press.

Welters, L. 1995. Ethnicity in Greek dress. In *Dress and ethnicity*, ed. J. B. Eicher, 53–77. Oxford: Berg.

Wenger, E. 1998. *Communities of practice: Learning, meaning and identity*. Cambridge: Cambridge University Press.

Were, G. 2005. Pattern, efficacy and enterprise: On the fabrication of connections in Melanesia. In *Clothing as material culture*, ed. S. Küchler and D. Miller, 159–74. Oxford: Berg.

Wesch, M. 2007. Anthropology 2.0: Some challenges and possibilities of radically collaborative digital technology. *Visual Anthropology Review* 23(2). http://mediatedcultures.net/beyondtext/wesch1.htm (accessed 5 March 2007).

Westermann, Mariët. 2005. Introduction: The objects of art history and anthropology. In *Anthropologies of art*, ed. Mariët Westermann. Williamstown: Clark Art Institute; New Haven, CT: Yale University Press.

White, J. 1999. Islamic chic. In *Istanbul: Between the global and the local*, ed. C. Keyder, 77–91. Lanham, MD: Rowman Littlefield.

Whorf, Benjamin L. 1956. *Language, thought and reality: Selected writings of Benjamin Lee Whorf*. Ed. J. B. Carroll. Cambridge, MA: MIT Press.

Wickett, E. 2007. Video for development. *Visual Anthropology* 20 (2): 123–41.

Wilk, Richard. 1993. It's destroying a whole generation: Television and moral discourse in Belize. *Visual Anthropology* 5 (3–4).

Williams, Drid. 1972. Review of Lomax's choreometrics. *Dance Research Journal* 6 (2): 25–29.

———. 1975. The role of movement in selected symbolic systems. PhD thesis, Oxford University.

———. 1979. The human action sign and semasiology. *Committee on Research in Dance (CORD) Annual* 10:39–64.

———. 1982. Semasiology: A semantic anthropologists view of human movements and actions. In *Semantic Anthropology*, ed. D. Parkin, 161–82. ASA 22. London: Academic Press.

———. 1991/2004. *Anthropology and the dance: Ten lectures*. Champaign: University of Illinois Press. Rev. ed. Metuchen, NJ: Scarecrow Press.

———. 1995. Space, intersubjectivity and the conceptual imperative: Three ethnographic cases. In *Human action signs in cultural context: The visible and the invisible in movement and dance*, ed. B. Farnell, 44–81. Metuchen, NJ: Scarecrow Press.

———. 1996a. Ceci nes pas un "wallaby." *Visual Anthropology* 8:197–217.

———, ed. 1996b. Signs of human action. *Visual Anthropology* 8 (2–4). Special issue.

———. 2007. On choreometrics. *Visual Anthropology* 20 (2–3): 233–39.

Williams, Drid, and Brenda Farnell. 1991. *The Laban script: A beginning text on movement writing*. Canberra: Institute for Torres Strait Islander and Aboriginal Studies.

Willmott, C. 2005. The lens of science: Anthropometric photography and the Chippewa, 1890–1920. *Visual Anthropology* 1 (4): 309–37.

Wilson, E. 1985. *Adorned with dreams: Fashion and modernity*. London: Virago.

Wilson, Pam, and Michelle Stewart, eds. 2008. *Global indigenous media: Cultures, practices, and politics*. Durham, NC: Duke University Press.

Wilson, Peter. 1988. *The domestication of the human species*. New Haven, CT: Yale University Press.

Winkler, K. 1994. Rape trauma: Contexts of meaning. In *Embodiment and experience: The existential ground of culture and self*, ed. Thomas J. Csordas, 248–68. Cambridge: Cambridge University Press.

Winkler, M., and L. Cole, eds. 1994. *The good body: Asceticism in contemporary culture*. New Haven, CT: Yale University Press.

Winston, Brian. 1995. *Claiming the real: The Griersonian documentary and its legitimations*. London: British Film Institute.

———. 1998. *Claiming the real: Documentary film revisited*. London: British Film Institute.

Winzeler, Robert. 1998. Two patterns of architectural change in Borneo. In *Indigenous architecture in Borneo: Traditional patterns and new developments*, ed. R. Winzeler, 88–118. Phillips, ME: Borneo Research Council Proceedings.

———. 2004. *The architecture of life and death in Borneo*. Honolulu: University of Hawai'i Press.

Wittenborn, Rainer, and Claus Biegert. 1981. *James Bay Project: A river drowned by water*. Montreal: Montreal Museum of Fine Art.

Wittgenstein, L. 1956. *Bemerkungen über die Grundlagen der Mathematik/Notes on the foundations of mathematics*. Oxford: Basil Blackwell.

———. 1977. *Bemerkungen über die Farben/Remarks on colour*. Berkeley: University of California Press.

Wogan, Peter. 2006. Audience reception and ethnographic film: Laughing at first contact. *Visual Anthropology Review* 22 (1): 14–33.

Wolbert, Barbara. 1998. Überlegungen zu einer symmetrischen Anthropologie der Kunst. *Anthropos* 93 (1–3): 189–96.

———. 2000. The anthropologist as photographer: The visual construction of ethnographic authority. *Visual Anthropology* 13 (4): 321–43.

Wolf, Gotthard. 1967. Organization and aims of the encyclopaedia cinematographica. In *Catalog*, pp. 4–11. Göttingen: Institut für den Wissenschaftlichen Film.

Woodhead, Leslie. 1992. Collaborating with anthropology through television. *Visual Anthropology Review* 8 (1): 118–21.

Woodward, S. 2005. Looking good, feeling right: Aesthetics of the self. In *Clothing as material culture*, ed. S. Küchler and D. Miller, 21–39. Oxford: Berg.

Worth, Sol. 1972. Towards an anthropological politics of symbolic forms. In *Reinventing anthropology*, ed. D. Hymes. New York: Vintage.

———. 1981. *Studying visual communication*. Ed. Larry Gross. Philadelphia: University of Pennsylvania Press.

Worth, Sol, and John Adair. 1973. *Through Navajo eyes*. Bloomington: Indiana University Press.

———. 1997. *Through Navajo eyes*. With a new introduction, afterword, and notes by Richard Chalfen. Albuquerque: University of New Mexico Press. (Orig. pub. 1972.)

Worth, S., and L. R. Sibley. 1994. Maja dress and the Andalusian image of Spain. *Clothing and Textiles Research Journal* 12 (4): 51–60.

Wortham, Erica Cusi. 2000. News from the mountains: Redefining the televisual borders of Oaxaca. In *Sphere 2000*, 17–24. New York: World Studio Foundation.

———. 2002. Narratives of location: Televisual media and the production of indigenous identities in Mexico. PhD thesis, Department of Anthropology, New York University.

Wright, Chris. 2004. Material and memory: Photography in the Western Solomon Islands. *Journal of Material Culture* 9 (1): 73–85.

———. 2007. Photo-objects. http://www.materialworld.blog.com (accessed 19 April 2007).

Wright, Terence. 1992. Television narrative and ethnographic film. In *Film as ethnography*, ed. Peter Ian Crawford and David Turton, 274–82. Manchester: University of Manchester Press.

Wundt, Wilhem. 1973. *The language of gestures*. Trans. J. S. Thayer, C. M. Greenleaf, and M. D. Silberman. The Hague: Mouton. (Orig. pub. 1921.)

Young, Michael. 1998. *Malinowski's Kiriwina: Fieldwork photography, 1915–18*. Chicago: University of Chicago Press.

Zeidler, Sebastian. 2004. Introduction. *October*, no. 107, 3–13. Special issue dedicated to the work of Carl Einstein, containing also an English translation of *Negerplastik*.

Zeitlyn, David. 2000. Archiving anthropology [20 paragraphs]. *Forum Qualitative Sozialforschung/Forum: Qualitative Social Research* 1 (3). http://www.qualitative-research.net/fqs-texte/3-00/3-00zeitlyn-e.htm (accessed 2 March 2007).

Zerner, Charles. 1983. Animate architecture of the Toraja. *Arts of Asia*, September–October, 96–106.

Zijlmans, Kitty, and Wilfried van Damme, eds. 2008. *World art studies*. Amsterdam: Valiz.

Zimmerman, Andrew. 2001. *Anthropology and anti-humanism in imperial Germany*. Chicago: University of Chicago Press.

Zimmerman, Patricia, and Eric Barnouw, eds. 1995. The Flaherty: Four decades in the cause of independent cinema. *Wide Angle* 17:1–4.

Filmography

Many of the titles listed are distributed by Documentary Educational Resources, Watertown, MA, abbreviated here as DER.

Asch, Timothy, and Napoleon Chagnon. 1970. *The feast*. DVD. DER.
———. 1975. *Ax fight*. DER.
Ascher, Robert. 1986. *Cycle*. No longer in distribution.
———. 1988. *Bar Yohai*. No longer in distribution.
———. 1991. *Blue: A Tlingit odyssey*. No longer in distribution.
———. 1995. *The golem*. No longer in distribution.
Balikci, Asen. 1966. *Netisilik Eskimo life*. Educational Development Corporation. 22 DVDs. DER.
Barbash, Ilisa, and Lucien Taylor. 1993. *In and out of Africa*.
Baron, Rebecca. 2005. *How little we know of our neighbors*. Chicago: Video Data Bank.
Barret, E. 1976. *Quilting Women*. 28 minutes. Appalshop, Inc.
Bennett, Compton, and Andrew Marton, directors. 1950. *King Solomon's mine*. Video. Warner Corporation, Warner Mega Classics Collection.
Biella, Peter. Forthcoming. *Maasai interactive*. Ethnography and interactive DVD courseware (with 530 photographs, 3.5 hours of transcribed, translated, and subtitled audio in Swahili and Maa, and 1,000 pages of text). Belmont, CA: Wadsworth/ Thompson Learning.
Biella, Peter, Napoleon Chagnon, and Gary Seaman. 1997. *Yanomamö interactive: The ax fight*. CD-ROM. New York: Harcourt Brace and Company.
Birdwhistell, Ray. 1969. *Microcultural incidents at 10 zoos*. 34 minutes. University Park: Penn State Media.
Bole-Becker, L., and B. Becker. 1997. *Unraveling the stories: Quilts as a reflection of our lives*. 57 minutes. Sound and Light, Ltd.

Brabbee, M. 2005. *Highway Courtesans*. 71 minutes. Hindi with English subtitles. http://womenmakemovies.com.

Buñuel, Luis. 1933. *Las hurdes [Land without bread]*. New York: Kino International.

Carver, H. P. 1930. *The silent enemy: An epic of the American Indian*. Video. Burden-Chanler Productions. Image Entertainment.

Connelly, Bob, and Robin Anderson. 1983. *First contact*. DVD. Arundel Productions. DER.

Cooper, Meriam, and Ernest Scheodsack. 1925/1992. *Grass*. Video. Famous Players-Lasky Corporation. Image Entertainment.

Coover, Roderick. 2003. *Cultures in web*. CD-ROM. Eastgate Systems.

Curling, Chris, and Melissa Llewelyn-Davies. 1983. *The southeast Nuba*. BBC Television. Media Collection.

Curtis, Edward. 1914. *In the land of the head hunters* (re-released, 1972, as *In the land of the war canoes*). Image Entertainment. Video.

Deren, Maya. 1948. *Meditation on violence*. New York: Filmmakers' Cooperative.

Deren, Maya, and Alexander Hamid. 1943. *Meshes of the afternoon*. New York: Filmmakers' Cooperative.

Dunlop, Ian. 1966. *The desert people*. From *People of the western Australian desert* (19-part series, 1966–1970). Film Australia.

Durington, Matthew. 2008. *Record store*. DVD. Berkeley Media.

Elder, Sarah, and Leonard Kamerling, producers. 1988. *Drums of Winter*. DVD. DER.

Engelbrecht, Beate. 1999. *Building season in Tiébélé: A royal compound in change, Kasena, Burkina Faso*. Göttingen: Institut für den Wissenschaftlichen Film.

Ferrero, P. 1980. *Quilts in women's lives*. 28 minutes. New Day Films.

Flaherty, Robert. 1922. *Nanook of the north*. 79 minutes. Les Frères Revillon.

———. 1926. *Moana*. 85 minutes. Hollywood: Famous Players–Lasky Corporation.

Friedrich, Su. 1990. *Sink or swim*. San Francisco: Canyon Cinema.

Fusco, Coco, and Paula Heredia. 1993. *Couple in a cage: Guatianaui odyssey*. Chicago: Video Data Bank.

Gardner, Robert. 1951a. *Blunden Harbour*. Seattle: Orbit Films.

———. 1951b. *Dances of the Kwakiutl*. Seattle: Orbit Films.

———. 1964. *Dead Birds*. DVD. DER.

———. 1973. *Rivers of Sand*. DVD. DER.

———. 1986. *Forest of Bliss*. DVD. DER.

Glass, Aaron. 2004. *In search of the Hamat'sa*. DVD, 33 minutes. Program for Culture and Media, New York University.

Grant, Jenna. 2005. *Sakamapeap*. Distributed by the filmmaker.

Haddon, Alfred C. 1898. [Torres Strait] footage. Cambridge University Museum of Archaeology and Anthropology.

Hardacker, Jennifer. 2008. *Nightgardener*. Distributed by the filmmaker.

Hindle, William. 1968. *Chinese firedrill*. New York: Filmmakers' Cooperative.

Howes, Arthur, and Amy Hardie. 1989/2001. *Kafi's story*. 53 minutes. California Newsreel.

Kirkpatrick, J. 2003. *Transports of delight: The ricksha arts of Bangladesh*. Blooming-ton: Indiana University Press.

Kudlácek, Marina. 2002. *In the mirror of Maya Deren*. New York: Zeitgeist Films.

Laird, Charles. 2004. *Through these eyes*. DVD. National Film Board of Canada. DER.

Lockhart, Sharon. 1999. *Teatro Amazonas*. New York: Barbara Gladstone Gallery.

Lumière, Louis. 1895. *Leaving the Lumière factory. The movies begin: A treasury of early cinema, 1894–1913*. Video.

Lydall, Jane, and Joanna Head. 1990. *The women who smile*. London: BBC.

MacDougall, David. 2000. *Doon School chronicles*. Berkeley: Berkeley Media LLC.

MacDougall, David, and Judith MacDougall. 1979. *Lorang's way*. DVD. Berkeley Media LLC.

———. 1980. *Wedding camels*. DVD. Berkeley Media LLC.

Marshall, John. 1957. *The hunters*. DVD. DER.

———. 1980. *N'ai, a life history of a San woman*. DVD. DER.

———. 2004. *A Kalahari family*. DVD. DER.

McLaren, Les, and Annie Stiven. 1996. *Taking pictures*. DVD. Ronin Films. DER.

McLaren, Norman. 1952. *Pen point percussion*. Toronto: National Film Board of Canada.

Mead, Margaret, and Gregory Bateson. 1951. *Karba's first years, Bathing babies in three cultures*, and *Trance and dance in Bali*. 16mm. All from the series *Character formation in different cultures*. 16mm. University of North Carolina Library and Penn State Media.

Minh-ha, Trihn. 1982. *Reassemblage*. New York: Women Make Movies.

Moser, Brian. 1971. *Last of the Cuiva*. 16mm. From the series *Disappearing World* (Granada Television). George Mason University and RAI Collection.

Myerhoff, Barbara. 1976. *Number our days*. 28 minutes. Lynn Littman, director. Los Angeles: Direct Cinema.

Pink, Sarah. 1998. *The bullfighter's braid: Unravelling photographic research*. CD-ROM. University of Derby.

Putti, R. 2005. *Gente in Mostra : Una ricerca di antropologia visiva*. DVD, 20 min-utes. Centro Televisivo di Ateneo. Università degli Studi di Siena.

Quay, Stephen, Timothy Quay, and Alan Passes. 1995. *Institute Benjamenta, or This dream people call human life*. New York: Zeitgeist Films.

———. 2005. *Piano tuner of earthquakes*. New York: Zeitgeist Films.

Rosler, Martha. 1975. *Semiotics of the kitchen*. Chicago: Video Data Bank.

Rouch, Jean. 1955. *Les maîtres fous [The mad masters]*. Video. DER.

———. 1961. *La pyramide humaine*. Paris: Les Filmes de la Pléiades.

———. 1965. *Jaguar*. Video. DER.

———. 1971. *Petit á petit [Little by little]*. Available only on Region 2 DVD, in French, as part of *Jean Rouch—Coffret 4* (Arcades Video).

Rouch, Jean, and Edgar Morin. 1961. *Chronique d'un été [Chronicle of a summer]*. VHS. Argos Films. First Run/Icarus.

Ruby, Jay. 2004–2006. *Oak Park stories*. Four CD-ROMs and a DVD. DER.

————. 2004. *The Taylor family*. CD-ROM. DER.

————. 2005. *Rebekah and Sophie*. CD-ROM. DER.

Sandall, Roger. 1969. *The Mulga seed ceremony*. 16mm. Australian Institute for Aboriginal Studies. Educational Media Collection, University of Washington.

Singh, Rani. 2006. *The old weird America: Harry Smith's anthology of american folk music*. New York: Harry Smith Archives.

Strand, Chick. 1964. *Eric and the monsters*. Not in distribution at this time.

————. 1967a. *Anselmo*. San Francisco: Canyon Cinema.

————. 1967b. *Waterfall*. San Francisco: Canyon Cinema.

————. 1970. *Mosori Monika*. San Francisco: Canyon Cinema.

Tiragallo, F., and M. Da Re. 1999. *Ordire: La preparazione della tessitura ad Armungia*. 32 minutes. Museo storico etnografico di Armungia, postproduction Arte-video scrl.

Worth, Sol, and John Adair. 1966. *Intrepid Shadows, The Navajo Silversmith, A Navajo Weaver, Old Antelope Lake, Second Weaver, The Shallow Well Project, The Spirit of the Navajos*. Video. Museum of Modern Art, New York.

Contributors

MARCUS BANKS is professor of visual anthropology at the University of Oxford; he has published widely on ethnographic and nonfiction film and on visual methodology, including *Visual Methods in Social Research* (Sage, 2001) and *Using Visual Data in Qualitative Research* (Sage, 2007).

SANDRA DUDLEY has a DPhil in social anthropology from the University of Oxford, formerly worked at the Pitt Rivers Museum, and is currently director of the MA in Interpretation, Representation and Heritage in the School of Museum Studies, University of Leicester. She has published on material anthropology, dress, museums, exile, and southeast Asia, with publications including *Materialising Exile* (Berghahn, 2010), *Museum Materialities* (Routledge, 2010), and *Textiles from Burma* (Philip Wilson, 2001).

ELIZABETH EDWARDS is professor in the cultural history of photography and senior research fellow at the University of the Arts London. She was formerly head of photograph collections at Pitt Rivers Museum and lecturer in visual anthropology at the Institute of Social and Cultural Anthropology, University of Oxford. She has published extensively, for some twenty years, on the relationship between photography, anthropology, history, and material culture, especially in cross-cultural environments. She published *Raw Histories: Photographs, Anthropology and Museums* (Oxford, 2001), and her new ethnography, *The Camera as Historian: Photography and Historical Imagination, 1885–1918*, will be published by Duke University Press in 2011.

BRENDA FARNELL is associate professor of sociocultural/linguistic anthropology and American Indian studies at the University of Illinois at Urbana-Champaign. She is the author of *"Do You See What*

I Mean?" Plains Indian Sign Talk and the Embodiment of Action and the CD-Rom *WIYUTA: Assiniboine Storytelling with Signs*. She has edited *Human Action Signs in Cultural Context: The Visible and the Invisible in Movement and Dance* and is coeditor of the *Journal for the Anthropological Study of Human Movement* (*JASHM*).

MATTHEW DURINGTON is an assistant professor of anthropology in the Sociology, Anthropology and Criminal Justice Department at Towson University. His research interests include visual anthropology, ethnographic media production, suburban culture, gated communities in South Africa, and indigenous land rights in southern Africa. His current ethnographic media projects include *Record Store* and *The Hunters Redux*, in addition to academic publications addressing visual anthropology and housing issues in South Africa.

FAYE GINSBURG is the David B. Kriser Professor of Anthropology at New York University, where she also directs the Graduate Program in Culture and Media, the Center for Media, Culture, and History, and the Center for Religion and Media. She is author or editor of four books, most recently *Media Worlds: Anthropology on New Terrain*, edited with Lila Abu-Lughod and Brian Larkin. Her current book in progress is entitled *Mediating Culture: Indigenous Identity in the Age of Media*.

CRISTINA GRASSENI lectures in anthropology at the University of Bergamo, Italy. Among her publications in English are *Skilled Visions: Between Apprenticeship and Standards* (Berghahn, 2007), *Developing Skill, Developing Visions: Identity and Locality in an Italian Alpine Community* (Berghahn, 2009), and several articles on visual anthropology, the anthropology of food, and the anthropology of science.

MICHAEL HERZFELD is professor of anthropology at Harvard University. A former editor of *American Ethnologist* (1994–1998) and the winner of the J. I. Staley Prize (1994) and Rivers Memorial Medal (1994), he is the author of ten books, including *Cultural Intimacy: Social Poetics in the Nation-State* (2nd ed., 2005), *The Body Impolitic: Artisans and Artifice in the Global Hierarchy of Value* (2004), and *Evicted from Eternity: The Restructuring of Modern Rome* (2009). He has also made a film, *Monti Moments: Men's Memories in the Heart of Rome* (2007).

STEVE HUGHES (MA, PhD, University of Chicago) currently teaches at the School of Oriental and African Studies, University of London, where he is director of studies for the MA Anthropology of Media programme. His research interests focus on the social and cultural history of mass media in Tamil south India.

SARAH PINK is professor of social sciences at Loughborough University, UK. Her books include *Doing Visual Ethnography* (2001), *The Future of Visual Anthropology* (2005), and *Visual Interventions* (2007).

KATHRYN RAMEY has a PhD in anthropology and an MFA in filmmaking from Temple University. Her research interests include the anthropology of visual communication, the film avant-garde, and the anthropology of art and aesthetics. She is an award-winning filmmaker and an assistant professor at Emerson College in Boston.

JAY RUBY is a recently retired visual anthropologist who has explored the relationship between culture and the pictorial world for forty years. His latest publications include *Picturing Culture* (University of Chicago Press, 2000) and five *Oak Park Stories* digital ethnographies on CD-ROM.

ARND SCHNEIDER is professor of social anthropology at the Department of Social Anthropology, University of Oslo. He writes on contemporary art and anthropology, visual anthropology, and international migrations. He coorganized *Fieldworks: Dialogues between Art and Anthropology* at the Tate Modern, London, 2003. Among his books are *Futures Lost: Nostalgia and Identity among Italian Immigrants in Argentina* (Peter Lang, 2000), *Appropriation as Practice: Art and Identity in Argentina* (Palgrave, 2006), and *Contemporary Art and Anthropology* (coedited with Christopher Wright (Berg, 2006).

ROXANA WATERSON studied social anthropology at the University of Cambridge, UK, and is an associate professor in the Department of Sociology, National University of Singapore, where she has taught since 1987. She is the author of *The Living House: An Anthropology of Architecture in Southeast Asia* (Oxford University Press, 1990; 3rd ed., Thames & Hudson, 1997) and numerous articles on houses and society among the Sa'dan Toraja of Sulawesi, Indonesia. She also teaches courses in visual anthropology and ethnographic videomaking.

Index

Abu-Lughod, Lila, 72, 302, 308, 310, 312
Adair, John, 134, 198, 205, 237, 277–78
Adam, Leonhard, 122
Adamowicz, Elza, 198
affordance, 21
Ahmed, M., 53
Allerton, C., 47, 64, 65
Alloula, Malek, 172, 173
Alsayyad, Nezar, 83–84
American Museum of Natural History, 111, 167, 206
Amerlinck, Mari-Jose, 89–90
Anderson, Robin, 201
Ang, Ien, 293, 300, 304, 310–11
Anselmo, 267
anthropology of vision, 19–44
Appadurai, Arjun, 60, 176–77
apprenticeship, 20, 22, 23, 29, 30, 38, 41, 315, 321–22, 330
Architectural Anthropology, 89–90
architecture. *See* built environment
Ardener, Edwin, 329
Armbrust, Walter, 308
art, 4, 7, 108–35; appropriation from non-Western culture, 118–22, 128, 130; camouflage, intellectual, 113–15, 117; embodiment and, 110–13, 116–17; interdisciplinary projects, 108–10, 118, 123–29; and mimesis, 113, 130–31; past, relationship with present, 109; and reenactment, 115–16, 117; reestablishment as a

unitary subject, 131; "speaking terms" between artists and anthropologists, 132; versus artifact, 4, 131
Arthur, Linda, 58
artifacts, 113, 130; cognitive, 20, 27, 31–32, 39; and communication, 20; and cultural appropriation 113; films as, 5; maps as, 33; and sense in film, 277; versus art, 4, 131; visual inscriptions as, 29, 36, 42
artifactuality, 70
Asch, Timothy, 169, 192, 198, 200, 204, 207, 222, 269, 274, 294, 295, 296–97
Ascher, Marcia, 276
Ascher, Robert, 111, 276–79, 284, 286
Asquith, Lindsay, 78, 103–4
Atanarjuat, the Fast Runner, 248
audience, 288–312; anthropological engagement with audience studies, 304–11; anthropology of media, 305–11; audience studies, crisis in, 292–93; educational mode of address, 296–98; ethnographic audience research, 308–11; ethnographic engagement with audience studies, 302–4; ethnographic film spectatorship, 305; film studies versus cultural studies, 299–302; history of audience studies, 292–93; history of ethnographic film